Business Cycles, Indicators, and Forecasting

Studies in Business Cycles
Volume 28

National Bureau of Economic Research
Conference on Research in Business Cycles

Business Cycles, Indicators, and Forecasting

Edited by James H. Stock and
Mark W. Watson

The University of Chicago Press

Chicago and London

JAMES H. STOCK is professor of political economy at the Kennedy School
of Government, Harvard University. MARK W. WATSON is professor of
economics at Northwestern University. Both are research associates of the
National Bureau of Economic Research.

The University of Chicago Press, Chicago 60637
The University of Chicago Press, Ltd., London
© 1993 by the National Bureau of Economic Research
All rights reserved. Published 1993
Printed in the United States of America

02 01 00 99 98 97 96 95 94 93   1 2 3 4 5
ISBN: 0-226-774880-0 (cloth)

Library of Congress Cataloging-in-Publication Data

Business cycles, indicators, and forecasting / edited by James H. Stock
and Mark W. Watson.
    p.   cm.—(Studies in business cycles ; v. 28)
    Includes bibliographical references and index.
    1. Economic forecasting—Congresses. 2. Economic indicators—
Congresses. 3. Business cycles—Congresses. 4. Economic forecasting—United States—Congresses. 5. United States—Economic conditions—Congresses. 6. Economic indicators—United States—Congresses. 7. Business cycles—United States—Congresses. I. Stock,
James H. II. Watson, Mark W. III. Series: Studies in business cycles ;
no. 28.
HB3730.B8457 1993
338.5′ 42—dc20   93-19498
                                                              CIP

Relation of the Directors to the Work and Publications of the National Bureau of Economic Research

1. The object of the National Bureau of Economic Research is to ascertain and to present to the public important economic facts and their interpretation in a scientific and impartial manner. The Board of Directors is charged with the responsiblity of ensuring that the work of the National Bureau is carried on in strict conformity with this object.

2. The President of the National Bureau shall submit to the Board of Directors, or to its Executive Committee, for their formal adoption all specific proposals for research to be instituted.

3. No research report shall be published by the National Bureau until the President has sent each member of the Board a notice that a manuscript is recommended for publication and that in the President's opinion it is suitable for publication in accordance with the principles of the National Bureau. Such notification will include an abstract or summary of the manuscript's content and a response form for use by those Directors who desire a copy of the manuscript for review. Each manuscript shall contain a summary drawing attention to the nature and treatment of the problem studied, the character of the data and their utilization in the report, and the main conclusions reached.

4. For each manuscript so submitted, a special committee of the Directors (including Directors Emeriti) shall be appointed by majority agreement of the President and Vice Presidents (or by the Executive Committee in case of inability to decide on the part of the President and Vice Presidents), consisting of three Directors selected as nearly as may be one from each general division of the Board. The names of the special manuscript committee shall be stated to each Director when notice of the proposed publication is submitted to him. It shall be the duty of each member of the special manuscript committee to read the manuscript. If each member of the manuscript committee signifies his approval within thirty days of the transmittal of the manuscript, the report may be published. If at the end of that period any member of the manuscript committee withholds his approval, the President shall then notify each member of the Board, requesting approval or disapproval of publication, and thirty days additional shall be granted for this purpose. The manuscript shall then not be published unless at least a majority of the entire Board who shall have voted on the proposal within the time fixed for the receipt of votes shall have approved.

5. No manuscript may be published, though approved by each member of the special manuscript committee, until forty-five days have elapsed from the transmittal of the report in manuscript form. The interval is allowed for the receipt of any memorandum of dissent or reservation, together with a brief statement of his reasons, that any member may wish to express; and such memorandum of dissent or reservation shall be published with the manuscript if he so desires. Publication does not, however, imply that each member of the Board has read the manuscript, or that either members of the Board in general or the special committee have passed on its validity in every detail.

6. Publication of the National Bureau issued for informational purposes concerning the work of the Bureau and its staff, or issued to inform the public of activities of Bureau staff, and volumes issued as a result of various conferences involving the National Bureau shall contain a specific disclaimer noting that such publication has not passed through the normal review procedures required in this resolution. The Executive Committee of the Board is charged with review of all such publications from time to time to ensure that they do not take on the character of formal research reports of the National Bureau, requiring formal Board approval.

7. Unless otherwise determined by the Board or exempted by the terms of paragraph 6, a copy of this resolution shall be printed in each National Bureau publication.

(Resolution adopted October 25, 1926, as revised through September 30, 1974)

Contents

Acknowledgments

This volume consists of papers presented at a conference held at the offices of the National Bureau of Economic Research, Cambridge, Massachusetts, 3 and 4 May 1991. Any opinions expressed in this volume are those of the respective authors and do not necessarily reflect the views of the National Bureau of Economic Research or any of the sponsoring organizations. Funding for the conference was provided by the Hewlett Foundation.

Introduction

James H. Stock and Mark W. Watson

The provision of reliable economic forecasts has long been one of the principal challenges facing economists. This continues to be an important way in which the economics profession contributes to the operation of business and government. The past ten years have seen major advances in computational power, data availability, and methods for time-series and econometric analysis. These technological advances have in turn led to the development of new methods for economic forecasting with sufficient scope to provide serious competition to more traditional structural econometric models and to judgmental forecasts, at least for the primary economic aggregates such real GDP and the GDP deflator.

This volume consists of papers presented at a conference held at the offices of the National Bureau of Economic Research, Cambridge, Massachusetts, 3 and 4 May 1991. The purpose of the conference was to provide a forum for discussing and investigating new methods for economic forecasting and for the analysis of business cycles. This conference continues the long-standing involvement of the NBER with economic forecasting and the leading and coincident indicators. Indeed, it was in a 1938 *NBER Bulletin* that NBER researchers Arthur Burns and Wesley Mitchell initially proposed their system of coincident, leading, and lagging indicators (see Mitchell and Burns [1938] 1961). Under the guidance of Geoffrey Moore, Victor Zarnowitz, and their associates, Burns and Mitchell's proposal evolved into the system of economic indicators maintained today by the U.S. Department of Commerce.

The papers in this volume document several of the new macroeconomic forecasting techniques and models developed over the past ten years, compare

James H. Stock is professor of political economy at the Kennedy School of Government, Harvard University. Mark W. Watson is professor of economics at Northwestern University. Both are research associates of the National Bureau of Economic Research.

1

their performance to traditional econometric models, and propose methods for forecasting and time-series analysis. The volume starts with an exhaustive study by Victor Zarnowitz and Phillip Braun of the historical performance of economic forecasts. The data for their study are the responses to a quarterly survey of professional forecasters conducted by the NBER in conjunction with the American Statistical Association from 1968 to 1990. The forecasters surveyed used mostly traditional econometric models, augmented to various degrees by individual judgment. Because these data constitute actual forecasts, they provide a framework for evaluating historical forecast performance and for making hypothetical comparisons of actual forecasts to forecasts that would have been produced had other techniques been used.

The traditional focus of economic forecasting has been the forecasting of growth rates (in the case of the real GNP, e.g.) or levels (say, in the case of interest rates) of economic variables. However, nontechnical audiences—the business press, politicians, and business people—are often less interested in growth rate forecasts than in answers to simple questions, such as "Are we going to be in a recession next year?" or, "When will the current recession end?" To address such questions, the forecaster must construct conditional probability distributions of future paths of output or other key variables, a task made possible by the recent advances in computational power. The next group of papers (the papers by James H. Stock and Mark W. Watson, Ray C. Fair, and Christopher A. Sims) takes advantage of these computational advances to study different approaches to forecasting growth rates and discrete events, in particular, to forecasting whether the economy will be entering a recession. The specific models used for these forecasts are quite different: Stock and Watson use a monthly time-series model based on a range of leading economic indicators, Fair uses a structural econometric model, and Sims uses a reduced-form Bayesian vector autoregressive (VAR) system. The common element in the papers by Stock and Watson and by Fair is the use of stochastic simulation to produce probability forecasts of discrete recession/expansion events. All three papers study the performance of their forecasting systems during the 1990–91 recession and draw lessons from this experience.

The third group of papers consists of a pair of empirical studies of historical relations among specific economic time series. A number of recent studies have found that the spread between the short-term commercial paper rate and the rate on matched-maturity U.S. Treasury bills—the "paper-bill" spread— has had a strong predictive relation to aggregate economic activity. Benjamin M. Friedman and Kenneth N. Kuttner document this relation, summarize several hypotheses for why this predictive relation exists, and provide empirical evidence on the extent to which these hypotheses plausibly explain the power of this spread as a leading indicator.

In their paper, Francis X. Diebold, Glenn D. Rudebusch, and Daniel E. Sichel use the historical NBER business-cycle chronology to document the striking differences between prewar and postwar U.S. business-cycle dynamics. Before World War II, the probability of an expansion ending increased with each additional month, while the probability of a recession ending was almost independent of duration. After World War II, the opposite has been true. Diebold et al. also find that the characterizations of prewar European business-cycle durations are similar to those of the United States.

The papers in the final group have substantial methodological as well as empirical components. Danny Quah and Thomas J. Sargent develop techniques for analyzing dynamic factor models in high-dimensional systems. Previous applications of dynamic factor models have involved fewer than ten variables. However, recent computational advances and improved algorithms make it possible to contemplate applications to systems with many more variables. In their study, Quah and Sargent find that the dynamics of employment in over fifty sectors of the U.S. economy are well explained using only two unobservable dynamic factors.

Clive W. J. Granger, Timo Teräsvirta, and Heather Anderson develop a family of nonlinear time-series models for forecasting economic variables. They apply their techniques to the possibility of forecasting postwar growth in real GNP using a nonlinear model involving the index of leading indicators.

What follows is a more detailed summary of the individual papers.

Historical Performance of Economic Forecasters

From 1968 to 1990, the NBER and the American Statistical Association (ASA) collaborated in the quarterly collection of quantitative economic forecasts made by professional forecasters in private firms, academic institutions, government, and nonprofit organizations with an interest in economic forecasting. These forecasts covered a broad range of macroeconomic series, including income, production, consumption, investment, profits, government purchases, unemployment, inflation, and interest rates. These surveys provided a public service by facilitating the comparison of forecasts and the construction of composite forecasts. They also serve a scientific purpose: after twenty-two years of collection, the results from these surveys, along with the actual outcomes of the variables being forecast, provide an opportunity to study historical forecast performance and thereby learn how forecasts can be improved.

In their paper, "Twenty-two Years of the NBER-ASA Quarterly Economic Outlook Surveys: Aspects and Comparisons of Forecasting Performance," Zarnowitz and Braun use these data to study the performance of professional forecasters over this period. The authors start by discussing the uses and history of economic forecasting and by providing a history of forecast appraisals. They then describe the content and evolution of the NBER-ASA survey and document the construction of the associated data base.

Zarnowitz and Braun then turn to an extensive analysis of the survey forecasts, leading to several main conclusions. (1) At any point in time, and for any economic variable, there is typically great dispersion across forecasts, which typically increases with the forecast horizon. (2) Macroeconomic variables differ greatly in the ease with which they are forecast: growth in real GNP and consumption were forecast better than inflation, residential investment, and changes in business inventories. (3) Perhaps surprisingly, over this period there were no large systematic improvements in forecast accuracy: although inflation forecast accuracy increased, the accuracy of real GNP forecasts decreased. (4) Combined forecasts, in the form of group mean forecasts, are generally more accurate than individual forecasts. Moreover, the group mean forecast for many variables, including real output, outperforms time-series models, in particular, variants of vector autoregressions, when the comparison is conducted in a simulated "real-time" setting (i.e., when the time-series models are estimated, and forecasts constructed, using only those data available contemporaneously to the forecasts made by the survey participants).

The Prediction of Recessions and Expansions

In "A Procedure for Predicting Recessions with Leading Indicators: Econometric Issues and Recent Experience," Stock and Watson describe an approach to forecasting recessions in the U.S. economy that they have been using since October 1988 and analyze its out-of-sample performance. Unlike the earlier literature in this area, which has focused on predicting turning points, the problem here is posed as one of forecasting a discrete variable indicating whether the economy is in a recession. Stock and Watson's approach is to define recessions and expansions as different patterns of economic activity so that whether the economy will be in a recession is equivalent to whether the path of overall economic activity falls in a recessionary or an expansionary pattern. With quantitative definitions for these two patterns, the probability that the economy is in a recession during a future month can then be computed by the stochastic simulation of a model that forecasts future economic activity.

The specific forecasting system used for the stochastic simulation is a reduced-form monthly time-series model, developed in earlier work, based on seven leading and four coincident economic indicators. This model was estimated using data from January 1959 through September 1988. Since then, it has been used to produce three indexes of overall economic activity on a monthly basis: an experimental coincident index (the XCI); an experimental leading index (the XLI), which is a forecast of the growth in the XCI over the subsequent six months; and an experimental recession index (the XRI), which estimates the probability that the economy will be in a recession six months hence.

These indexes performed well from 1988 through the summer of 1990—for example, in June, 1990, the XLI model forecast a 0.4 percent (annual rate) decline in the XCI from June through September when in fact the decline was only slightly greater, 0.8 percent. However, the XLI and the XRI failed to forecast the sharp declines of October and November 1990. Even so, the short-horizon recession probabilities produced by the model performed relatively well during this episode. After investigating a variety of possible explanations for the forecast failure, Stock and Watson conclude that the main source was the failure of the individual leading indicators included in the model to forecast the sharp drop in aggregate growth, either individually or collectively. In short, the XLI and the XRI relied on financial variables during a recession that, unlike the previous three recessions, was not associated with a particularly tight monetary policy.

This poor forecasting record entering the 1990 recession is typical of a wide range of economic indicators. Of a broad set of forty-five coincident and leading indicators, Stock and Watson find that almost all performed poorly during this episode; even the best had large forecast errors by historical standards, and, moreover, they performed relatively poorly in the recessions of the 1970s and early 1980s. This in turn suggests that there was only limited room for improvement in the performance of the recession forecasts.

In "Estimating Event Probabilities from Macroeconomic Models Using Stochastic Simulation," Fair also considers the problem of forecasting recessions. In contrast to Stock and Watson's reduced-form approach based on monthly data, Fair studies recession forecasts using his quarterly structural econometric model, a nonlinear dynamic simultaneous equation system consisting of 30 stochastic equations, 98 identities, and 179 estimated coefficients. Because his system has exogenous variables, he can study recession forecasts that incorporate three different types of uncertainty: uncertainty in the future path of the endogenous variables, given future values of the exogenous variables and the model coefficients; uncertainty in the exogenous variables, given the model coefficients; and uncertainty (arising from estimation error) about the model coefficients themselves.

Fair considers business-cycle events defined in terms of real GNP, and he examines three alternative discrete events: (1) at least two consecutive quarters of negative growth in real GNP during the next five quarters; (2) at least two quarters of negative real GNP growth during the next five quarters; and (3) at least two quarters of the next five having inflation exceeding 7 percent at an annual rate. Because the event "two consecutive quarters of negative real GNP growth" is a conventional, if sometimes inaccurate, rule-of-thumb definition of a recession, the first of these events corresponds to a recession occurring sometime during the next five quarters.

On a computational level, Fair's approach is to draw a set of exogenous variables, disturbances, or coefficients, depending on which of the three types of simulation is being performed, and to use these to compute a stream of forecasts over 1990:I–1991:I. The fraction of times that the forecast registers the indicated type of event yields the probability of that event occurring.

Fair's initial focus is the five quarters 1990:I–1991:I. Even though his mean forecasts predict positive growth in four of the five quarters, the probabilities of the two contraction events are rather high: for the full stochastic simulation (with uncertainty arising from endogenous variables, exogenous variables, and coefficients), the probability of two consecutive declines in GNP approaches 40 percent.

Fair then turns to the more computationally demanding task of computing a sequence of event probabilities over the period 1954:I–1990:I and compares the event forecasts produced by his model to those produced by a "naive" model, a univariate autoregression for GNP. For each of the two recession events, Fair's model (with endogenous variable and coefficient uncertainty, using future values of the exogenous variables) outperforms the naive model using conventional probability scores. Overall, these results are encouraging and suggest pursuing further work using stochastic simulation to predict discrete events.

One of the most important advances in forecasting methodology during the 1980s was the development and refinement of small multivariate time-series forecasting models, in particular, vector autoregressions (VARs). Since first introducing VARs to economists, Christopher Sims and his students have pursued a research program aimed in part at improving the forecasts made by VARs. A key aspect of this program has been the ongoing production of quarterly forecasts from a Bayesian VAR. This model was originally developed and maintained by Robert Litterman at the Federal Reserve Bank of Minneapolis. Sims took over the responsibility for this model and its forecasts in 1987.

The paper by Sims in this volume—"A Nine-Variable Probabilistic Macroeconomic Forecasting Model"—documents the current version of this model and summarizes the changes that have been made to it over the years. Sims then provides various measures of the model's performance, both in sample and out of sample. The version of the model currently in use incorporates nine variables and can be thought of as a third-generation VAR. Because a nine-variable, five-lag VAR would have a very large number of coefficient estimates (forty-five regression coefficients per equation, plus a constant), unrestricted estimation of this system would result in imprecise coefficient estimates and thus a good chance of poor out-of-sample performance. Sims uses Bayesian techniques to restrict the otherwise large number of parameters. Sims has also modified Litterman's original model to incorporate two deviations from the standard linear/Gaussian framework, conditional heteroskedasticity and nonnormal errors. Also, the model has been modified to permit cointegration among the variables. These modifications and the priors incorporated into the model are documented in Sims's paper.

Sims next examines the performance of his model. The early VARs had produced good forecasts of real variables, but their forecasts of inflation were substantially worse than forecasts from traditional structural econometric equations. According to Sims's evidence, his subsequent model modifications improved the inflation forecasts without deteriorating the real forecasts. The final evidence examined in Sims's paper is the performance of the model in the 1990 recession. Like almost all (unadjusted) formal quantitative economic models, this VAR failed to forecast the negative GNP growth in the fourth quarter of 1990 and the first quarter of 1991. Sims concludes by exploring the lessons of this episode for future work.

Historical Empirical Studies

A series of recent papers has shown that the difference between interest rates on commercial paper and U.S. Treasury bills—the "paper-bill spread"—has, for the past three decades, exhibited a systematic relation to subsequent fluctuations of real economic activity. Friedman and Kuttner's paper "Why Does the Paper-Bill Spread Predict Real Economic Activity?" documents the empirical facts about this spread as a leading economic indicator and studies various economic reasons why this spread has such a strong historical forecasting record.

Friedman and Kuttner start by documenting the value of this spread as a predictor of economic activity. Commercial paper represents the unsecured, discounted short-term (up to 270 days) liability of either nonfinancial business corporations or financial intermediaries. The paper-bill spread outperforms any other interest rate or any monetary aggregate as a predictor of output. In contrast to the monetary aggregates, the authors argue, this spread clearly forecasts real rather than nominal economic activity; it predicts nominal magnitudes only to the extent that nominal magnitudes reflect real ones. In his discussion of Friedman and Kuttner's paper, Ben S. Bernanke presents additional evidence concerning the striking predictive performance of this spread as a leading economic indicator.

Friedman and Kuttner turn next to a description of several factors that can account for the levels of and changes in the spread. One explanation of the mean level is the difference in tax treatments between commercial paper and Treasury bills when the interest is received by entities domiciled in states or municipalities with an income tax; the authors calculate that an effective state/municipal tax rate of 8.1 percent would suffice to explain the spread between six-month commercial paper and six-month Treasury bills. A second factor in the spread is that commercial paper is subject to potential default by private obligors, a factor that is exacerbated by the junior standing of commercial paper as unsecured debt. A third factor underlying this spread is the greater liquidity of the Treasury-bill market than the commercial paper market. Although the total value of commercial paper outstanding in 1989 was $579 billion, as recently as 1960 the volume outstanding was only $6.5 billion. In contrast, the U.S. Treasury market has been well developed throughout the postwar period, with a total value outstanding of $482 billion in 1990. This growth of the commercial paper market during this period, along with legal restrictions on the use of commercial paper, raises the possibility that the commercial paper market had substantially less liquidity than the Treasury-bill market for much of this episode. To quantify these factors, Friedman and Kuttner provide a decomposition of changes in the level of the paper-bill spread among changes in the level of interest rates (as suggested by the tax and default arguments), changes in quality as measured by the P2-P1 commercial paper premium, and residual, unexplained changes. They find that all three components are statistically and economically large.

Having documented these historical relations, Friedman and Kuttner study three hypotheses about why this spread predicts aggregate economic activity. The first concerns changes in perceptions of default risk: a widening of the spread reflects an increasing fear of a downturn, business failures, and concomitant defaults on debt. The second hypothesis is that the paper-bill spread is an indicator of monetary policy. The third hypothesis emphasizes changes in borrowers' cash flows: to the extent that borrowers' cash flows vary cyclically, borrowing requirements might rise toward the end of an expansion (because of constant costs in the face of declining sales), with the result that the increasing spread would reflect an increasing supply of commercial paper and an increasing commercial paper rate. When these hypotheses are studied empirically using a more structural approach based on imperfect substitutability between commercial paper and Treasury bills, empirical support is found for each of these three hypotheses.

In "Further Evidence on Business-Cycle Duration Dependence," Diebold et al. use formal statistical techniques to take a new look at an idea found in popular discussions of the business cycle: that business cycles exhibit duration dependence. That is, the probability that an expansion or a recession will end depends on the length of that expansion or recession. The authors' previous research on duration dependence in the U.S. business cycle found evidence of substantial differences between the prewar and the postwar business cycle: during the postwar period, contractions exhibit duration dependence, but expansions do not, while the opposite is true during the prewar period. This paper extends this line of research to France, Germany, and Great Britain.

The analysis of duration dependence in business cycles is made difficult by the small number of observations of recessions or expansions contained in even one century of data. Thus, techniques for the analysis of duration dependence appropriate for large samples—the estimation of nonparametric or semiparametric hazard models—are inapplicable here because they require too many observations. Instead, Diebold et al. employ a quadratic hazard model that is parsimonious yet flexible enough to allow the nonmonotone hazards that might be found in business-cycle data.

The application of this quadratic hazard model to the U.S. business-cycle chronology confirms the authors' earlier findings, obtained using a simpler hazard specification, about the differences between duration dependence during the prewar and postwar periods. For example, they find that the hazard rate for postwar recessions rises from .07 to .29 over the course of twelve months.

Their results for France, Germany, and Great Britain indicate that prewar expansions exhibit positive duration dependence in all three countries and that in none of the countries do prewar contractions exhibit positive duration dependence. There is also evidence for duration dependence in prewar whole cycles in these three countries, which the authors attribute to the positive duration dependence of the expansion phase. Overall, these results are qualitatively the same for the United States, which leads the authors to suggest that, during the prewar period, there were substantial similarities across countries in business-cycle dynamics.

Methods for Analyzing Economic Time Series

Much of the aggregate economic data of primary interest to economic forecasters has disaggregated components. For example, the U.S. Bureau of Labor Statistics reports total private employment and employment disaggregated by industry. However, the richness provided by these disaggregated data has largely been ignored in many recent developments in the area of economic forecasting. From the point of view of economic theory, a study of the comovements of these data might elucidate the extent to which different sectors respond to aggregate shocks and might even help identify the number of separate aggregate shocks to the economy. From the point of view of economic forecasting, the use of these data might result in better measures of these different aggregate shocks, which could in turn be used to improve aggregate forecasts. However, the very richness of the data—the large number of disaggregated sectors—has posed a technical barrier to the simultaneous modeling of these comovements.

In "A Dynamic Index Model for Large Cross Sections," Quah and Sargent embark on a project to model simultaneously the comovements of a large number of disaggregated series. They examine dynamic factor models, in which the comovements of the series are presumed to arise from a reduced number of factors. These factors can affect different series with different lags and dynamic specifications. Because of computational limitations, these models have in the past been fit to small systems, for example, with four time series. The main technical advance in the paper is the development of procedures, based on the "EM" algorithm, for the fitting of these models to a large panel of time series.

In their empirical application, Quah and Sargent examine the comovements in U.S. employment in fifty-four industries over the period 1948–89. Their striking finding is that a large fraction of the variation in employment can be described by two common factors. Their results demonstrate that the construction of such large-scale dynamic factor models is both feasible and potentially valuable both for forecasting and for data description purposes.

Most statistical analysis of economic times series is done using linear models. However, economic theory typically predicts linear relations only as special cases; more often, the processes are likely to be nonlinear, in the sense that optimal forecasts will involve nonlinear rather than linear functions of the observed variables. In "Modeling Nonlinearity over the Business Cycle," Granger et al. outline a family of nonlinear time-series models and tests that might usefully be applied to economic data. Their main focus is on smooth-transition regression models, which allow for regression coefficients to take on two values and to shift between these two values in a continuous way.

The empirical focus of their paper is the relation between GNP and the Department of Commerce's index of leading indicators. Their objective is to ascertain whether a nonlinear model provides better forecasts of real GNP than a linear model does, in particular, whether a nonlinear model would have predicted the onset of the 1990 recession better than a linear one would have. Overall, in this application, the results are mixed: although formal statistical tests provide some evidence of nonlinearity, and although the nonlinear model provides quite different forecasts than the linear model, neither model performed particularly well in the slow-growth period leading to the recession and in the sharp contraction during the autumn of 1990.

Reference

Mitchell, W. C., and A. B. Burns. [1938] 1961. Statistical indicators of cyclical revivals. Reprinted in *Business cycle indicators,* ed. G. H. Moore. Princeton, N.J.: Princeton University Press.

1 Twenty-two Years of the NBER-ASA Quarterly Economic Outlook Surveys: Aspects and Comparisons of Forecasting Performance

Victor Zarnowitz and Phillip Braun

Human action has to a large extent always been oriented toward the future. Since ancient times, men and women hoped to outwit fate and survive by magic divination; they also hoped to outwit nature and others by shrewd calculation. Attempts to predict the future, therefore, are as old as magic, but they are also as old as commerce, saving, and investment. Their motivation must always have been largely economic, despite the inevitable frustrations of economic forecasting.

Great foresight in business matters is presumably highly profitable and rare. Its possessor will do well to exploit it directly for personal enrichment and hence should not be inclined to offer its products to the public in the open market. An economist who perceives competitive markets as working with reasonable efficiency should not expect any forecasts of stock prices or interest rates to be both freely traded and consistently much better than average. Forecasting macroeconomic aggregates such as real GNP and its major expenditure components is likely to have less potential for direct profitability than forecasting financial variables. Hence, it is presumably less vulnerable to that old American adage rebuking expert advisers: "If you're so smart, why ain't you rich?" (cf. McCloskey 1988).

For reasons explained in section 1.1 below, to be interesting and robust, macroforecast assessments should cover a broad range of forecasters, variables, and economic conditions. The forecasts must be explicit, verifiable,

Victor Zarnowitz is professor emeritus of economics and finance at the University of Chicago, Graduate School of Business, and a research associate of the National Bureau of Economic Research. Phillip Braun is assistant professor of finance at Northwestern University, Kellogg Graduate School of Management.

The authors thank Ray Fair, Christopher Sims, Allen Sinai, James Stock, Mark Watson, and the participants in the discussion at the NBER meeting on 4 May 1991 for helpful comments; Christopher Culp for research assistance; Cynthia Davis for typing; and the NBER for financial assistance.

and sufficient to allow a responsible appraisal. Unfortunately, most of the available time series of forecasts are short, and none are free of some gaps, discontinuities, and inconsistencies. Relying on a small sample of specific forecasts from an individual source risks overexposure to isolated hits or misses due to chance. It is therefore necessary to concentrate on a set of forecasts from numerous and various sources. This is likely to improve the coverage by types of information and methods used as well.

The way to collect the required data is to conduct regularly, for a sufficiently long time and with appropriate frequency, a survey that would be reasonably representative of the professional activities of macroeconomic forecasters. A joint project of the National Bureau of Economic Research (NBER) and the Business and Economic Statistics Section of the American Statistical Association (ASA) had the purpose of accomplishing just that. The NBER-ASA survey assembled a large amount of information on the record of forecasting annual and quarterly changes in the U.S. economy during the period 1968:IV–1990:I (eighty-six consecutive quarters). It reached a broadly based and diversified group of people regularly engaged in the analysis of current and prospective business conditions. Most of the economists who responded came from corporate business and finance, but academic institutions, government, consulting firms, trade associations, and labor unions were also represented. The forecasts covered a broad range of principal aggregative time series relating to income, production, consumption, investment, profits, government purchases, unemployment, the price level, and interest rates. The surveys also collected data on the methods and assumptions used by the participants and on the probabilities that they attached to alternative prospects concerning changes in nominal or real GNP and the implicit price deflator.

The NBER-ASA data have their shortcomings, most important of which are probably the high turnover of participants and the large frequency of gaps in their responses. The data collected represent a mixture of public and private predictions. The survey members, generally professional forecasters, were identified by code only. Their anonymity helped raise the survey response rates but may have had otherwise ambiguous consequences (encouraging independence of judgment or reducing the sense of individual responsibility?).

The initiative to develop and maintain the quarterly NBER-ASA survey was strongly motivated by the desire to make it "the vehicle for a scientific record of economic forecasts" (Moore 1969, 20). The expectation that such a survey would be of considerable service to both the profession and the public was shared by Moore with others who helped implement his proposal (including one of the authors of this paper, who had the responsibility for reporting on the NBER-ASA survey during the entire period of its existence). In retrospect, it seems fair to say that the assembled data do indeed provide us with rich and in part unique information, which can help support much-needed research on the potential and limitations of forecasting economic change.

Twenty-two years of a survey that attracted numerous responses from a variety of sources each quarter add up to a mass of information about the processes and results of macroeconomic forecasting. Although many studies have already used some of this material, much of it remains to be explored. This report is the first to examine all the variables included in the NBER-ASA forecasts, for all horizons and over the entire period covered. It concentrates on the properties of the distributions of summary measures of error, by variable and span of forecast, viewed against the background of descriptive statistics for the predicted time series. Other subjects of interest include the role of characteristics and revisions of "actual" data in the evaluation of the forecasts, differences by subperiod (roughly the 1970s vs. the 1980s), the relation between the individual and the group mean or "consensus" forecasts from the surveys, the comparative accuracy of the survey results and predictions with a well-known macroeconometric model, and comparisons with forecasts from state-of-the-art multivariate and univariate time-series models.

Section 1.1 of this paper examines some general problems and the history of forecast evaluations and surveys. Section 1.2 presents the NBER-ASA data and the methods used. Sections 1.3–1.5 discuss the results of the analysis and form the core of the paper. Section 1.6 draws the conclusions.

1.1   The Diversity of Forecasts and Their Evaluation

1.1.1   Some Reflections on Predictability and Uncertainty

It can be readily observed that, at any time, predictions of a given variable or event can and in general do differ significantly across forecasters. Indeed, modern macroeconomic forecasts display a great diversity, which must be taken into account in thinking about how to assemble and evaluate the related data.

Although changes in the economy are predicted primarily to meet the demand for forecasts by public and private decision makers, they are also predicted to test theories and analytic methods and to argue for or against points of policy. Some conditions and aspects of the economy are much more amenable to prediction than others. Furthermore, individual forecasters differ with respect to skills, training, experience, and the espoused theories and ideologies. They compete by trying to improve and differentiate their models, methods, and products. They respond to new developments in the economy and new ways to observe and analyze them. In sum, there are both general and specific reasons for the observed diversity of forecasts.

Comparisons among forecasts that are differentiated in several respects are difficult yet unavoidable. The quality of a forecast is inherently a relative concept. Common standards of predictive performance must therefore be applied to properly classified forecasts along each of the relevant dimensions.

Surely, the main value of a forecast lies in its ability to reduce the uncertainty about the future faced by the user. In general, a forecast will perform better in this regard the smaller and closer to randomness its errors are. However, the value of a forecast depends not only on its accuracy and unbiased nature but also on the predictability of the variable or event concerned. Some events and configurations of values are common, others rare. Where the probability of occurrence for the forecasting target is high, uncertainty is low, and prediction is easy but not very informative. Where that probability is low, uncertainty is high, and prediction is difficult but potentially very valuable (cf. Theil 1967).

For example, total stocks of the nation's wealth and productive capital normally change little from one month or quarter to the next, barring a catastrophic war or a natural disaster, and so can be predicted with small relative errors. Much the same applies to other typically "slow" stock variables such as total inventories of goods or monetary aggregates and the overall price level (but not in periods of rapid inflation!). In contrast, income and expenditure aggregates represent "fast" flow variables, some of which (e.g., corporate profits, investment in plant and equipment, housing starts, and change in business inventories) are highly volatile over short horizons and apt to be very difficult to forecast accurately. Rates of change in indexes of price levels fall in the same category.

There are also situations that are unique or nearly so where no objective or subjective probabilities based on past history or experience are believed to apply and where "true" (nonergodic) uncertainty rules (as in Knight 1921, 233). According to Keynes (1936, 149), "Our knowledge of the factors which will govern the yield of an investment some years hence is usually very slight and often negligible," yet businesspeople must make decisions to make or buy plant and equipment despite this recognized state of ignorance. In economics, as in history, statistical-stochastic methods have limited applicability (cf. Hicks 1979; Solow 1985). Forecasters cannot afford to be deterred by such considerations and assume some predictability throughout, never full uncertainty.

Across many variables, uncertainty depends on the "state of nature" (more explicitly, on the state of the economy or the phase of the business cycle). Thus, it is much easier to predict continued moderate growth once it is clear that the economy has entered a period of sustained expansion than it is to predict the occurrence and timing of a general downturn after the expansion has lasted for some time and may be slowing down.

Influential public macro forecasts could in principle be either self-invalidating or self-validating. Thus, if the government believes a forecast of a recession next year, it might succeed in stimulating the economy so as to make the expansion continue. On the other hand, if consumers generally come to expect a recession because of such a forecast, individuals may try to protect themselves by spending less now and dissaving later when the bad times arrive. Businesspeople, acting on similar expectations, may reduce investment expenditures and financing, production, and inventory costs. But such actions, although individually rational, would collectively help bring about the recession no one wants.

Indeed, an early theoretical monograph on forecasts of general business conditions concluded, on these grounds, that they *cannot* be accurate, particularly if they are made public (Morgenstern 1928). However, it is not necessarily true that a known forecast must be falsified by agents' reaction to it, even if that reaction does affect the course of events. Conceptually, the reaction can be known and taken into account for bounded variables related by continuous functions (Grunberg and Modigliani 1954).[1] But the public prediction can be correct only if the corresponding private prediction is correct, which of course is often not the case. Forecasting remains difficult whether or not its results are published. The premise of a generally shared belief and confidence in a commonly held forecast is so unrealistic as to deprive theoretical exercises based on it of much practical interest.

1.1.2   A Brief History of Forecast Appraisals and Surveys

Qualitative judgments about contemporary levels of, and changes in, general business activity are among the oldest economic data. A compilation of such records provided partial evidence for the NBER work on identifying and dating the business cycles of history (Thorp 1926; Burns and Mitchell 1946). A look at these "business annals," which go back to the 1830s, reminds one of the importance of public perceptions and expectations concerning aspects of general economic and financial activity: employment, production, prices, interest rates.

This expectational element in the dynamics of economic life has probably long attracted great attention from students of current events and men and women of affairs. It did not much concern those early theorists, who were preoccupied with problems of long-run static equilibrium. But some prominent economists in the classical tradition stressed the role that variations in expectations and "confidence" play in business cycles (Marshall), or hypothesized the occurrence of sequences of overoptimism and overpessimism (Pigou), or attributed to bankers and entrepreneurs predictive errors resulting in malinvestments (Hayek). Keynes and some of his later followers elaborated on the destabilizing role of uncertainty. Along with the formal models of interacting economic processes came the theories of expectation formation, first that of adaptive and later that of rational expectations. In the last twenty years or so, incomplete information and expectational errors acquired prime importance in many models of economists of various persuasions (monetarist, new-classical, new-Keynesian). The corresponding literature grew rapidly.

Lack of quantitative data has long hampered the progress of economics,

---

1. Interestingly, Morgenstern's monograph and Grunberg and Modigliani's paper are in a sense precursors of the contemporary rational expectations models in which behavior follows forecasts that are consistent with the assumptions of the models and free of any systematic errors.

causing empirical work and tests to lag well behind the formulation of theories and hypotheses. Numerical data on forecasts and expectations are particularly scarce, except for the very recent period of great expansion in economic and financial prediction and consulting activities. Hence, the literature on macroeconomic forecasting has a brief history, although it too has grown rapidly of late.[2]

The first forecasting services in the United States to gain considerable success date back to the years immediately preceding World War I and the 1920s. They used lead-lag relations to predict business-cycle turning points, relying mainly on the tendency of stock prices to lead and short-term interest rates to lag business activity. The sequence, best known as the Harvard "ABC" curves, had a basis in theory and fact, but it was a crudely oversimplified predecessor of the indicator system subsequently developed at the NBER. It performed rather well in the period 1903–14 and in the depression of 1920–21, and it would have applied generally in recent times as well (cf. Moore 1969), but the Harvard service failed to foresee the onset and extent of the Great Depression, which doomed this and related forecasting efforts. A 1988 postmortem study, using the Harvard data and modern vector autoregressive (VAR) model techniques, concludes that the large declines in output that followed the 1929 stock market crash could not have been forecast (Dominguez, Fair, and Shapiro 1988).[3] This, however, is disputed by a very recent paper that applies the Neftci sequential analysis method to the Harvard index (Niemira and Klein 1991).

Monthly forecasts from six sources for the period 1918–28 were scored for accuracy in Cox (1929), to our knowledge the first methodical appraisal of ex ante predictions of U.S. business activity. Cox found evidence of a moderate forecasting success despite the poor showing at the 1923–24 recession.

The earliest compilation of quantitative macro forecasts, so far as we can tell, was the informal survey conducted since 1947 by Joseph Livingston, the late syndicated financial columnist based in Philadelphia. Twice a year he collected predictions of such variables as industrial production and the consumer price index and summarized the results in a business outlook column published in June and December. The forecasters were mostly business and financial economists, but some academics were also included. The Livingston data represent a unique and valuable source of information on forecasts for the early post–World War II period, and, in the 1970s, they began to be widely used in research, primarily on price expectations. But Livingston adjusted his published "consensus forecasts" (means of the collected individual predictions) in an attempt to take into account any large revisions in the actual data that may have occurred between the mailing of his questionnaire and the sub-

---

2. The same applies to the literature on microeconomic prediction, which is additionally restricted by the fact that much of the material on micro forecasts is confidential.
3. Forecasts of a Yale service developed by Irving Fisher were not better in 1929 than those of the Harvard service, developed by Warren Persons (see Dominguez, Fair, and Shapiro 1988).

mission of his column to the press. Carlson (1977) recalculated the semiannual Livingston forecasts of CPI and WPI inflation rates for 1947–75 from the original data so as properly to reflect the timing of the predictions and the information incorporated in them.[4]

As quantitative macroeconomic data and forecasts began to accumulate in the 1950s and 1960s, valid examinations of the accuracy and properties of the latter became increasingly possible (Okun 1959; Theil 1961, 1966; Suits 1962; Stekler 1968). A comprehensive NBER study initiated in 1963 resulted in a systematic collection and appraisal of annual and quarterly, public and private, judgmental and econometric forecasts of important economic aggregates and indexes as well as such events as business-cycle peaks and troughs (Zarnowitz 1967, 1972; Fels and Hinshaw 1968; Mincer 1969; Moore 1969; Cole 1969; Evans et al. 1972; Haitovsky, Treyz, and Su 1974).

In 1968, a regular quarterly survey of general economic forecasts was established at the initiative of Geoffrey Moore, then president of the ASA, to be conducted cooperatively by the NBER and the Business and Economic Statistics Section of the ASA.[5] This was the first major organized effort to build up reliable information about the potential and limitations of short-term aggregative economic forecasts, which would provide a broad base for research and improvements in this field. The ASA "agreed to carry out the surveys for a period long enough to assure accumulation of useful experience and evidence," while the National Bureau "assumed responsibility for the tabulation of forecasts, computation of error statistics and other measures, and research in evaluating the results and their analytical implications" (Zarnowitz 1968, 1–2). The cooperation was to last twenty-two years. One measure of its success is that, in 1990, the Federal Reserve Bank of Philadelphia undertook to continue the survey essentially in the same way as it was conducted by the NBER and the ASA.

1.2 The NBER-ASA Survey: Characteristics, Measures, and Data

1.2.1 Coverage

Table 1.1 identifies each of the variables covered by title, source, symbol, Commerce series number, and the form in which we use the data. During the period 1968:IV–1981:II (col. 5), direct forecasts were made for seven nominal indicators and three real indicators; also, predictions for GNP in constant dollars were derived from those for GNP in current dollars and the implicit price deflator. During the period 1981:III–1990:I (col. 6), direct forecasts were made for six nominal and eleven real variables. Seven major expenditure com-

---

4. Later studies of the Livingston forecasts generally used them as amended by Carlson, but many earlier studies suffer from measurement errors in the published group averages.

5. The Business and Economic Statistics Section had long been engaged in producing annual surveys of forecasts by its members.

Table 1.1   List of Variables Covered in the NBER-ASA Quarterly Economic Outlook Surveys, 1968:IV–1981:II and 1981:III–1990:I

Row	Variable (Symbol) (1)	Unit (R or N)[a] (2)	Source[b] (3)	Series No.[c] (4)	Period Covered 68:IV–81:II (5)	Period Covered 81:III–90:I (6)	Form[d] (7)
1	Gross national product (GNP)	$bil. (N)	1	200	✓	✓	%Δ
2	GNP implicit price deflator (IPD)	b.y. = 100 (N)	1	310	✓	✓	%Δ
3	GNP in constant dollars (RGNP)	const. $bil. (R)	1	50	✓	✓	%Δ
4	Industrial production (IP)	b.y. = 100 (R)	4	47	✓	✓	%Δ
5	Unemployment rate (UR)	% (R)	3	43	✓	✓	level
6	Corporate profits after taxes (CP)	$bil. (N)	1	16	✓	✓	%Δ
7	Plant and equipment expenditures (PE)	$bil. (N)	2	61	✓		%Δ
8	Private nonfarm housing starts (HS)	a.r., mil. (R)	2	28	✓	✓	level
9	Change in business inventories (CBI)	$bil. (N)	1	245	✓		level
10	Consumer expenditures for durable goods (CD)	$bil. (N)	1	232	✓		%Δ
11	National defense purchases (DEF)	$bil. (N)	1	564	✓		%Δ
12	Personal consumption expenditures (PCE)	const. $bil. (R)	1	231		✓	%Δ

13	Nonresidential fixed investment (NFI)	const. $bil. (R)	1	86	✓	%Δ
14	Residential fixed investment (RFI)	const. $bil. (R)	1	89	✓	%Δ
15	Federal government purchases (FGP)	const. $bil. (R)	1	263	✓	%Δ
16	State and local government purchases (SLGP)	const. $bil. (R)	1	267	✓	%Δ
17	Change in business inventories (RCBI)	const. $bil. (R)	1	30	✓	level
18	Net exports of goods and services (NX)	const. $bil. (R)	1	255	✓	level
19	Consumer price index (CPI)	% change (N)	3	320	✓	level
20	Treasury-bill rate, 3 month (TRB)	% (N)	4	114	✓	level
21	New high-grade corporate bond yield (CBY)	% (N)	5	116	✓	level

[a]R = real; N = nominal; b.y. = base year; a.r. = annual rate; const. $ = in constant dollars.

[b]Sources are as follows: 1 = U.S. Department of Commerce, Bureau of Economic Analysis; 2 = U.S. Department of Commerce, Bureau of the Census; 3 = U.S. Department of Labor, Bureau of Labor Statistics; 4 = Board of Governors of the Federal Reserve System; 5 = Citibank and U.S. Department of the Treasury.

[c]As listed in the *Business Conditions Digest* and the *Survey of Current Business.*

[d]As used in the computation of forecast errors. %Δ = percentage change.

ponents of real GNP, the consumer price index, the Treasury-bill rate, and the corporate bond yield were added to the list; four nominal series (expenditures for consumer durables, plant and equipment, and national defense and change in business inventories) were dropped.

The change in 1981 resulted from new initiatives undertaken by the NBER in the preceding year. A special questionnaire mailed to a long list of professional forecasters (both past and present survey participants and others) collected much useful information about the reactions to the design and uses of the NBER-ASA survey, the improvements suggested, and the assumptions and procedures favored. There was strong sentiment for expanding the survey by including several additional variables. The problem was how to comply with these wishes without either losing the essential continuity or overloading the survey and risking discouraging future participation. An advisory committee helped make the desirable changes.[6]

A large number of individuals participated in the earliest surveys, but many were not prepared to fill out a detailed questionnaire each quarter and soon dropped out. Of the more than 150 people who responded to the survey at one time or another, many did so only sporadically, and some submitted incomplete questionnaires. To exclude such occasional forecasters, we decided to use only the responses of those who answered at least ten surveys, providing information for most variables and horizons. Note that the surveys need not be consecutive; had we required long records of uninterrupted participation, few respondents would have qualified.

Table 1.2 shows how this selection was accomplished and with what results. Using the forecasts of spending on consumer durables for 1968–81, the number of respondents fell from a total of 156 to eighty-six in the sample, but the average number of surveys covered per respondent was greatly increased (e.g., doubling from eleven to twenty-two, according to the medians). The average number of respondents per survey was reduced only slightly, remaining above forty. The variability of coverage over time was lowered considerably throughout (cf. cols. 1 and 2).

The participation rates in the surveys were much smaller in 1981–90 than in 1968–81. In terms of the forecasts of real nonresidential investment, the number of respondents fell from a total of seventy-four to twenty-nine in the sample. Again, however, the selection process achieved relatively good results. The retained forecasters averaged about twenty surveys, more than double the number for all survey participants. The median number of surveys covered per respondent declined only slightly, from twenty-one to eighteen.

---

6. The committee was established with the support of the Business and Economic Statistics Section of the ASA and its 1980 and 1981 chairs, Arnold Zellner and George Tiao. The members included Rosanne Cole, Ray C. Fair, Edgar R. Fiedler, Albert A. Hirsch, F. Thomas Juster, Geoffrey H. Moore, George L. Perry, W. Allen Spivey, and Victor Zarnowitz. For more detail on these initiatives, see Zarnowitz (1982, 11–13).

Table 1.2   **NBER-ASA Quarterly Economic Outlook Surveys, All Forecasts and Sampled Forecasts: Selected Distributional Statistics, 1968–90 and Two Subperiods**

		1968:IV–1981:II		1981:III–1990:I		1968:IV–1990:I	
		All	Sample	All	Sample	All	Sample
Row	Statistic	(1)	(2)	(3)	(4)	(5)	(6)
		Number of Surveys					
1	Total number	51	51	35	35	86	86
	Surveys per respondent:						
2	Mean	14.8	24.2	10.3	20.8	21.0	28.5
3	Standard deviation	13.0	10.4	9.9	7.5	16.1	13.5
4	Median	11	22	6	20	12	25
5	Interquartile range	21	18	14.8	9.5	26	21
6	Maximum	46	46	35	35	70	70
7	Minimum	1	10	1	10	1	10
		Number of Respondents					
8	Total number	156	86	74	29	159	111
	Respondents per survey:						
9	Mean	45.8	40.8	21.7	17.2	39.0	36.8
10	Standard deviation	14.5	11.3	5.9	3.3	15.9	14.1
11	Median	44	42	21	18	37	34.5
12	Interquartile range	24	16	10	6	26.2	22.5
13	Maximum	86	61	33	22	78	67
14	Minimum	22	20	10	9	12	12

Note: The counts refer to the forecasts one and two quarters ahead for the following variables: 1968:IV–1981:II (51 surveys), consumer expenditures for durable goods (CD); 1981:III–1990:I (35 surveys), nonresidential fixed investment (NFI); 1968:IV–1990:I (86 surveys), unemployment rate (UR). The sample includes the forecasters who participated in at least 10 surveys in terms of these observations (see row 7).

Here, too, the relevant dispersion measures were all substantially reduced (cf. cols. 3 and 4).

Finally, the sample for the total period 1968–90, based on forecasts of the unemployment rate, consists of 111 out of a total of 159 people. The coverage of surveys per respondent ranges from ten to seventy, with a mean of about twenty-eight; the corresponding figures for respondents per survey are twelve to sixty-seven and thirty-seven. Here the dispersion statistics show relatively small declines in the transition from "all" to "sample" (cf. cols. 5 and 6). All in all, the turnover among the survey participants was considerable, which should be remembered when looking at the results of our study.[7]

7. Missing observations (gaps in response) limit our ability to use these data to study such problems as the dependencies over time in the forecast errors (but see Zarnowitz 1985, sec. 3).

Table 1.3   Percentage Distributions of Respondents by Primary Affiliation: Four
                   NBER-ASA Economic Outlook Surveys, 1968–80

		Quarterly Surveys			
		December 1968	December 1970	November 1975	November 1980
Row	Primary Affiliation[a]	(1)	(2)	(3)	(4)
1	Manufacturing	39.3	45.6	21.3	40.0
2	Financial institutions	21.4	21.7	23.4	20.0
3	Commercial banking	11.9	6.5	12.8	13.3
4	Other	9.5	15.2	10.6	6.7
5	Consulting and research	11.9	10.9	23.4	20.0
6	Academic	7.1	4.4	10.6	6.7
7	Government	8.3	8.7	8.5	6.7
8	Other[b]	11.9	8.7	12.8	6.7
9	Total present[c]	100.0	100.0	100.0	100.0
		(84)	(46)	(47)	(30)

[a]As reported by the participants in the given survey (those who did not respond to the question on primary affiliation are excluded).

[b]Includes a very few responses from labor union and trade association economists, but mainly "not elsewhere classified," i.e., not included in the categories listed above.

[c]Total number of respondents is listed in parentheses. The component percentages may not add up exactly to 100.0 because of rounding.

1.2.2   Forecasters' Affiliations and Methods

In 1968–80, the questionnaire asked the participating forecasters about their primary affiliation, but later the question was dropped. As illustrated in table 1.3, academic economists represented on average about 7 percent and government economists about 8 percent of the membership (rows 5 and 6). All other respondents, except for a few from labor unions and trade associations, came from the business world. Most of the time, manufacturing accounted for at least one-third and up to 40 percent of the participants, commercial banking and other financial institutions for one-fifth or more and consulting and research firms also for 20 percent or more in 1975–80, less in earlier years (rows 1–4).

These distributions resemble those for the universe of business forecasters as represented by the respondents to the annual economic outlook surveys of the National Association of Business Economists (NABE) in 1975–89. Here from one-third to more than 40 percent of respondents were in the industrial economy (manufacturing, energy, utilities), 25–30 percent in finance, 12 percent or more in consulting and research, 4 percent in other private services, and 6–12 percent in government and academe. The assessments of some of the NABE surveys looked for but found no systematic differences in forecasting performance between these industry groups.[8]

Another question asked regularly through 1981 concerned the relative importance assigned by survey participants to each of several items on a short list of forecasting methods or tools. Business economists use a variety of procedures to predict the major expenditure components of GNP, combine these predictions in nominal and real terms, and check and adjust the resulting forecasts for consistency with logic, theory, and the currently available information. This "informal GNP model" is an eclectic and flexible approach in which a major rule is played by the forecaster's judgment (Butler and Kavesh 1974). Over 70 percent of the NBER-ASA survey respondents reported using it, and over 50 percent on average ranked it first (table 1.4, col. 1). About one-fifth of the group favored econometric models, whether their own or outside, and one-fourth had their own econometric models (not necessarily comprehensive and first ranked). Users of outside models accounted for more than 40 percent of the early members and more than half of those in the late 1970s and early 1980s (cols. 2 and 3).

Leading indicators were employed by about 70 percent of the survey membership in 1968–70, but later that share declined to closer to 50 percent. They were ranked second by most respondents. Similar majorities referred to anticipations surveys, which generally were given lower ranks. Other methods, such as time-series models, were specified by fewer than 20 percent of the participants and preferred by about half of them (cols. 4–6).

These findings leave no doubt about one point, namely, that the listed methods were predominantly used in various combinations. Very few individuals preferred any one method to the exclusion of others. Presumably, there is a good reason for this in that the different methods tend to complement each other. For example, new readings on monthly cyclical indicators and the latest results from an investment or consumer anticipations survey may be used to modify forecasts from econometric models or the informal approach.

There seems to be little or no systematic relation between the forecasters' rankings of the methods and the accuracy of their predictions, allowing for the difference between the targeted variables, spans, etc. This is suggested by cross-sectional (survey-by-survey) regressions of individual forecast errors on dummy variables representing the first-ranked methods as well as by comparisons of properly standardized average errors over time (Zarnowitz 1971; Su and Su 1975). The lower panel in table 1.4 (rows 5–8) presents average root mean square errors (RMSEs) for groups classified by their self-declared methodological preferences. These measures are based on a large number of individual forecasts of rates of change in nominal GNP and real GNP (RGNP),

---

8. We are indebted to David L. Williams, secretary-treasurer of the NABE, for help in collecting these data.

Table 1.4 Average Ranks and Accuracy of Forecasting Methods Used in the NBER-ASA Surveys, 1968–81

Row	Statistic	Informal GNP Model (1)	Econometric Models		Leading Indicators (4)	Anticipations Surveys (5)	Other Methods[a] (6)
			Own (2)	Outside (3)			
1	% using[b]	75	24	48	62	57	16
2	% ranking first[c]	55	11	9	11	2	8
3	% ranking second	13	7	15	29	21	4
4	% ranking lower[d]	6	7	25	22	35	4
				Average Root Mean Square Error[e]			
5	GNP,[f] % change	.96	1.09	.89	1.00	.99	1.15
6	RGNP, % change	1.14	1.25	1.05	1.24	1.22	1.27
7	IPD, % change	.71	.76	.72	.79	.85	.83
8	UR, level	.58	.66	.52	.62	.71	.59

[a] A "write-in" response but often not specified.

[b] Based on seven surveys 1968:IV–1970:II (496 replies), six surveys 1974:I–1975:II (308 replies), and six surveys 1980:I–1981:II (187 replies). The August 1969 survey was held in connection with the ASA annual meeting and attracted a very large number of respondents (128, including 46 regular panelists). Participation in the other surveys covered varied from 24 to 83. The averages are weighted according to the numbers of the replies.

[c] Most important.

[d] Ranks third to sixth (least important).

[e] According to first-ranked method (ties for the first rank are not included). Refers to 79 individuals who participated in at least 12 of the 46 quarterly surveys in the period from 1968:IV through 1980:I. For more detail, see Zarnowitz (1983).

[f] Symbols are defined in table 1.1.

IPD (implicit price deflator) inflation, and the levels of the unemployment rate; they omit occasional forecasters and aggregate across predictions for the current quarter and three quarters ahead. The differences between the RMSEs are generally small and of uncertain significance.[9]

1.2.3   Basic Measures of Error in Forecasts of Changes and Levels

For series with upward trends, for example, GNP in current and constant dollars and the implicit price deflator, the most relevant forecasts are those of percentage change. Let the current survey quarter and the four quarters that follow be denoted by $t = 1, \ldots, 5$, respectively. The most recent quarter for which data are available precedes the date of the survey ($t = 0$). Then the predicted *average* changes refer to the spans 0–1, 0–2, ..., 0–5, and the implied *marginal* (or intraforecast) changes refer to the spans 0–1, 1–2, ..., 4–5.

For approximately stationary series such as the unemployment rate, real inventory investment, and real net exports, the most relevant forecasts are those of levels in the original units. They refer to quarters $1, \ldots, 5$.

Our data consist of more than 17,000 individual time series of forecasts defined by source, variable, and horizon. For example, for 1968–90, there are 111 respondents in our sample, reporting on seven variables over five spans each, yielding 3,885 series ($= 111 \times 7 \times 5$; however, consideration of four marginal changes for five of these variables adds another subset of 2,220 series). The tables presented below record the distributions of the summary measures of error across these individual series for each variable, period, and horizon covered. We distinguish three measures—the mean error (ME), the mean absolute error (MAE), and the root mean square error (RMSE)—and compute several location and dispersion statistics for each. These statistics include means, standard deviations, medians, interquartile ranges, skewness, and kurtosis (denoted by M, SD, MD, IQR, SK, and KU, respectively). Not all the detail of this compilation can be presented here, of course, but it is available for purposes of verification and further research.

1.2.4   Data Revisions and Forecast Accuracy

Some of the variables covered by the surveys, such as the consumer price index and the interest rates, are subject to few or no revisions. Others, notably the aggregates and indexes taken from the national income and product accounts (NIPAs), are revised frequently, and some of the revisions are large. An old but still controversial issue is which revision or vintage of such data should be used in evaluating the accuracy of forecasts. The preliminary figures are most closely related to the latest figures that were available to the

---

9. Most of these differences actually disappear when rounded off to one decimal point. Providing detail by span of forecast and for some other variables would not alter the picture significantly (see Zarnowitz 1983, 84–85). However, it is probably worth noting that the group ranking first the outside econometric models had the smallest average RMSEs for most variables (col. 3). This group included large companies using well-known econometric service bureaus as well as their own staffs of professional economists.

forecasters, but they may themselves be partly predictions or "guesstimates" and may seriously deviate from "the truth," as represented by the last revision of the data. On the other hand, the final data may be issued years after the forecast was made and may incorporate major benchmark revisions. That the forecasters should be responsible for predicting all measurement errors to be corrected by such revisions is surely questionable.

Appraisals of forecasts differ: Some are based on early data (e.g., Zarnowitz 1967), others on late data, generally prebenchmark revisions (e.g., McNees 1979; Zarnowitz 1985). Judgmental forecasts that rely heavily on recent preliminary figures may look best when compared with early data; econometric model forecasts that incorporate long series of revised data may be more favored by evaluations using later vintages.

For the NBER-ASA percentage change forecasts of GNP, RGNP, and IPD, table 1.5 shows the MAEs and RMSEs obtained by comparisons with fifteen-day, forty-five-day, early July, and late July data. In general, and with exceptions, the errors tend to increase monotonically the more revised the data are. However, the differences between the successive error measures in each segment and column of the table are relatively small, typically less than 0.1 percent. This is fortunate because it suggests that the choice of which vintage of the data to use may not be so critical. Even so, larger differences may occur in particular subperiods and offset each other over the total period covered. Our results certainly do not detract from the importance of measurement errors in the forecasting context, which has been demonstrated to be large (Cole 1969).

To save space and avoid relying on the extremes of either very preliminary or repeatedly revised data, we shall henceforth use the forty-five-day estimate in most of our text references and all tabular presentations. But no single data vintage is an optimal standard here; the choice of any is inevitably more or less arbitrary and too restrictive.

1.3   Forecasts of Nominal and Real GNP Growth and Inflation

1.3.1   Graphic Comparisons of Predictions

A convenient way to relate the distributions of survey forecasts and the actual data visually is to plot the former in the form of box diagrams and the latter as a continuous series, quarter by quarter, to common scales. Figures 1.1–1.3 apply this device to predictions of nominal and real GNP growth and IPD inflation rates. There is one graph for each variable and horizon. The midpoint of each box marks the location of the group's mean forecast; the top and bottom mark the mean plus or minus one standard deviation. A longer vertical line bisects each box and connects the highest and lowest forecasts recorded on the same occasion. A heavy curve superimposed on the array of the boxes and vertical lines represents the actual outcomes (forty-five-day estimates).

The graphs make it clear that the curves cross most of the boxes. This

Table 1.5 **Mean Absolute Errors and Root Mean Square Errors of Forecasts of Nominal and Real GNP Growth and Inflation: Comparisons with Different Vintages of Target Data, 1968–90**

Row	Vintage of Actual Data[a]	Mean Absolute Errors by Span (Qs)[b]					Root Mean Square Errors by Span (Qs)[c]				
		0–1 (1)	0–2 (2)	0–3 (3)	0–4 (4)	0–5 (5)	0–1 (6)	0–2 (7)	0–3 (8)	0–4 (9)	0–5 (10)
		Gross National Product (GNP)									
1	15-day	.59	1.08	1.55	1.92	2.36	.77	1.41	2.03	2.54	3.13
2	45-day	.62	1.12	1.60	1.99	2.48	.86	1.45	2.07	2.58	3.20
3	Early July	.65	1.15	1.65	2.02	2.54	.85	1.48	2.10	2.60	3.26
4	Late July	.69	1.17	1.66	2.03	2.52	.89	1.50	2.10	2.60	3.23
		Gross National Product in Constant Dollars (RGNP)									
5	15-day	.61	1.06	1.51	1.96	2.44	.81	1.40	2.04	2.70	3.35
6	45-day	.64	1.09	1.56	2.00	2.47	.85	1.44	2.08	2.74	3.38
7	Early July	.67	1.09	1.57	1.99	2.46	.88	1.44	2.07	2.69	3.33
8	Late July	.68	1.11	1.58	2.01	2.48	.90	1.44	2.05	2.66	3.30
		Implicit Price Deflator (IPD)									
9	15-day	.40	.71	1.07	1.49	1.98	.50	.92	1.37	1.92	2.56
10	45-day	.42	.77	1.16	1.63	2.14	.54	.99	1.50	2.10	2.79
11	Early July	.42	.77	1.18	1.66	2.17	.53	.99	1.52	2.14	2.83
12	Late July	.41	.79	1.21	1.70	2.21	.53	.99	1.53	2.16	2.84

[a]15-day: preliminary data released in the month following the target quarter of the forecast. 45-day: revised data released a month later. Early July: generally first July revision; where this is not available, the preceding revision. Late July: generally second July revision; where this is not available, the preceding revision.

[b]Mean of the MAEs of the individual forecasts, where MAE $= 1/N \sum |E_t|$; $E_t = P_t - A_t$; $P_t =$ predicted value; $A_t =$ actual value of the given vintage. The average errors refer to percentage changes from quarter $t, t + 1, t + 2, t + 3,$ and $t + 4$ (1, 2, 3, and 4), respectively, where t refers to the quarterly date of the survey. Thus, 0–1 denotes the change from quarter $t - 1$ to quarter t, 0–2 denotes the change from quarter $t - 1$ to quarter $t + 1$, etc. All measures refer to percentage change errors and are given in percentages.

[c]Mean of the RMSEs of the individual forecasts, where RMSE $= \sqrt{1/n \sum (P_t - A_t)}$.

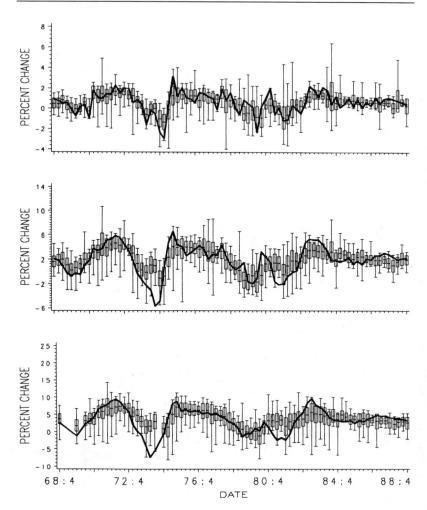

Fig. 1.1   Forecast distributions and actual values of percentage changes in real GNP, three horizons, 1968:IV–1990:I

H

M + SD

M   H = high; M = mean; SD = standard deviation; L = low.

M – SD

L

means that the realizations fall within one standard deviation of the mean or "consensus" predictions most of the time. However, some large declines in actual values are widely missed or underestimated, such mis- or underestimations showing up as boxes lying conspicuously above the troughs or valleys in the curves. Similarly, widespread underpredictions of some large actual rises

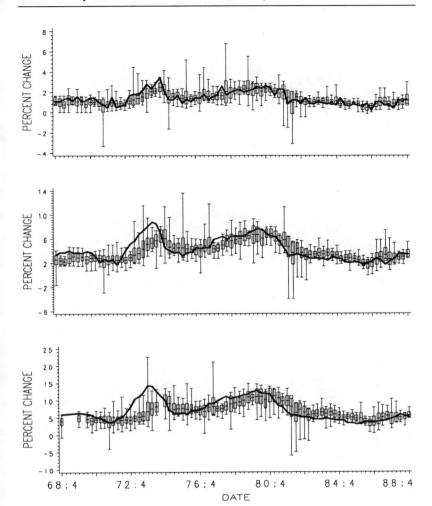

Fig. 1.2 Forecast distributions and actual values of percentage changes in IPD, three horizons, 1968:IV–1990:I

show up as boxes situated below the local peaks for concentrations of high values. Occasionally, the actual outcome would be missed by all respondents to the survey, as seen in instances where the entire vertical line of forecasts lies above or below the curve.

These errors are clearly associated with business cycles. Figure 1.1 shows clusters of large overestimates of real GNP growth in all major slowdowns and recessions covered: 1969–70, 1973–74, 1981–82, and 1985–86. It also shows clusters of large underestimation errors in all recoveries and booms: 1972, 1975, late 1980, 1983–84, and 1987. So overprediction of growth occurs mainly when the economy weakens and declines, underprediction when it rises strongly. Both types of error can be seen as particularly pronounced

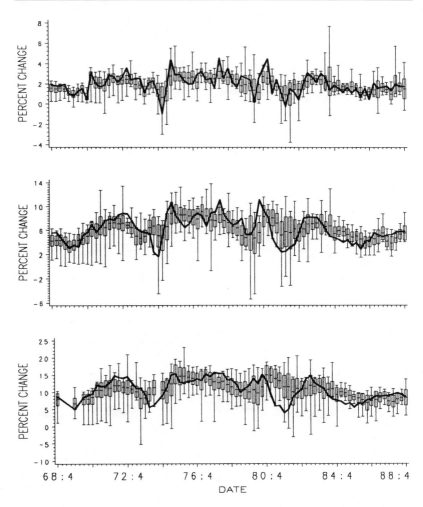

Fig. 1.3   Forecast distributions and actual values of percentage changes in nominal GNP, three horizons, 1968:IV–1990:I

and persistent in forecasts with longer spans. Overall, the errors of overprediction in bad times tended to be larger than those of underprediction in good times.

Figure 1.2 shows that inflation was at times widely underpredicted in 1969–71, even though it was then fairly stable. In 1973–74, a period of supply shocks and deepening recession, inflation rose sharply and was greatly underestimated by most survey participants. Here the curves can be seen to rise above most of the boxes and even to peak above the highest forecasts for the longer horizons. The same tendency to underpredict also prevailed in 1976–80, although in somewhat weaker form. In this period, inflation rose more gradually, while the economy first expanded vigorously and then, in 1979–80, experienced another oil shock, a slowdown, and a short recession. In between, during the recovery of 1975–76, inflation decreased markedly and was mostly overestimated. Another, much longer disinflation occurred in 1981–85, a phase that followed the shifts to a tight monetary policy in late 1979 and included the severe 1981–82 recession and then a strong recovery. Here again most forecasters are observed to overpredict inflation. Finally, in 1986–89, inflation, which began to drift upward, was generally well predicted most of the time (except in the mid-quarter of 1987, when it dipped suddenly and was overestimated).

In sum, there is also a cyclical pattern to the errors of inflation forecasts. Accelerated inflation was associated predominantly with underprediction, disinflation with overprediction errors.

Figure 1.3, which compares the forecast distributions and actual values for nominal GNP growth rates, shows a broad family resemblance to the corresponding graphs for real GNP growth in figure 1.1. For example, both nominal and real growth tended to be underpredicted in such boom years as 1972 and 1983 and overpredicted in such recession years as 1974 and 1981–82. But inflation expectations and their relation to real growth forecasts are also important here. Predictions of nominal GNP are often helped by inverse correlations between the changes in IPD and RGNP and the associated offsets between the forecast errors for the two variables.[10] Thus, in the inflationary recession of 1973–74 associated with the first occurrence of major supply and oil shocks, real growth was overpredicted and inflation underpredicted. The reverse combination of too low RGNP and too high IPD forecasts can be observed in the recoveries of 1974 and 1983–84. However, there are also episodes of positive correlation; for example, in 1981–82, both real growth and inflation were overpredicted, which resulted in nominal growth forecasts that turned out much too high.

1.3.2 Distributions of Summary Measures of Error

Table 1.6 presents the statistics on the distributions of the mean errors in the sampled NBER-ASA survey forecasts of GNP, RGNP, and IPD. For the forecasts of average changes in GNP, the means are all negative, but the corresponding medians have mixed signs. The averages for the marginal change errors are predominantly positive. The dispersion measures (SD and IQR) are very large relative to the averages. Thus, these statistics (rows 1–4) fail to show clearly any dominant under- or overprediction bias. Similar observations can be made about the real GNP forecasts (rows 7–10). However, underestimation errors definitely prevail in the inflation (IPD) forecasts. Here all the averages, M and MD, are negative, and the relative size of the corresponding AD and IQR figures is less.

---

10. This has been noted before, in Zarnowitz (1979, 15).

Table 1.6   Distribution of Mean Errors in Individual Forecasts of Nominal and Real GNP Growth and Inflation, 1968–90

Row	Statistic	Average Errors by Span (Qs)					Marginal Errors by Span (Qs)			
		0–1 (1)	0–2 (2)	0–3 (3)	0–4 (4)	0–5 (5)	1–2 (6)	2–3 (7)	3–4 (8)	4–5 (9)
		Gross National Product (GNP)								
1	Mean (M)	−.09	−.11	−.11	−.14	−.30	−.01	.01	.04	.08
2	Standard deviation (SD)	.26	.56	.91	1.19	1.61	.31	.38	.36	.37
3	Median (MD)	−.05	−.06	.04	.15	.00	.01	.06	.09	.13
4	Interquartile range (IQR)	.24	.48	.72	.91	1.30	.27	.29	.31	.31
5	Skewness (SK)	−1.94	−1.57	−1.60	−2.65	−2.78	−.55	−1.41	−1.64	−1.92
6	Kurtosis (KU)	12.14	12.42	11.90	12.81	13.80	10.89	8.49	8.50	8.66
		Gross National Product in Constant Dollars (RGNP)								
7	Mean (M)	−.01	.09	.25	.45	.48	.10	.16	.22	.28
8	Standard deviation (SD)	.24	.48	.77	1.06	1.39	.29	.35	.34	.43
9	Median (MD)	−.00	.13	.34	.62	.64	.10	.20	.27	.29
10	Interquartile range (IQR)	.27	.46	.69	.98	1.20	.28	.36	.38	.51
11	Skewness (SK)	−1.30	−1.58	−1.84	−2.04	−2.06	−1.17	−1.75	−1.34	−.89
12	Kurtosis (KU)	4.64	6.76	7.29	7.57	8.13	4.78	6.63	4.24	1.97
		Implicit Price Deflator (IPD)								
13	Mean (M)	−.07	−.19	−.36	−.57	−.65	−.12	−.15	−.19	−.21
14	Standard deviation (SD)	.16	.34	.57	.83	1.24	.20	.25	.27	.35
15	Median (MD)	−.07	−.17	−.34	−.54	−.74	−.11	−.14	−.16	−.21
16	Interquartile range (IQR)	.15	.39	.75	1.09	1.79	.27	.35	.36	.52
17	Skewness (SK)	.06	.32	.09	.14	−.06	.28	−.10	.26	−.04
18	Kurtosis (KU)	1.35	.76	.50	.92	−.11	.42	.36	1.91	−.24

Note: Columns 1–5 refer to the errors in forecasts of average changes; cols. 6–9 refer to the errors in forecast of marginal changes (for 0–1, the average and marginal changes are the same). ME, SD, MD, and IQR (rows 1–4, 7–10, and 13–16) are in percentage points; entries for SK and KU (rows 5–6, 11–12, and 17–18) are dimensionless ratios. IQR = $Q_3 - Q_1$ is the difference, third quartile minus first quartile of the distribution (where MD = Q_2). SK = μ_3/σ^3 is the ratio of the third moment around the mean to the third power of the standard deviation SD = σ. KU = μ_4/σ^4 is the ratio of the fourth moment around the mean to the fourth power of SD.

The M and MD statistics tend to increase monotonically in absolute value with the length of the span, strongly for the forecasts of average change, less so for those of the marginal change. For each of three variables, the SD and IQR statistics tend to be much larger the longer the span and the more remote the forecast target (cf. rows 1–4, 7–10, and 13–16).

There is evidence that the distributions for GNP and RGNP are skewed to the left (i.e., SK < 0), with medians larger than the means. For IPD, SK is very small throughout, and M and MD are very close (cf. rows 5, 11, and 17).

The distributions for GNP and RGNP show larger values for kurtosis, indicating the presence of long, thick tails (for the normal distribution, KU = 3). Again, the situation is very different for IPD, where the KU statistics are very low (cf. rows 6, 12, and 18).

Tables 1.7 and 1.8, each of which has the same format as table 1.6, show the distribution statistics for the mean absolute errors and the root mean square errors, respectively. The RMSEs are, of course, larger than the corresponding MAEs, and the statistics in table 1.8 are generally larger than their counterparts in table 1.7 (e.g., they are on average about 30–60 percent higher for the GNP measures). Otherwise, the two sets have very similar characteristics, which can be summed up as follows.

For both the MAEs and the RMSEs of the individual forecasts, the means and medians increase with the span regularly, strongly for the average changes, less so for the marginal changes. The main reason is that errors cumulate over time, but it is also true that the more distant target quarters are predicted somewhat less accurately than the near ones. The dispersion statistics SD and IQR also increase as the forecast horizon lengthens, except for the marginal IPD errors.

SK is greater than zero everywhere here, and the SK statistics are generally large for GNP and RGNP but small for IPD. Consistently, the MDs tend to be smaller than the MEs. The distributions tend to be skewed to the right.

Several of the KU statistics for GNP and RGNP are quite large. Little kurtosis is observed in the IPD forecasts, except for the shortest ones.

We conclude that the survey respondents tended to underestimate inflation but not (or, in any event, much less) the nominal and real GNP growth rates. The IPD forecast distributions were more nearly symmetrical and had fewer outliers than the distributions for GNP and RGNP.

1.3.3   Individual versus Group Mean Forecasts

Combining corresponding forecasts that come from different sources or use different techniques tends to produce significant gains in accuracy. This is by now well known from many studies, including some based on the NBER-ASA surveys.[11] In what follows, we extend and update the evidence on this point.

---

11. See Zarnowitz (1984), which uses the data for 1968–79. An early demonstration that simple averaging can reduce forecast errors is in Zarnowitz (1967, 123–26). For a survey of the literature, see Clemen (1989).

Table 1.7   Distribution of Mean Absolute Errors in Individual Forecasts of Nominal and Real GNP Growth and Inflation, 1968–90

Row	Statistic	Average Errors by Span (Qs)					Marginal Errors by Span (Qs)			
		0–1 (1)	0–2 (2)	0–3 (3)	0–4 (4)	0–5 (5)	1–2 (6)	2–3 (7)	3–4 (8)	4–5 (9)
		Gross National Product (GNP)								
1	Mean (M)	.62	1.12	1.60	1.99	2.48	.76	.84	.85	.88
2	Standard deviation (SD)	.23	.43	.64	.81	1.12	.22	.23	.23	.26
3	Median (MD)	.56	1.02	1.49	1.84	2.31	.73	.81	.82	.86
4	Interquartile range (IQR)	.28	.39	.41	.61	.98	.20	.22	.26	.28
5	Skewness (SK)	1.69	2.38	3.11	3.51	3.85	1.61	1.69	1.16	1.11
6	Kurtosis (KU)	4.18	8.21	13.31	18.79	22.53	4.15	5.44	2.46	2.21
		Gross National Product in Constant Dollars (RGNP)								
7	Mean (M)	.64	1.09	1.56	2.00	2.47	.78	.85	.93	.96
8	Standard deviation (SD)	.23	.37	.51	.63	.84	.20	.20	.24	.26
9	Median (MD)	.59	1.00	1.41	1.82	2.26	.76	.82	.92	.94
10	Interquartile range (IQR)	.22	.33	.46	.63	.89	.29	.29	.34	.33
11	Skewness (SK)	1.59	1.77	1.82	1.76	1.92	1.09	.70	.30	.33
12	Kurtosis (KU)	2.89	4.12	4.12	4.13	6.12	2.20	.87	-.18	.36
		Implicit Price Deflator (IPD)								
13	Mean (M)	.42	.77	1.16	1.63	2.14	.50	.56	.61	.65
14	Standard deviation (SD)	.13	.23	.35	.45	.59	.12	.13	.16	.18
15	Median (MD)	.38	.72	1.08	1.55	2.07	.49	.54	.57	.62
16	Interquartile range (IQR)	.14	.23	.47	.51	.69	.15	.18	.16	.19
17	Skewness (SK)	1.84	1.29	1.11	.71	.64	.85	1.17	1.11	.98
18	Kurtosis (KU)	4.53	2.51	2.21	.85	.84	1.36	1.25	2.20	1.76

Note: See table 1.6.

Table 1.8   Distribution of Root Mean Square Errors in Individual Forecasts of Nominal and Real GNP Growth and Inflation, 1968–90

| | | Average Errors by Span (Qs) | | | | | Marginal Errors by Span (Qs) | | | |
| | | 0–1 | 0–2 | 0–3 | 0–4 | 0–5 | 1–2 | 2–3 | 3–4 | 4–5 |
Row	Statistic	(1)	(2)	(3)	(4)	(5)	(6)	(7)	(8)	(9)
						Gross National Product (GNP)				
1	Mean (M)	.81	1.45	2.07	2.58	3.20	1.02	1.12	1.13	1.19
2	Standard deviation (SD)	.30	.55	.76	.92	1.25	.31	.30	.30	.38
3	Median (MD)	.74	1.33	1.93	2.45	3.06	.97	1.10	1.11	1.14
4	Interquartile range (IQR)	.38	.47	.61	.69	1.14	.25	.29	.39	.40
5	Skewness (SK)	1.20	2.17	2.36	2.34	2.43	1.63	1.34	1.55	1.51
6	Kurtosis (KU)	1.52	6.48	7.32	9.47	10.59	3.97	3.65	.06	4.61
						Gross National Product in Constant Dollars (RGNP)				
7	Mean (M)	.85	1.44	2.08	2.74	3.38	1.05	1.16	1.27	1.32
8	Standard deviation (SD)	.35	.49	.67	.82	1.04	.31	.28	.33	.38
9	Median (MD)	.77	1.32	1.90	2.57	3.12	.98	1.15	1.26	1.31
10	Interquartile range (IQR)	.34	.54	.80	.83	1.18	.38	.39	.50	.51
11	Skewness (SK)	1.78	1.54	1.54	1.30	1.22	1.37	.47	.18	.46
12	Kurtosis (KU)	4.02	3.42	3.29	2.04	1.90	3.08	.20	-.11	.86
						Implicit Price Deflator (IPD)				
13	Mean (M)	.54	.99	1.50	2.10	2.79	.65	.72	.79	.85
14	Standard deviation (SD)	.19	.32	.43	.57	.75	.20	.18	.24	.25
15	Median (MD)	.47	.91	1.43	2.06	2.79	.61	.70	.74	.81
16	Interquartile range (IQR)	.18	.30	.55	.79	1.08	.22	.24	.22	.33
17	Skewness (SK)	1.82	1.44	.89	.54	.18	1.44	.94	1.51	1.21
18	Kurtosis (KU)	3.35	2.78	1.15	1.06	-.04	3.00	1.58	4.19	3.64

Note: See table 1.6.

Averaging all predictions in each survey for a given variable and horizon results in a time series of group mean (or median) forecasts. These are often called "consensus" forecasts, whether or not there is much actual consensus among the respondents. The group mean predictions based on our GNP, RGNP, and IPD sample forecasts have considerably smaller errors than the average individual respondent, as shown by comparisons of the ME, MEA, and RMSE entries in table 1.9 (cf. cols. 1 and 4, 2 and 5, and 3 and 6). The absolute or squared errors tend to increase with the span of forecast for both individuals and group means, but less so for the latter.

For each individual time series of forecasts, a series of group mean forecasts has been computed with strictly matching coverage in terms of the survey dates and target characteristics. Table 1.10 shows the locational statistics for the distributions of the ratios of the individual RMSEs to the corresponding group RMSEs. These measures indicate that the group mean forecasts were more accurate than about 75 percent of the sampled respondents' forecasts. Thus, most of the first- or lower-quartile (Q_1) ratios are close to one (but some for RGNP are lower), most of the median (Q_2) ratios are 1.1–1.2, and most of the third- or upper-quartile (Q_3) ratios are 1.3–1.5 (cf. rows 2–4, 7–9, and 12–14). These distributions are bounded from below (any ratio greater than zero) and are heavily skewed to the right (e.g., the entries for the best forecasts in table 1.10 are 0.5–0.9, those for the worst 3–7).

Unlike their numerators and denominators, the ratios of the individual to the group RMSEs do not depend systematically on the length of the forecast or distance to the target quarter. Also, the diversity of the individual forecasts by source, variable, and horizon is greatly reduced by the normalization with the group means. Thus, the ratios for the same quartiles are not very different for GNP, RGNP, and IPD.

1.3.4   Some Overall Accuracy and Variability Measures

The preceding tables offer some insight into the structure of errors calculated from the survey forecasts, but not into their relative levels. The latter will be assessed by comparisons with benchmark predictions from time-series models selected to fit the characteristics of the variables concerned and with forecasts from other sources. But, first, we take a quick look at the average values of the outcomes for the target series so as to gain some idea about the orders of magnitude involved.

Columns 7–9 in table 1.9 show, successively, the means, standard deviations, and root mean square values (RMSVs) of the actual percentage changes in the targeted variables. The absolute values of the average errors in the individual forecasts and, a fortiori, in the group mean forecasts are generally very small compared with the average actual changes, particularly for GNP and IPD (cf. cols. 1 and 7). The average RMSEs of the individual forecasts are about 30–37 percent of the RMSVs for the nominal GNP growth and inflation and 68–72 percent of the RMSVs for the real GNP growth rates (cf. cols.

Table 1.9   Individual and Group Mean Forecasts and Actual Values of Nominal and Real GNP Growth and Inflation: Selected Statistics on Accuracy and Variability, 1968–90

Row	Span (Qs)	Individual Forecasts[a]			Group Mean Forecasts[b]			Actual Values (%Δ)[c]		
		M (1)	MAE (2)	RMSE (3)	M (4)	MAE (5)	RMSE (6)	M (7)	SD (8)	RMSV (9)
				Gross National Product (GNP)						
1	0–1	−.09	.62	.81	−.08	.49	.64	1.98	.96	2.20
2	0–2	−.11	1.12	1.45	−.10	.84	1.11	4.00	1.00	4.31
3	0–3	−.11	1.60	2.07	−.07	1.22	1.61	6.07	2.14	6.44
4	0–4	−.14	1.99	2.58	−.02	1.56	2.06	8.20	2.63	8.61
5	0–5	−.30	2.48	3.20	−.09	1.91	2.51	10.38	3.12	10.84
				Gross National Product in Constant Dollars (RGNP)						
6	0–1	−.01	.64	.85	−.02	.50	.64	.61	1.03	1.20
7	0–2	.09	1.09	1.44	.02	.83	1.11	1.23	1.77	2.16
8	0–3	.25	1.56	2.08	.16	1.17	1.61	1.86	2.40	3.04
9	0–4	.45	2.00	2.74	.33	1.42	2.05	2.50	2.95	3.87
10	0–5	.48	2.47	3.38	.40	1.70	2.47	3.15	3.45	4.67
				Implicit Price Deflator (IPD)						
11	0–1	−.07	.42	.54	−.04	.28	.35	1.36	.65	1.51
12	0–2	−.19	.77	.99	−.12	.55	.70	2.74	1.25	3.01
13	0–3	−.36	1.16	1.50	−.22	.84	1.13	4.16	1.84	4.55
14	0–4	−.57	1.63	2.10	−.34	1.21	1.64	5.60	2.43	6.10
15	0–5	−.65	2.14	2.79	−.37	1.63	2.23	7.08	3.03	7.70

Note: On the symbols used, see previous tables and the text.

[a]Means of the corresponding statistics for individual forecasts (as shown in tables 1.6–1.8, rows 1, 7, and 13, cols. 1–5).

[b]Survey-by-survey "consensus" forecasts based on the sampled data, as explained in the text.

[c]45-day estimates, as used in tables 1.6–1.8. RMSV = root mean square value computed as $\sqrt{(ME)^2 + (SD)^2}$.

Table 1.10   Individual-to-Group Mean Ratios of Root Mean Square Errors: Selected Distributional Statistics for Forecasts of Nominal and Real GNP Growth and Inflation, 1968–90

		Average Errors by Span (Qs)					Marginal Errors by Span (Qs)			
Row	Statistics	0–1 (1)	0–2 (2)	0–3 (3)	0–4 (4)	0–5 (5)	1–2 (6)	2–3 (7)	3–4 (8)	4–5 (9)
		Gross National Product (GNP)								
1	Lowest-error forecast (MIN)	.84	.72	.88	.79	.78	.85	.85	.82	.68
2	First quartile (Q₁)	1.10	1.07	1.07	1.08	1.03	1.05	1.07	1.06	1.07
3	Median (MD)	1.22	1.23	1.19	1.20	1.18	1.15	1.11	1.13	1.14
4	Third quartile (Q₃)	1.62	1.46	1.38	1.36	1.43	1.33	1.25	1.28	1.32
5	Highest-error forecast (MAX)	7.34	5.35	5.90	5.78	5.57	3.12	2.88	2.56	4.26
		Gross National Product in Constant Dollars (RGNP)								
6	Lowest-error forecast (MIN)	.82	.63	.77	.82	.82	.76	.87	.86	.83
7	First quartile (Q₁)	1.11	1.09	1.04	1.06	1.06	1.06	1.06	1.04	1.03
8	Median (MD)	1.30	1.20	1.17	1.14	1.14	1.17	1.14	1.13	1.11
9	Third quartile (Q₃)	1.58	1.40	1.36	1.38	1.33	1.31	1.30	1.28	1.31
10	Highest-error forecast (MAX)	4.84	3.87	6.45	5.76	6.69	3.29	3.77	4.40	3.84
		Implicit Price Deflator (IPD)								
11	Lowest-error forecast (MIN)	.83	.88	.82	.55	.53	.67	.88	.81	.71
12	First quartile (Q₁)	1.13	1.03	1.02	.99	1.00	1.03	1.02	1.02	1.02
13	Median (MD)	1.24	1.21	1.15	1.12	1.12	1.17	1.12	1.11	1.11
14	Third quartile (Q₃)	1.56	1.39	1.34	1.27	1.23	1.39	1.32	1.23	1.29
15	Highest-error forecast (MAX)	3.55	4.30	3.55	3.74	3.37	3.27	2.68	2.86	3.71

Note: All entries show ratios $RMSE_i/RMSE_g$, where the subscripts i and g refer to the individual and group mean forecasts, respectively. MIN and MAX denote the lowest and highest ratios in each distribution. Q_1 and Q_3 denote the lower and upper quartile ratios, and MD denotes the median ratio.

3 and 9). The RMSEs of the group mean forecasts are about 23–29 percent of the RMSVs for nominal GNP growth and inflation and 51–53 percent of the RMSVs for real GNP growth (cf. cols. 6 and 9).

1.3.5   Have Any Forecasters Excelled Consistently?

Each forecaster in our sample of 111 was ranked by the accuracy of his or her predictions, separately for each forecast target as defined by the date of the survey (t), variable, and span (e.g., for the GNP 0–1 predictions made in 1970:I). Let r_{it} be the rank of the ith respondent in the time t survey, which increases from the smallest to the largest squared error. The number of surveys covered per respondent (m_i) varied widely across individuals, and the number of respondents per survey (n_t) varied widely across time (see table 1.2, col. 6). In view of this variability, it was necessary to normalize the ranks by the number of participants in the particular survey. This is done by calculating $R_t = 100 r_{it}/n_t$. The best forecast in each set would have $r_{it} = 1$, and hence $R_{it} = 100/n_t$. The worst forecast would have $r_{it} = n_t$, and hence $R_{it} = 100$. This setup permits us to consider the question, How stable were the accuracy rankings of the forecasters over time?

When the ranks are aggregated across the corresponding sets for each individual, measures of central tendency and dispersion are obtained that characterize the distributions over time of the ranks. Thus, for a given variable and span, the overall rank of the ith forecaster is $R_i = 1/m \sum_t^m R_{it}$, and the corresponding standard deviation equals $[1/m \sum_t^m (R_{it} - R_i)^2]^{1/2}$. We compute such means, standard deviations, medians, quartiles, and ranges for each of the 111 individuals covered. Table 1.11 presents simple averages of some of these measures in columns 1–4. For example, the grand means (Ms) in column 1 represent $\bar{R} = 1/111 \sum_i R_i$.

In addition, columns 5–10 of table 1.11 summarize the distributions across individuals of the mean normalized ranks R_i. The selected statistics include SD, quartiles, and extremes. For example, here SD $= [1/111 \sum_i (R_i - \bar{R})^2]^{1/2}$ (col. 5).

The entries in column 1 are all very close: 53–55 for GNP, 52 for RGNP, and 54–59 for IPD. The corresponding medians (not shown) are similarly clustered but one to two points larger. In fact, there is very little variation between the entries in any column of table 1.11. That is, the distributions of the normalized ranks are very similar for any of the three variables covered and for any of the five spans.

Typically, any forecaster would rank high at some times and low at others. Indeed, the *average* range of 85–90 (col. 4) is close to the *maximum* range possible for the R_{it} ranks (which cannot exceed 99 and would not be much larger than 90 for relatively small values of n_t). The forecaster's rank would fall in the center half of the distribution (i.e., in the interquartile range IQR) nearly 50 percent of the time and within $\pm$ SD of the mean perhaps up to 66 percent of the time (cols. 2 and 3). There is no evidence of a high skewness or

Table 1.11   Ranking Forecasters According to Their Accuracy in Predicting Nominal and Real GNP and Inflation Rates: Selected Measures, 1968–90

Row	Span (Qs)	Distribution over Time of Individual Normalized Ranks (R_{it}): Means of:				Distribution across Individuals of Mean Normalized Ranks (R_i)					
		M (1)	SD (2)	IQR (3)	Range (4)	SD (5)	MIN (6)	Q_1 (7)	MD (8)	Q_3 (9)	MAX (10)
		Gross National Product (GNP)									
1	0–1	53	27	46	87	10	38	48	53	59	95
2	0–2	53	27	46	87	11	32	45	51	59	98
3	0–3	53	27	46	88	11	36	46	51	58	100
4	0–4	53	27	46	86	11	33	47	52	58	99
5	0–5	53	26	45	85	12	30	46	51	58	100
		Gross National Product in Constant Dollars (RGNP)									
6	0–1	52	28	50	90	9	29	47	52	56	77
7	0–2	52	28	47	89	10	30	47	51	57	94
8	0–3	52	28	47	88	9	35	46	51	57	89
9	0–4	52	28	48	88	9	34	45	51	58	87
10	0–5	52	28	48	86	10	31	45	51	57	99
		Implicit Price Deflator (IPD)									
11	0–1	59	28	48	89	10	40	52	57	65	93
12	0–2	56	28	48	89	10	39	49	56	62	95
13	0–3	55	28	47	88	10	33	48	54	60	98
14	0–4	54	28	46	88	10	29	48	54	60	93
15	0–5	54	27	46	86	11	29	45	54	59	94

Note: The basic unit of measurement is the normalized rank $R_{it} = 100(r_{it}/n_t)$, where r_{it} = rank of the ith forecaster in the time t set of predictions for a given variable and span, and n_t = number of forecasters in the same set. The ranks are assigned according to the squared errors $(P − A)^2$, from the smallest to the largest. The entries in cols. 1–4 represent the means of the summary measures for the distributions of the individuals' ranks over time (e.g., M in col. 1 refers to $\bar{R} = 1/n \sum_{1}^{n} R_i$, where $R_i = 1/m \sum_{1}^{m} R_{it}$; similarly for the standard deviations in col. 2, etc.). The entries in cols. 5–10 characterize the distributions across the individuals of R_i. All statistics are rounded off, with no decimals shown. For symbols, see the preceding tables and the text.

a high kurtosis in these distributions. To sum up, the forecasting performance of any one individual relative to another is likely to be highly variable over time.

On the other hand, the dispersion of the corresponding forecasts and their errors across individuals will tend to be limited by the commonality of the targets of the forecasters and of the information and methods available to them. The correlations between the forecasters' errors are expected to be positive and may be high. Our measures presumably reflect all these regularities. Interestingly, the standard deviations in column 2 are 26–28, but those in column 5 are only 9–12 (note that the definition of the former includes time t explicitly, while the definition of the latter does not). Similarly, the IQRs in column 3 are 45–50, those implied by columns 7 and 9 are 9–15, and the corresponding total ranges are 85–90 and 30–59 (cf. cols. 4 and 6–10). These numbers seem consistent with the results obtained in some previous studies indicating that fluctuations over time contribute more than differences across forecasters to the overall variation in forecast errors (see Zarnowitz 1974, 578–79).

For each of the forecast targets identified in lines 1–15 of table 1.11, the ranks according to R_i form a relatively tight cluster between the values of Q_1 and Q_3 that average 47 and 59, respectively (cols. 7–9). One-quarter of the group performed poorly relative to the others, with R_i values ranging from well above 60 to 100 (cols. 9–10). However, our attention centers on the top-ranking quarter, with R_i values averaging in the 30s and 40s (cols. 6–7). The latter can be said to have excelled with respect to the given category of forecast targets.

All these subsets, of course, consist of individuals who are coded and can be identified. It is important to ask next what the correlations of the ranks are between the different variables and spans. For example, do those who best predicted the growth of real GNP also tend to excel in predicting inflation? Do those who rank high in forecasting over the shortest horizons also rank high in forecasting over the longer horizons?

Table 1.12 indicates that the answers to these questions are on the whole positive. The correlations among our normalized ranks, both across the variables for each span (rows 1–3) and across the spans for each variable (rows 4–13), are all positive and sufficiently high not to be due to chance. Forecasters who predict relatively well (poorly) any one of these targets are also likely to predict well (poorly) any of the other targets. Not surprisingly, the correlations are higher the more closely related the forecast targets are. Thus, they are higher for GNP and RGNP than for RGNP and IPD and higher for successive spans (e.g., 0–1 and 0–2) than for more distant spans (e.g., 0–1 and 0–5). Similar results have been found for other variables and periods and for marginal as well as average change forecasts (cf. Zarnowitz 1984, 17–19).

Table 1.12   Respondents to NBER-ASA Surveys Ranked According to the
Accuracy of Their Forecasts of Nominal and Real GNP Growth and
IPD Inflation Rates: Correlations among the Ranks and across
Variables and Horizons, 1968–90

		Correlated for Forecast Horizons (in Qs)				
Row	Variables	0–1 (1)	0–2 (2)	0–3 (3)	0–4 (4)	0–5 (5)
1	GNP, RGNP	.73	.74	.68	.64	.64
2	GNP, IP	.56	.64	.68	.59	.59
3	RGNP, IPD	.47	.52	.54	.51	.42

		Correlated for Variables		
	Horizons	GNP	RGNP	IPD
4	0–1, 0–2	.82	.77	.79
5	0–1, 0–3	.73	.68	.65
6	0–1, 0–4	.68	.67	.51
7	0–1, 0–5	.73	.62	.47
8	0–2, 0–3	.87	.87	.83
9	0–2, 0–4	.75	.74	.75
10	0–2, 0–5	.79	.72	.67
11	0–3, 0–4	.92	.86	.92
12	0–3, 0–5	.87	.80	.86
13	0–4, 0–5	.92	.86	.92

Note: The correlations are based on the normalized ranks described in the text and table 1.11. On the symbols used, see previous tables and the text.

1.3.6   Comparisons with Bayesian Vector Autoregressive (BVAR) Forecasts

We use a BVAR model with five variables: RGNP, IPD, M2 (broad money supply), LI (the composite index of leading indicators), and TBR (the three-month Treasury-bill rate). TBR is a level series; the others are series of growth rates. The model is estimated on quarterly series, each taken with six lags. The data are those presently available (i.e., they incorporate all revisions), and, in this sense, the forecasts based on them are ex post. But the forecasts are generated sequentially, using only the information preceding the date of the forecast.

Unlike the forecasters, who can take advantage of the early information provided by the monthly and weekly time series released during the survey quarter, the BVAR model does not draw on any such data. On the other hand, unlike the BVAR model, which is based on the present, revised series, the forecasters work under the disadvantage of having access only to the latest preliminary data, that is, data containing measurement errors that have yet to be eliminated by revisions.

Because the quarterly data for the survey quarter (1) are not known to the forecasters, our first approach was to impute the same lack of knowledge to our BVAR model. Here, then, the shortest prediction is for 0–1, the longest for 0–5. But, as pointed out by Christopher Sims during the conference, this approach (now called "variant A") ignores any effects on the survey forecasts of the most recent economic news. Since the knowledge of the news on balance presumably helps the forecasters, variant A in this respect handicaps our BVAR, as it would more generally any model based strictly on quarterly time series only.

For this reason, we also present the results of alternative calculations ("variant B"), which assume full knowledge of the actual values in quarter 1, or effectively perfect foresight. Here, for 0–1, the error of the BVAR model is identically zero, and no comparisons with the survey forecasts are available; the shortest prediction is for 1–2. Thus, the two variants represent contrasting extremes: in A there is no knowledge; in B there is full knowledge of period 1 values. Variant B handicaps the real-life forecaster, who has only partial and indirect knowledge of the target variable in the current (survey) quarter.

It follows that the truth about the relative accuracy of the individual forecasts from the surveys and the BVAR forecasts falls somewhere between variants A and B. Table 1.13 provides the evidence, showing in columns 1–3 that the measures of error of BVAR variant A for spans 0–1, 0–2, . . . , etc. are approximately equal to the corresponding measures of error of BVAR variant B for spans 0–2, 0–3, . . . , etc., respectively (cf. rows 1 and 7, 2 and 8, and so on). As would be expected, the RMSE ratios in columns 4–8 are throughout lower for variant A than for variant B, when comparing entries for the corresponding spans (rows 2 and 7, 3 and 8, and so on). That is, variant B calculations show the BVAR model forecasts in a relatively more favorable light than variant A calculations do.

We present the results for both variants of the retroactively used time-series models for comparisons relating to GNP, RGNP, and IPD (this covers both our own and outside, multivariate and univariate models). For the other variables, only variant A is used. More often than not, the "true" outcomes are probably closer to the variant A than to the variant B comparisons because the forecasters' information about recent and current developments is in fact quite limited and deficient and because the forecasters use preliminary data and the time-series models use revised data. When all is considered, it can be argued that variant B handicaps the forecasters more than variant A handicaps the models.

The RMSE ratios in table 1.13, columns 4–8, indicate that at least 75 percent of the individual forecasts of GNP, 50 percent of those of IPD, and 25 percent of those of RGNP were more accurate than the variant A BVAR forecasts. Thus, the Q_3 ratios are less than 1.0 for nominal growth and close to 1.0 for inflation. For real growth, the MD ratios approach unity at spans of 2 to 3 quarters and exceed it at longer spans. The ratios based on the variant B

Table 1.13   BVAR Forecasts (Two Variants) versus Individual Forecasts from NBER-ASA Surveys: Summary Measures of Error and RMSE Ratios for GNP, RGNP, and IPD, 1968–90

Row	Span (Qs)	BVAR Forecasts[a]			RMSE Ratios, Individual to BVAR Forecasts[b]				
		M (1)	MAE (2)	RMSE (3)	MIN (4)	Q_1 (5)	MD (6)	Q_3 (7)	MAX (8)
		Gross National Product (GNP): Variant A							
1	0–1	.07	.84	1.11	.32	.54	.66	.91	1.89
2	0–2	.18	1.47	1.92	.34	.57	.68	.83	2.00
3	0–3	.26	2.08	2.73	.38	.58	.70	.83	2.44
4	0–4	.33	2.59	3.45	.24	.59	.68	.85	2.61
5	0–5	.38	3.23	4.23	.25	.54	.67	.82	2.41
		GNP: Variant B							
6	0–1	0	0	0	N.A.	N.A.	N.A.	N.A.	N.A.
7	0–2	.07	.87	1.14	.43	.75	.85	1.03	2.89
8	0–3	.17	1.49	1.96	.53	.78	.91	1.03	1.90
9	0–4	.26	2.12	2.80	.49	.81	.91	1.05	1.82
10	0–5	.33	2.63	3.53	.63	.86	.96	1.13	2.29
		GNP in Constant Dollars (RGNP): Variant A							
11	0–1	.08	.78	1.00	.29	.59	.75	.99	3.65
12	0–2	.20	1.09	1.51	.36	.73	.89	1.07	2.25
13	0–3	.28	1.53	2.03	.43	.79	.93	1.13	2.36
14	0–4	.35	1.76	2.34	.52	.96	1.08	1.29	2.74
15	0–5	.39	2.05	2.64	.41	1.00	1.13	1.40	2.90

RGNP: Variant B

16	0–1	0	0	0	N.A.	N.A.	N.A.	N.A.	N.A.
17	0–2	.09	.78	1.01	.48	.83	.96	1.16	3.87
18	0–3	.20	1.11	1.53	.46	1.00	1.15	1.33	2.85
19	0–4	.29	1.56	2.06	.63	1.06	1.19	1.37	3.68
20	0–5	.36	1.79	2.38	.71	1.18	1.40	1.61	3.14

Implicit Price Deflator (IPD): Variant A

21	0–1	.05	.37	.48	.55	.81	.97	1.16	3.68
22	0–2	.11	.76	.97	.49	.76	.87	1.02	3.62
23	0–3	.17	1.18	1.53	.40	.72	.86	1.02	2.95
24	0–4	.23	1.65	2.18	.38	.72	.87	1.04	2.74
25	0–5	.28	2.19	2.94	.37	.72	.86	1.06	3.94

IPD: Variant B

26	0–1	0	0	0	N.A.	N.A.	N.A.	N.A.	N.A.
27	0–2	.04	.37	.47	.70	1.07	1.23	1.51	3.69
28	0–3	.10	.76	.97	.71	.95	1.09	1.30	2.83
29	0–4	.16	1.17	1.53	.57	.98	1.10	1.24	2.56
30	0–5	.21	1.64	2.18	.61	.95	1.08	1.24	4.23

Note: N.A. = not available.

[a] Based on a model with five variables (RGNP, IPD, M2, LI, and TBR) and six quarterly lags, estimated sequentially with presently available data. Variant A assumes that the last known values of the variables to be predicted refer to the quarter $t − 1$ (denoted 0); variant B assumes that they refer to the current quarter t (denoted 1).

[b] $RMSE_i/RMSE_{bv}$, where the subscript i refers to the individual forecasts from the NBER-ASA surveys and the subscript bv refers to the corresponding Bayesian vector autoregressive (BVAR) forecasts (variant A in rows 1–5, 11–15, and 21–25; variant B in rows 6–10, 16–20, and 26–30). MIN and MAX denote the lowest and highest ratios in each distribution, Q_1 and Q_3 denote the lower- and upper-quartile ratios, and MD denotes the median ratio.

BVAR forecasts still show most of the survey forecasts to be superior for GNP, but not for IPD or RGNP. Here the ratios rise above 1.0 for all horizons at Q_3 for GNP, at MD for IPD, and even at Q_1 for RGNP.

The BVAR mean errors are all positive, unlike the MEs for the NBER-ASA survey forecasts, which are mostly negative for GNP and IPD and mostly positive but somewhat mixed for RGNP. (For this and the rest of the paragraph, see table 1.13, cols. 1–3, and table 1.9, cols. 1–6.) Comparisons of the MAEs and RMSEs of BVAR with the corresponding measures for the average individual survey forecast produce a mixed picture, depending on the series and criteria used. However, the comparisons with the group means are generally adverse for BVAR of either variant.

Such variables as the leading index and the short-term interest rate act as strong codeterminants of growth in total output, as suggested by regression estimates and out-of-sample predictions with VAR models (Zarnowitz and Braun 1990; Zarnowitz 1992, chap. 11). Our findings here are consistent with these results. The BVAR forecasts of RGNP perform relatively well, which holds a potentially useful lesson for the forecasters to take proper account of these relations. But the BVAR forecasts of GNP and IPD are apparently weaker.

1.3.7   Comparing Forecasts for the First and Second Halves of 1968–90

The period 1968:IV–1979:III was one of upward drifts and large instability in both inflation and unemployment; of business contractions in 1969–70 and 1973–75; of the Vietnam War and price control disturbances in the early years; and of severe supply (mainly oil price) shocks in the middle and late years. The period 1979:IV–1990:I was one of more successful attempts to slow inflation by restrictive monetary policy; of sharp rises in prices and interest rates followed by downward trends in the wake of two back-to-back recessions in 1980 and 1981–82; of a long expansion that followed, interrupted by slowdowns in 1984–86 and 1989; and of new trade and financial problems. It is of interest to ask how the macro forecasts fared in these two so different periods of approximately equal length.

The errors of the individual forecasts from the NBER-ASA surveys were on average larger in 1979–90 than in 1968–79 for GNP but smaller for IPD, judging from the comparisons of the RMSEs in table 1.14, columns 1 and 5. For RGNP, the differences between the two subperiods are small and mixed, depending on the horizon of the forecasts.

The average individual (i)-to-group mean (g) RMSE ratios differ little between 1968–79 (1.04 ≤ i/g ≥ 1.34) and 1979–90 (1.15 ≤ i/g ≥ 1.31). They decreased somewhat in the latter period for short GNP and RGNP forecasts, increased more for longer IPD forecasts, but remained approximately unchanged in most cases (cf. cols. 2 and 6).

The individual-to-BVAR (bv) RMSE ratios for GNP rose from 0.6 or less in 1968–79 to around 0.8 in 1979–90; those for RGNP rose as well, from an

Table 1.14 Individual, Group Mean, and BVAR Forecasts of Percentage Changes in GNP, RGNP, and IPD: Selected Comparisons by Span and Subperiods, 1968–79 and 1979–90

Rows	Span (Qs)	Forecasts for 1968:IV–1979:III				Forecasts for 1979:IV–1990:I			
		Median $RMSE_i$[a] (1)	RMSE Ratios			Median $RMSE_i$[a] (5)	RMSE Ratios[b]		
			i/g (2)	i/bv (3)	g/bv (4)		i/g (6)	i/bv (7)	g/bv (8)
		Gross National Product (GNP)							
1	0–1	.60	1.34	.53	.48	.86	1.15	.79	.71
2	0–2	1.13	1.20	.58	.50	1.56	1.17	.78	.69
3	0–3	1.68	1.18	.60	.51	2.23	1.18	.81	.70
4	0–4	2.04	1.21	.60	.49	3.08	1.15	.81	.71
5	0–5	2.24	1.19	.51	.47	3.80	1.18	.82	.70
		Gross National Product in Constant Dollars (RGNP)							
6	0–1	.69	1.29	.62	.57	.80	1.20	.88	.76
7	0–2	1.25	1.18	.78	.69	1.34	1.15	1.01	.82
8	0–3	1.87	1.17	.85	.76	1.80	1.15	1.03	.86
9	0–4	2.59	1.14	.99	.84	2.30	1.16	1.16	.94
10	0–5	3.13	1.13	1.04	.92	2.84	1.15	1.24	.99
		Implicit Price Deflator (IPD)							
11	0–1	.50	1.29	.90	.73	.37	1.22	.87	.74
12	0–2	1.00	1.14	.90	.80	.64	1.31	.70	.56
13	0–3	1.57	1.08	.89	.84	.93	1.28	.60	.51
14	0–4	2.25	1.04	.92	.89	1.37	1.26	.64	.50
15	0–5	3.06	1.05	.99	.95	1.94	1.25	.63	.49

[a]Median of the root mean square errors of the individual forecasts from the quarterly NBER-ASA surveys.

[b]Ratio of the median RMSE of the individual forecasts (i) to the RMSE of the corresponding group mean forecast (g) in cols. 2 and 6. Ratio of the median RMSE of the individual forecasts (i) to the RMSE of the corresponding BVAR model forecast (bv) in cols. 3 and 7. Ratio of the RMSE of the group mean forecast (g) to the RMSE of the corresponding BVAR model (bv) in cols. 4 and 8.

approximate range of 0.6–1.0 to 0.9–1.2; and those for IPD declined from 0.9–1.0 to 0.6–0.9 (cols. 3 and 7). These i/bv ratios, then, show that, on average, the NBER-ASA survey forecasts outperformed our BVAR forecasts, except for RGNP in 1979–90. The group mean predictions from the surveys were throughout more accurate than BVAR; that is, the ratios g/bv are less than one in all cases (cols. 4 and 8). As might be expected, the changes in i/bv and g/bv between the two subperiods paralleled each other directionally.

There is no evidence here that, on the whole, the forecasts either improved or deteriorated in the 1980s as compared with the 1970s. The BVAR benchmark proved a little more effective in 1979–90 than in 1968–79 for nominal and real GNP growth and somewhat less effective for inflation.

1.4   Other Forecasts for 1968–90

1.4.1   Percentage Change Forecasts: Industrial Production and Corporate Profits

Table 1.15 shows that the average errors of the forecasts of IP (industrial production) and CP (corporate profits) tended to be positive but widely dispersed and strongly increasing with the span (cols. 1–3). The RMSEs increased in a similar fashion (cols. 4–6). Comparisons with the average size and variability of the actual changes (cols. 9–11) indicate a moderate level of accuracy for the IP forecasts but poor overall performance for the CP forecasts (where the mean and median RMSEs exceed the actual SD and RMSV values). The large positive values of SK and KU for the IP predictions up to three quarters ahead suggest skewness to the right and fat tails; the latter may also characterize the longer CP predictions (cols. 7–8).

Combining the individual forecasts by simple averaging reduces the errors substantially for IP (except for the longest span) but not for CP, where the gains from using the group mean or consensus forecast are small (cf. table 1.15, cols. 4 and 6, with table 1.16, col. 1). Accordingly, the RMSE ratios i/g are smaller for CP than for IP, but it is still true for both variables that only about the best 25 percent of the sample are more accurate than the group mean forecasts (see table 1.16, cols. 2–4).

The BVAR model forecasts (variant A only) outperform the group mean forecasts for profits. The comparisons for the production index yield closer and mixed results, which favor the survey group's predictions for the shorter and the BVAR predictions for the longer horizons. (Compare the corresponding entries in cols. 1–4 and 5–8 of table 1.16.)

In almost all cases, both IP and CP forecasts had larger RMSEs in 1979–90 than in 1968–79 (table 1.17, cols. 1 and 5). Compared with BVAR variant A, the survey forecasts look better in the earlier than in the later subperiod, particularly for IP (cf. cols. 3 and 4 with cols. 7 and 8, respectively).

Table 1.15   Selected Measures of Forecast Accuracy and Actual Values: Percentage Changes in Industrial Production and Corporate Profits, by Span, 1968–90

Row	Span (Qs)	Mean Error			Root Mean Square Error					Actual Value[a]		
		M (1)	SD (2)	MD (3)	M (4)	SD (5)	MD (6)	SK (7)	KU (8)	M (9)	SD (10)	RMSV (11)
					Index of Industrial Production (IP)[b]							
1	0–1	.04	.58	.02	1.66	1.08	1.54	7.89	73.16	.76	2.17	2.29
2	0–2	.83	1.07	.30	3.13	1.80	2.93	7.66	69.68	1.52	3.79	4.08
3	0–3	.67	1.58	.63	4.52	2.10	4.26	6.28	52.71	2.28	5.04	5.53
4	0–4	1.04	1.90	1.09	5.45	1.35	5.34	.80	1.58	3.06	6.08	6.81
5	0–5	1.06	2.27	1.35	6.19	1.37	6.02	.36	1.05	3.83	6.95	7.94
					Corporate Profits after Taxes (CP)[c]							
6	0–1	.26	2.49	−.02	9.50	2.03	9.39	.04	1.08	1.33	7.36	7.48
7	0–2	1.00	4.58	.76	14.42	2.86	14.71	−.39	1.95	2.78	11.13	11.47
8	0–3	2.58	6.54	2.64	18.58	3.32	18.75	−.14	4.23	4.17	13.54	14.17
9	0–4	4.11	8.20	4.39	22.38	4.29	22.58	.05	7.34	5.55	15.56	16.52
10	0–5	6.29	9.66	6.41	26.30	4.94	26.47	.93	9.07	7.01	17.82	19.15

[a]Refers to the period 1970:I–1989:IV.
[b]Based on the second revision of the monthly data.
[c]Based on the first July revision of the quarterly data.

Table 1.16   Individual, Group Mean, and BVAR Forecasts of Percentage Changes in Industrial Production and Corporate Profits: Selected Comparisons, by Span, 1968–90

		Group Mean	RMSE Ratios i/g			BVAR[a]	RMSE Ratios i/bv		
Row	Span (Qs)	RMSE (1)	Q_1 (2)	MD (3)	Q_3 (4)	RMSE (5)	Q_1 (6)	MD (7)	Q_3 (8)
				Index of Industrial Production (IP)[b]					
1	0–1	1.17	1.13	1.26	1.54	1.56	.85	1.00	1.32
2	0–2	2.44	1.06	1.16	1.30	2.83	.90	1.04	1.45
3	0–3	3.50	1.07	1.16	1.28	3.66	.99	1.20	1.58
4	0–4	4.55	1.06	1.13	1.24	4.25	1.04	1.25	1.74
5	0–5	6.16	1.05	1.13	1.26	4.78	1.04	1.21	1.66
				Corporate Profits after Taxes (CIP)[c]					
6	0–1	9.24	1.00	1.08	1.14	7.22	1.25	1.41	1.58
7	0–2	13.68	1.01	1.08	1.16	11.22	1.15	1.32	1.49
8	0–3	17.36	1.00	1.06	1.14	14.35	1.14	1.29	1.44
9	0–4	20.98	1.00	1.06	1.14	16.62	1.18	1.31	1.48
10	0–5	24.41	.98	1.05	1.12	19.16	1.14	1.33	1.51

[a]For IP, based on a model with six variables (RGNP, IPD, M2, LI, TBR, and IP) and six quarterly lags, estimated sequentially with presently available data. For CP, based on a model with six variables (RGNP, IPD, M2, LI, TBR, and CP) and six quarterly lags, estimated sequentially with presently available data. BVAR variant A is used throughout.
[b]Based on the second revision of the monthly data.
[c]Based on the first July revision of the quarterly data.

1.4.2 Level Forecasts: Unemployment Rate and Housing Starts

For UR (unemployment rate; table 1.18, rows 1–5), the mean errors are predominantly negative, suggesting some underprediction, but they also show considerable dispersion. Level errors, unlike average change errors, do not cumulate, but the RMSEs still increase substantially with the distance to the target quarter. The summary error measures are quite small relative to the statistics for the actual values of UR. For short forecasts, the distributions of the RMSEs are skewed to the right and have fat tails, judging from the large SK and KU values.

For HS (housing starts; rows 6–10), the mean errors are close to zero and have mixed signs. They do not depend on the distance to the target (unlike the mean errors for UR, which increase with the distance). The RMSE and SD values, as usual, increase for the longer forecasts, but they remain fairly small compared with the measures for the actual values of HS. The SK and KU figures are small.

Combining the individual forecasts results in substantial gains in accuracy for both variables, but particularly for UR (cf. table 1.19, col. 1, and table

Table 1.17   **Individual, Group Mean, and BVAR Forecasts of Percentage Changes in Industrial Production and Corporate Profits: Selected Comparisons, by Span and Subperiod, 1968–79 and 1979–90**

| | | Forecasts for 1968:IV–1979:III | | | | Forecasts for 1979:IV–1990:I | | | |
| | | Median RMSE | RMSE Ratios | | | Median RMSE | RMSE Ratios | | |
Raw	Span (Qs)	(1)	i/g (2)	i/bv (3)	g/bv (4)	(5)	i/g (6)	i/bv (7)	g/bv (8)
				Index of Industrial Production (IP)					
1	0–1	1.65	1.23	1.00	.91	1.49	1.30	1.22	.83
2	0–2	2.95	1.16	1.01	.92	3.13	1.09	1.42	1.07
3	0–3	4.17	1.17	1.09	.95	4.54	1.11	1.65	1.21
4	0–4	4.96	1.14	1.14	1.00	5.84	1.10	1.70	1.29
5	0–5	5.37	1.18	1.03	1.28	6.98	1.08	1.64	1.35
				Corporate Profits after Taxes (CP)					
6	0–1	9.13	1.06	1.48	1.40	10.08	1.06	1.37	1.20
7	0–2	14.12	1.08	1.32	1.25	15.06	1.05	1.44	1.25
8	0–3	17.62	1.05	1.17	1.13	19.06	1.08	1.47	1.29
9	0–4	20.93	1.06	1.17	1.09	22.66	1.07	1.52	1.32
10	0–5	23.52	1.06	1.12	1.06	25.93	1.06	1.47	1.31

Note: The symbols i, g, and bv refer to the individual, group mean, and BVAR forecasts, variant A, respectively. $RMSE_i$ is the median of the RMSEs of the sampled forecasts (cols. 1 and 5). The i/g ratio is $RMSE_i/RMSE_g$ for strictly matching observations, and the i/bv ratio is $RMSE_i/RMSE_{bv}$, with medians of the individual forecasts used in each case (cols. 2 and 6 and cols. 3 and 7, respectively). The g/bv ratio is $RMSE_g/RMSE_{bv}$ (cols. 4 and 8). See also the notes to tables 1.13 and 1.14.

1.18, cols. 4 and 6). The RMSE ratios i/g are generally higher for UR than for HS, but, once again, the Q_1 ratios are close to one throughout; that is, about 75 percent of the individual forecasts are less accurate than the group means in either case (table 1.19, cols. 2–4). The variant A BVAR forecasts are about as accurate as the group mean forecasts for target quarters 3–5 of both UR and HS; for closer targets, the comparisons favor the surveys for UR and the BVAR for HS (cf. the corresponding entries in cols. 1-4 and 5–8).

Table 1.20 shows that, on the whole, the NBER-ASA forecasters predicted UR somewhat better and HS somewhat worse in 1968–79 than in 1979–90 (cf. cols. 1 and 5). The relative performance of the group mean and the individual forecasts was very similar in the two periods (cols. 2 and 6); that of the BVAR variant A model improved in most cases for UR but showed no systematic change for HS (cols. 3–7 and 4–8).

Table 1.18 Selected Measures of Forecast Accuracy and Actual Values: Levels of the Unemployment Rate and Housing Starts, by Target Quarter, 1968–90

Row	Target Quarter	Mean Error			Root Mean Square Error					Actual Value		
		M (1)	SD (2)	MD (3)	M (4)	SD (5)	MD (6)	SK (7)	KU (8)	M (9)	SD (10)	RMSV (11)
					Unemployment Rate (UR)[a]							
1	1	.02	.08	.03	.26	.21	.21	4.93	27.12	6.50	1.61	6.70
2	2	−.01	.13	.01	.52	.20	.49	3.83	19.92			
3	3	−.08	.20	−.07	.77	.23	.73	2.31	11.73			
4	4	−.20	.28	−.19	.98	.26	.97	1.22	5.93			
5	5	−.22	.34	−.29	1.15	.25	1.13	.53	.65			
					Housing Starts (HS)[b]							
6	1	−.04	.06	−.03	.23	.04	.23	−.01	.08	1.65	.38	1.69
7	2	−.03	.09	−.02	.29	.05	.29	.18	.67			
8	3	−.00	.12	.01	.34	.07	.34	.61	2.23			
9	4	.03	.15	.03	.38	.09	.38	.72	3.32			
10	5	.06	.18	.08	.42	.10	.41	.69	2.45			

[a]Based on presently available data (no important revisions).
[b]Based on the second revision of the monthly data.

Table 1.19   **Individual, Group Mean, and BVAR Forecasts of Levels of the Unemployment Rate and Housing Starts: Selected Comparisons, by Target Quarter, 1968–90**

Row	Target Quarter	Group Mean RMSE (1)	RMSE Ratios i/g			BVAR[a] RMSE (5)	RMSE Ratios i/bv		
			Q_1 (2)	MD (3)	Q_3 (4)		Q_1 (6)	MD (7)	Q_3 (8)
					Unemployment Rate (UR)[b]				
1	1	.16	1.19	1.42	1.73	.28	.72	.84	.96
2	2	.41	1.05	1.17	1.32	.50	.89	1.02	1.23
3	3	.65	1.01	1.10	1.23	.66	.96	1.16	1.38
4	4	.86	.98	1.09	1.20	.78	1.07	1.25	1.50
5	5	1.00	.99	1.10	1.20	.85	1.14	1.30	1.71
					Housing Starts (HS)[c]				
6	1	.21	.99	1.06	1.16	.13	1.52	1.78	1.99
7	2	.25	1.00	1.07	1.18	.20	1.30	1.41	1.60
8	3	.29	1.02	1.08	1.19	.27	1.15	1.25	1.38
9	4	.33	.98	1.10	1.16	.32	.99	1.13	1.22
10	5	.36	.99	1.07	1.18	.37	.93	1.04	1.16

[a]For IP, based on a model with six variables (RGNP, IPD, M2, LI, TBR, and UR) and six quarterly lags, estimated sequentially with presently available data. For HS, based on a model with six variables (RGNP, IPD, M2, LI, TBR, and HS) and six quarterly lags, estimated sequentially with presently available data. See the text and the appendix. BVAR variant A is used throughout.
[b]Based on presently available data.
[c]Based on the second revision of the monthly data.

1.5   Comparisons with Selected Econometric and Time-Series Model Forecasts

1.5.1   The University of Michigan Research Seminar in Quantitative Economics

The Michigan Research Seminar in Quantitative Economics (RSQE) has the longest record of the several well-known service bureaus working with macroeconometric forecasting models. RSQE kindly provided us with the record of their forecasts, and we were able to compare them with the NBER-ASA survey forecasts for ten variables. It is important to note that the quarterly Michigan forecasts begin in 1970:IV and were not made in the first quarter in the years 1975 and 1976 and in the second quarter in the years 1971–75 and 1977–79.[12] We matched the Michigan (Mi) and the NBER-ASA (i) forecasts period by period. Further, the Michigan predictions were made typically in March, June (occasionally May), August (rarely September) and November

12. RSQE predicts normally eight times in each year.

Table 1.20   Individual, Group Mean, and BVAR Forecasts of the Unemployment Rate and Housing Starts: Selected Comparisons, by Target Quarter and Subperiod, 1968–79 and 1979–90

| | | Forecasts for 1968:IV–1979:III | | | | Forecasts for 1979:IV–1990:I | | | |
| | | Median | RMSE Ratios | | | Median | RMSE Ratios | | |
Row	Target Quarter	RMSE$_i$ (1)	i/g (2)	i/bv (3)	g/bv (4)	RMSE$_i$ (5)	i/g (6)	i/bv (7)	g/bv (8)
				Unemployment Rate (UR)					
1	1	.21	1.34	.84	.58	.21	1.39	.82	.57
2	2	.45	1.15	.95	.80	.52	1.19	1.16	.84
3	3	.66	1.06	.98	.95	.83	1.10	1.39	1.30
4	4	.84	1.06	1.09	1.04	1.09	1.10	1.51	1.20
5	5	.96	1.08	1.11	1.02	1.28	1.09	1.17	1.37
				Housing Starts (HS)					
6	1	.23	1.07	1.58	1.39	.23	1.03	1.93	1.80
7	2	.30	1.08	1.39	1.24	.28	1.05	1.43	1.26
8	3	.37	1.10	1.27	1.14	.30	1.07	1.23	1.01
9	4	.42	1.08	1.11	1.07	.31	1.05	1.14	.98
10	5	.45	1.05	1.01	1.01	.34	1.04	1.08	.98

Note: See table 1.17.

(in 1974–75, December). The NBER-ASA survey questionnaire was usually mailed in the first half of each quarter, but it was only in the last month of the quarter that all responses were collected. Thus, at least some of the survey forecasts had the advantage of later timing (which means more potentially useful up-to-date information) vis-à-vis the Michigan forecasts.

Comparing the ME, MAE, and RMSE statistics for the Michigan and the NBER-ASA group means forecasts show the latter to have been more accurate for GNP, RGNP, and IPD (cf. cols. 1–3 and 4–6 of table 1.21). Consistent evidence comes from the RMSE ratios that have ranges of approximately 0.7– 0.9, 0.9–1.1, and 1.0–1.3 for Q_1, MD, and Q_3, respectively (cols. 7–9). Thus, generally about half or more of the individual forecasts from the surveys were at least somewhat more accurate than the Michigan forecasts.

The results for the other variables are mixed. As shown in table 1.22, the Michigan predictions of real consumption show on the whole larger errors than the NBER-ASA "consensus," but not by much, and not for the longest horizon (rows 1–5). They are better than 50 percent of the individual survey forecasts for the two shortest spans and better than 75 percent for the three longest spans. The comparisons for real nonresidential investment favor the group averages by modest margins, except again for the longest span covered. For real residential investment, the Michigan forecasts are definitely better

Table 1.21   **Michigan (RSQE) Econometric Forecasts and NBER-ASA Survey Forecasts of Nominal and Real GNP Growth and IPD Inflation Rates, by Span, 1970–90**

		Michigan Forecasts			Group Mean Forecasts			RMSE Ratios i/Mi		
Row	Span (Qs)	M (1)	MAE (2)	RMSE (3)	M (4)	MAE (5)	RMSE (6)	Q_1 (7)	MD (8)	Q_3 (9)
					Gross National Product (GNP)					
1	0–1	− .09	.80	1.08	− .09	.51	.66	.56	.73	.95
2	0–2	.13	1.24	1.60	− .07	.91	1.18	.73	.89	1.05
3	0–3	.34	1.45	1.91	.02	1.33	1.73	.95	1.11	1.27
4	0–4	.51	1.81	2.38	.04	1.64	2.15	N.A.	1.00	1.26
5	0–5	.97	2.15	2.95	− .02	1.99	2.61	.76	1.00	1.19
					Gross National Product in Constant Dollars (RGNP)					
6	0–1	.01	.77	1.02	− .05	.51	.66	.56	.75	.99
7	0–2	.25	1.09	1.49	.01	.88	1.16	.75	.91	1.13
8	0–3	.46	1.34	1.77	.14	1.19	1.64	.91	1.09	1.28
9	0–4	.77	1.58	2.18	.19	1.32	1.89	.81	.97	1.30
10	0–5	1.20	1.96	2.88	.29	1.61	2.32	.75	.94	1.18
					Implicit Price Deflator (IPD)					
11	0–1	− .10	.39	.51	− .03	.27	.34	.71	.88	1.17
12	0–2	− .14	.72	.87	− .08	.52	.68	.81	.97	1.17
13	0–4	− .15	1.00	1.32	− .12	.76	1.05	.78	.90	1.05
14	0–4	− .27	1.40	1.98	− .14	1.12	1.56	.78	.89	1.02
15	0–5	− .28	1.78	2.42	− .18	1.57	2.20	.87	.98	1.12

Note: The Michigan forecasts cover the period 1970:IV–1990:I, except for the following quarters: 1971:II, 1972:II, 1973:II, 1974:II, 1975:I, 1975:II, 1976:I, 1977:II, 1978:II, and 1979:II. We match the NBER-ASA forecasts to the Michigan forecasts period by period. The ratios in cols. 7–9 are $RMSE_i/RMSE_{Mi}$, where the subscript i refers to individual forecasts from the NBER-ASA surveys and the subscript Mi refers to the Michigan forecasts.

than all but the shortest group mean forecasts. National defense expenditures are predicted better by the surveys through span 0–3 and better by Michigan (Mi) for the two longer spans. More than half of the RMSE ratios i/Mi for NFI (nonresidential fixed investment), RFI (residential fixed investment), and DEF (national defense expenditures) are less than one (rows 6–20).

The pattern that the NBER-ASA group mean forecasts have an edge for the two shortest spans and the Michigan forecasts for the two longest spans holds for the unemployment rate and the Treasury-bill rate (TBR) in table 1.23 (rows 1–5 and 6–10). The middle span shows about equal RMSEs for the two sets. The corporate bond yield (CBY) predictions from Michigan outperform those from the surveys for all but the shortest span (rows 11–15).

Table 1.22   Michigan (RSQE) Econometric Forecasts and NBER-ASA Survey Forecasts of Percentage Changes in Consumption, Investment, and Defense Expenditures, by Span, 1981–90 and 1968–81

		Michigan Forecasts			Group Mean Forecasts			RMSE Ratios i/Mi		
Row	Span (Qs)	M (1)	MAE (2)	RMSE (3)	M (4)	MAE (5)	RMSE (6)	Q_1 (7)	MD (8)	Q_3 (9)
				Personal Consumption Expenditures (PCE)						
1	0–1	− .12	.56	.76	− .14	.47	.59	.82	.89	1.56
2	0–2	− .19	.73	.89	− .24	.64	.77	.78	.97	1.25
3	0–3	− .26	.93	1.15	− .39	.84	.99	.98	1.15	1.41
4	0–4	− .35	1.10	1.34	− .51	1.04	1.25	.94	1.21	1.52
5	0–5	− .41	1.21	1.51	− .66	1.28	1.56	.92	1.30	1.51
				Nonresidential Fixed Investment (NFI)						
6	0–1	− .63	2.04	2.65	− .49	1.68	2.10	.71	.93	1.18
7	0–2	− 1.04	3.25	4.26	− .93	2.74	3.52	.81	1.00	1.29
8	0–3	− 1.09	4.91	5.94	− 1.38	4.03	5.23	.70	.87	1.09
9	0–4	− .95	6.47	7.48	− 1.71	5.57	7.09	.76	.93	1.16
10	0–5	− .84	7.71	8.68	− 2.16	7.57	9.11	.82	1.10	1.33
				Residential Fixed Investment (RFI)						
11	0–1	− .34	2.53	3.54	− .87	2.15	3.29	.79	1.36	1.57
12	0–2	− .30	3.89	5.93	− 1.99	4.34	7.55	.92	1.20	1.79
13	0–3	.31	5.26	7.57	− 3.72	6.51	11.43	.92	1.11	1.37
14	0–4	1.36	6.59	9.02	− 5.43	8.43	14.32	.94	1.16	1.29
15	0–5	2.32	8.19	10.56	− 7.51	10.55	17.46	.93	1.14	1.26
				National Defense Expenditures (DEF)						
16	0–1	− .09	2.18	2.54	− .07	1.44	2.00	.85	.98	1.20
17	0–2	− .28	2.89	3.65	.56	2.28	3.08	.84	1.04	1.19
18	0–3	− .49	3.75	4.52	− 1.49	3.13	4.09	.74	.92	1.15
19	0–4	− .65	4.03	4.76	− 2.14	4.34	5.23	.79	1.01	1.25
20	0–5	− .95	5.84	6.83	− 3.64	5.45	7.07	.67	.80	.99

Note: See table 1.21.

1.5.2 Sims's Probabilistic Forecasts

In addition to outside econometric model forecasts, we wished to compare the results of the NBER-ASA surveys to outside time-series forecasts. We are indebted to Chris Sims for data on predictions from both sophisticated BVAR and univariate ARIMA models.

Recall that our own BVAR model used earlier in this paper includes RGNP, IPD, TBER, M2, and LI plus the variable predicted (if not one of the above). The Sims model includes the first three variables in our set plus six others:

Table 1.23   **Michigan (RSQE) Econometric Forecasts and NBER-ASA Forecasts of the Unemployment Rate, Treasury-Bill Rate, and Corporate Bond Yield, by Target Quarter, 1968–90 and 1981–90**

Row	Target Quarter	Michigan Forecasts			Group Mean Forecasts			RMSE Ratios i/Mi		
		M (1)	MAE (2)	RMSE (3)	M (4)	MAE (5)	RMSE (6)	Q_1 (7)	MD (8)	Q_3 (9)
				Unemployment Rate, 1968–90 (UR)						
1	1	.05	.14	.17	.02	.13	.17	1.07	1.32	1.72
2	2	.08	.33	.44	.05	.33	.43	1.03	1.15	1.35
3	3	.05	.49	.67	.03	.51	.68	1.01	1.16	1.32
4	4	−.01	.58	.78	.00	.61	.85	1.08	1.21	1.38
5	5	−.11	.69	.93	−.02	.71	.96	1.01	1.18	1.33
				Treasury-Bill Rate, 1981–90 (TBR)						
6	1	−.04	.24	.31	.01	.15	.20	.96	1.17	1.58
7	2	−.05	.79	1.07	.15	.69	.91	.85	.96	1.19
8	3	−.01	1.13	1.39	.38	1.11	1.40	.97	1.11	1.32
9	4	.07	1.37	1.64	.62	1.45	1.80	1.05	1.25	1.39
10	5	.21	1.67	1.90	.87	1.72	2.16	1.06	1.25	1.52
				Corporate Bond Yield, 1981–90 (CBY)						
11	1	−.44	.48	.63	−.19	.31	.38	.73	.97	1.26
12	2	−.31	.64	.81	−.07	.66	.83	1.17	1.28	1.55
13	3	−.20	.84	1.08	.16	1.05	1.25	1.23	1.36	1.50
14	4	−.12	1.17	1.43	.37	1.32	1.53	1.08	1.23	1.39
15	5	−.03	1.39	1.68	.57	1.48	1.74	1.02	1.12	1.32

Note: See table 1.21.

M1, UR, NFI, the S&P 500 stock price index, a commodity price index, and the trade-weighted value of the dollar.[13] It is a nine-variable, five-lag model, whereas ours is a five- or six-variable, six-lag model.

Sims's model is an extension of the model constructed in 1980 and used in quarterly forecasting during 1980–86 by Litterman (1986). It is three variables larger than the original Litterman model, and it allows time variation in coefficients, predictable time variation in forecast error variance, and nonnormality in disturbances (Sims 1989). The modifications give rise to nonnormal, nonlinear models and hence to considerable complications in estimation and analysis (Sims and Todd 1991). The Sims model (like our own BVAR) forecasts are simulations of real-time forecasts in that they use only data from time periods before the periods to be predicted. But, for several reasons, including

13. The data are generally expressed in log-level form, except for TBR, which was not logged.

the use of current versions of the data, they are far from being true ex ante forecasts (again, the same applies to our BVAR as well).

In evaluating the BVAR forecasts (both Sims's and our own), we used the current data, which is consistent with their construction and believed to be fair. Use of preliminary figures would have resulted in finding larger errors.

Again, like for our own BVAR (see table 1.13 and text above), the comparisons of the Sims model forecasts with the NBER-ASA survey forecasts for GNP, RGNP, and IPD are presented in two variants, A and B (table 1.24). For reasons already explained, variant A favors the real-time predictions that incorporate contemporary news evaluations, while variant B favors the predictions based on the ex post constructed time-series models.

Using variant A, Sims's forecasts (S) are found to have on the whole larger errors than the group mean forecasts from the NBER-ASA surveys for both GNP and RGNP (table 1.24, rows 1–5 and 11–15; cf. cols. 1–3 and 4–6). The corresponding ratios $RMSE_i/RMSE_s$ are relatively low, approaching 1.00 only for Q_3 (cols. 7–9), which means that most individual forecasts from the surveys are more accurate than the Sims model forecasts. In contrast, the Sims forecasts are considerably more accurate than the group mean forecasts for IPD inflation, and here the RMSE ratios i/S mostly exceed 1.00, even for Q_1 (rows 21–25).

Using variant B as a criterion (rows 6–10, 16–20, and 26–30), we still see the group mean forecasts as retaining on balance an advantage over the Sims forecasts for GNP, but it is a much-reduced advantage and one essentially limited to the longer spans. For RGNP, the NBER-ASA consensus predictions are somewhat more accurate than the Sims model predictions for the spans 0–4 and 0–5, whereas the opposite is true for the shorter spans. For IPD, the Sims forecasts have smaller errors throughout. (Compare cols. 1–3 for variant B with the corresponding entries in cols. 4–6.) Looking at the RMSE ratios i/S (cols. 7–9), we find them to exceed 1.00, that is, to favor the Sims model, for GNP at Q_3 only, for RGNP at MD and Q_3, and for IPD at Q_1, MD, and Q_3.

Interestingly, the original Litterman BVAR performed relatively well for real GNP and unemployment but worse for IPD, which motivated both Litterman and Sims to make changes designed to improve their inflation forecasts. But simulations disclosed "a tendency for improvements in the retrospective forecast performance of the BVAR model for inflation to be accompanied by deterioration in its performance for real variables" (Sims 1989, 1). A similar trade-off was observed in working with our own BVAR.

According to the measures in table 1.25 (based on variant A only), most of the NBER-ASA survey forecasts for the unemployment rate (1968–90), the Treasury-bill rate (1981–90), and the rate of growth in real nonresidential fixed investment (1981–90) exceeded the corresponding Sims model forecasts considerably in overall accuracy. This can be concluded from both the com-

Table 1.24   **Sims Model Forecasts (Two Variants) and NBER-ASA Survey Forecasts of Nominal and Real GNP Growth and IPD Inflation, by Span, 1968–90 and 1981–90**

		Sims Model Forecasts (S)			Group Mean Forecasts			RMSE Ratios i/S		
Row	Span (Qs)	M (1)	MAE (2)	RMSE (3)	M (4)	MAE (5)	RMSE (6)	Q_1 (7)	MD (8)	Q_3 (9)
		Gross National Product, 1968–90 (GNP): Variant A								
1	0–1	.01	.86	1.09	−.08	.49	.64	.51	.66	.89
2	0–2	.01	1.31	1.68	−.10	.84	1.11	.62	.79	.94
3	0–3	−.05	1.87	2.34	−.07	1.22	1.61	.62	.79	.93
4	0–4	−.11	2.32	2.93	−.02	1.56	2.06	.65	.79	.98
5	0–5	−.20	2.74	3.48	−.09	1.91	2.51	.65	.80	1.08
		GNP, 1968–90: Variant B								
6	0–1	0	0	0				N.A.	N.A.	N.A.
7	0–2	.00	.85	1.08				.70	.84	.98
8	0–3	.02	1.29	1.66				.81	.93	1.10
9	0–4	.08	1.85	2.33				.74	.88	1.09
10	0–5	.15	2.29	2.90				.78	.88	1.10
		GNP in Constant Dollars, 1968–90 (RGNP): Variant A								
11	0–1	.03	.78	.99	−.02	.50	.64	.63	.77	.98
12	0–2	.05	1.18	1.50	.02	.83	1.11	.73	.86	1.06
13	0–3	.04	1.68	2.12	.16	1.17	1.61	.75	.89	1.05
14	0–4	.02	2.10	2.66	.33	1.42	2.05	.79	.93	1.08
15	0–5	−.03	2.54	3.15	.40	1.70	2.47	.80	.96	1.12
		RGNP, 1968–90: Variant B								
16	0–1	0	0	0				N.A.	N.A.	N.A.
17	0–2	−.02	.79	1.00				.81	.96	1.11
18	0–3	−.03	1.19	1.51				.99	1.12	1.27
19	0–4	−.03	1.70	2.14				.97	1.12	1.30
20	0–5	.00	2.11	2.68				1.01	1.13	1.36
		Implicit Price Deflator, 1968–90 (IPD): Variant A								
21	0–1	.01	.30	.38	−.04	.27	.34	.71	.88	1.17
22	0–2	.04	.54	.68	−.12	.55	.70	1.81	.97	1.17
23	0–4	.08	.75	.95	−.22	.84	1.13	1.24	1.46	1.73
24	0–4	.12	1.01	1.25	−.34	1.21	1.64	1.35	1.58	1.85
25	0–5	.16	1.29	1.59	−.37	1.63	2.23	1.40	1.68	1.99
		IPD, 1968–90: Variant B								
26	0–1	0	0	0				N.A.	N.A.	N.A.
27	0–2	−.02	.31	.39				1.31	1.52	1.81
28	0–3	−.05	.55	.69				1.43	1.63	1.91

(continued)

Table 1.24   (continued)

Row	Span (Qs)	Sims Model Forecasts (S)			Group Mean Forecasts			RMSE Ratios i/S		
		M (1)	MAE (2)	RMSE (3)	M (4)	MAE (5)	RMSE (6)	Q_1 (7)	MD (8)	Q_3 (9)
29	0–4	−.09	.76	.96				1.51	1.68	1.90
30	0–5	−.14	1.02	1.26				1.47	1.71	1.98

Note: Sims's model is a nine-variable, five-lag quarterly probabilistic model (see the text for more detail). The Sims forecasts contain no gaps and refer to the same periods as those covered by the NBER-ASA survey forecasts (individual and group means). The entries in cols. 7–9 represent ratios $RMSE_i/RMSE_S$, where the subscript i refers to individual forecasts from the surveys and the subscript S refers to the Sims model forecasts. Q_1 and Q_3 denote the lower- and upper-quartile ratios, and MD denotes the median ratio. Variant A assumes that the last known values of the variables to the predicted refer to the quarter $t - 1$ (denoted 0); variant B assumes that they refer to the current quarter t (denoted 1). N.A. = not available.

parisons with group mean predictions from the surveys (cf. cols. 1–3 and 4–6) and the low i/S ratios (cols. 7–9).

The Sims model and our own BVAR forecasts have errors of generally similar orders of magnitude. The Sims predictions are more accurate for GNP and IPD, less accurate for RGNP and UR. The results for NFI and TBR are mixed (favoring Sims at the two longest horizons only).[14]

1.5.3   Univariate Time-Series Models

Predictions from ARIMA models make popular benchmarks for evaluating forecasters' performance. We use ARIMA as specified in Sims and Todd (1991), where they are reported to have worked well relative to the Simsian BVAR for financial variables and business fixed investment in 1980–90 (pp. 9–10). However, our measures show that, throughout, Sims's BVAR forecasts had smaller overall errors than the corresponding ARIMA forecasts, whether the comparisons cover the variants A or the variants B (cf. tables 1.24 and 1.25, cols. 1–3, with tables 1.26 and 1.27, cols. 2–4).

The results of comparing the NBER-ASA survey forecasts with their counterparts of the Sims-Todd ARIMA type are less clear-cut. Most of the forecasters did better than the time-series models according to the variant A calculations, as is evident from the individual-to-ARIMA (i/Ar) ratios in columns 5–7 of tables 1.26 and 1.27. But, when variant B is used, the forecasters are no longer clearly ahead for RGNP and fall somewhat behind for IPD (table 1.26, rows 16–20 and 26–30).

Beginning in 1976:II, Charles Nelson has produced ARIMA forecasts of rates of change in nominal and real GNP and the implicit price deflator synchronously with other real-time forecasts, updating them each quarter on the

14. For the RMSEs of the BVAR forecasts, see table 1.13, col. 3 (GNP, RGNP, IPD), and tables 1.19, 1A.6, and 1A.8, col. 5 (UR, NFI, and TBR, respectively).

Table 1.25   Sims Model Forecasts (Variant A) and NBER-ASA Survey Forecasts of the Unemployment Rate, the Treasury-Bill Rate, and Growth in Real Nonresidential Investment, by Target Quarter or Span, 1968–90 and 1981–90

Row	Target Quarter or Span (Qs)	Sims Model Forecasts M (1)	MAE (2)	RMSE (3)	Group Mean Forecasts M (4)	MAE (5)	RMSE (6)	RMSE Ratios i/S Q_1 (7)	MD (8)	Q_3 (9)
				Unemployment Rate, 1968–90 (UR)						
1	1	.09	.39	.55	.03	.13	.16	.35	.45	.55
2	2	.14	.56	.79	.04	.32	.41	.54	.65	.81
3	3	.18	.76	1.03	–.00	.49	.65	.59	.71	.93
4	4	.21	.95	1.23	–.08	.63	.86	.64	.78	.94
5	5	.23	1.10	1.40	–.10	.73	1.00	.66	.79	.98
				Treasury-Bill Rate, 1981–90 (TBR)						
6	1	–.34	1.27	1.57	.01	.15	.20	.20	.24	.29
7	2	–.54	1.47	1.84	.13	.68	.90	.52	.62	.70
8	3	–.60	1.69	2.13	.35	1.09	1.38	.62	.71	.82
9	4	–.71	1.96	2.48	.61	1.41	1.77	.67	.76	.86
10	5	–.86	2.19	2.69	1.07	1.87	2.49	.75	.86	.97
				Nonresidential Fixed Investment, 1981–90 (NFI)						
11	0–1	–.16	2.31	2.93	–.45	1.61	2.01	.72	.85	1.01
12	0–2	–.31	3.61	4.16	–.88	2.67	3.43	.63	.72	1.01
13	0–3	–.74	5.23	6.05	–1.19	3.93	4.99	.60	.67	.85
14	0–4	–.90	4.50	6.69	–1.74	5.51	6.89	.60	.65	.93
15	0–5	–1.63	4.95	7.31	–2.31	7.29	8.69	.54	.65	.75

Note: See table 1.24.

Table 1.26　　ARIMA Model Forecasts (Two Variants) and NBER-ASA Survey Forecasts of Nominal and Real GNP Growth and IPD Inflation, by Span, 1968–90

Row	Span (Qs)	ARIMA Model (Ar) (1)	ARIMA Forecasts			RMSE Ratios i/Ar		
			M (2)	MAE (3)	RMSE (4)	Q_1 (5)	MD (6)	Q_3 (7)
			Gross National Product (GNP): Variant A					
1	0-1	N.A.	-.11	.95	1.18	.48	.61	.82
2	0-2		-.29	1.64	2.05	.53	.64	.74
3	0-3		-.55	2.51	3.04	.51	.61	.73
4	0-4		-.85	3.32	4.00	.51	.58	.69
5	0-5		-1.19	4.11	4.96	.49	.61	.74
			GNP: Variant B					
6	0-1	N.A.	0	0	0	N.A.	N.A.	N.A.
7	0-2		.12	.94	1.18	.64	.77	.86
8	0-3		.32	1.62	2.02	.71	.81	.95
9	0-4		.59	2.48	3.01	.61	.71	.87
10	0-5		.91	3.28	3.96	.59	.74	.94
			Gross National Product in Constant Dollars (RGNP): Variant A					
11	0-1	1,1,0	-.06	.80	1.03	.60	.74	.94
12	0-2		-.14	1.33	1.68	.67	.79	.94
13	0-3		-.27	1.91	2.33	.71	.82	1.00
14	0-4		-.40	2.37	2.88	.77	.86	1.05
15	0-5		-.54	2.82	3.39	.76	.93	1.11

RGNP: Variant B

		1,1,0						
			0	0	0	N.A.	N.A.	N.A.
16	0-1		0	0	0	N.A.	N.A.	N.A.
17	0-2		.06	.81	1.04	.78	.93	1.08
18	0-3		.16	1.33	1.68	.91	1.04	1.21
19	0-4		.28	1.93	2.35	.93	1.07	1.29
20	0-5		.43	2.39	2.91	.99	1.11	1.34

Implicit Price Deflator (IPD): Variant A

		1,1,2						
21	0-1		.05	.38	.50	.72	.93	1.11
22	0-2		.15	.80	1.00	.71	.87	1.10
23	0-3		.29	1.27	1.60	.68	.90	1.11
24	0-4		.49	1.84	2.29	.65	.93	1.16
25	0-5		.74	2.47	3.07	.63	1.02	1.28

IPD: Variant B

		1,1,2						
			0	0	0	N.A.	N.A.	N.A.
26	0-1		0	0	0	N.A.	N.A.	N.A.
27	0-2		−.05	.39	.51	.94	1.10	1.39
28	0-3		−.16	.80	1.01	.97	1.17	1.37
29	0-4		−.32	1.27	1.62	.88	1.11	1.33
30	0-5		−.53	1.86	2.32	.79	1.14	1.40

Note: N.A. = not available (forecasts obtained from those for RGNP and IPD). The specifications of the ARIMA models are as in Sims and Todd (1991, table 1). For more detail, see Sims and Todd (1991, 3–4). The entries in cols. 5–6 represent ratios RMSE$_i$/RMSE$_{A}$, where the subscript i refers to individual forecasts from the NBER-ASA surveys and the subscript Ar refers to the ARIMA model forecasts.

Table 1.27   ARIMA Model Forecasts (Variant A) and NBER-ASA Survey Forecasts of the Unemployment Rate, the Treasury-Bill Rate, and Growth in Real Nonresidential Investment, by Target Quarter or Span, 1968–90 and 1981–90

Row	Target Quarter or Span (Qs)	ARIMA Model (Ar) (1)	ARIMA Forecasts			RMSE Ratios i/Ar		
			M (2)	MAE (3)	RMSE (4)	Q_1 (5)	MD (6)	Q_3 (7)
				Unemployment Rate (UR)				
1	1	1,1,0	−.25	.45	.65	.30	.36	.44
2	2		−.44	.67	.96	.44	.52	.60
3	3		−.63	.87	1.26	.50	.58	.68
4	4		−.80	1.07	1.50	.56	.63	.74
5	5		−.94	1.21	1.67	.58	.66	.76
				Treasury-Bill Rate (TBR)				
6	1	0,1,1	−.39	1.37	1.96	.15	.19	.26
7	2		−.66	1.60	2.14	.42	.49	.61
8	3		−.80	1.88	2.59	.53	.60	.72
9	4		−.96	2.26	3.19	.57	.65	.72
10	5		−1.19	2.51	3.49	.59	.69	.78
				Nonresidential Fixed Investment (NFI)				
11	0–1	1,1,0	−.07	1.63	2.37	.58	.84	1.21
12	0–2		−.16	3.32	4.27	.65	.78	.98
13	0–3		−.22	5.10	6.26	.58	.64	.81
15	0–4		−.22	6.76	8.11	.50	.59	.65
16	0–5		−.16	8.19	9.69	.40	.48	.56

Note: See table 1.26.

Table 1.28 Joutz Model Forecasts and NBER-ASA Survey Forecasts of Nominal and Real GNP Growth and IPD Inflation, by Span, 1976–90

Row	Span (Qs)	Joutz Model Forecasts (J)			Group Mean Forecasts (g)			RMSE Ratios i/J		
		M (1)	MAE (2)	RMSE (3)	M (4)	MAE (5)	RMSE (6)	Q_1 (7)	MD (8)	Q_3 (9)
					Gross National Product (GNP)					
1	0–1	.04	.72	.96	−.05	.55	.70	.73	.89	1.25
2	0–2	.09	1.21	1.52	−.02	.89	1.16	.85	1.08	1.26
3	0–3	.16	1.65	2.08	.08	1.30	1.69	1.00	1.18	1.64
4	0–4	.28	2.05	2.58	.18	1.63	2.15	.94	1.14	1.39
					Gross National Product in Constant Dollars (RGNP)					
5	0–1	.02	.64	.85	−.08	.53	.65	.86	1.07	1.40
6	0–2	.08	1.05	1.31	−.10	.81	1.03	.84	1.03	1.45
7	0–3	.18	1.38	1.68	−.05	1.03	1.35	.95	1.21	1.55
8	0–4	.30	1.53	1.90	−.04	1.12	1.57	.89	1.12	1.51
					Implicit Price Deflator (IPD)					
9	0–1	.01	.29	.37	.04	.24	.30	.86	1.07	1.40
10	0–2	.00	.53	.65	.09	.43	.52	.78	.96	1.30
11	0–3	−.03	.73	.96	.15	.61	.75	.80	.98	1.21
12	0–4	−.04	1.05	1.33	.21	.89	1.06	.79	.97	1.28

announcement of the first preliminary numbers for the preceding quarter. Comparisons with five econometric models for the period 1976:II–1982:IV have shown these ex ante "benchmark" forecasts to be of competitive accuracy (Nelson 1984). Since 1988, Frederick Joutz has been preparing the ARIMA forecasts on a current basis (the same way as Nelson had before), and he kindly let us have the results for the purposes of a comparative analysis.

Table 1.28 shows that the NBER-ASA group mean forecasts (g) were on average consistently more accurate than the Joutz ARIMA (J) forecasts (cf. cols. 2–5 and 3–6). The RMSE ratios g/J rose with the span from 0.73 to 0.88 for GNP and from 0.76 to 0.83 for RGNP; they varied irregularly between 0.78 and 0.81 for IPD. The RMSE ratios i/J (cols. 7–9) average 0.8–0.9 for Q_1, 1.0–1.1 for MD, and 1.3–1.5 for Q_3. Our analysis confirms the findings that these ARIMA forecasts are indeed competitive and that their relative accuracy tends to improve with their horizon for GNP and RGNP (but not for IPD, where they are weakest).

1.6   A General Evaluation and Conclusions

In presenting and discussing more than thirty tables on multiperiod quarterly forecasts for a score of variables by a total of more than one hundred individuals, we had to make some hard choices about which problems to confront and which measures to use. Forecasts for two-thirds of the time series covered were treated less comprehensively and relegated to an appendix, to make the paper easier to read. Even so, the inevitable abundance of detail risks obscuring the overall picture. Therefore, lest we miss the forest for the trees, a statement of general findings, conclusions, and qualifications is very necessary at this point.

1. The distributions of the error statistics show that there is much dispersion across the forecasts, which typically increases with the length of the predictive horizon. Forecasters differ in many respects, and so do their products. The idea that a close "consensus" persists, that is, that current matched forecasts are generally all alike, is a popular fiction. The differentiation of the forecasts usually involves much more than the existence of just a few outliers. However, it is also true that forecasters depend on common information, interact, and influence each other. This naturally induces some common trends. The more independent information the individuals possess, the more their predictions can differ. Thus, a clustering of forecasts could be due either to genuine agreement or to common ignorance, while dissent may reflect uncertainty.[15]

2. Errors of the average change forecasts cumulate over the spans 0–1, . . . , 0–5 with great regularity for a variety of time series. To a large extent,

---

15. Compare Zarnowitz and Lambros (1987), a study that compares the point and probabilistic forecasts from the NBER-ASA surveys. Time and space restrictions prevented us from including in this paper the survey responses to questions on the probabilities of alternative GNP and IPD outcomes and turning points. See also Braun and Yaniv (1991).

this occurs because of the progression to larger changes in the corresponding actual values. But the errors of marginal change and level forecasts, too, often increase with the distance to the target quarter, although by much smaller margins and with much less regularity. As might be expected, the further out in the future the target, the less can be inferred about it from the past, and the worse it is usually forecast. The less random and more predictable the series, the better this rule holds, in the sense that the forecasts will be more forward looking and more appropriately differentiated with the distance to the target period.[16]

3. Macroeconomic variables differ greatly in the extent to which they can be forecast. The more persistent (autocorrelated) series are, of course, more accurately predicted than series with high random variability. Thus, real GNP and consumption are far easier to forecast than residential investment and, especially, change in business inventories. Inflation was underestimated and poorly predicted by most forecasters most of the time. Negative correlations between RGNP and IPD forecast errors have long been observed (see Zarnowitz 1979, table 4 and text), and offsetting performance for inflation and real variables appears to be frequently encountered in studies of forecasting methods and results.

4. A comparison of the summary measures of error for 1968:IV–1979:III and 1979:IV–1990:I reveals no large and systematic differences that would indicate either deterioration or improvement in the overall performance of the respondents to the NBER-ASA surveys. The accuracy of GNP forecasts may have decreased somewhat, but that of inflation forecasts increased. The 1970s and the 1980s differed significantly in a number of economically important dimensions, but it is difficult to say that either subperiod presented the forecasts with definitely greater problems than the other. Each experienced two business recessions, which is noted because previous research has shown that turning-point errors played a major role in downgrading the forecasting records (for a recent summary, see Zarnowitz 1992).

5. Group mean forecasts are generally much more accurate than the majority of individual forecasts. These consensus predictions are computed by simple averaging across the corresponding responses to each successive survey; we made no effort to use other than equal weighting. This paper, then, provides many examples of the rule that combining forecasts often results in substantial improvements. The method is very accessible and inexpensive. The gains are enhanced by the diversification of the forecasts that are combined; for example, our group mean forecasts should be better the more different and complementary the information embodied in their components. For some variables and periods, the combinations work much better than for oth-

16. It should be noted that annual forecasts are generally more accurate than all but the very short quarterly forecasts, owing to cancellation of errors for the quarters within the year (Zarnowitz 1979). In this paper, annual forecasts are not considered.

Table 1.29   Nine Sets of Forecasts Ranked According to Their Average RMSEs, Three
                  Variables, 1968:IV–1990:I

Row	Forecast	Gross National Product (GNP)		GNP in Constant Dollars (RGNP)		Implicit Price Deflator (IPD)	
		ARMSE (1)	Rank (2)	ARMSE (3)	Rank (4)	ARMSE (5)	Rank (6)
1	NBER-ASA median	1.90	4	1.94	7	1.53	7
2	NBER-ASA consensus	1.586	1	1.58	3	1.21	5
3	Michigan (RSQE)	1.98	5	1.87	5	1.42	6
4	BVAR variant A	2.69	8	1.90	6	1.62	8
5	BVAR variant B	1.89	3	1.40	1	1.03	3
6	Sims variant A	2.30	7	2.08	8	.97	2
7	Sims variant B	1.594	2	1.47	2	.66	1
8	Sims-Todd ARIMA variant A	3.05	9	2.26	9	1.69	9
9	Sims-Todd ARIMA variant B	2.03	6	1.60	4	1.09	4

Source: Row 1 is based on entries in table 1.10, row 3, cols. 1–5; row 2 on table 1.9, col. 6; row 3 on table 1.21, col. 3; rows 4 and 5 on table 1.13, col. 3; rows 6 and 7 on table 1.24, col. 3; and rows 8 and 9 on table 1.26, col. 4.

Note: ARMSE (average root mean square error) is computed by taking the mean of the RMSEs across the five spans 0–1, . . . , 0–5. The smallest ARMSE is ranked 1, the largest ARMSE 9, for each of the three variables.

ers. In principle, one would prefer to combine the information in a single model rather than combining the forecasts. In practice, the latter will typically be much easier.

6. Consider first comparisons with time-series models constructed on the assumption that the last-known values of the variables concerned refer to the prior quarter $t - 1$ (variant A). The assumption is certainly valid for the quarterly variables in the real-time forecasts, but it results in some bias against the time-series forecasts. Table 1.29 sums up the evidence in the form of the RMSEs averaged across spans. For the subset consisting of the median individual and the consensus forecasts from the NBER-ASA surveys, the Michigan econometric model, our BVAR variant A model, the Sims variant A probabilistic model, and the Sims-Todd ARIMA variant A model (rows 1–4, 6, and 8), the consensus (group mean) survey forecasts rank first for GNP and RGNP and second for IPD (following the Sims [variant A] model).

7. The alternative assumption, that the last-known values of the variables refer to the current quarter t (variant B), is rather strongly biased in favor of the ex post forecasts with time-series models. The average root mean square errors (ARMSEs) are all much lower for the variant B predictions than for their variant A counterparts (cf. rows 4, 6, and 8 with rows 5, 7, and 9). When all nine sets of forecasts listed in table 1.29 are considered, the Sims variant B model ranks second, second, and first for GNP, RGNP, and IPD, respec-

Table 1.30   **Six Sets of Forecasts Ranked According to Their RMSEs Averaged across Spans, Twenty-one Variables, 1968:IV–1990:I, 1968:IV–1981:II, and 1981:II–1990:I**

		Average Root Mean Square Error (ARMSE) and the Corresponding Rank[b]					
Row	Variable[a]	NBER-ASA Surveys Median Individual Forecast (1)	Group (Consensus) Forecast (2)	BVAR Model Forecast (3)	Michigan (RSQE) Forecast (4)	Sims Probabilistic Model Forecast (5)	ARIMA Model Forecast (6)
			1968:IV–1990:I				
1	GNP	1.90	1.59	2.69	1.98	2.30	3.05
		(2)	(1)	(5)	(3)	(4)	(6)
2	RGNP	1.94	1.58	1.90	1.87	2.08	2.26
		(4)	(1)	(3)	(2)	(5)	(6)
3	IPD	1.53	1.21	1.62	1.42	.97	1.69
		(4)	(2)	(5)	(3)	(1)	(6)
4	IP	4.02	3.56	3.42	N.A.	N.A.	N.A.
		(3)	(2)	(1)			
5	CP	18.38	17.13	13.71	N.A.	N.A.	N.A.
		(3)	(2)	(1)			
6	UR	.71	.62	.61	.60	1.00	1.21
		(4)	(3)	(2)	(1)	(5)	(6)
7	HS	.33	.29	.26	N.A.	N.A.	N.A.
		(3)	(2)	(1)			
			1968:IV–1981:II				
8	CD	5.65	5.05	5.93	N.A.	N.A.	N.A.
		(2)	(1)	(3)			
9	PE	11.49	11.08	4.35	N.A.	N.A.	N.A.
		(3)	(2)	(1)			
10	DEF	3.92	3.34	8.19	4.46	N.A.	N.A.
		(2)	(1)	(4)	(3)		
11	CBI	11.38	12.38	13.94	N.A.	N.A.	N.A.
		(1)	(2)	(3)			
			1981:III–1990:I				
12	RCBI	19.69	18.96	26.69	N.A.	N.A.	N.A.
		(2)	(1)	(3)			
13	NX	47.29	44.19	21.02	N.A.	N.A.	N.A.
		(3)	(2)	(1)			
14	PCE	1.30	1.24	5.69	1.13	N.A.	N.A.
		(3)	(2)	(4)	(1)		
15	NFI	6.06	1.11	5.25	5.80	5.43	6.14
		(5)	(1)	(2)	(4)	(3)	(6)
16	RFI	9.59	1.22	8.70	10.81	N.A.	N.A.
		(3)	(1)	(2)	(4)		
17	FGP	4.96	1.38	8.54	N.A.	N.A.	N.A.
		(2)	(1)	(3)			

(continued)

Table 1.30   (continued)

| | | Average Root Mean Square Error (ARMSE) and the Corresponding Rank[b] | | | | | |
| | | NBER-ASA Surveys Median Individual Forecast | Group (Consensus) Forecast | BVAR Model Forecast | Michigan (RSQE) Forecast | Sims Probabilistic Model Forecast | ARIMA Model Forecast |
Row	Variable[a]	(1)	(2)	(3)	(4)	(5)	(6)
18	SLGP	1.47	.94	1.27	N.A.	N.A.	N.A.
		(3)	(1)	(2)			
19	CPI	1.19	.52	.76	N.A.	N.A.	N.A.
		(3)	(1)	(2)			
20	TBR	1.71	1.35	2.03	1.26	2.14	2.67
		(3)	(2)	(4)	(1)	(5)	(6)
21	CBY	1.64	1.28	1.72	1.13	N.A.	N.A.
		(3)	(2)	(4)	(1)		

Note: N.A. = not available.

[a]On the symbols used, see previous tables and the text.

[b]ARMSE = average of the RMSEs across the five horizons (0–1, . . . , 0–5, or 1, . . . , 5). Entries in parentheses represent ranks according to ARMSE (smallest to largest).

tively. The corresponding ranks of BVAR variant B are also high: third, first, and third. The NBER-ASA consensus forecasts are now almost tied for the first rank with the Sims variant B and rank only third for RGNP and fifth for IPD (cf. rows 2, 5, and 7).

8. Table 1.30 sums up the evidence on the comparative accuracy of the several sets of forecasts included in this study, using the longest series of predictions available for each variable. Here again, root mean square errors averaged across the spans serve as the basis for ranking the forecasts, but only the variant A time-series predictions are used. By this criterion, the group forecasts from the NBER-ASA surveys earned ten first and ten second ranks for the twenty-one variables covered. The median individual forecasts ranked first or second six times, third eleven times, and lower four times. Our BVAR model had equal numbers in the first, second, and third ranks (five each), plus six lower ranks. The Michigan (RSQE) forecasts, available for ten variables, ranked first four times, second once, third three times, and fourth twice. The Sims probabilistic model forecasts, available for six variables, were mostly less accurate, and the ARIMA model forecasts were throughout least accurate.

9. Finally, table 1.31, using sums of the ranks across variables, shows that the group (consensus) forecasts from the survey performed best overall in each of the periods covered; the Michigan forecasts were second best; the median individual forecasts, the BVAR model forecasts, and the Sims forecasts share mostly the ranks third or fourth (there are ties); and the ARIMAs rank last. Note that major deviations from this ordering appear for some variables; notably, Michigan is best for UR, Sims for IP. Also, these results con-

Table 1.31   **Six Sets of Forecasts Ranked According to Their Overall Accuracy across Variables, by Period, 1968:IV–1990:I, 1968:IV–1981:II, and 1981:II–1990:I**

Row	Number of Variables[a]	Individual Median Forecast (1)	Group (Consensus) Forecast (2)	BVAR Model Forecast (3)	Michigan (RSQE) Forecast (4)	Sims Probabilistic Model Forecast (5)	ARIMA Model Forecast (6)
				Ranking According to the Sum of Ranks across Variables[b]			
				1968:IV–1990:I			
1	7 (1–7)	Third (23)	First (13)	Second (18)	N.A.	N.A.	N.A.
2	4 (1–3, 6)	Third (14)	First (7)	Fourth (15)	Second (9)	Fourth (15)	Sixth (36)
				1968:IV–1981:II			
3	4 (8–11)	Second (8)	First (6)	Third (11)	N.A.	N.A.	N.A.
				1981:II–1990:I			
4	10 (12–21)	Third (30)	First (14)	Second (27)	N.A.	N.A.	N.A.
5	5 (14–16, 20, 21)	Third (17)	First (8)	Fourth (18)	Second (11)	N.A.	N.A.
6	2 (15, 20)	Fourth (8)	First (3)	Third (6)	Second (5)	Fourth (8)	Sixth (12)

Note: N.A. = not available.

[a]Identified by rows in table 1.30 (in parentheses).

[b]Sum of the ranks from table 1.30 is given in parentheses.

ceal the differences between the forecast horizons, which are sometimes important (e.g., the Michigan forecasts would rate higher for the longer, and lower for the short, spans).

10. It is important to emphasize that these comparisons concentrate on only one aspect of the forecasts and need not imply an overall superiority of any of them. For example, the econometric and time-series models are clearly much better defined, more easily explained, more easily replicated, and more internally consistent than the survey forecasts. But the survey data collectively embody a great deal of apparently useful knowledge and information available to professional forecasters. An interesting project, which must be left for future research, would be to identify the best of the individual forecasts from the surveys and to combine them with each other and with very different model forecasts. Regressions of actual values on predictions from different sources and models would serve as one method for implementing this objective. Given rich data from active forecasters and interesting models, studies of this type should yield useful lessons.

Appendix
Forecasts of Diverse Macroeconomic Series, 1968–81 and 1981–90

Selected Nominal Aggregates, 1968–81

Current-dollar expenditures on durable consumer goods, business plant and equipment, and national defense (CD, PE, and DEF, respectively) all contribute strongly to the cyclical nature and volatility of quarterly changes in GNP. DEF is generally treated as an important exogenous variable.

The statistics for mean errors suggest that underestimates prevailed in the forecasts of CD and PE and overestimates in those of DEF, but there is much dispersion across the individual respondents here, which increases strongly with the forecast horizon (table 1A.1, cols. 1–3). The RMSE measures show much the same kind of progression (cols. 4–6). The forecast errors generally are at least smaller than the actual percentage changes in CD, PE, and DEF, but often not by much, as can be seen by comparing the corresponding entries in columns 4–6 and 9–11. Most of the SK and KU values are small, and only a few for CD and DEF may be significant (cols. 7 and 8).

The gains from averaging across the individual forecasts are modest for CD and DEF and, perhaps surprisingly, barely existent for PE (table 1A.2, cols. 1–4). The RMSE ratios for PE are closely clustered, indicating lack of differentiation among the forecasts for this variable. One possible reason may be the availability and influence of the quarterly anticipation series for plant and equipment outlays.

The RMSEs of our BVAR forecasts are larger than those of the group mean forecasts for CD and much larger for DEF. In contrast, BVAR is found to be much more accurate than the survey averages for PE. Indeed, the RMSE ratios i/bv are relatively very low for CD and DEF and very high for PE throughout. (Compare the corresponding measures in cols. 1–4 and 5–8.)

Finally, the NBER-ASA survey questionnaire used through 1981:II asked for forecasts of the levels of inventory investment in current dollars (CBI), another important but highly volatile and hard-to-predict variable. Table 1A.3 shows that the mean errors and root mean square errors for CBI increased markedly with the span while the corresponding standard deviation did not (rows 1–5). The M and MD statistics for mean errors are all positive here; the RMSE for target quarter 5 (i.e., $t + 4$) is about equal to the actual RMSV.

Apparently, CBI is another of those rare cases in which combining the individual survey forecasts is of little help. The group mean's RMSE is relatively large, and even the lower-quartile i/g ratios are close to one (see table 1A.4, rows 1–5). However, our BVAR model performs somewhat worse still here (cf. cols. 1–4 and 5–8).

Table 1A.1 Selected Measures of Forecast Accuracy and Actual Values: Percentage Changes in Expenditures for Consumer Durable Goods, Plant and Equipment, and National Defense, by Span, 1968–81

Row	Span (Qs)	Mean Error			Root Mean Square Error					Actual Value		
		M (1)	SD (2)	MD (3)	M (4)	SD (5)	MD (6)	SK (7)	KU (8)	M (9)	SD (10)	RMSV (11)
		Consumer Expenditures for Durable Goods (CD)										
1	0–1	−.79	.73	−.87	3.60	1.06	3.42	.88	.72	1.93	4.52	4.91
2	0–2	−1.10	1.26	−1.18	5.35	1.80	4.95	3.97	24.35	3.96	6.00	7.19
3	0–3	−1.30	1.59	−1.26	6.30	1.52	5.96	1.45	2.69	5.89	7.12	9.24
4	0–4	−.97	2.07	−.87	6.94	1.83	6.45	1.73	4.01	7.86	7.57	10.91
5	0–5	−1.23	2.61	−.74	8.39	3.50	7.46	4.01	23.83	9.96	8.68	13.21
		Plant and Equipment Expenditures (PE)										
6	0–1	−.71	1.02	−.51	5.49	1.75	5.69	.06	−.89	2.34	6.10	6.53
7	0–2	−1.24	1.89	−1.24	8.49	2.52	9.00	.40	−.19	4.66	9.36	10.46
8	0–3	−1.69	2.55	−1.95	11.51	2.84	11.82	−.07	−.70	6.89	11.99	13.83
9	0–4	−1.83	3.12	−1.95	13.78	3.26	14.17	−.32	−.46	8.86	14.19	16.73
10	0–5	−2.77	4.18	−2.46	16.46	3.68	16.79	−.60	.01	10.83	15.97	19.30
		National Defense Expenditures (DEF)										
11	0–1	.16	.55	.24	2.33	.56	2.25	.54	.71	1.43	2.51	2.89
12	0–2	.21	.97	.35	3.48	.97	3.41	.72	2.28	2.97	4.27	5.20
13	0–3	.17	1.52	.40	4.19	1.21	4.05	1.02	2.88	4.75	5.98	7.64
14	0–4	.04	2.06	.34	4.80	1.57	4.51	1.80	6.39	6.60	7.58	10.05
15	0–5	−.23	2.62	N.A.	5.79	1.94	5.38	2.21	8.93	8.60	9.55	12.85

Note: On the symbols used, see previous tables and the text.

Table 1A.2   **Individual, Group Mean, and BVAR Forecasts of Percentage Changes in Expenditures for Consumer Durable Goods, Plant and Equipment, and National Defense: Selected Comparisons, by Span, 1968–81**

Row	Span (Qs)	Group Mean RMSE (1)	RMSE Ratios i/g			BVAR RMSE (5)	RMSE Ratios i/bv		
			Q_1 (2)	MD (3)	Q_3 (4)		Q_1 (6)	MD (7)	Q_3 (8)
					Consumer Expenditures for Durable Goods (CD)				
1	0–1	3.23	.95	1.12	1.34	3.98	.72	.93	1.05
2	0–2	4.70	1.01	1.11	1.23	5.23	.88	1.02	1.15
3	0–3	5.38	1.02	1.13	1.31	6.27	.88	.98	1.19
4	0–4	5.50	1.06	1.16	1.36	6.74	.84	.96	1.13
5	0–5	6.42	1.04	1.17	1.43	7.45	.83	.99	1.18
					Plant and Equipment Expenditures (PE)				
6	0–1	5.82	1.01	1.05	1.09	2.19	1.87	2.72	3.04
7	0–2	8.96	1.01	1.07	1.10	3.16	2.19	2.83	3.33
8	0–3	11.54	1.00	1.06	1.10	4.47	2.36	2.79	3.20
9	0–4	13.76	1.00	1.05	1.12	5.51	2.39	2.70	3.30
10	0–5	15.69	.98	1.05	1.13	6.41	2.50	2.89	3.55
					National Defense Expenditures (DEF)				
11	0–1	1.78	1.07	1.19	1.38	2.85	.66	.75	.87
12	0–2	2.73	1.05	1.16	1.34	5.78	.47	.54	.63
13	0–4	3.31	1.02	1.17	1.38	8.53	.38	.45	.54
14	0–4	3.91	1.03	1.20	1.44	10.55	.35	.43	.50
15	0–5	4.96	1.05	1.22	1.44	13.25	.32	.38	.48

Note: On the symbols used, see previous tables and the text.

Components of Real GNP, 1981–90

After mid-1981, the survey collected forecasts of the main GNP expenditure categories in constant dollars. We start with real inventory investment (RCBI), to follow up on the preceding discussion. It turns out that the RCBI forecasts for 1981–90, like the CBI forecasts for 1981–90, have RMSEs that are large relative to the average actual levels and their variability, especially for the more distant target quarters (table 1A.3, rows 6–10). The average MEs are negative but very small, the SDs large and stable. Again, little is gained by averaging the individual forecasts, but the group mean forecasts do have a distinct advantage over the BVAR forecasts (table 1A.4, rows 6–10).

Similarly, real net exports (NX) were on the whole poorly predicted in the 1980s, as seen from the large relative size of the summary error measures in table 1A.3, rows 11–15. For NX, too, the group mean forecasts do not help much, but, in this case, the BVAR forecasts are found to be much more accurate (table 1A.4, rows 11–15).

Table 1A.3 Selected Measures of Forecast Accuracy and Actual Values: Nominal and Real Inventory Investment and Real Net Exports, by Span, 1968–81 and 1981–90

Row	Target Quarter	Mean Error			Root Mean Square Error					Actual Value		
		M (1)	SD (2)	MD (3)	M (4)	SD (5)	MD (6)	SK (7)	KU (8)	M (9)	SD (10)	RMSV (11)
					Change in Business Inventories, 1968–81 (CBI)							
1	1	.43	2.07	.45	9.33	3.65	9.76	.13	–.26	7.30	11.27	13.43
2	2	.92	2.42	1.10	9.94	3.62	10.24	–.19	–.49			
3	3	1.59	2.28	1.73	10.92	3.95	11.59	–.46	–.84			
4	4	2.57	2.53	2.78	11.63	3.77	11.84	–.34	–.43			
5	5	3.54	2.78	3.34	23.01	3.90	13.45	–.53	–.21			
					Change in Business Inventories in Constant Dollars, 1981–90 (RCBI)							
6	1	–.20	2.94	–.18	18.27	4.64	18.58	.58	1.35	14.58	20.37	25.05
7	2	–.47	3.57	.27	18.90	3.72	19.26	–.02	–.07			
8	3	–1.09	3.26	–.83	19.70	3.78	19.35	.47	.35			
9	4	–.08	3.73	–.64	20.46	4.10	20.25	.41	–.22			
10	5	–.69	4.41	–.58	21.06	4.47	21.03	.70	.75			
					Net Exports of Goods and Services in Constant Dollars, 1981–90 (NX)							
11	1	9.33	6.02	7.48	28.83	9.87	31.32	–.90	.35	–53.19	66.09	84.84
12	2	14.52	8.81	12.99	37.89	12.21	40.35	–1.15	.94			
13	3	21.36	10.72	18.35	47.60	12.79	48.36	–1.02	1.21			
14	4	27.04	12.72	27.36	54.15	12.06	55.81	–1.09	1.68			
15	5	31.53	15.13	28.56	60.21	12.31	60.63	–1.38	2.89			

Note: On the symbols used, see previous tables and the text.

Table 1A.4   Individual, Group Mean, and BVAR Forecasts of Nominal and Real Inventory Investment and Real Net Exports: Selected Comparisons, by Span, 1968–81 and 1981–90

		Group Mean	RMSE Ratios i/g			BVAR,[a]	RMSE Ratios i/bv		
Row	Target Quarter	RMSE (1)	Q_1 (2)	MD (3)	Q_3 (4)	RMSE (5)	Q_1 (6)	MD (7)	Q_3 (8)
		Change in Business Inventories, 1968–81 (CBI)							
1	1	10.57	.98	1.07	1.15	10.70	.83	1.03	1.15
2	2	10.75	.97	1.07	1.18	13.32	.72	.89	1.02
3	3	12.69	.99	1.07	1.16	14.17	.76	.95	1.07
4	4	13.41	1.00	1.06	1.12	16.24	.78	.91	1.09
5	5	14.50	1.00	1.05	1.12	15.28	.81	.99	1.12
		Change in Business Inventories in Constant Dollars, 1981–90 (RCBI)							
6	1	17.87	.96	1.03	1.14	19.78	.76	.91	1.08
7	2	18.35	.99	1.06	1.12	25.95	.52	.72	.82
8	3	19.19	1.00	1.05	1.13	28.45	.50	.66	.80
9	4	19.40	.97	1.06	1.20	29.38	.52	.68	.95
10	5	20.01	.98	1.02	1.11	29.89	.55	.68	.84
		Net Exports of Goods and Services in Constant Dollars, 1981–90 (NX)							
11	1	28.04	1.00	1.03	1.07	13.28	2.06	2.30	2.60
12	2	36.45	1.00	1.04	1.14	17.71	2.00	2.21	2.65
13	3	44.91	.98	1.03	1.11	19.66	2.17	2.45	2.78
14	4	52.11	.98	1.03	1.10	23.08	2.16	2.36	2.51
15	5	59.44	.97	1.02	1.08	31.39	1.79	1.94	2.13

Note: On the symbols used, see previous tables and the text.

One would expect total consumption (PCE), the largest and smoothest component of real GNP, to be the easiest to predict and in fact the best predicted. A relatively small but smooth and presumably also well-predicted series should be that of state and local government purchases (SLGP). Federal government purchases (FGP) are more autonomous and volatile, hence more difficult to forecast. Residential fixed investment (RFI) is another hard problem for the forecasters, although for different reasons: it is highly cyclical and an early leading series (construction lags behind housing permits and starts are short). Nonresidential fixed investment (NFI) has more persistence, more of an upward trend, and lags at cyclical turning points, which should make it more easily predicted than RFI. Also, NFI is anticipated with long leads by new capital appropriations and contracts and orders for plant and equipment—but these monthly series on business investment commitments are themselves very volatile.

The evidence on the forecasts of percentage changes in PCE, NFI, RFI,

Table 1A.5   **Selected Measures of Forecast Accuracy and Actual Values: Percentage Changes in Consumption, Investment, and Government Components of Real GNP, by Span, 1981–90**

Row	Span (Qs)	Mean Error			Root Mean Square Error					Actual Value		
		M (1)	SD (2)	MD (3)	M (4)	SD (5)	MD (6)	SK (7)	KU (8)	M (9)	SD (10)	RMSV (11)
		Personal Consumption Expenditures (PCE)										
1	0–1	−.14	.20	−.14	.83	.30	.68	1.61	2.17	.78	.69	1.04
2	0–2	−.26	.29	−.29	1.10	.42	.94	1.81	2.67	1.58	.99	1.86
3	0–3	−.47	.46	−.44	1.45	.51	1.27	1.96	3.74	2.44	1.22	2.73
4	0–4	−.63	.65	−.59	1.80	.64	1.60	1.96	4.33	3.33	1.41	3.62
5	0–5	−.85	.85	−.74	2.23	.86	2.00	2.03	4.02	4.22	1.69	4.55
		Nonresidential Fixed Investment (NFI)										
6	0–1	−.59	.91	−.71	2.85	2.10	2.43	5.07	26.62	1.05	2.00	2.80
7	0–2	−1.22	1.42	−1.26	4.53	1.91	4.07	3.99	18.39	2.21	4.40	4.92
8	0–3	−1.47	1.88	−1.51	6.76	2.51	5.86	2.32	5.35	3.46	6.18	7.08
9	0–4	−2.31	2.38	−2.36	8.47	2.14	7.97	1.43	1.69	4.87	7.85	9.24
10	0–5	−2.76	3.14	−2.97	10.33	2.55	9.99	1.35	1.81	6.46	9.26	11.29
		Residential Fixed Investment (RFI)										
11	0–1	−.85	1.08	−.67	4.16	1.52	3.83	1.89	4.70	1.18	4.84	4.98
12	0–2	−1.87	2.27	−1.42	7.56	2.48	7.18	.67	−.24	2.95	9.01	4.27
13	0–3	−2.93	3.19	−2.32	10.23	3.28	10.14	.36	−.21	5.06	12.59	13.57
14	0–4	−4.12	3.93	−3.56	12.68	4.26	12.42	.28	−.67	7.39	15.78	17.42
15	0–5	−5.58	5.23	−4.94	14.95	5.07	14.40	.21	−.95	9.90	18.71	21.17
		Federal Government Purchases (FGP)										
16	0–1	−.60	1.33	−.51	3.99	.81	3.77	.60	−.37	1.16	4.15	4.31
17	0–2	−.79	1.50	−.90	5.25	1.32	5.03	1.49	3.63	2.22	5.24	5.69
18	0–3	−.94	1.75	−1.21	5.35	1.43	5.01	1.78	4.47	3.09	5.28	6.12
19	0–4	−.74	2.36	−1.35	5.91	3.06	5.27	3.75	17.22	4.00	4.85	6.29
20	0–5	−1.55	2.70	−1.81	6.16	1.71	5.74	1.14	1.48	5.27	6.05	8.02
		State and Local Government Purchases (SLGP)										
21	0–1	−.13	.28	−.17	.90	.33	.85	1.87	4.40	.52	.70	.87
22	0–2	−.24	.52	−.26	1.24	.56	1.15	2.77	9.44	1.12	1.07	1.55
23	0–3	−.38	.72	−.40	1.57	.77	1.52	2.61	9.42	1.72	1.32	2.17
24	0–4	−.62	.88	−.58	1.89	.92	1.79	2.98	12.01	2.34	1.54	2.80
25	0–5	−.92	1.09	−1.13	2.35	1.11	2.03	2.82	11.02	2.99	1.85	3.52

Note: On the symbols used, see previous tables and the text.

FGP, and SLGP is generally consistent with these priors. Thus, forecasts of growth in PCE four quarters ahead have errors averaging about half the actual percentage change (table 1A.5, rows 1–5). This is not great, but fair, and in sharp contrast to the apparent failure of forecasts of inventory investment (the least predictable of the components of aggregate demand). The RMSEs of the NFI forecasts are much smaller than their counterparts for RFI (but the actual percentage changes are also smaller for NFI; compare the corresponding entries in rows 6–10 and 11–15). The SLGP forecasts are definitely much more accurate than the FGP forecasts (cf. rows 16–20 and 21–25).

The forecasts share some characteristics across all the variables. All the M and MD statistics for mean errors are negative, suggesting a prevalence of underprediction errors (cols. 1 and 3). The absolute values of these statistics increase with the span in each case. Indeed, all the summary error measures, except SK and KU, show such increases, as do the statistics for actual values.[17] The means of the RMSEs are generally larger than the medians, and SK is greater than zero. The KU statistics are large in some cases, particularly for NFI (short forecasts) and SLGP.

Combining the individual forecasts into group means reduces the RMSEs for each variable and span, as can be seen by comparing column 1 of table 1A.6 with column 6 (and a fortiori with col. 4) of table 1A.5. At the lower quartile Q_1, the RMSE ratios i/g are close to one throughout; the range of the median ratios is about 1.1–1.3, and that of the Q_3 ratios is 1.2–1.7. The group mean forecasts perform best (the ratios are highest) for PCE and SLGP (see table 1A.6, cols. 2–4).

Our BVAR forecasts have larger RMSEs than the NBER-ASA group mean forecasts 80 percent of the time, according to the paired entries in columns 1 and 5 of table 1A.6. They are very poor for PCE and definitely inferior for FGP, whereas elsewhere the differences are much smaller (cf. cols. 1–4 and 5–8).

Consumer Price Inflation and Interest Rates, 1981–90

Forecasters underpredicted CPI inflation just as they did IPD inflation (see the negative signs of the mean errors in table 1A.7, rows 1–5, cols. 1 and 3). The RMSEs of these forecasts are discouragingly large compared to the descriptive statistics for the actual values (cf. cols. 4 and 6 with 11, in particular). Note that the NBER-ASA survey questionionnaire asked directly for forecasts of the level of *CPI inflation* at an annual rate in the current quarter and the following four quarters (not for forecasts of the CPI itself).

In contrast, the forecasts of the three-month Treasury-bill rate (TBR) had relatively small errors according to these comparisons (rows 6–10). The fore-

---

17. A few deviations from the rule appear in the longest forecasts; they are apparently due to outliers and small-sample problems.

Table 1A.6   **Individual, Group Mean, and BVAR Forecasts of Percentage Changes in Consumption, Investment, and Government Components of Real GNP: Selected Comparisons, by Span, 1981–90**

Row	Span (Qs)	Group Mean RMSE (1)	RMSE Ratios i/g Q₁ (2)	MD (3)	Q₃ (4)	BVAR RMSE (5)	RMSE Ratios i/bv Q₁ (6)	MD (7)	Q₃ (8)
			Personal Consumption Expenditures (PCE)						
1	0–1	.58	1.08	1.23	1.73	1.97	.31	.36	.48
2	0–2	.79	1.12	1.22	1.41	3.78	.22	.24	.28
3	0–3	.98	1.11	1.25	1.51	5.65	.20	.22	.27
4	0–4	1.18	1.15	1.24	1.71	7.66	.18	.20	.25
5	0–5	1.47	1.10	1.27	1.66	9.37	.18	.21	.24
			Nonresidential Fixed Investment (NFI)						
6	0–1	2.01	1.10	1.19	1.34	2.23	.90	1.02	1.19
7	0–2	3.43	1.03	1.11	1.26	3.64	.95	1.04	1.17
8	0–3	4.99	1.04	1.12	1.26	5.31	.96	1.04	1.19
9	0–4	6.89	1.00	1.06	1.22	6.83	.99	1.09	1.23
10	0–5	8.69	.99	1.05	1.18	8.25	1.02	1.09	1.26
			Residential Fixed Investment (RFI)						
11	0–1	3.01	1.05	1.26	1.45	3.97	.79	.97	1.21
12	0–2	5.83	.96	1.25	1.43	5.24	1.10	1.30	1.80
13	0–3	8.42	.94	1.21	1.41	8.33	.90	1.15	1.51
14	0–4	10.63	.93	1.24	1.42	11.30	.80	1.02	1.35
15	0–5	12.62	.96	1.15	1.45	14.64	.71	.98	1.23
			Federal Government Purchases (FGP)						
16	0–1	3.31	1.00	1.14	1.27	4.61	.72	.80	.95
17	0–2	4.22	1.02	1.10	1.29	7.26	.59	.65	.82
18	0–3	4.11	1.04	1.18	1.37	9.02	.50	.54	.66
19	0–4	3.79	1.13	1.31	1.48	10.39	.39	.52	.63
20	0–5	4.55	1.07	1.30	1.48	11.44	.44	.53	.65
			State and Local Government Purchases (SLGP)						
21	0–1	.61	1.14	1.23	1.51	.49	1.40	1.64	2.07
22	0–2	.75	1.02	1.19	1.39	.82	1.09	1.44	1.62
23	0–3	.91	1.00	1.17	1.27	1.20	1.11	1.41	1.60
24	0–4	1.07	1.13	1.19	1.40	1.68	1.13	1.29	1.54
25	0–5	1.35	1.01	1.13	1.30	2.18	1.04	1.28	1.53

Note: On the symbols used, see previous tables and the text.

Table 1A.7   Selected Measures of Forecast Accuracy and Actual Values: Consumer Price Inflation, the Treasury-Bill Rate, and the Corporate Bond Yield, 1981–90

Row	Target Quarter	Mean Error			Root Mean Square Error					Actual Value		
		M (1)	SD (2)	MD (3)	M (4)	SD (5)	MD (6)	SK (7)	KU (8)	M (9)	SD (10)	RMSV (11)
		Consumer Price Index, % Change (CPI)										
1	1	−.61	.47	−.50	1.20	.39	1.08	.34	−1.37	1.02	.54	1.16
2	2	−.58	.48	−.46	1.18	.43	1.15	.11	−1.41			
3	3	−.57	.50	−.46	1.20	.42	1.20	.19	−1.36			
4	4	−.53	.50	−.51	1.21	.38	1.26	.10	−1.50			
5	5	−.51	.53	−.50	1.23	.39	1.24	.00	−1.41			
		Treasury-Bill Rate, 3-Month, % (TBR)										
6	1	.03	.24	−.03	.49	.36	.40	2.50	8.01	8.38	2.48	8.74
7	2	.19	.49	.24	1.51	.51	1.52	.06	2.75			
8	3	.39	.68	.61	1.85	.50	1.80	.11	.85			
9	4	.65	.59	.83	2.03	.56	2.23	−1.55	2.14			
10	5	1.05	.68	1.03	2.48	.71	2.62	−.42	1.09			
		Corporate Bond Yield, % (CBY)										
11	1	−.26	.30	−.24	.72	.35	.63	2.01	5.65	11.64	2.34	11.87
12	2	−.00	.48	.12	1.59	.59	1.37	.66	−.26			
13	3	.21	.61	.31	1.86	.49	1.81	.78	.51			
14	4	.39	.72	.58	2.05	.43	2.02	.39	−.28			
15	5	.60	.74	.69	2.25	.66	2.36	.88	1.58			

Note: On the symbols used, see previous tables and the text.

Table 1A.8   **Individual, Group Mean, and BVAR Forecasts of Consumer Price Inflation, the Treasury-Bill Rate, and the Corporate Bond Yield: Selected Comparisons, by Span, 1981–90**

Row	Target Quarter	Group Mean RMSE (1)	RMSE Ratios i/g Q₁ (2)	RMSE Ratios i/g MD (3)	RMSE Ratios i/g Q₃ (4)	BVAR,[a] RMSE (5)	RMSE Ratios i/bv Q₁ (6)	RMSE Ratios i/bv MD (7)	RMSE Ratios i/bv Q₃ (8)
				Consumer Price Index, % Change (CPI)					
1	1	.53	1.01	1.03	1.12	.54	1.63	2.63	3.22
2	2	.46	1.01	1.03	1.12	.74	1.02	1.63	2.29
3	3	.48	1.01	1.03	1.18	.78	1.05	1.80	2.06
4	4	.54	1.01	1.02	1.09	.80	1.07	1.63	1.79
5	5	.58	1.01	1.02	1.08	.95	.92	1.36	1.59
				Treasury-Bill Rate, 3-month, % (TBR)					
6	1	.20	1.45	1.83	2.46	.96	.29	.38	.56
7	2	.90	1.09	1.26	2.11	1.62	.59	.81	1.17
8	3	1.38	1.02	1.31	1.54	2.03	.65	.80	1.08
9	4	1.77	1.00	1.14	1.29	2.51	.68	.77	.94
10	5	2.49	1.01	1.08	1.18	3.03	.67	.78	.95
				Corporate Bond Yield, % (CBY)					
11	1	.38	1.17	1.57	1.81	.77	.56	.77	.98
12	2	.83	1.15	1.48	2.52	1.26	.72	.95	1.75
13	3	1.24	1.09	1.25	1.74	1.74	.77	.92	1.25
14	4	1.51	1.03	1.19	1.46	2.19	.69	.88	1.03
15	5	2.42	.98	1.11	1.20	2.65	.60	.83	1.02

Note: On the symbols used, see previous tables and the text.

casts of the (new high-grade) corporate bond yield (CBY) were even more accurate (rows 11–15).

Despite the already noted weakness of most of the individual CPI forecasts, the corresponding group mean forecasts perform relatively well. Their RMSEs are considerably smaller than those of the BVAR model and less than half those of the average individual forecasts (cf. table 1A.8, rows 1–5, and table 1A.7, rows 1–5, cols. 4 and 6). The i/g ratios cluster close to one between Q_1 and Q_2, which indicates that the forecasts concerned are remarkably alike.

For the interest rates TBR and CBY, combining the individual forecasts greatly reduces errors, but with notable exceptions at the most distant target quarter (5). Here the RMSEs are much larger for the BVAR than the group mean forecasts, and, correspondingly, the i/bv ratios are much lower than the i/g ratios (cf. table 1A.8, rows 6–15, cols. 1–4 and 5–8).

References

Braun, P. A., and I. Yaniv. 1991. A case study of expert judgment: Economists' probabilistic forecasts. University of Chicago. Mimeo.

Burns, A. F., and W. C. Mitchell. 1946. *Measuring business cycles*. New York: NBER.

Butler, W. F., and R. A. Kavesh. 1974. Judgmental forecasting of the gross national product. In *Methods and techniques of business forecasting*, ed. W. F. Butler, R. A. Kavesh, and R. B. Platt. Englewood Cliffs, N.J.: Prentice-Hall.

Carlson, J. A. 1977. Study of price forecasts. *Annals of Economic and Social Measurement* 6 (1): 27–56.

Clemen, R. T. 1989. Combining forecasts: A review and annotated bibliography. *International Journal of Forecasting* 5 (4): 559–83.

Cole, R. 1969. *Errors in provisional estimates of gross national product*. New York: Columbia University Press (for the NBER).

Cox, G. V. 1929. *An appraisal for American business forecasts*. Chicago: University of Chicago Press.

Dominguez, K. M., R. C. Fair, and M. D. Shapiro, 1988. Forecasting the Depression: Harvard versus Yale. *American Economic Review* 78 (4): 595–612.

Evans, M. K., Y. Haitovsky, and G. I. Treyz, assisted by V. Su. 1972. An analysis of the forecasting properties of U.S. econometric models. In *Econometric models of cyclical behavior*, ed. B. G. Hickman, 2 vols. New York: Columbia University Press (for the NBER).

Fels, R., and C. E. Hinshaw. 1968. *Forecasting and recognizing business cycle turning points*. New York: Columbia University Press (for the NBER).

Grunberg, E., and F. Modigliani. 1954. The predictability of social events. *Journal of Political Economy* 62 (6): 465–78.

Haitovsky, Y., G. I. Treyz, and V. Su. 1974. *Forecasts with quarterly macroeconometric models*. New York: Columbia University Press (for the NBER).

Hicks, J. R. 1979. *Causality in economics*. New York: Basic.

Keynes, J. M. 1936. *The general theory of employment, interest and money*. London: Macmillan.

Knight, F. M. 1921. *Risk, uncertainty, and profit*. Boston: Houghton Mifflin.

Litterman, R. B. 1986. Forecasting with Bayesian vector autoregressions—five years of experience. *Journal of Business and Economic Statistics* 4 (1): 25–38.

McCloskey, D. N. 1988. The limits of expertise: If you're so smart, why ain't you rich? *American Scholar* (Summer), 393–406.

McNees, S. K. 1979. The forecasting record of the 1970s. *New England Economic Review* (September/October) 57(3): 1–21.

Mincer, J. 1969. *Economic forecasts and expectations: Analyses of forecasting behavior and performance*. New York: Columbia University Press (for the NBER).

Moore, G. H. 1969. Forecasting short-term economic change. *Journal of the American Statistical Association* 64 (March): 1–22.

Morgenstern, O. 1928. *Wirtschaftsprognose: Eine Untersuchung ihrer Voraussetzungen and Möglichkeiten*. Vienna: Springer.

Nelson, C. R. 1984. A benchmark for the accuracy of econometric forecasts of GNP. *Business Economics* 19 (3): 52–58.

Niemira, M., and P. A. Klein. 1991. Forecasting the Great Depression using cyclical indicators: Another look. New York: Mitsubishi Bank. Mimeo.

Okun, A. M. 1959. A review of some economic forecasts for 1955–57. *Journal of Business* 32 (July): 199–211.

Sims, C. A. 1989. A nine-variable probabilistic macroeconomic forecasting model. Discussion Paper no. 14. Institute for Empirical Macroeconomics. Minneapolis: Federal Reserve Bank of Minnesota, May. Mimeo.

Sims, C. A., and R. M. Todd. 1991. Evaluating Bayesian vector autoregressive forecasting procedures for macroeconomic data: Part 2. Paper presented at the NSF-NBER Seminar on Bayesian Inference in Econometrics and Statistics, St. Paul, Minnesota, April.

Solow, R. M. 1985. Economic history and economics. *American Economic Review* 75 (2): 328–31.

Stekler, H. O. 1968. Forecasting with econometric models: An evaluation. *Econometrica* 36: 437–63.

Su, V., and J. Su. 1975. An evaluation of the ASA/NBER business outlook survey forecasts. *Explorations in Economic Research* 2: 588–618.

Suits, D. B. 1962. Forecasting and analysis with an econometric model. *American Economic Review* 52:104–32.

Theil, H. 1961. *Economic forecasts and policy.* 2d rev. ed. Amsterdam: North-Holland.

———. 1966. *Applied economic forecasting.* Amsterdam: North-Holland; Chicago: Rand McNally.

———. 1967. *Economics and information theory.* Amsterdam: North-Holland; Chicago: Rand McNally.

Thorp, W. L. 1926. *Business annals.* New York: NBER.

Zarnowitz, V. 1967. *An appraisal of short-term economic forecasts.* New York: Columbia University Press (for the NBER).

———. 1968. The new ASA-NBER survey of forecasts by economic statisticians. *American Statistician* 23 (1): 12–16.

———. 1971. New plans and results of research in economic forecasting. In *Fifty-first annual report.* New York: NBER.

———. 1972. Forecasting economic conditions: The record and the prospect. In *The business cycle today,* ed. V. Zarnowitz. New York: Columbia University Press (for the NBER).

———. 1974. How accurate have the forecasts been? In *Methods and techniques of business forecasting,* ed. W. F. Butler, R. A. Kavesh, and R. B. Platt. Englewood Cliffs, N.J.: Prentice-Hall.

———. 1979. An analysis of annual and multiperiod quarterly forecasts of aggregate income, output, and the price level. *Journal of Business* 52 (1): 1–33.

———. 1982. Improvements and new studies of the economic outlook survey. *NBER Reporter* (Summer), 11–13.

———. 1983. Some lessons from research in macroeconomic forecasting. *Economic Outlook USA* 10 (4): 83–86.

———. 1984. The accuracy of individual and group forecasts from business outlook surveys. *Journal of Forecasting* 3 (1): 11–26.

———. 1985. Rational expectations and macroeconomic forecasts. *Journal of Business and Economic Statistics* (4): 293–311.

———. 1991. Has macro-forecasting failed? Working Paper no. 3867. Cambridge, Mass.: NBER, October. (This paper will be reprinted in the proceedings of the Cato Institute's ninth annual monetary conference: *Money, macroeconomics, and forecasting.* Washington, D.C.: Cato Institute, in press.)

———. 1992. *Business cycles: Theories, history, indicators, and forecasting.* Chicago: University of Chicago Press.

Zarnowitz, V., and P. Braun. 1990. Major macroeconomic variables and leading indexes: Some estimates of their interrelations. In *Analyzing modern business cycles: Essays honoring Geoffrey H. Moore,* ed. P. A. Klein. Armonk, N.Y.: M. E. Sharpe.

Zarnowitz, V., and L. A. Lambros. 1987. Consensus and uncertainty in economic prediction. *Journal of Political Economy* 95 (3): 591–621.

Comment   Allen Sinai

Victor Zarnowitz and Phillip Braun (ZB) have produced an impressive paper on the record of macroeconomic forecasts and forecasting performance, probably the most encyclopedic ever on this topic. The data set, while not without deficiencies, is rich in content, comprehensive, and spans an unusually long period, 1968–90. There is a representative enough sample of forecasters and a long enough time frame to promote confidence in the implications for forecasts and forecasting performance suggested by the work.

The macro variables covered were big and small (e.g., ranging from gross national product [GNP] to the change in business inventories), important and less so in the macro scheme of things, showed both little and considerable variability, and presented a wide range of ease or difficulty in forecasting. The forecasters sampled and forecasting methods used represent a reasonable cross section of those who engage in macro forecasting, although classification of the types of forecasts and forecasters is difficult because of the mix in background and methods of the forecasters.

One problem with the data was considerable variability in the survey respondents, over time and across individuals. On average, the response rate was not very high and was quite variable. The number of respondents shrank dramatically in the 1980s compared with the 1970s. There was no systematic statistically based process for generating the observations used to calculate the results. Inferences drawn from so nonrandom a sample, especially one on which distributional summary statistics are calculated, may be more suggestive than confirmational and should be interpreted cautiously.

ZB nearly exhaust the possible range of questions about macro forecasts and macro forecasting, providing numerous insights on forecasting accuracy and performance that can help consumers of economic forecasts in understanding what to expect from forecasts and forecasters.

This Comment discusses several aspects of the ZB paper, drawing out what might be of interest to the historian of forecast performance, to the forecasting practitioner, and to those who are consumers of macroeconomic forecasts. Of interest is what the forecasts of macroeconomic variables reveal about forecast accuracy, what forecasters can learn from past forecasting performance to help

Allen Sinai is chief economist and president, Lehman Brothers Economic Advisors, and adjunct professor, Lemberg Program for International Economics and Finance, Brandeis University.

forecasting in the future, and what consumers of macroeconomic forecasts can reasonably expect from forecasts and forecasters. A couple of specific criticisms are separately treated.

Forecasts and Forecasting Performance

The ZB paper provides the most comprehensive and exhaustive survey of macroeconomic forecasts presented to date.[1] The sample period covered twenty-two years with eleven variables from 1968:IV to 1981:II and seventeen through 1990:I, included a large number of forecasters, contained a variety of forecasting methods, involved numerous organizational sites from which the forecasts were made, and provided a varied, often volatile set of macroeconomic conditions and events to forecast. Topics covered relative to forecasts and forecasting performance included accuracy (for specific variables and in general), the variability of forecasts, near-term versus longer-run forecasts, "consensus" versus individual forecasts, and forecast performance (by organization, by period, and by method).

Some deficiencies of the data must be noted, however. How representative the sample of forecasts and forecasters is affects the validity of any inferences drawn.

First, the sample generating the forecast observations was not of uniform size and composition in a cross-sectional or time-series sense. Nor was it randomly selected by any sampling method. There were 86 respondents used in the period 1968:IV–1981:2. The mean number per survey, 40.8, was less than half the total. The standard deviation was 11.3, or 27.6 percent of the mean for this subperiod, an indication of considerable variability in the responses across surveys. The sample from 1981:III to 1990:I contained 29 individuals, only one-third the number in the prior subperiod, although the responses were more consistent. The mean number of respondents per survey was 17.2 and the standard deviation 3.3.

Respondent participation was not strong, with only 24.2 surveys per respondent, on average, out of 51 in 1968:IV–1981:II and a standard deviation of 10.4, or 43 percent of the mean. The mean number of surveys per respondent was 20.8 out of 35 but with a smaller standard deviation of 7.5, or 36.1 percent of the mean.

---

1. McNees has summarized and presented the results of macroeconomic forecasts in numerous articles (e.g., McNees 1979, 1981, 1988; McNees and Ries 1983), but his sample generally has been limited to econometrics-based forecasts. Victor Zarnowitz, and now Phillip Braun, has been collecting a large number of macroeconomic variable forecasts for the North-Holland publication *Economic Forecasts*. Numerous forecasters are surveyed whose methods of forecasting vary considerably. This effort is fairly recent, but the data set will provide an excellent basis for analysis at some point. The *Eggert Blue Chip Survey* collects forecasts from about fifty-three forecasters who are based at different types of organizations and who use different methods to forecast. This could provide data useful for analyzing forecasts and forecasting performance if it would ever be made available for that purpose. The *Wall Street Journal* surveys fifty or so forecasters twice a year, publishing the results in early January and in early July, and has been doing so regularly since 1981. This is yet another source of data on macroeconomic forecasts and forecasting performance.

A smaller sample of participants can produce greater variability in the various summary measures of forecast accuracy, those for central tendency or spread. A wide dispersion of forecasts would have a similar effect. How to correct for the variability of survey responses across time and of respondents by survey is not clear. Means and standard deviations of the individual and group mean forecasts are likely biased in such a situation.

Second, certain differences between forecasters were not accounted for, nor were any adjustments made for the time spent in forecasting. Those who participated in a few surveys might not have been similar in interest to those who responded to many surveys or have had similar training, experience, or ability. "Part-time" forecasting, on average, probably produces less accuracy, "full-time" forecasting more, and "commercially based" forecasting perhaps the most accuracy.

Third, coverage varied across individuals and over time, with turnover of participants high, again a problem for the drawing of inferences from the calculated results.

Fourth, since the sample participants were largely from business but spread across other areas including finance, research and consulting, academic institutions, government, and others, skill levels, possible influences of the work environment on forecasting, and methods used could have been very different. Forecast comparisons need to correct for these factors.

Fifth, the forecasting method most often identified was "informal judgment." This provided another sort of heterogeneity in the sample since the informal judgment method of forecasting is amorphously defined and for at least some forecasters potentially a surrogate for an otherwise identifiable forecast method.

Such features of the data probably bias the results more than if each forecaster exhibited a similar configuration of characteristics and the sample size were the same over time. Doubt is cast on the validity of conclusions drawn because the sample may not have been representative of the population. The inferences claimed from the study must therefore be regarded as tentative and in need of further investigation.

Any weaknesses of the data did not carry over into the assessment of forecasting performance, however. ZB provide a complete and comprehensive set of results and make a major contribution to the issue of forecast accuracy, producing numerous insights and implications for practitioners and users of macroeconomic forecasts.

A full range of summary measures of forecast performance is provided, for both short- and longer-run forecasts. Almost everything is there—mean errors; marginal errors; mean absolute errors (MAEs); root mean square errors (RMSEs); measures of dispersion such as standard deviation, median, interquartile range, skewedness, and kurtosis; early quarter and late quarter forecasts; group mean as consensus versus individual forecasts; levels and percentage changes; zero- to five-quarters-ahead forecasts; Bayesian vector autoregression (BVAR) forecasts; subperiod forecast assessment (1968:IV–1979:III and 1979:IV–1990:I); Michigan (RSQE) model econometric forecasts versus those from the NBER-ASA survey; Sims model (BVAR) forecasts versus the NBER-ASA versus the Sims-Todd ARIMA—in thirty-one tables of data and eight appendix tables, quite a collection of results!

The analysis is also very complete, ranging over issues of absolute accuracy in forecasts of changes and levels; the effects of data revision on accuracy; the distribution of errors in the short run (current to one or two quarters out) and in the long run (as much as five quarters out); accuracy for major variables such as nominal GNP, real GNP, and inflation but also for other macroeconomic variables such as the unemployment rate, housing starts, capital goods spending, net exports, and certain interest rates; individual versus "consensus" or group mean forecasts; how well certain forecasters forecast certain variables; a comparison of forecasts before and after the big change of Federal Reserve policy in October 1979; econometric model performance of the Michigan model versus the NBER-ASA; the NBER-ASA versus time-series methods such as BVAR, the Sims version of BVAR, and ARIMA.

Many of the conclusions drawn have been put forward before, for example, larger forecast errors the longer the forecast horizon and the superior performance of group mean or consensus forecasts relative to most individual forecasts. The supporting evidence is more substantial in ZB than in other studies, however.

Some results are new and interesting. There is new evidence particularly on the performance of BVAR and other time-series forecasting methods versus the NBER-ASA forecasts, which were mostly informal judgment. These relatively new methods of forecasting have been subjected to little evaluation, in terms of accuracy, relative to others such as informal judgment, econometrics, or the leading economic indicators barometric approach. The results from the BVAR approach of ZB were mixed, where two variants were used, one with an assumption of no current-quarter knowledge (variant A) and the other assuming perfect foresight in the quarter (variant B). But the results appear promising enough to warrant additional examination of BVAR as an alternative or supplemental macroeconomic forecasting tool.

Other time-series methods, represented in models developed by Christopher Sims and by Sims and R. Todd, BVAR- and ARIMA-type specifications, were analyzed for the major variables. Some ARIMA forecasts of Charles Nelson's and Frederick Joutz's were also evaluated.

Here, the results were again mixed, with forecasts of some variables showing up relatively well against the NBER-ASA surveys and some not, depending especially on whether the assumption was no current-quarter knowledge or perfect foresight. If the former, the ARIMA comparisons were unfavorable. If the latter, the ARIMA comparisons were competitive. Consensus or group mean forecasts almost uniformly were superior to the ARIMA methods, regardless of which type. The Sims BVAR results were competitive, suggesting BVAR as a forecasting technique worth using, if only at least on a collateral basis.

Group mean forecasts consistently did better than most individual forecasts and the various time-series methods of forecasting, not a new result, but one underscored and most impressive in ZB for the degree and widespread nature of the supporting evidence. This is a significant and important finding for both practitioners and users of macroeconomic forecasts.

A few interesting topics were not analyzed. There was no discussion or evaluation of forecast accuracy on cyclical turns. ZB did not deal with the question of forecasting turning points in major variables. It would have been of interest to see how the NBER-ASA forecasts did on turning points and in identifying the extent and length of downturns and expansions and to see how consistent forecasts were across different cyclical episodes. The 1970s and 1980s were quite volatile, in a business-cycle sense, with both endogenous swings and external shocks, policy and other, perturbing the economy more than usual. How macro forecasts did under such conditions could have been highlighted given the data available, would have been instructive on issues of accuracy, and would have been of interest to practitioners of forecasting.

A useful historical analysis would have carefully examined the forecasts in periods after "shocks" such as the fourfold oil price increase of 1973–74 and the radical change of Federal Reserve policy in October 1979.

A notion of rational expectations is that forecasts, especially those of econometric models and implicitly others that use a structural approach, might not do well after a change in structure. Looking at forecast performance for a few years before and after the structural changes that occurred and across forecasting methods such as econometric, informal judgment, the barometric approach of the leading economic indicators, and anticipatory surveys could have provided a test of this rational expectations idea.

A historical description of how the forecasts fared over business-cycle episodes, à la McNees (1988) and McNees and Ries (1983), would also have been of interest. This cannot be extracted from the tables, although it certainly exists in the ZB data set.

Interesting also was the attempt at a before-and-after comparison of forecast accuracy where the new Fed policy (NFP) under Federal Reserve chairman Volcker constituted the dividing line between 1968:IV–1979:III and 1979:IV–1990:I. Regardless of the forecasting method, a worse performance might have been expected in the period 1979:IV–1990:I than in 1968:IV–1979:III. The structure of the economy certainly shifted during the late 1970s and early 1980s, at first because of oil price shocks and then because of the NFP.

The period comparisons, eleven years each, were interpreted by ZB as not showing any significant improvement or worsening of forecasts between them. But some of the ZB data do not support this assertion. Table 1.14 shows that, in the period 1979–90, the individual forecasts were worse on nominal GNP, worse part of the time on real GNP, and better on inflation. The group mean forecasts were significantly worse on nominal GNP, slightly worse on real GNP near term, and distinctly better on inflation.

In any case, disaggregation over time, rather than the lumping together of so much experience into eleven-year subsamples, would be necessary if differences were to be assessed fully. Macro forecasting is a lot easier in expansion (e.g., the years 1983–88) than over a shorter period of time such as 1981–82, which was characterized by a great deal of volatility.

There is considerable averaging in the two eleven-year spans, perhaps wiping out or diminishing what might appear to be differences in forecasting performance if the specific episodes had been isolated for comparisons over a shorter span of time.

Also of interest was the comparison of the NBER-ASA survey results with the econometric approach to forecasting as represented by the Michigan model (RSQE) forecasts. The Michigan model comparison with the NBER-ASA forecasts were unfavorable and did not support some earlier work that has indicated "model plus judgment" as superior to "judgmental" forecasting alone. The NBER-ASA survey showed about half or more of individual forecasts to be at least somewhat more accurate than Michigan in the major variables real GNP, inflation, and unemployment.

The comparison of the NBER-ASA surveys with the Michigan model really does not put the econometric approach in the best light, however. The Michigan model was chosen principally because it had the longest forecast history of those methods that were econometrics based, matching better the span of the NBER-ASA surveys. The more general system methods for macro forecasting, pioneered by Lawrence R. Klein and the various Klein and Wharton models and by Otto Eckstein (1983) at Data Resources, probably were not well represented by the Michigan model.

The National Economic Information System, Eckstein's terminology, is used more or less by many large-scale macroeconometric model builders, especially commercial vendors, including Data Resources, Wharton Econometric Forecasting Associates (WEFA), Evans Economics, Lawrence Meyer and Associates, and the Boston Company Economic Advisors. It stresses intensive monitoring, screening, and filtering of high-frequency data in the forecasts of early periods, typically spends more time assessing and estimating exogenous variables and policy inputs, and applies significant numbers of staff to the forecasting task. The National Economic Information System approach also encompasses many more types of studies, simulations, and collateral research that feed into the macroeconometric forecasts than perhaps might be followed by Michigan.

An interesting comparison would be to take macroeconometric model forecasts including those of the Michigan RSQE, perhaps the data kept by Steve McNees from the NBER-NSF Model Comparison Seminars, and to compare the collective results of those forecasts over a sample period that matches a portion of the NBER-ASA surveys. This would produce a more useful and informative comparison of the econometric approach with informal judgment (the NBER-ASA survey) than ZB actually performed. Group mean forecast comparisons between the two, NBER-ASA and econometrics based, would provide the most instructive test.

Presumably, these organizations who use the econometric approach in profit-making enterprises ought to produce, on average, more accurate forecasts than the NBER-ASA survey. The fees paid by the market are supposed to reflect some added value, perhaps related to the accuracy of the forecasting.

An important contribution of ZB was the notion of assessing accuracy relative to the variability of what is being predicted, an important point often neglected in the evaluation of forecasts and forecasting performance and in model building. Looking at forecast errors relative to actual changes or prospective changes, instead of actual levels, gives an idea of how much one can reasonably expect to forecast and a way to judge forecasts. Some variables are just inherently less easily forecast than others. In such a situation, forecasts that miss more could actually be better than forecasts of variables that follow an easily predicted path, or more accurate, or more valuable for decisions.

Some Lessons for the Forecasting Practitioner

A few lessons or "messages" for forecasting practitioners emerge from the ZB work. First, forecast errors grow larger the longer the time span of a projection. All variables in the individual forecasts showed this property, as did also the group mean or consensus forecasts. This is neither a lesson nor a surprise, just a reaffirmation of how hard it is to make conditional forecasts of any variable with any method going out a long period of time because of events, right-hand-side variable perturbation, and noise between the time of the forecast and the time of the forecast realization. The lesson for the practicing forecaster is to forecast continuously or to develop systems that do so, monitoring external impulses and internal propagation mechanisms that might move variables of interest on a high-frequency basis.

Second, there is the finding, very well documented in ZB, that group mean forecasts (consensus) outperform most individual forecasts. Combining forecasts that come from different sources or that are generated by different techniques tends to produce significant gains in accuracy. This finding, at least in ZB, is accompanied by the notion that it is invariant to the forecast horizon and other time-series methods. Some individual forecasts do better than the consensus, about 25 percent of them for nominal GNP, real growth, and the implicit GNP deflator. For the practitioner who might use forecasts of inputs in his or her own forecast, this suggests averaging the sources of those inputs or generating several attempts at them by using different forecasting methods.

Third, there is much evidence relating to comparisons between forecasting methods. The methods included those used in the NBER-ASA survey itself, a potpourri of methods that most in the survey indicated as informal judgment, the BVAR approach as specified by ZB, a more sophisticated BVAR model provided by Sims, the Sims-Todd ARIMA, and the Michigan model (the "model-plus-manager" approach). The results (tables 1.26–1.31), measured by average root mean square error (ARMSE), tended to favor the informal GNP approach represented by the group mean forecasts of the NBER-ASA survey. Some time-series approaches performed impressively, particularly the Sims BVAR (variant B) and the ZB form of the BVAR (variant B). Other results were mixed, depending on the sample period and variables examined. The Michigan model generally did well in comparison with the various time-series methods.

A lesson here is the running of BVAR forecasting models as a collateral system, using some current-quarter information. The BVAR results are worth noting. Establishing such systems as potential generators of forecasts should be tried. The structural econometric model approach of the Michigan model showed favorably compared to most other methods except the group mean forecasts of the NBER-ASA. Along with the NBER-ASA and BVAR forecasts, the econometric method of forecasting ranked well. It is clear that macroeconomic forecasting cannot yet be expected to produce better results through any "black box" approach, regardless of the technique. The ARIMA results tended to rank lowest. BVAR forecasting, although clearly worthy of use at least as a collateral information input, consistently ranked below the group mean forecasts of the NBER-ASA and did no better than the econometric approach.

A fourth lesson relates to systematic under- or overprediction of macroeconomic time series. This is especially true of forecasts just after turning points, a topic not covered by ZB, with carryover in a time-series sense a prevalent characteristic. This tendency has actually been long known in forecasting. The implication for forecasters is to adjust forecasts from knowledge of this tendency, assuming that it will exist and persist. Many users of macro forecasts adjust consensus forecasts with this in mind, particularly the projections of financial market participants.

Fifth, judging accuracy by some standard of what is inherently characteristic of the series to be predicted is suggested by relating forecast changes to actual changes. If there is a lot of variability, then the standard for accuracy can be relaxed compared with cases where the variable being forecast has a smoother pattern. Validation in model building and forecast evaluation can make use of this notion.

What Users of Forecasts Can Learn

There is much in ZB of use to consumers of macroeconomic forecasts, who, in decision making, can make adjustments to the forecasts that are provided in order to understand, interpret, and use them in a practical way. First, the cumulation of errors across the forecast horizon should make users skeptical of long-term forecasts, basically disbelieving them, and understanding this as the rule rather than the exception. Indeed, *forecast* is probably the wrong word to describe long-run projections that are conditional on so many events that can change between the time the forecast is made and the realization. The long-run projections should be taken as *scenarios* or planning paths.

Second, the use of consensus forecasts or averages from many sources can be a valuable informational input for planning. The superior accuracy of the group mean forecasts was impressive, widespread, and one of the significant themes in the ZB paper. Users of macroeconomic forecasts should put this notion to good use, averaging the forecasts of individual forecasters as one information input or averaging projections generated by different methods of forecasting. However, the group mean results of the NBER-ASA survey did show that about 25 percent of the individual forecasts were superior to the consensus, so it should be noted that significant value can be obtained from certain individual forecasts if accuracy is the main criterion.

Third, while time-series models are perhaps a useful adjunct or alternative informational input, they do not seem to offer a great deal in terms of accuracy. Users need to be skeptical of time-series or black box kinds of statistical projections. At the same time, an informationally dense BVAR approach seems worthy of note.

Finally, users should understand the systematic nature, either under- or overprediction, in macroeconomic forecasts, documented by ZB, and incorporate the systematic serially autocorrelated errors of macroeconomic forecasts into planning.

Some Additional Observations

There are some myths in the ZB paper. One has to do with the notion that forecasting macroeconomic aggregates like real GNP and its components has less potential for direct profitability than forecasting financial variables. I would not say this. In financial market work, there is room for the heavy use of forecasts of macro aggregates and their components, not as financial variables in themselves, but as inputs that will drive financial markets in a predictable way. The macro aggregates also can have implications for inflation, monetary policy, the trade balance, and currencies. As an example, the Federal Reserve drives markets through changes in short-term interest rates. Actual interest rate forecasts can be irrelevant. Understanding what may happen to the inputs that affect Fed policy can be much more valuable. Indeed, good forecasts of the macro aggregates can be more forward looking than the information contained in forecasts of interest rates, making the macro input very important. Virtually all decision makers use macro aggregates as a backdrop for planning, implicitly or explicitly.

A second mistaken notion relates to the assertion that the main value of the forecast lies in the ability to reduce uncertainty about the future faced by the user. Forecasts are a dime a dozen. Probably more valuable than a point forecast is a process that enhances understanding of the phenomenon being forecast or a clear statement of the way the forecasts are being generated.

Conclusion

The ZB paper is an important and significant contribution to the literature on macroeconomic forecasting, with a valuable set of data, not even fully analyzed—and not without deficiencies—but probably the best set of data around.

The ZB record of the history of forecasting performance, insights into tendencies from the forecasts, comparison of the NBER-ASA informal model results with other forecasting methods, and striking observations that averages of individual forecasts are more accurate than individual forecasts alone constitute a major contribution of a paper that carefully uses a rich data set to provide a basic reference. The ZB contribution will be an essential reference document on macroeconomic forecasts and forecasting.

References

Braun, P., S. Shishado, and J. Vuchelin, eds. Monthly. *Economic forecasts: A monthly worldwide survey.* Amsterdam: North-Holland.

Eckstein, Otto. 1983. *The DRI model of the U.S. economy.* New York: McGraw-Hill.

McNees, Stephen K. 1979. The forecasting record for the 1970s. *New England Economic Review* (September/October), 33–53.

———. 1981. The recent record of thirteen forecasters. *New England Economic Review* (September/October), 5–21.

———. 1988. How accurate are macroeconomic forecasts? *New England Economic Review* (July/August), 15–36.

McNees, Stephen K., and John Ries. 1983. The track record of macroeconomic forecasts. *New England Economic Review* (November/December), 5–18.

2

A Procedure for Predicting Recessions with Leading Indicators: Econometric Issues and Recent Experience

James H. Stock and Mark W. Watson

Since the pioneering work on leading indicators by Mitchell and Burns ([1938] 1961) and their collaborators at the NBER, the prediction of business-cycle turning points has been one of the core problems of business-cycle analysis. This paper describes one approach to forecasting the future state of the business cycle or, more simply, to predicting recessions. The paper has three objectives. The first is to provide the mathematical details of this approach to forecasting recessions. The second is to evaluate the empirical performance of the resulting recession probability forecasts. This evaluation focuses on the sharp economic downturn in the fall of 1990, which provided an opportunity to examine the performance of a range of leading economic indicators under the unusual conditions of a broadly weak economy facing the prospect of oil supply disruptions and war in the Persian Gulf. The third objective is to draw some general conclusions about the use of leading indicators for macroeconomic forecasting.

The methodology for estimating the probability that the economy will be in a recession at a future date is described in section 2.1. Rather than trying to forecast turning points (see, e.g., Kling 1987; Hymans 1973; Neftci 1982; Wecker 1979; and Zellner, Hong, and Gulati 1987), the scheme focuses on forecasting a 0/1 variable that indicates whether the economy will be in a recession in a given month. The basic idea is to define recessions and expansions as different patterns of economic activity in such a way that whether the

James H. Stock is professor of political economy at the Kennedy School of Government, Harvard University. Mark W. Watson is professor of economics at Northwestern University. Both are research associates of the National Bureau of Economic Research.

The authors thank Rob Engle, Kenneth Wallis, and Jeff Wooldridge for helpful comments on an earlier draft and Gustavo Gonzaga for research assistance. This work was supported in part by National Science Foundation grant SES-89–10601.

economy will be in a recession in, say, six months is equivalent to whether the path of overall economic activity six months hence falls in a recessionary or an expansionary pattern. With quantitative definitions for these two patterns, the probability that the economy is in a recession during a future month can then be computed by the stochastic simulation of a model that forecasts future economic activity.

The recession and growth forecasts examined here were produced by the model developed in Stock and Watson (1989). This model was estimated using data from January 1959 through September 1988. Since then, it has been used to produce three indexes of overall economic activity on a monthly basis: an experimental coincident index (the XCI); an experimental leading index (the XLI), which is a forecast of the growth in the XCI over the subsequent six months; and an experimental recession index (the XRI), which estimates the probability that the economy will be in a recession six months hence. The in-sample performance of the recession forecasts (the XRI) is examined in section 2.2. This investigation provides little evidence of misspecification in the recession definition, in the algorithm used to compute the recession probabilities, or in the linear structure of the forecasting model used to construct the XCI and the XLI.

The data since October 1988 provide true out-of-sample observations on the performance of the experimental indexes, including the recession index. Since May 1989, the XCI, XRI, and XLI have been publicly released on a monthly basis, with release dates approximately coinciding with the release of the Composite Index of Leading Indicators produced by the Department of Commerce (DOC). The performance of the experimental indexes over this period is studied in section 2.3. In brief, forecasts of growth rates through September 1990 performed quite well, with growth rate forecast errors half what they were in sample. However, the experimental indexes failed to forecast the sharp decline that began in October 1990.

Section 2.4 investigates a variety of possible sources for the poor performance of the indexes over the fall of 1990. The main conclusion is that the source of the large forecast errors and of the failure of the recession index to forecast the downturn is not the recession definition or the mathematical structure of the model but rather the choice of specific leading indicators used to construct the indexes. An analysis of a broad set of 45 coincident and leading indicators, including the seven in the experimental index, demonstrates that almost all performed quite poorly during this episode. Only a few, such as housing building permits, consumer expectations, a measure of business sentiment, oil prices, help wanted advertising, and stock prices, signaled that the economy would suffer a sharp contraction. It is of course easy to recognize that these particular indicators performed well ex post; the challenge is how they could have been identified ex ante. These and other conclusions are summarized in section 2.5.

2.1   Calculation of Recession Probabilities

This section outlines the procedure used to calculate the probability that the economy will be in a recession at time τ, conditional on leading and coincident economic indicators observed through time t. Let R_τ be an indicator variable that equals one if the economy is in a recession and zero otherwise. Throughout, x_s denotes a vector of coincident variables, and y_s denotes a vector of leading indicators that are useful in predicting future economic activity. It is assumed that x_s is stationary in first-differences and that the leading indicators have been transformed so that y_s is stationary.

The objective is to calculate the probability of being in a recession in month τ, given data on (x_s, y_s) through month t; this probability is denoted $P_{\tau|t}$. The approach to computing $P_{\tau|t}$ has three components: the specification of the conditional probability model for the state of the economy; the definition of the recession event R_τ in terms of the state of the economy; and the estimation of the model parameters. These three components are addressed in turn in the following subsections.

2.1.1   The Model

The probability model used to describe the evolution of $(\Delta x_t, y_t)$ is a dynamic single index model of the form proposed by Sargent and Sims (1977) and used, for example, by Geweke (1977) and Singleton (1980). This is discussed at length in Stock and Watson (1989, 1991) and is only sketched here. The comovements at all leads and lags among the coincident variables are modeled as arising from a single common source c_t, a scalar unobserved time series that can be thought of as the overall state of the economy. The idiosyncratic components of the growth of each of the coincident variables (the part not arising from leads and lags of c_t) is assumed to be stationary and uncorrelated with the idiosyncratic components of the other variables, but otherwise it can have a rich serial correlation structure. In particular,

(1) $$\Delta x_t = \beta + \gamma(L)\Delta c_t + u_t,$$

(2) $$D(L)u_t = \varepsilon_t,$$

(3) $$\phi(L)\Delta c_t = \delta + \eta_t,$$

where (ε_t, η_t) are serially uncorrelated with a diagonal covariance matrix, and where $D(L) = \text{diag}[d_{ii}(L)]$. To fix the timing of c_t, one of the elements of $\gamma(L)$, say, $\gamma_i(L)$, is set equal to γ_{i0} (in the empirical model, $\gamma_i[L] = \gamma_{i0}$ for three of the four coincident variables used).

Leading indicators are added to the model to help predict future values of c_t by replacing (3) with the autoregressive system,

(4) $$\Delta c_t = \mu_c + \lambda_{cc}(L)\Delta c_{t-1} + \lambda_{cy}(L)y_{t-1} + v_{ct},$$

(5) $$y_t = \mu_y + \lambda_{yc}(L)\Delta c_{t-1} + \lambda_{yy}(L)y_{t-1} + v_{yt},$$

where $v'_t = (v'_{ct}, v'_{yt})$ is serially uncorrelated with mean zero and is independent of ε_t.

The model (1), (2), (4), and (5) can be solved to obtain linear minimum mean square error linear forecasts of future values of Δy_t and x_t or to estimate the unobserved state Δc_t or c_t. This is readily implemented using the Kalman filter, as described in Stock and Watson (1991). With the additional assumption, which is made throughout, that (ε_t, v_t) are jointly normal with constant conditional covariances, these linear projections are also conditional expectations.

2.1.2   Definition of Recessions and Expansions

A key aspect of this analysis is obtaining a quantifiable definition of a recession. Burns and Mitchell (1946, 3) provide a somewhat vague but nonetheless useful description of a recession as a substantial prolonged decline in economic activity that occurs broadly across various sectors of the economy. More recent working definitions used by business-cycle analysts refine these ideas and emphasize the "three Ds": for a slowdown to be a recession, it should be sufficiently long (duration), it should involve a substantial decline in economic activity (depth), and it should involve multiple sectors or all the sectors of the economy rather than simply reflecting an isolated decline in a single sector or region (diffusion).

The generally accepted business-cycle chronology is maintained by the NBER's Business Cycle Dating Committee. In practice, each individual on the committee must trade off these various parts of the definition to decide whether a particular episode warrants classification as a recession. The committee eschews numerical rules; this would limit its flexibility in deeming a particular episode a recession when there are unforeseen extenuating circumstances that are not amenable to being incorporated in a formulaic definition.

The definition of a recession adopted here attempts to capture, in a simple way, the institutional process in which recessions are categorized. We define a recession in terms of the growth of the unobserved state of the economy, Δc_t; this embodies the requirement that the recession be economywide, not specific to only one or two individual series. We treat the problem of classifying a sequence $\{\Delta c_t\}$, were it observed, as a pattern recognition problem: if the sequence falls in a recessionary pattern, then it is classified as a recession; if it falls in an expansionary pattern, it is an expansion. The recessionary and expansionary patterns that are possible in a sequence $(\Delta c_{t-k+1}, \ldots, \Delta c_t)$ of length k constitute subsets of $\Re^k$; whether such a sequence is an expansion or a recession depends on which subset the sequence falls in.

We suppose there to be two elementary recessionary patterns. In the first, D_1, Δc_t falls below a threshold $b_{r,t}$ for six consecutive months; in the second,

D_2, Δc_t falls below $b_{r,t}$ for seven of nine consecutive months, including the first and last months. That is,

(6) $D_{1\tau} = \{\Delta c_s, s = \tau - 5, \ldots, \tau : \Delta c_s \leq b_{r,s}, s = \tau - 5, \ldots, \tau\}$,

(7) $D_{2\tau} = \{\Delta c_s, s = \tau - 8, \ldots, \tau : \Delta c_{\tau - 8} \leq b_{r,\tau - 8}, \Delta c_\tau \leq b_{r,\tau}$,
       $\#(\Delta c_s \leq b_{r,s}, s = \tau - 7, \ldots, \tau - 1) \geq 5\}$,

where $\#(\cdot)$ denotes the number of times that the event occurs. Given the thresholds $\{b_{r,t}\}$, the economy is in a recession in month t if and only if that month falls in a recessionary pattern. Since a recessionary pattern $D_{1\tau}$ can commence anytime between $t - 5$ and t for the month to be in a recession, the set of recessionary patterns constituting a recession at date t is

(8) $$D_t = \left(\bigcup_{\tau = t}^{t+5} D_{1\tau} \right) \cup \left(\bigcup_{\tau = t}^{t+8} D_{2\tau} \right) \in \Re^{17}.$$

Thus, the recession event R_t is

(9) $$R_t = 1[(\Delta c_{t-8}, \ldots, \Delta c_t, \ldots, \Delta c_{t+8}) \in D_t],$$

where $1(\cdot)$ is the indicator function. An expansion event is defined symmetrically. Specifically,

(10) $U_{1\tau} = \{\Delta c_s, s = \tau - 5, \ldots, \tau : \Delta c_s > b_{e,s}, s = \tau - 5, \ldots, \tau\}$,

(11) $U_{2\tau} = \{\Delta c_s, s = \tau - 8, \ldots, \tau : \Delta c_{\tau - 8} > b_{e,\tau - 8}, \Delta c_\tau > b_{e,\tau}$,
       $\#(\Delta c_s > b_{e,s}, s = \tau - 7, \ldots, \tau - 1) \geq 5\}$,

(12) $$U_t = \left(\bigcup_{\tau = t}^{t+5} U_{1\tau} \right) \cup \left(\bigcup_{\tau = t}^{t+8} U_{2\tau} \right) \in \Re^{17},$$

(13) $$E_t = 1[(\Delta c_{t-8}, \ldots, \Delta c_t, \ldots, \Delta c_{t+8}) \in U_t].$$

The complement of U_t and D_t in $\Re^{17}$ is nonempty; that is, these definitions leave room for indeterminant sequences. Because the recession/expansion classification is dichotomous, these indeterminant events are ruled out in computing the probability of a recession. Thus, the probability that the economy is in a recession in month τ, conditional on coincident and leading indicators observed through month t and the cutoff values, is

$$\Pr[R_\tau = 1 | (R_\tau = 1) \cup (E_\tau = 1), x_t, x_{t-1}, \ldots, x_1, y_t, y_{t-1}, \ldots, y_1; b_r, b_e),$$

where b_r and b_e are the collection of cutoff values.

This probability is conditional on the sequence of cutoffs $(b_{r,t}, b_{e,t})$. One approach is to treat these as unknown time-invariant parameters, which could then be estimated. There are, however, at least two arguments for treating these parameters as random. First, this definition is in terms of c_t, while the process of identifying actual recessions involves the examination of a broad set of indicators; one interpretation of this is that the cutoff used in the recession definition should itself depend on macroeconomic variables that are omitted from this analysis. Second and alternatively, the process by which the Business Cycle Dating Committee reaches a decision involves different assessments of what constitutes a recession among the different members of the committee; one model of this is that each committee member has in mind some pair $(b_{r,t}, b_{e,t})$ for month t but that these vary across committee members and indeed over time for each member. Both arguments suggest that $(b_{r,t}, b_{e,t})$ can usefully be treated as random, and this approach is adopted here. Specifically, $b_{r,t}$ and $b_{e,t}$ are modeled as

$$(14) \qquad b_{r,t} = \mu_r + \zeta_t, \quad b_{e,t} = \mu_e + \zeta_t, \quad \zeta_t \text{ i.i.d. } N(0, \sigma_\zeta),$$

where ζ_t is independent of (ε_t, ν_t).

The probability that the economy is in a recession in month τ, given information through month t, is thus

$$
\begin{aligned}
P_{\tau|t} = {} & \int \Pr[R_\tau = 1 | (R_\tau = 1) \cup (E_\tau = 1), x_t, x_{t-1}, \ldots, x_1 \\
& y_t, y_{t-1}, \ldots, y_1 ; b_e(\tilde{\zeta}_\tau), b_r(\tilde{\zeta}_\tau)] dF_\zeta(\tilde{\zeta}_\tau) \\
= {} & E[R_\tau | (R_\tau = 1) \cup (E_\tau = 1), x_t, x_{t-1}, \ldots, x_1 \, y_t, y_{t-1}, \ldots, y_1],
\end{aligned}
$$
(15)

where $\tilde{\zeta}_\tau = (\zeta_{\tau-8}, \ldots, \zeta_{\tau+8})'$, and $F_\zeta(\cdot)$ is the c.d.f. of $\tilde{\zeta}_\tau$.

The conditional probability $P_{\tau|t}$ involves integrating over a thirty-four-dimensional Gaussian distribution (a seventeen-fold integration to compute the conditional probability

$$\Pr[R_\tau = 1 | (R_\tau = 1) \cup (E_\tau = 1), x_t, x_{t-1}, \ldots, y_t, y_{t-1}, \ldots ; b_r(\tilde{\zeta}_\tau), b_e(\tilde{\zeta}_\tau)]$$

and an additional seventeen-fold integration over $\tilde{\zeta}_\tau$). In practice, the integration is performed by Monte Carlo simulation using the following algorithm:

   i. Compute the conditional mean $m_{\tau|t}$ and covariance matrix $\Omega_{\tau|t}$ of $\tilde{c}_\tau(-8, 8)$, where $\tilde{c}_\tau(-k_1, k_2) = (\Delta c_{\tau-k_1}, \ldots, \Delta c_\tau, \ldots, \Delta c_{\tau+k_2})$, given data through month t. (In steady state, $\Omega_{\tau|t}$ is a function of $\tau - t$, not τ or t separately.)

   ii. Draw a pseudorandom realization of $\tilde{c}_\tau(-8, 8)$ from the $N(m_{\tau|t}, \Omega_{\tau|t})$ conditional distribution of $\tilde{c}_\tau$.

   iii. Draw a realization of $\tilde{b}_{r,\tau}$ and $\tilde{b}_{e,\tau}$, where $\tilde{b}_{i,\tau} = (b_{i,\tau-8}, \ldots, b_{i,\tau+8})$, as $(\tilde{b}_{r,\tau}, \tilde{b}_{e,\tau}) = (\mu_e + \tilde{\zeta}_\tau, \mu_r + \tilde{\zeta}_\tau)$ according to (14).

   iv. For each realization of $[\tilde{c}_\tau(-8, 8), \tilde{b}_{r,\tau}, \tilde{b}_{e,\tau}]$, evaluate R_t and E_t according to (9) and (13), respectively.

   v. Repeat ii–iv (in practice enough times to obtain a minimum of two thousand draws of E_t or R_t), and compute $P_{\tau|t}$ as $\#(R_t)/[\#(R_t) + \#(E_t)]$.

It is worth emphasizing that this definition of a recession treats the identification of recessions (more generally, cycles) as a pattern recognition algorithm that could be applied to many series. This contrasts with approaches in which R_t is related to the time-series properties of the process, in which R_t is useful in predicting future c_t given its past. An example of the latter situation is Hamilton's (1989) model in which a discrete variable, empirically identified as a recession/expansion indicator, enters the conditional mean of the time series. One can usefully think of the latter situation as being one in which the definition of the recession event is intrinsic to the time-series model generating the data; a recession is then not well defined if the process is in fact linear and Gaussian. In contrast, the pattern recognition approach developed here can be applied whether the series is linear, Gaussian, or stationary.

2.1.3   Estimation of the Model Parameters

The estimation strategy is based on a partition of the joint density of the leading indicators, the coincident variables, and the recession indicator. Let Y_t = $(y_1, \ldots, y_t)$, $X_t = (x_1, \ldots, x_t)$, $S_t = (R_1, \ldots, R_t)$, and $C_t = (c_1, \ldots, c_t)$. The joint density of (Y_T, X_T, S_T) can be factored

$$(16) \qquad f(Y_T, X_T, S_T | \theta, \mu) = f_1(S_T | Y_T, X_T; \mu, \theta) f_2(Y_T, X_T | \theta).$$

This factorization is done without loss of generality and serves to define the parameter vector μ as the additional parameters introduced in the conditional density f_1. In terms of the model in section 2.1.1 and the definition of the recession variable R_t, θ is the vector of parameters given in (1), (2), (4), and (5), and μ is the vector of parameters describing the distribution of the recession threshold parameters, so $\mu = (\mu_e, \mu_r, \sigma_\zeta)$ as defined in (14).

In general, as long as θ appears in f_1, computing the maximum likelihood estimator (MLE) will entail maximization of the joint density $f(Y_T, X_T, S_T | \theta, \mu)$. The MLE simplifies to a two-stage process if θ does not appear in f_1, which would occur were R_t defined in terms of the observable variables (X_t, Y_t) and the parameters μ, for example, if Δc_t were replaced by Δx_{1t} in the definitions of D_{it} and E_{it} in section 2.1.2. However, because c_t is unobserved, θ enters f_1, and the MLE does not have a convenient simplification. Intuitively, because c_t is unobserved, R_t provides another dependent variable (in this case, discrete valued) that, in conjunction with the continuous variables, potentially provides useful information for estimation.

Unfortunately, because R_t is a discrete-valued time-series variable, the implementation of the MLE for (16) is numerically imposing. The parameters are therefore estimated in a two-stage process, estimating θ first, then μ. The estimation of θ is described at length in Stock and Watson (1989, 1991) and is not discussed here. In the second stage, μ is estimated conditional on the first-stage estimate of θ. While this simplifies the estimation of θ, maximization of the conditional likelihood $f_1(S_T | Y_T, X_T; \mu, \theta)$ remains numerically demanding. Estimation therefore proceeds by minimizing the mean square error $\Sigma_{t=t_1}^{T}(R_t - P_{t|T})^2$ (where $t_1 = t + 36$ so that the probabilities could be computed using the steady-state state covariance matrix Ω). The resulting estimators for μ_r, μ_e, and σ_ζ, computed by a grid search, are $\hat{\mu}_r = -1.5$, $\hat{\mu}_e = -0.25$, and $\hat{\sigma} = 0.8$.[1]

The estimated model and various in-sample specification tests are discussed in Stock and Watson (1989, 1991), to which the reader is referred for details.

2.1.4 Treatment of Data Irregularities

The form of the model in sections 2.1.1–2.1.3 used for monthly forecasting incorporates two modifications for data irregularities that arise when working with monthly data releases. Both involve conceptually straightforward (but computationally and notationally involved) modifications of the basic Kalman filter for the state space representation of the model (1), (2), (4), and (5). The general strategy for handling data irregularities is to make an appropriate modification of the state vector, the state transition equation, and the measurement equation. We now turn to the specifics.

One coincident indicator (manufacturing and trade sales) is reported by the Department of Commerce with a lag of an additional month. Let α_t denote the state vector in the state space representation of (1), (2), (3), and (4); let $\bar{\alpha}_{t|t}$ denote the expected value of the state vector given observations on all variables except x_{it} through month t and on x_{it} through month $t - 1$, and let $\alpha_{t|t}$ denote the expected value of α_t given data on all variables through date t. Because complete data are available through $t - 1$, the Kalman filter can be applied to the unmodified model to form $\alpha_{t-1|t-1}$. At date t, the state space model is altered by modifying the measurement equation (1) to exclude the equation for the coincident variable in question. Alternatively, the equation could be included, an arbitrary finite observation used for the variable in question, and a measurement error term appended to (1) with infinite variance (in practice approximated by a large constant).

The second important modification of the standard Kalman filter is to handle revisions in many of the coincident and leading variables. Let z_{it}^j denote the value of z_{it} published at date $t + j$, where z_{it} indicates an element of the vector $z_t = (\Delta x_t', y_t')$. Thus, $j = 0$ corresponds to the initial release of z_{it}, $j = 1$ corresponds to the first monthly revision, etc. The revision error is $z_{it} - z_{it}^j = e_{it}^j$, and the model is modified to account for this additional error. The appropriate modification to the model depends on the covariance properties of e_{it}^j. We find it useful to consider two extreme assumptions concerning e_{it}^j, analogous to the "news" and "noise" assumptions of Mankiw and Shapiro (1986) (see also Mankiw, Runkle, and Shapiro 1984). The first assumption—noise—corresponds to the classical errors-in-variable model

---

1. The sensitivity to the choice of optimand was checked by recomputing the estimates using the pseudolikelihood obtained by treating R_t as an independent Bernoulli random variable with probability $P_{t|T}$. The point estimates for μ_r, μ_e, and σ were close for the two optimands, and, more important, the estimated probabilities $P_{t|T}$ were virtually indistinguishable. For both optimands, the surface of the objective function was rather flat in a neighborhood of the optimized values. Evidence of this insensitivity is given in sec. 2.4.1 below.

(17) $$z_{it}^j = z_{it} + e_{it}^j,$$

where e_{it}^j is uncorrelated with z_{it}. Because this is a dynamic model, it is further assumed that e_{it}^j is uncorrelated with all values of the actual data, that is, $E(e_{it}^j z_{k\tau}) = 0$ for all j, i, k, t, and τ, and that measurement errors are uncorrelated across series, that is, $E(e_{it}^j e_{k\tau}^n) = 0$ for all j, n, t, and τ when $k \neq i$.

The second assumption—news—corresponds to the optimal forecasting model

(18) $$z_{it} = z_{it}^j + e_{it}^j,$$

where e_{it}^j is uncorrelated with z_{it}^j. Thus, z_{it}^j is viewed as an unbiased forecast of z_{it}, and e_{it}^j contains information (news) about z_{it} not contained in z_{it}^j.

The modifications needed to incorporate a single "noise" variable in univariate models are discussed in Harvey et al. (1981). The modification to handle multiple noise variables in this application is a straightforward generalization of this single variable modification. The modifications necessary to incorporate a "news" variable into the model are simpler: if the preliminary variable is an optimal forecast of the final variable, and if (as is assumed) the data collection agency uses a superset of the information in (X_t, Y_t) to produce this optimal forecast of the final series, then optimal estimates and forecasts of α_t can be constructed by substituting the preliminary data in place of the actual data and running the Kalman filter on the unmodified model. However, while no modification is necessary to produce $\alpha_{t|t}$, it is necessary to modify its covariance matrix to reflect the increased uncertainty associated with the preliminary data. The details of the Kalman filter modifications for measurement error are provided in Stock and Watson (1988).[2]

2.1.5 Summary of the Estimated Indexes and Their Interpretation

Since its estimation in early 1989, this model has been used to produce three indexes on a monthly basis: an experimental coincident index (XCI), an experimental leading index (XLI), and an experimental recession index (XRI). The XCI is the estimate of the state at time t, that is, $XCI = c_{t|t}$. The XLI is the estimate of its growth over the subsequent six months, $c_{t+6|t} - c_{t|t}$ (because x_t is in logarithms, $c_{t+6} - c_t$ is the six-month growth in c_t; the XLI is reported at annual percentage growth rates, i.e., $200[c_{t+6|t} - c_{t|t}]$). And the XRI is the probability that the economy will be in a recession in six months ($XRI = P_{t+6|t}$). The coincident and leading variables used in the model, which were selected by a modified stepwise regression procedure (see Stock and Watson 1989), are listed in panels A and B, respectively, of table 2.1. Since mid-1990, we have also been tracking a second set of indexes (the XLI2 and the XRI2), based solely on nonfinancial indicators. The coincident indi-

---

2. The empirical implementation allows for a maximum of $j = 12$ revisions. The covariance matrices of $e_{it} = (e_{it}^1, \ldots, e_{it}^{12})'$ were estimated using data from 1981:1 through 1985:12.

Table 2.1   **Coincident and Leading Indicators in the XRI and XRI2**

Mnemonic	Transformation	Description
		A. Coincident Indicators
IP	Growth rates	Industrial production, total
GMYXP8	Growth rates	Personal income, total less transfer payments, 1982$
MT82	Growth rates	Manufacturing and trade sales, total, 1982$
LPMHU	Growth rates	Employee-hours in nonagricultural establishments
		B. Leading Indicators in the XLI
HSBP	Levels	Housing authorizations—new private housing
MDU82S	Growth rates	Manufacturers' unfilled orders: durable goods industries, 1982$, smoothed
EXNWT2S	Growth rates	Trade-weighted nominal exchange rate between the United States and the United Kingdom, West Germany, France, Italy, and Japan, smoothed
LHNAPSS	Growth rates	Part-time work in nonagricultural industries because of slack work (U.S. Department of Labor, The Employment Situation, Household Survey), smoothed
FYGT10S	Differences	Yield on constant-maturity portfolio of 10-year U.S. Treasury bonds, smoothed
CP6_GM6	Levels	Spread between interest rate on a 6-month commercial paper and the interest rate on 6-month U.S. Treasury bills (Federal Reserve Board)
G10_G1	Levels	Spread between the yield on constant-maturity portfolio of 10-year U.S. T-bonds and the yield on 1-year U.S. T-bonds (Federal Reserve Board)
		C. Leading Indicators in the XLI2
HSBP	Levels	Housing authorizations—new private housing
MDU82S	Growth rates	Manufacturers' unfilled orders: durable goods industries, 1982$, smoothed
EXNWT2S	Growth rates	Trade-weighted nominal exchange rate between the United States and the United Kingdom, West Germany, France, Italy, and Japan, smoothed
LPHRM	Levels	Average weekly hours of production workers in manufacturing
IPXMCA	Differences	Capacity utilization rate in manufacturing, total (Federal Reserve Board)
LHEL	Growth rates	Index of help wanted advertising in newspapers (The Conference Board)
IVPAC	Levels	Vendor performance: percentage of companies reporting slower deliveries

Note: The series described as "smoothed" were passed through the filter $(1 + 2L + 2L^2 + L^3)$. All variables except exchange rates and interest rates are seasonally adjusted.

cators entering the XLI2 are those in panel A, and the leading indicators entering the XLI2 are given in panel C of table 2.1.

Empirically, the XCI can be thought of as a monthly proxy for real GNP. Simple regression relations between the XCI produced by the estimated model, aggregated to a quarterly level, and real GNP are presented in table 2.2. The correlation between the six-month growth of the XCI and real GNP is large, approximately .88. Although the mean growth of the XCI and real GNP are approximately equal over this period, XCI growth is more volatile, and the regression coefficient of GNP growth onto XCI growth is .58. This implies that XCI growth of zero corresponds approximately to GNP growth of 1.3 percent.

2.2   In-Sample Analysis of Probabilities

This section examines the within-sample performance of the estimated recession probabilities. The analysis focuses on three types of potential misspecification: misspecification of the probability model, so that the information in the included leading and coincident indicators is not fully incorporated into the predicted probabilities; omission of alternative indicators that help predict recessions; and misspecification associated with the possible duration dependence in recessions and expansions, that is, with the possibility that the length of the current recession (expansion) might usefully predict when the next expansion (recession) will occur.

The probabilities examined here are based on the model outlined in section 2.1, estimated in early 1989 using data from 1959:1 to 1988:9. The seven leading indicators used in the XLI were selected from a "short list" of fifty-five series. Any such selection of a few variables from many exacerbates the usual risks of overfitting, so the in-sample analysis in this section provides only limited guidance in assessing the performance of the model. Still, rejection by these in-sample diagnostics would suggest specification problems in the way the probabilities are calculated.

Table 2.2   **Relation between the XCI and Real GNP: OLS Regressions of the Form $\ln(\text{RGNP}_t/\text{RGNP}_{t-k}) = \alpha + \beta \ln(\text{XCI}_t^Q/\text{XCI}_{t-k}^Q) + e_t$ (1962: I–1988:III, where XCI_t^Q is the XCI, aggregated to a quarterly level)**

k (quarters)	$\hat{\alpha}$	$\hat{\beta}$	R^2	SEE
1	1.286	.577	.65	2.37
	(.264)	(.042)		
2	1.296	.578	.78	1.50
	(.173)	(.030)		

Note: Autocorrelation-robust standard errors (computed using 6 lagged autocovariances with a Bartlett kernel) are reported in parentheses. Estimation used quarterly observations. The quarterly XCI^Q series was constructed by averaging the values of the XCI over the months in the quarter.

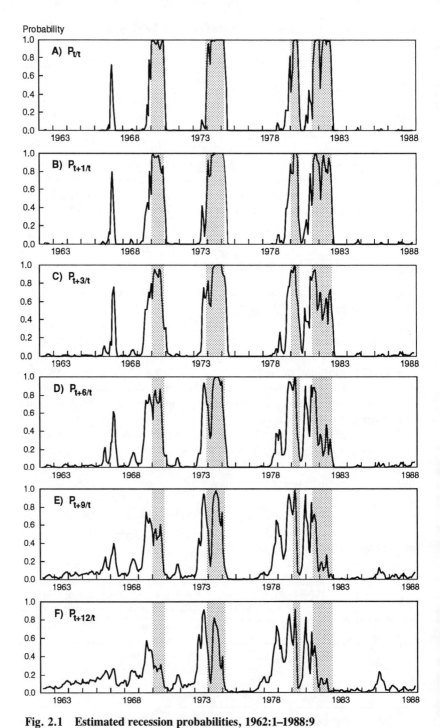

Fig. 2.1 Estimated recession probabilities, 1962:1–1988:9

Note: The dates on the horizontal axes denote t, the date through which the data are available for computing $P_{t+k/t}$. The figure is based on data revised through 1988:9.

The recession probabilities $P_{t+k|t}$, as estimated through 1988:9, are plotted in figure 2.1 for various horizons. (The dating convention plots $P_{t+k|t}$ at time t.) At a horizon of one month, the probabilities are sharp; the forecasts become substantially less precise as the horizon increases beyond six months.

The performance of these predictions is investigated in tables 2.3–2.5. Panel A of table 2.3 presents, for each horizon, the average predicted probability, $\bar{P}$, the proportion of recession realizations $\bar{R}$, the R^2 of the predictions, and the RMSE (root mean square error) of the prediction. The table suggests a slight bias in the predictions: $\bar{P} > \bar{R}$ for all horizons. (Because the probabilities are nonlinear functions of μ_r, μ_e, and σ, minimizing the mean square

Table 2.3   **Predictive Performance of Recession Probabilities $P_{t+k|t}$: Summary Statistics**

		A. Overall			
		Forecast Horizon (Months)			
Statistic[a]	1	3	6	9	12
$\bar{P}$	.180	.186	.187	.185	.183
$\bar{R}$	.146	.147	.148	.150	.151
R^2	.789	.687	.577	.482	.367
RMSE	.176	.215	.251	.279	.309

		B. Statistics by Cell			
		Forecast Horizon (Months)			
Cell	Statistic[a]	1	3	6	9	12
$.0 \leq$	$\bar{P}$	.015	.022	.042	.061	.086
P	$\bar{R}$	.004	.000	.016	.024	.040
$< .25$	N	261	250	251	249	248
	N_R	1	0	4	6	10
$.25 \leq$	$\bar{P}$	.368	.362	.349	.349	.343
P	$\bar{R}$	.067	.211	.308	.387	.525
$< .50$	N	15	19	26	31	40
	N_R	1	4	8	12	21
$.50 \leq$	$\bar{P}$	.627	.613	.639	.630	.613
P	$\bar{R}$	.364	.577	.571	.643	.519
$< .75$	N	11	26	21	28	27
	N_R	4	15	12	18	14
$.75 \leq$	$\bar{P}$	.918	.896	.895	.889	.845
P	$\bar{R}$	.896	.789	.781	.684	.444
< 1.0	N	48	38	32	19	9
	N_R	43	30	25	13	4

[a]For definitions, see the text.

Table 2.4   **In-Sample Regression Tests for Omitted Variables in $P_{t+k|t}$ (p-values of test statistics) Based on OLS Regressions, 1962:1–1988:9 − k**

Variable	Forecast Horizon (Months)				
	0	1	3	6	9
Constant	.064	.058	.141	.327	.475
Coincident Indicators					
IP	.740	.549	.961	.545	.293
GMYXP8	.914	.317	.624	.950	.089
MT82	.614	.655	.558	.746	.389
LPMHUADJ	.482	.249	.396	.594	.414
Leading Indicators in the XRI					
HSBP	.770	.865	.978	.122	.349
MDU82S	.094	.126	.241	.497	.861
EXNWT2FS	.755	.422	.425	.425	.342
LHNAPSS	.837	.385	.143	.476	.544
FYGT10FS	.734	.750	.004	.209	.461
CP6_GM6F	.823	.894	.858	.246	.985
G10_GLF	.859	.830	.277	.221	.727
XLI	.311	.382	.499	.654	.647
Leading Indicators in the XRI2					
LPHRM	.258	.275	.475	.847	.625
IPXMCA	.613	.478	.555	.458	.305
LHEL	.839	.567	.558	.755	.965
IVPAC	.176	.135	.012	.607	.216
Financial Indicators					
FSPCOMF	.083	.156	.041	.442	.589
FM1D82	.734	.493	.304	.275	.951
FM2D82	.841	.289	.260	.560	.998
FMBASE	.561	.867	.475	.553	.743
CCI30M	.738	.991	.882	.502	.354
FCBCUCY	.202	.209	.263	.743	.263
FYFFF	.981	.785	.198	.332	.948
BAA_G10F	.588	.615	.024	.244	.785
YLD_DUMF	.401	.200	.882	.800	.703
Employment Indicators					
LUINC	.977	.942	.896	.596	.530
LHU5	.932	.454	.282	.758	.533
LHELX	.983	.750	.938	.558	.751

Table 2.4   (continued)

| Variable | \multicolumn{5}{c}{Forecast Horizon (Months)} |
	0	1	3	6	9
\multicolumn{6}{c}{Consumption and Retail Sales}
IPCD	.685	.262	.417	.661	.424
GMCD82	.814	.628	.421	.689	.827
RTR82	.498	.493	.249	.707	.905
\multicolumn{6}{c}{Inventories and Orders}
MPCON8	.363	.334	.659	.225	.921
MOCM82	.285	.243	.225	.498	.462
MDO82	.173	.079	.086	.880	.388
IVMT82	.353	.231	.199	.667	.668
IVM1D8	.640	.218	.139	.811	.295
IVM2D8	.490	.506	.559	.556	.438
IVM3D8	.919	.093	.146	.397	.524
\multicolumn{6}{c}{Additional Indicators}
DLBLNPAP	.506	.705	.686	.577	.648
PMI	.370	.400	.266	.835	.498
PMNO	.290	.365	.446	.966	.529
HHSNTN	.414	.153	.057	.626	.471
HHST	.092	.813	.072	.850	.211
PW561	.482	.864	.798	.782	.731
PW561R	.505	.722	.828	.816	.765
FTM333	.601	.440	.216	.231	.527
FTM333R	.624	.485	.349	.472	.573
\multicolumn{6}{c}{Composite Indexes and Measures of Duration}
DLEAD	.686	.589	.125	.721	.268
DL3D	.790	.585	.478	.080	.032
DL3U	.355	.441	.572	.431	.858
IP3D	.011	.060	.596	.465	.423
IP3U	.145	.303	.459	.605	.762
MTREC	.002	.128	.627	.541	.368
MTEXP	.595	.463	.518	.148	.079
MTTOT	.538	.282	.615	.511	.912

Note: The p-values refer to Wald tests of the hypothesis that the coefficients on $(z_t, \ldots, z_{t-5})$ in the regression of $R_{t+k} - P_{t+k|t}$ on a constant and $z_t, \ldots, z_{t-5}$ are zero, where k refers to the forecast horizon (months). The tests were computed using autocorrelation- and heteroskedasticity-robust covariance matrices, constructed as weighted averages of $k + 5$ autocovariances with Bartlett kernel weights. A p-value of .000 denotes a p-value $< .0005$. The regressions were estimated from 1962:1–1988:9 − k. The variables are defined in the appendix.

Table 2.5   **In-Sample Regression Tests for Omitted Variables in $P_{t+k|t}$ (p-values of test statistics) Based on WLS Regressions, 1962:1–1988:9 − k**

Variable	Forecast Horizon (Months)				
	0	1	3	6	9
Constant	.001	.000	.001	.123	.035
Coincident Indicators					
IP	.670	.760	.841	.658	.503
GMYXP8	.587	.853	.559	.882	.639
MT82	.932	.731	.682	.571	.899
LPMHUADJ	.981	.762	.466	.955	.492
Leading Indicators in the XRI					
HSBP	.741	.840	.889	.844	.656
MDU82S	.352	.437	.466	.700	.455
EXNWT2FS	.593	.481	.799	.479	.172
LHNAPSS	.625	.678	.801	.699	.584
FYGT10FS	.882	.898	.573	.806	.706
CP6_GM6F	.973	.779	.953	.782	.547
G10_GLF	.701	.565	.461	.877	.300
XLI	.499	.535	.743	.933	.330
Leading Indicators in the XRI2					
LPHRM	.735	.409	.461	.596	.510
IPXMCA	.486	.564	.372	.150	.131
LHEL	.398	.369	.677	.875	.954
IVPAC	.757	.692	.468	.857	.743
Financial Indicators					
FSPCOMF	.630	.364	.483	.934	.755
FM1D82	.690	.803	.678	.767	.837
FM2D82	.870	.618	.692	.691	.837
FMBASE	.830	.776	.559	.609	.879
CCI30M	.628	.555	.494	.602	.501
FCBCUCY	.737	.874	.302	.899	.684
FYFFF	.744	.772	.773	.843	.445
BAA_G10F	.941	.915	.258	.829	.486
YLD_DUMF	.719	.955	.865	.777	.422
Employment Indicators					
LUINC	.969	.934	.842	.950	.841
LHU5	.827	.851	.438	.826	.973
LHELX	.663	.806	.527	.801	.540

Table 2.5 (continued)

| Variable | \multicolumn{5}{c}{Forecast Horizon (Months)} | | | | |
	0	1	3	6	9
	\multicolumn{5}{c}{Consumption and Retail Sales}				
IPCD	.831	.710	.639	.853	.538
GMCD82	.993	.797	.860	.740	.979
RTR82	.974	.648	.517	.697	.879
	\multicolumn{5}{c}{Inventories and Orders}				
MPCON8	.758	.849	.899	.480	.894
MOCM82	.507	.293	.499	.768	.859
MDO82	.375	.528	.759	.772	.654
IVMT82	.400	.491	.594	.787	.624
IVM1D8	.903	.545	.737	.608	.670
IVM2D8	.893	.861	.396	.897	.552
IVM3D8	.984	.662	.422	.969	.823
	\multicolumn{5}{c}{Additional Indicators}				
DLBLNPAP	.779	.865	.855	.678	.711
PMI	.539	.665	.736	.390	.841
PMNO	.584	.408	.660	.427	.854
HHSNTN	.728	.882	.721	.956	.792
HHST	.235	.788	.634	.906	.794
PW561	.054	.897	.980	.701	.910
PW561R	.078	.812	.942	.772	.866
FTM333R	.651	.896	.332	.883	.675
	\multicolumn{5}{c}{Composite Indexes and Measures of Duration}				
DLEAD	.870	.755	.749	.918	.611
DL3D	.924	.877	.932	.890	.806
DL3U	.151	.705	.875	.861	.576
IP3D	.388	.435	.613	.670	.611
IP3U	.333	.564	.195	.676	.860
MTREC	.012	.005	.040	.917	.752
MTEXP	.378	.434	.114	.000	.134
MTTOT	.620	.575	.098	.084	.054

Note: Computed by weighted least squares regression as discussed in the text, with weights $w_t = \min\{P_{t+k|t}(1 - P_{t+k|t}), .01\}$. See the note to table 2.4.

error [MSE] need not result in unbiased forecasts: reducing the sample bias would increase the sample MSE.)

Panel B of table 2.3 takes a closer look at the predictions by partitioning the observations into cells based on the predicted value. In the table, N represents the number of observations in the cell, N_R represents the number of these observations that turned out to be periods of recession. For example, of the

251 times within sample that $P_{t+6|t}$ fell within $(0, 0.25)$, only four of those turned out to be recessionary months; if a value of $P_{t+6|t}$ below .25 is interpreted as a signal of "no recession," this corresponds to a false negative rate (the probability of a recession given a forecast of no recession) of 1.6 percent. Similarly, if $P_{t+6|t} \geq 0.75$ is interpreted as a recession signal, then this signal had a within-sample false positive rate of 22 percent (7/32). This interpretation of false negative and positive rates corresponds to monthly forecasts of whether the economy will be in a recession, which is different than whether the economy will shift from an expansion to a recession, or vice versa, in the next six months. The latter concept is of practical interest, but, given the few turning points in the sample, it is one for which a false positive/negative rate cannot be computed as reliably.

Tables 2.4 and 2.5 present the primary within-sample evidence concerning possible misspecification in the probability model. From (15), $P_{t+k|t}$ is the conditional expectation of R_{t+k} given data through t. One way to test whether the estimated probabilities satisfy this condition is to ask whether the errors $R_{t+k} - P_{t+k|t}$ can be predicted as linear functions of the observable indicators. This is done using regressions of the form

(19) $$R_{t+k} - P_{t+k|t} = \alpha + \beta(L)z_t + e_t,$$

where z_t denotes an indicator observable at time t, transformed to be stationary so that conventional asymptotic theory can be used to interpret the regression results. Under the null hypothesis that the model (1), (2), (4), and (5) and the algorithm in section 2.1.2 are correctly specified, α and $\beta(L)$ will equal zero. Because R_t is a probability, e_t in (19) will be heteroskedastic, having a conditional variance under the null of $P_{t+k|t}(1 - P_{t+k|t})$. In addition, the k-step-ahead forecast error will be serially correlated. Were R_t observable at t, under the null hypothesis e_t would be $MA(k - 1)$; however, because turning points are declared only with a delay (typically of six to eighteen months), the order of the dependence of e_t is presumably greater.

Results of specification tests based on (19) are presented in tables 2.4 and 2.5.[3] In table 2.4, the p-values are computed by estimating (19) by OLS and computing heteroskedasticity- and autocorrelation-robust standard errors. Because the errors are conditionally heteroskedastic, table 2.5 reports p-values based on weighted least squares (WLS) regressions, where the weights are based on the conditional variance under the null, $P_{t+k|t}(1 - P_{t+k|t})$, and p-values were computed using an autocorrelation-robust covariance matrix.[4]

---

3. The dates of the cyclical peaks and troughs used to construct R_t for the subsequent empirical analysis are the official dates of the NBER Business Cycle Dating Committee, with one exception: the committee dated the 1969 cyclical peak as 1969:12, while throughout we use 1969:10. According to the recession definition in sec. 2.1.2, the earlier date is more consistent with the rules used to define the other historical turning points, and 1969:10 was the date used to estimate the model and to produce the results in Stock and Watson (1989).

4. The p-values ignore complications associated with the correlation between sampling error in the estimated parameters of the model and the regressors in (19).

The tests in tables 2.4 and 2.5 are computed using the data as revised through October 1988, with the exception of the series labeled "additional indicators," for which the data as revised through 1991:2 are used. (See the appendix for definitions of and sources for the series.)

The first blocks of tables 2.4 and 2.5 examine the first type of misspecification, in which the coincident and leading variables in the model might have predictive content for $P_{t+k|t}$. Because these included variables have no predictive content for the errors from the linear part of the model (1), (2), (4), and (5) (Stock and Watson 1989), rejections here would suggest misspecification in the definition of a recession. The XLI is also included in this panel. Aside from the regression on a constant, which reflects the bias discussed in the context of table 2.3, neither the OLS nor the WLS results indicate rejections at the 5 percent level at any horizons.

The next several blocks examine whether alternative leading and coincident indicators, not included in the model, have predictive content for R_{t+k} given $P_{t+k|t}$. The variables LPHRM through IVM3D8 were included in the original short list of fifty-five variables from which the seven included indicators were selected. Because the selection was done in the context of linear predictions of $c_{t|t}$, evidence of predictive content here would be evidence that the candidate variable has marginal value in predicting recessions and expansions, even though it does not in predicting overall economic growth rates. The results provide no strong evidence that the in-sample performance of the recession probabilities could have been improved by incorporating these indicators into the XRI model. If anything, the p-values tend to be rather high, reflecting the use of these indicators in the preliminary analysis.

The "additional indicators" in tables 2.4 and 2.5 are series arguably related to the 1990 downturn but not on the original short list of fifty-five leading indicators. These indicators will be examined in more detail in section 2.4 below; the relevant point here is that, on the basis of the 1962:1–1988:9 sample, taken individually none provide a significant improvement in the performance of the recession probabilities.

The final block of results in tables 2.4 and 2.5 examines the marginal predictive content of the DOC Composite Index of Leading Indicators (DLEAD) and of various nonlinear cyclical measures. Like the variables that compose it, the DOC leading index makes an insignificant contribution. There is some evidence that a variable constructed using the "three consecutive declines" rule of thumb, in which a recession is signaled when the DOC leading index declines for three consecutive months, has some marginal predictive content for long horizons and that such a rule of thumb, applied to IP alone, has marginal predictive value for short horizons.

The final three variables examine the possibility that the business cycle exhibits duration dependence. Cyclical duration dependence has been examined by Neftci (1982) and others, most recently including Diebold, Rudebusch, and Sichel (chap. 6 in this volume). The linear model, combined with the pattern recognition approach to identifying recessions used here, assumes that there is no duration dependence in expansions and recessions beyond that implied by the minimum six-month lengths of the events $D_{i\tau}$ and $U_{i\tau}$. This assumption can be checked by examining whether variables related to the duration of the current expansion/recession have additional predictive content. An obvious candidate variable is the duration M_t of the current expansion or recession. Although this is not known at time t with certainty because the dating committee identifies turning points only ex post, it can be estimated using the model of section 2.1. Let $M_{t|t}^r$ be the expectation of M_t in month t, conditional on being in a recession, that is, $M_{t|t}^r = E(M_t|R_t = 1, x_t, x_{t-1}, \ldots, y_t, y_{t-1}, \ldots)$; similarly define $M_{t|t}^e$ for expansions; and let $M_{t|t} = M_{t|t}^r P_{t|t} + M_{t|t}^e (1 - P_{t|t})$ be the expected length of the current spell whether or not it is a recession. The time series $M_{t|t}^r$, $M_{t|t}^e$, and $M_{t|t}$ were estimated using the model of section 2.1.[5]

The results for these duration dependence variables provide some evidence of this form of nonlinearity. Both the OLS and the WLS results suggest that $M_{t|t}^r$ (MTREC in tables 2.4 and 2.5) is a useful predictor for short forecast horizons; the WLS results indicate that $M_{t|t}^e$ (MTEXP) is a useful predictor for the six-month horizon as well. Thus, there appears to be some potential misspecification associated with the duration of recessions. There are several possible sources of this misspecification; for example, the linear model (1), (2), (4), and (5) might incorrectly ignore nonlinear feedback, perhaps from R_t, or the linear model might be correctly specified but the recession definition itself (i.e., the process by which recessionary patterns are identified in time series)

---

5. $M_{t|t}^r$ was constructed as follows. Using the algorithm in sec. 2.1.2, generate a historical realization of $\bar{c}_t(-m - 8, 8)$, and, using adjacent septendecimtuples $\bar{c}_\tau(-8, 8)$, classify each month for $\tau = t - m, \ldots, t$ as being in a recession or an expansion. This results in a vector of pseudorandom realizations of $(R_{t-m}, \ldots, R_t)$, constructed using data through t. In the computations, $m = 12$, and historical (true) values of R_t were appended for $\tau < t - 12$. Let L_{ti}^r be the length of the final string of 1s through time t ($t = 1962:1, \ldots, 1988:9$) if $R_t = 1$, and let L_{ti}^e be the length of the final string of 0s if $R_t = 0$. Then $M_{t|t}^r$ is the average of L_{ti}^r over the $R_t = 1$ Monte Carlo draws and similarly for $M_{t|t}^e$. This construction provides an approximation to the joint conditional distribution of $(R_{t-m}, \ldots, R_t)$ or to the distribution of functions of these random variables such as M_t. This approximation, however, has two difficulties. First, because $b_{r,t}$ and $b_{e,t}$ are treated as random and varying over t, the event U_τ computed using $b_{r,t}$ differs from U_τ computed using $b_{r,t+1}$ (say). Second, even if $b_{r,t}$ and $b_{e,t}$ were constant ($\zeta_t = \zeta$), the marginal distribution of R_t constructed using this procedure will differ from that based on the algorithm in sec. 2.1.2: the marginals in sec. 2.1 are implicitly

$$\Pr[R_i|R_t \cup E_t] = \Pr\{R_i|R_t \cup E_t, R_\tau \cup E_\tau \cup [\mathfrak{R}^{17}/(R_\tau \cup E_\tau)]\}, \tau \neq t\}$$

(where $\mathfrak{R}^{17}/[R_\tau \cup E_\tau]$ is the complement of $R_\tau \cup E_\tau$ in $\mathfrak{R}^{17}$), while those computed here are

$$\Pr[R_i|R_t \cup E_t] = \Pr[R_i|R_t \cup E_t, R_\tau \cup E_\tau, \tau \neq t].$$

It should be emphasized that this difficulty arises only when computing joint probabilities, not when computing sequences of marginal probabilities (e.g., $P_{t+k|t}$, $k = 0, 1, 2, \ldots$). Resolving this issue awaits further research.

have a temporal dependence that is not captured by the pattern recognition algorithm of section 2.1.2. Ascertaining which if either of these possibilities produces these rejections must await future research.

Taken together, these results suggest that there is little in-sample evidence of misspecification associated with the inefficient use of information in the included indicators or in candidate alternative leading indicators. Although there is some evidence of nonlinear misspecification related to duration dependence, the evidence is strongest at short forecasting horizons, and, in any event, this misspecification is not well proxied by any of the alternative leading indicators.

2.3   Out-of-Sample Performance

The XLI model was estimated using data through 1988:9. This section examines the performance of the XLI and the XRI over the period from 1988:10 through 1991:10, the month for which the most recent data were available to us. This provides thirty-seven months, including a cyclical peak in July 1990, with which to assess the performance of the indexes and to draw conclusions concerning the modification of the indexes.

2.3.1   Out-of-Sample Performance: An Overview

Forecasts of the growth in the XCI (annualized growth rates) made using the XLI model since 1988:1 are plotted in figure 2.2 for forecasting horizons of three, six, and nine months. The six-month-ahead forecast (panel B) is the XLI (i.e., $c_{t+6|t} - c_{t|t}$). The estimated recession probabilities $P_{t+k|t}$ for $k = -2, 0, 1, 2, 3, 6$, are presented in figure 2.3 and table 2.6.

As figure 2.2 makes plain, it is useful to consider the performance of the XLI over two episodes: prior to the summer of 1990 (approximately 1990:5) and subsequently. In the first episode, the performance of the XLI was very good, forecasting both the slowdown in the spring of 1989 and the growth that followed. During the fall of 1988 and the winter of 1989, interest rates rose substantially, by many reports in conjunction with an attempt by the Federal Reserve Board to control inflation; for example, the six-month Treasury-bill rate rose from 7.5 percent in October 1988 to 8.85 percent in March 1989. With the easing of interest rates in the spring of 1989, the financial market indicators in the XLI became more optimistic: by July, the commercial paper–Treasury-bill spread had fallen to 58 basis points, just above its postwar average and well below its March peak of 113 basis points. With this decline in interest rates and spreads, the XLI forecast increased growth: on the basis of unrevised data (i.e., as the XLI was originally computed), the XLI for March was − 1.1 percent, while, by July, the XLI had risen to 0.7 percent. The behavior of the XLI forecasts was broadly consistent with the overall outlook at the time as reported in the economic and financial press, which was one of

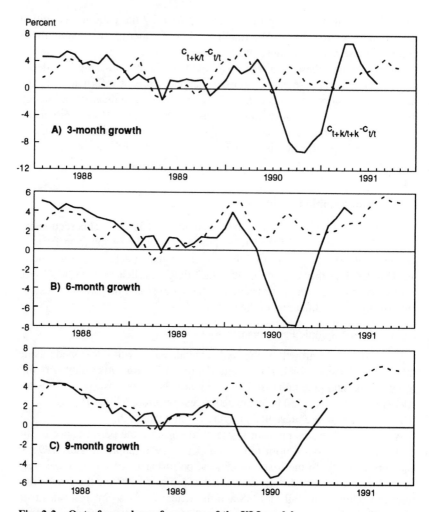

Fig. 2.2   Out-of-sample performance of the XLI model

Note: The series $c_{t+k|t} - c_{t|t}$ is based on preliminary data, and $c_{t+k|t+k} - c_{t|t}$ is based on revised data.

general concern over economic conditions in the early spring being replaced by cautious optimism in the late spring and early summer.[6]

As can be seen from figure 2.2, over this episode the XLI model provided very good forecasts of overall activity, not only at the six-month horizon for

6. For example, commenting on the 31 May 1989 release of the Department of Commerce's Leading Index in the *New York Times* (1 June 1989, C1), Michael P. Niemira of the Mitsubishi Bank stated, "The message is more strength still in the pipeline." The article later states, "Weakness in various measures of output and sales have signaled that economic growth is slowing and raised some concerns about a possible recession. The slowdown has also, however, raised hopes

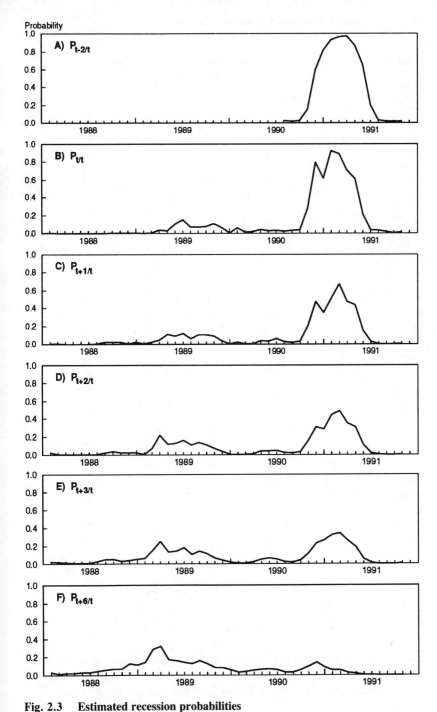

Fig. 2.3 Estimated recession probabilities

Note: The dates on the horizontal axes denote t, the date through which the data are available for computing $P_{t+k/t}$. The figure is based on data revised through 1988:9 and unrevised data since 1988:10. The series $P_{t-2/t}$ begins in 1990:7, and all other series begin in 1988:1.

Table 2.6   Estimated Recession Probabilities $P_{t+k|t}$, by Month

Date	$P_{t-2|t}$	$P_{t|t}$	$P_{t+1|t}$	$P_{t+2|t}$	$P_{t+3|t}$	$P_{t+6|t}$
1988:10	. . .	.01	.02	.02	.03	.07
1988:11	. . .	.01	.01	.02	.04	.13
1988:12	. . .	.01	.02	.02	.05	.11
1989:1	. . .	.00	.01	.01	.06	.14
1989:2	. . .	.01	.02	.07	.15	.29
1989:3	. . .	.04	.05	.22	.25	.32
1989:4	. . .	.03	.11	.12	.13	.17
1989:5	. . .	.10	.09	.13	.14	.16
1989:6	. . .	.15	.12	.16	.18	.14
1989:7	. . .	.07	.06	.11	.10	.13
1989:8	. . .	.07	.10	.14	.14	.16
1989:9	. . .	.08	.10	.11	.11	.13
1989:10	. . .	.11	.09	.07	.07	.09
1989:11	. . .	.07	.04	.04	.05	.09
1989:12	. . .	.01	.01	.01	.02	.06
1990:1	. . .	.06	.03	.01	.01	.03
1990:2	. . .	.02	.01	.00	.01	.05
1990:3	. . .	.02	.01	.01	.02	.05
1990:4	. . .	.04	.04	.05	.05	.06
1990:5	. . .	.03	.03	.05	.06	.07
1990:6	. . .	.04	.06	.05	.05	.05
1990:7	.03	.03	.03	.03	.02	.03
1990:8	.02	.04	.02	.02	.02	.03
1990:9	.03	.04	.03	.04	.05	.06
1990:10	.16	.28	.20	.16	.12	.10
1990:11	.59	.80	.48	.31	.23	.14
1990:12	.81	.62	.35	.28	.26	.09
1991:1	.93	.93	.52	.45	.33	.05
1991:2	.97	.87	.67	.49	.35	.04
1991:3	.98	.70	.48	.35	.26	.03
1991:4	.88	.61	.44	.31	.19	.02
1991:5	.65	.22	.15	.11	.05	.01
1991:6	.20	.04	.03	.02	.01	.01
1991:7	.04	.04	.01	.01	.01	.01
1991:8	.02	.02	.01	.01	.01	.01
1991:9	.02	.01	.01	.01	.01	.01
1991:10	.02	.01	.01	.01	.01	.01

Note: Recession probabilities were computed using unrevised (original) data.

which it had been optimized, but also at the three- and nine-month horizons. During this episode, the XRI indicated an increased probability of a recession: the XRI peaked at 32 percent in March 1989 and then quickly declined.

---

that the Federal Reserve might ease the tight grip it has kept on monetary policy for more than a year." In the *Wall Street Journal* that same day (p. A2), Gary Ciminero of Fleet/Norstar Financial Group was quoted as saying, "I think it [the DOC Leading Index] means that if we do encounter a

The second episode starts in the summer of 1990. On the basis of data through March 1990, the XLI was 3.1 percent, down from almost 5 percent in January and February 1990. In comparison, the XCI growth over the six months from March to September was 1.6 percent (annual rate), a forecast error of 1.5 percent, similar to previous out-of-sample performance and only approximately 1 percentage point in GNP units. The three-month-ahead forecast based on data through June 1990, for June–September, was −0.8 percent (annual rates); actual growth in the XCI over this period was −0.4 percent. However, the slowdown—correctly predicted over the next three months—was predicted to be short, to be followed by positive but slow growth. As a consequence, the recession probability—computed for each future month using data through June 1990—remained low, only 5 percent for each month from August through February 1991. This forecast of moderate growth in the fall of 1991 was, as it turned out, dramatically wrong: the XLI computed in August was 3.6 percent, while the actual growth of the XCI over this period was −7.3 percent, a forecast error of 10.9 percent (over 6 percent in GNP units at an annual rate). At the time of this writing (December 1991), the XLI appears to be back on track: the XCI increased by 3.9 percent at an annual rate between April and October 1991 (the most recent month for which data are available), and in April the XLI predicted that this growth would be 2.9 percent.

The performance within sample and during these two out-of-sample episodes is summarized in table 2.7 in terms of the RMSE and mean absolute errors (MAEs) of the forecasts.[7] The table shows that, during the first episode (1988:10–1990:4), the out-of-sample performance of the XLI was noticeably better than expected on the basis of the in-sample experience, with RMSEs and MAEs half what they were in sample. During the second episode (1990:5–1991:4; 1991:4 is the final month for which $c_{t+6|t+6}$ has been observed), forecast errors were approximately two times as large as within sample.

As can be seen from figure 2.3, the XRI has continued to estimate a six-month-ahead recession probability of under 20 percent; the XRI missed the July 1990 peak. It should be emphasized, however, that shorter-run forecasts indicated an increased probability of a recession, although not until October or November. For example, $P_{t|t}$, computed using data through October, was 28 percent; computed using data through November, it was 80 percent. Even so, the probability of a recession declined sharply with the horizon; in November, the three-month-ahead recession probability was only 23 percent.

An initial possibility is that the XLI continued to be a good forecast of

---

more significant slowdown in the economy, it's not going to occur in the next few months. I think we'll encounter a recession at the start of next year."

7. Note that k-month-ahead forecasts made during 1988:10 − k, . . . , 1988:9, $k \geq 1$, are partly out of sample, even though they are not included in the span used to compute the out-of-sample summary statistics in table 2.7.

Table 2.7   Performance of the XLI: Summary Statistics

Sample Period	RMSE	MAE
A. Forecasting Performance of the XLI		
1962:1–1988:9	2.89	2.32
1980:1–1988:9	3.50	2.94
1980:1–1990:8	3.54	2.83
1988:10–1990:8	3.72	2.32
1988:10–1990:4	1.35	1.13
1990:5–1991:4	6.26	4.96
B. Relation between XCI Growth and GNP		
1962:I–1988:III	2.34	1.84
1988:IV–1990:IV	1.32	1.07

Note: Panel A: The root mean square error (RMSE) and mean absolute error (MAE) are computed for the difference between the XLI ($c_{t+6|t} - c_{t|t}$) and the 6-month growth in the XCI ($c_{t+6|t+6} - c_{t|t}$). The dates in the first column correspond to the date that the forecast was made, so 1991:4 corresponds to the last observation for which there are data on $c_{t+6|t+6}$. Panel B: The statistics are computed for the residual from a regression (estimated over 1962:I–1988:III) of the quarterly growth of real GNP at annual rates on the quarterly growth of the XCI, where the XCI growth is the quarter-to-quarter growth of the monthly XCI, averaged across the months in the quarter.

economic activity but that the relation between overall economic activity (say, real GNP) and the XCI had deteriorated since 1988:9. This possibility is, however, readily dismissed: the out-of-sample relation between the XCI and real GNP was, if anything, closer than it had been in sample. This is documented in the final rows of table 2.7. Although there are currently only two observations on the quarterly XCI and real GNP during the second episode, the relation between the two appears to have been stable: the residuals from the 1962:I–1988:III regression of quarterly GNP growth onto quarterly XCI growth in table 2.2 yields forecast errors of −1.2 percent and 0.9 percent for 1990:III and 1990:IV, respectively, less than either the in-sample RMSE or the in-sample MAE.

The remainder of this paper explores possible explanations for the failure of the XLI and the XRI to predict the 1990 recession, with the objective of drawing lessons from this experience to guide revisions of the index and, more generally, future research on leading indicators. This section first documents the contributions of the individual variables to the XLI over 1990, then examines the importance of data revisions during the second episode. Section 2.4 turns to more fundamental issues of specification, construction of the index, and the choice of leading indicators.

2.3.2   Contributions of Individual Indicators to the Overall Index

The XLI model as described in section 2.2 is linear in the data and in c_t; as a result, $c_{t+k|t}$ can be written as a linear projection onto current and past values of the observable series

(20) $$c_{t+k|t} - c_{t|t} = \lambda k + \sum_{i=1}^{11} A_{ki}(L)z_{it},$$

where $z_t = (\Delta x_t', y_t')$ denotes the vector of four coincident and seven leading indicators in the XLI, where $A_{ki}(L)$ are lag polynomial weights, and where λ is a trend growth rate. These weights $A_{ki}(L)$ are readily computed numerically and are plotted in Stock and Watson (1989). The weighted averages $A_{ki}(L)z_{it}$ constitute the contribution of each of the eleven indicators to the deviation of the k-step-ahead forecast from its mean λk. An examination of these contributions for $k = 6$ therefore shows how each of the variables influenced the performance of the XLI on a month-by-month basis.

These historical contributions to the index are plotted in figure 2.4 over 1988:1–1991:10 and are presented in table 2.8 for January 1990 hence. Through the summer of 1990, the coincident indicators made negligible contributions to the index, usually 0.3 percent or less. The largest contributions to the index typically were made by building permits, exchange rates, the public-private yield spread, and the Treasury-bond yield spread.

This pattern changed during the second half of 1990. Although the public-private spread variable made positive contributions during July and August, its contribution in September and October was approximately zero. This was consistent with the doubling of this spread over this period, from thirty-nine basis points in July to seventy-nine basis points in November. The largest negative contributions came from housing authorizations and part-time work due to slack work. Three variables typically made substantial, incorrectly positive contributions to the index: the Treasury-bill yield curve, exchange rates, and, since December 1990, industrial production. The positive contribution of industrial production during this period reflects a mean reverting component in the model after the sharply negative values of IP in October and November. The yield curve and exchange rate contributions suggest that these variables might be partly to blame for the poor performance of the index. However, even if the contributions of these two variables are eliminated, then the XLI in September would still have been 1.7, while in fact the XCI declined by over 7 percent over this period.

In the winter and early spring of 1991, housing permits, unfilled orders, and part-time employment continued to provide negative signals. The appreciation of the dollar during the first quarter led exchange rates to provide a negative contribution to the XLI. The yield curve continued to steepen as short-term interest rates fell more quickly than long-term rates, leading to an

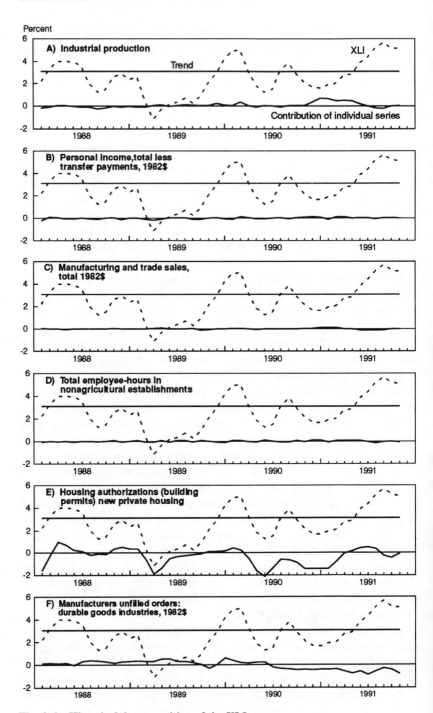

Fig. 2.4   Historical decomposition of the XLI
Note: The XLI and the historical contributions are based on preliminary data.

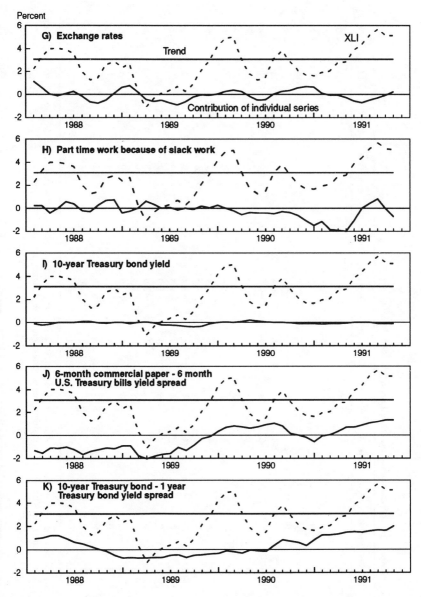

Fig. 2.4 (continued)

even more positive contribution from the yield curve spread. Finally, the commercial paper–Treasury-bill spread fell below its historical average, providing a positive contribution to the XLI. By the middle of 1991, all the indicators except exchange rates and unfilled orders were providing positive signals and suggesting stronger-than-average short-term growth in the XCI.

Table 2.8   Historical Contributions to the XLI, January 1990–February 1991

Month	IP	GMYXP8	MT82	LPMHU	HSBP	MDU82S	EXNWT2FS	LHNAPSS	FYGT10FS	CP6.GM6F	G10.G1F	XLI	$c_{t+6|t+6} - c_{t|t}$
1990:1	.0	-.0	.0	.0	.5	.4	.3	.0	.0	.7	-.1	5.0	4.0
1990:2	.4	.1	.0	.0	.3	.2	.4	-.2	.0	.8	-.2	5.0	2.5
1990:3	.0	.0	-.0	-.0	-.5	.1	.3	-.5	.1	.7	-.3	3.1	1.4
1990:4	-.0	-.0	-.0	-.0	-1.6	.2	-.1	-.4	.2	.6	-.0	1.8	.1
1990:5	.0	-.0	-.0	.0	-2.1	.2	-.5	-.4	.2	.8	-.1	1.3	-2.6
1990:6	.0	.0	.0	.0	-1.4	-.3	-.4	-.4	.0	.9	-.1	1.5	-4.7
1990:7	-.0	.0	-.0	-.0	-.6	-.3	.0	-.5	.0	1.0	.4	3.1	-6.8
1990:8	.0	-.0	-.0	-.0	-.6	-.4	.3	-.3	.0	.8	.8	3.8	-7.7
1990:9	.0	.0	-.0	.0	-.9	-.5	.4	-.4	-.0	.2	.8	2.9	-7.8
1990:10	.0	.0	.0	-.0	-1.4	-.4	.6	-.6	-.0	.0	.6	2.1	-5.5
1990:11	.3	.2	.0	.1	-1.4	-.5	.7	-1.1	-.1	-.2	.4	1.7	-2.4
1990:12	.7	.1	.0	.1	-1.4	-.4	.7	-1.5	-.0	-.6	.8	1.6	.2
1991:1	.7	-.0	.1	-.0	-.7	-.4	.2	-1.2	-.1	-.0	1.3	1.9	2.6
1991:2	.5	.1	-.0	.0	-.0	-.6	-.0	-1.8	-.1	.0	1.3	2.1	3.4
1991:3	.5	.1	-.0	.0	-.0	-.6	-.0	-1.9	-.1	.4	1.3	2.8	4.6
1991:4	.5	.0	-.0	.0	.2	-.8	-.2	-2.0	-.0	.7	1.5	2.9	3.9
1991:5	.2	.0	-.0	.0	.5	-.6	-.5	-1.1	.0	.7	1.5	3.9	...
1991:6	.0	.0	-.0	-.0	.5	-.9	-.7	.0	.0	.9	1.4	4.4	...
1991:7	-.1	-.0	-.0	-.1	.4	-.6	-.5	.4	.0	1.1	1.6	5.2	...
1991:8	-.2	.0	-.0	-.0	-.2	-.3	-.3	.8	-.0	1.2	1.7	5.7	...
1991:9	.0	.0	.0	.0	-.4	-.4	-.0	-.0	-.1	1.4	1.6	5.2	...
1991:10	.0	.0	-.0	-.0	-.0	-.8	.2	-.7	-.1	1.4	2.0	5.1	...

Note: The decompositions and the XLI are based on unrevised (original) data. The contributions are deviations from trend; the sum of the contributions, plus a trend of 3.1 percent, equals the XLI. For a discussion of the decompositions, see the text.

To understand the behavior of the XLI during the second half of 1990, it is useful to contrast the behavior of the financial variables around the cyclical peak of July 1990 to their behavior just before the cyclical peaks in November 1973, January 1980, and July 1981. In each of these three periods, the yield curve was strongly inverted: the spread between ten- and one-year Treasury-bond yields (G10_G1) was, respectively, -0.61, -1.59, and -1.39 in the month before each of these cyclical peaks, while its July 1990 value was 0.38. Similarly, the commercial paper–Treasury-bill yield spread (CP6_GM6) was 1.60, 0.96, and 1.13 in the month before these peaks but only 0.43 in June 1990 (approximately its postwar average value). Thus, the strong negative signals given by these variables prior to the previous recessions were replaced by neutral or slightly positive signals during the summer of 1990. Although the corporate paper–Treasury-bill spread had increased to 0.79 by November 1990, this increase occurred only after the general slowdown in September and October had become apparent.

In summary, this analysis of the historical contributions during the onset of the 1990 recession suggests two observations. First, the financial variables— in particular, the yield curve spread and, to a lesser extent, exchange rates— gave optimistic signals throughout this episode, even in the late fall, when the general public perception was that a recession was inevitable. Second, although none of the other variables gave strong positive signals, only three— part-time work, building permits, and unfilled orders—gave negative signals, and these negative contributions were still moderate, particularly in the second and third quarters of 1990.

Whether there were other variables that would have predicted this recession had they been incorporated into the index is the topic of the next section of the paper. First, however, we turn briefly to a discussion of data revisions during this episode.

2.3.3   Revisions to the Coincident Indicators

Some of the revisions to the data on the coincident indicators during the fall of 1990 were large. Table 2.9 presents these data as they were released over this period, in terms of monthly growth at annual percentage rates. On the basis of recent revisions, we see that industrial production growth was positive through September; estimates of the decline in IP in October ranged from almost 11 percent (annual rate) in the 1990:11 data release to only 7.6 percent in the 1991:1 release. An examination of table 2.9 reveals comparable revisions in the other coincident indicators. Even though measurement error models are explicitly incorporated into the XLI model as described in section 2.1, large revisions in the coincident indicators can nonetheless result in substantial changes in $c_{t+k|t}$ for k small (say, $k \leq 3$). This raises the possibility that the poor performance of the XLI and the XRI was, at least in part, due to their reliance on these substantially revised preliminary data.

This possibility is examined in figure 2.5, which presents the XLI com-

Table 2.9   **Coincident Indicator Data and Revisions, 1990:5–1991:2: Monthly Growth at Annual Rates**

	Data Released During the Month Following:					
Data for:	1990:9	1990:10	1990:11	1990:12	1991:1	1991:2
	A. Industrial Production					
1990:5	6.60	6.60	6.60	6.60	6.60	6.60
1990:6	7.65	7.65	7.65	7.65	7.65	7.65
1990:7	2.18	3.27	3.27	3.27	3.27	3.27
1990:8	1.09	.00	1.09	1.09	1.09	1.09
1990:9	3.26	1.09	−1.09	1.09	1.09	1.09
1990:10	. . .	−9.81	−10.92	−8.71	−7.62	−7.62
1990:11	. . .	. . .	−21.02	−22.06	−18.71	−17.60
1990:12	. . .	. . .	. . .	−7.82	−13.38	−12.25
1991:1	. . .	. . .	. . .	. . .	−5.62	−6.74
1991:2	. . .	. . .	. . .	. . .	. . .	−10.18
	B. Personal Income, Total, Less Transfer Payments, 1982$					
1990:5	.17	.17	.17	.17	.17	.17
1990:6	1.36	1.36	1.36	1.36	1.36	1.36
1990:7	3.05	3.25	2.92	2.92	2.92	2.92
1990:8	−5.93	−4.90	−5.36	−5.36	−5.36	−5.36
1990:9	−3.14	−4.55	−4.34	−4.34	−4.34	−4.34
1990:10	. . .	−8.23	−11.32	−11.78	−12.96	−12.75
1990:11	. . .	. . .	−.75	.75	1.05	2.30
1990:12	. . .	. . .	. . .	6.51	7.05	5.09
1991:1	. . .	. . .	. . .	. . .	−17.60	−17.06
1991:2	. . .	. . .	. . .	. . .	. . .	−.21
	C. Manufacturing and Trade Sales, Total, 1982$					
1990:5	11.24	11.24	11.24	11.24	11.24	11.24
1990:6	7.43	7.43	7.43	7.43	7.43	7.43
1990:7	−4.81	−7.52	−7.53	−7.53	−7.53	−7.53
1990:8	11.13	14.91	14.07	14.09	14.09	14.09
1990:9	. . .	−22.84	−18.78	−22.19	−22.19	−22.19
1990:10	. . .	. . .	−1.38	−1.68	−2.24	−2.18
1990:11	. . .	. . .	. . .	−19.96	−16.31	−20.41
1990:12	. . .	. . .	. . .	. . .	−23.54	−23.38
1991:1	. . .	. . .	. . .	. . .	. . .	−14.94
1991:2	. . .	. . .	. . .	. . .	. . .	. . .
	D. Total Employee-Hours in Nonagricultural Establishments					
1990:5	9.84	9.84	9.84	10.01	10.01	10.01
1990:6	5.65	5.65	5.65	9.23	9.23	9.23
1990:7	−3.32	−3.32	−3.32	−3.56	−3.56	−3.56
1990:8	−4.06	−4.71	−4.71	−4.74	−4.74	−4.74
1990:9	5.20	5.73	5.93	5.96	5.96	5.96

Table 2.9   (continued)

Data for:	Data Released During the Month Following:					
	1990:9	1990:10	1990:11	1990:12	1991:1	1991:2
1990:10	. . .	− 15.24	− 16.93	− 17.39	− 17.39	− 17.39
1990:11	. . .	. . .	3.85	4.13	4.13	4.13
1990:12	. . .	. . .	. . .	6.01	6.00	4.36
1991:1	. . .	. . .	. . .	. . .	− 18.88	− 15.77
1991:2	. . .	. . .	. . .	. . .	. . .	3.71

Source: Department of Commerce Electronic Bulletin Board, various releases.
Note: Data on manufacturing and trade sales are available with a two-month lag.

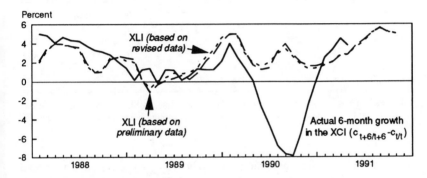

Fig. 2.5   Original and revised XLI
Note: The XLI and the growth in the SCI are at annual rates.

puted using the unrevised and the revised data as well as the actual growth of the XCI based on the most recently available revised data. Although the revisions in the coincident indicator data are large, these revisions had scant effect on the XLI: the change in the XLI based on the revised data is typically less than 0.4 percentage points. One explanation for this is that the XLI relies in large part on leading variables not subject to revision, in particular, the financial variables; another is that the predictive role of the coincident indicators, although substantial for very short horizons, diminishes markedly for longer horizons. In any event, the large revisions to the coincident indicators over the summer and fall of 1990 do not seem to be the source of the breakdown in the XLI and XRI forecasts.

2.4   Alternative Specifications: Recent Performance

This section investigates the failure of the XLI to predict the downturn in the fall of 1990. The analysis centers around two main possibilities. The first is that, given the list of indicators selected, the model was incorrectly speci-

Table 2.10   Sensitivity of $P_{t+6|t}$ to μ_r, μ_e, and σ_ζ: RMSE for $R_{t+6} - P_{t+6|t}$, in Sample (1962:1–1988:9) and out of Sample (1988:10–1990:8)

μ_r\\μ_e	.000	−.250	−.500	μ_r\\μ_e	.000	−.250	−.500
	A. $\sigma_\zeta = .6$				C. $\sigma_\zeta = 1.0$		
−1.250	.250	.248	.250	−1.250	.250	.247	.250
	.486	.483	.484		.485	.484	.482
−1.500	.249	.250	.250	−1.500	.249	.250	.250
	.486	.486	.476		.486	.486	.486
−1.750	.250	.251	.251	−1.750	.249	.251	.253
	.485	.486	.484		.483	.486	.485
	B. $\sigma_\zeta = .8$				D. Additional RMSEs		
−1.250	.250	.249	.250	$\mu_r = 0,\ \mu_e = 0,$			.258
	.486	.483	.482	$\sigma_\zeta = .8$:			.447
−1.500	.249	.250	.249	$\mu_r = 0,\ \mu_e = 0,$			.258
	.485	.486	.485	$\sigma_\zeta = 1.0$:			.489
−1.750	.250	.250	.250				
	.484	.487	.485				

Note: The upper entry in each (μ_r, μ_e, σ_ζ) cell is the in-sample RMSE; the lower entry is the out-of-sample MSE. For these calculations, the most recent turning point was the cyclical peak of 1990:7.

fied or "overfit," in the sense that it was too heavily parameterized. The second is that the list of indicators was flawed: had other indicators been included, would the XRI have predicted a recession?

These two questions are addressed in several steps. We first consider the effect of possible modifications of the definition of a recession on both the in-sample and the out-of-sample performance of the XRI. Because the main source of the failure in the XRI stems from the overly optimistic forecasts embodied in the XLI in August and September, it is not surprising that tuning the recession definition does not substantially improve the performance of the XRI. Next, we consider the possibility that the model is overparameterized, resulting in "overfitting" the in-sample data. This is examined by studying an alternative set of indexes, based on the seven leading indicators in the XLI, in which the number of estimated parameters is reduced and the structure of the index is simplified substantially. The performance of these indexes is comparable to the XLI, both in and out of sample, which leads us to conclude that overparameterization or model misspecification does not account for the poor performance of the XLI. The analysis therefore turns to the performance of the individual indicators constituting the index and of alternative leading indicators and indexes.

2.4.1   Changes in the Definitions of Recession/Expansion Events

The first possibility investigated is that the XRI would have performed better had it used a different definition of recessions. This is investigated, first, by considering the effect of changing the parameters (μ_r, μ_e, σ_ζ) that enter the definition of recession and expansion events and, second, by redefining recession events so that a recession can last only four months rather than six.

The results of these changes are summarized in table 2.10 and 2.11. Table 2.10 presents the RMSEs of the XRI forecast errors (i.e., $R_{t+6} - P_{t+6|t}$), both in and out of sample. The much larger RMSEs out of sample than in sample largely reflect the failure of the XLI to predict the downturn in the fall of 1990. In general, the RMSE, both in and out of sample, is insensitive to changes of $\pm$ .25 for μ_r and μ_e and of $\pm$ .2 for σ_ζ; minor modifications in the recession definition would not have resulted in more accurate recession probabilities.

Six-month-ahead recession probabilities for 1990, computed using alternative parameter values, are summarized in table 2.11. Although modest changes make negligible differences, increasing the recession cutoffs to $\mu_r =$

Table 2.11   **The Effect of Changing the Definition of a Recession on the XRI Probabilities ($P_{t+6|t}$) for January–December 1990**

	(μ_r, μ_e, σ_ζ) =					
	(−1.5, −.25, .8)	(−1.75, −.25, .8)	(−1.5, .0, .8)	(−1.5, −.25, .6)	(.0, .0, 1.0)	4-Month Recessions
	A. Recession Probabilities					
Jan.	.021	.023	.016	.010	.041	.023
Feb.	.026	.026	.036	.044	.062	.031
Mar.	.047	.023	.035	.041	.098	.066
Apr.	.056	.040	.038	.040	.102	.077
May	.048	.030	.057	.037	.098	.076
June	.030	.021	.040	.034	.120	.082
July	.023	.024	.023	.020	.082	.045
Aug.	.016	.022	.041	.016	.061	.037
Sep.	.029	.037	.048	.034	.130	.065
Oct.	.092	.102	.070	.088	.182	.100
Nov.	.134	.105	.136	.129	.238	.125
Dec.	.095	.073	.097	.097	.243	.116
	B. RMSEs					
1962:7– 1988:9	.250	.251	.249	.250	.258	.253
1988:10– 1990:8	.486	.486	.485	.486	.489	.485

Note: Panel A: The entries are the values of the XRI ($P_{t+6|t}$) that would have been computed for each month during 1990, had the indicated values of (μ_r, μ_e, σ_ζ) been used. To facilitate comparisons, the first column reports the value of the XRI; the next four columns report probabilities computed with alternative parameter values. The final column reports probabilities computed using the parameters used in the model, but with the minimum length of a recession taken to be 4 rather than 6 months. Panel B: The entries are the RMSEs of $R_{t+k} - P_{t+k|t}$ over the indicated (in-sample and out-of-sample) ranges.

$\mu_e = 0$ would have produced slightly higher probabilities; the XRI would have registered 13 percent in September rather than 3 percent. However, cutoffs this high are implausible: the pre-1988:10 RMSEs for these parameters exceed those for the chosen parameter values, and, more important, because the XCI is more volatile than GNP, recession cutoffs of $\mu_r = \mu_e = 0$ approximately correspond to a recession occurring if real GNP growth drops below 1.3 percent for two consecutive quarters. In the past, the Business Cycle Dating Committee has dated recessions as if the appropriate cutoff is approximately zero growth in real GNP.

The final modification considered here is reducing the length of the shortest recession from six to four months, with the result that (6) is replaced by

$$(6')\ D_{1\tau} = \{\Delta c_s,\, s = \tau - 3,\, \ldots,\, \tau\colon \Delta c_s \leq b_{r,s},\, s = \tau - 3,\, \ldots,\, \tau\},$$

and similarly for $U_{1\tau}$. As seen in the final column of table 5.11, this change has little effect on the XLI, in terms of either the in-sample RMSE or the probabilities over 1990.

In short, modifications of the recession definition—even major ones, such as permitting recessions with a duration as short as four months or as shallow as growth dipping below 1.3 percent in the units of annual GNP growth—have little effect on the recession probabilities computed over this episode.

2.4.2   Possible Overparameterization and Overfitting

Because the linear model outlined in section 2.1.1 has a large number of parameters, it is possible that the poor performance during the fall of 1990 can be attributed to "overfitting" in the sense of having too few observations per parameter. This possibility is investigated by constructing some simple alternative indexes that entail fitting considerably fewer parameters. These indexes are of the form

$$(21)\qquad\qquad \hat{y}_t = \sum_{i=1}^{n} \alpha_i \hat{y}_{it},$$

where $\hat{y}_{it}$ are the indexes (forecasts) constructed from each of the n individual leading indicators entering the index. The individual forecasts are computed as the projection of the growth of the XCI over the next six months onto current and lagged values of each candidate leading indicator y_{it} and onto current and lagged values of XCI growth; that is, $\hat{y}_{it}$ is the fitted value from the regression

$$(22)\qquad c_{t+6|T} - c_{t|T} = \omega + \beta_i(L)y_{it} + \gamma_i(L)\Delta c_{t|t} + v_t.$$

An index constructed according to (21) and (22), like the XLI, is linear in the leading indicators and has a representation analogous to (20).[8]

---

8. For related work that approaches the construction of indexes of leading indicators as a forecasting problem, see Auerbach (1982), Stekler and Schepsman (1973), and Vaccara and Zarnowitz (1978).

The parameters ω, $\beta_i(L)$, and $\gamma_i(L)$ in (22) were estimated by running the regression in (22) with contemporaneous values and five lags of y_{it} and with contemporaneous values and two lags of $\Delta c_{t|t}$. If, in fact, $\Delta c_{t|t}$ and y_{it} follow a VAR(p), this regression would be inefficient relative to estimating a VAR(p), but this procedure has two advantages: first, it produces conditionally unbiased projections (conditional on lags of y_{it}) if the true projection is linear (with the specified lag length); second, it reduces the number of parameters that need to be estimated for multistep forecasting.

Because the individual "indexes" $\hat{y}_{it}$ are each forecasts of $c_{t+6|T} - c_{t|T}$, the problem of constructing a composite index—that is, computing the weights $\{\alpha_i\}$ in (21) given the set of individual indexes to be included—reduces to the well-studied problem of the combination of forecasts. Two simple approaches are used here. The first is analogous to the weighting scheme effectively used to construct the DOC Leading Index; that is, all the weights are set to $1/n$.[9] The second approach is to produce the minimal mean squared error linear combination of forecasts, which is implemented by estimating α_i by OLS with $c_{t+6|T} - c_{t|T}$ as the dependent variable and $\hat{y}_{it}$ as the independent variable. The net effect of constructing indexes using this simple structure is to reduce substantially the number of parameters to be estimated, relative to the model of section 2.1.1.

Composite indexes based on (21) and (22) were estimated using data over the period 1959:1–1988:9. The RMSEs of the resulting indexes are summarized in table 2.12, along with the corresponding RMSEs for the XLI. (These and subsequent RMSEs for indexes of the form [21] and [22] are computed relative to the growth in the smoothed XCI, $c_{t+6|T} - c_{t|T}$.) Relative to the OLS-weighted index with the same seven leading indicators, the XLI performs better both in and out of sample, but it performs slightly worse than the equally weighted index out of sample. Overall, the performance is comparable across these three indexes for all subsamples.

The same exercise was repeated for the leading indicators composing the XLI2 (the alternative nonfinancial leading index). As with the indexes based on the XLI indicators, the performance is similar across indexes in all subsamples. The implication is that the fitting of many parameters in the XLI (or XLI2) model does not appear to be a key factor in the breakdown in the fall of 1990.

A second conclusion emerging from table 2.12 is that, although the XLI2 does markedly worse than the XLI in sample, it noticeably outperforms the XLI out of sample, with a reduction of almost one-quarter in the RMSE for forecasts into the fall of 1990. This, along with the findings of the previous section concerning the insensitivity of the XLI to the recession definition, suggests that the problems with the XLI resulted from omitting leading indi-

---

9. For discussions of the DOC weighting schemes, see Zarnowitz and Boschan (1975a, 1975b) and Zarnowitz and Moore (1982).

Table 2.12   Forecasting Performance of Alternative Composite Indexes: Six-Month-Ahead Forecast Horizon

Series	RMSE Computed over:				MAE Computed over:			
	62:1–88:9	88:10–90:8	88:10–90:4	90:5–90:8	62:1–88:9	88:10–90:8	88:10–90:4	90:5–90:8
Constant	4.38	3.55	1.75	7.61	3.12	2.45	1.39	7.53
XLI	2.76	3.42	1.39	7.62	2.20	2.15	1.08	7.24
XLI-equal	3.57	3.36	1.31	7.54	2.61	2.16	1.06	7.39
XLI-OLS	2.78	3.76	1.54	8.36	2.25	2.36	1.14	8.14
XLI2	3.80	2.61	1.57	5.24	2.83	1.93	1.35	4.67
XLI2-equal	3.94	3.20	1.38	7.07	2.83	2.10	1.08	6.93
XLI2-OLS	3.38	3.03	1.72	6.23	2.64	2.15	1.40	5.73

Note: "Constant" indicates forecasting $c_{t+6} - c_t$ by a constant only. The alternative composite indexes XLI-equal, XLI-OLS, XLI2-equal, and XLI2-OLS are constructed according to eqs. (21) and (22) in the text. In the "equally weighted" indexes, the weights in (21) are $\alpha_i = 1/n$, while, in the "OLS-weighted" indexes, $\{\alpha_i\}$ are estimated by ordinary least squares. XLI indicators: HSBP, MDU82S, EXNWT2FS, LHNAPSS, FYGT10FS, CP6–GM6F, G10–GLF; XLI2 indicators: HSBP, MDU82S, EXNWT2FS, LPHRM, IPXMCA, LHEL, IVPAC. All indexes were computed using the revised data as of 1991:2. RMSEs were computed relative to $(c_{t+6|T} - c_{t|T})$. All growth rates are in percentages, at annual rates.

cators that turned out to have important predictive content for the 1990 downturn and including others that did not.

2.4.3   Alternative Indicators: Diagnostic Tests

The tests based on the regressions (19) provide a useful framework for checking whether alternative leading or coincident indicators would have been useful in predicting R_t over 1988:10–1991:2. The p-values for the resulting Wald tests are reported in table 2.13. Because of the limited number of out-of-sample observations, only current values and two lags of each candidate indicator are used in the regressions. Also, in this out-of-sample period, there are only three nonoverlapping nine-month periods, so the most distant horizon considered is six months. Because there are fewer than five nonoverlapping observations on $P_{t+6|t}$, the six-month horizon results need to be interpreted cautiously as well.

The results provide strong evidence of misspecification during this period. The weights given to the included indicators—in particular, housing starts, exchange rates, and the ten-year bond rate—were ex post incorrect. This accords with the message of figure 2.4 above: exchange rates and the interest rate indicators yielded overoptimistic predictions during the summer and fall of 1990, and the XLI (and the XRI) would have performed better had building permits been given more weight.

Table 2.13 also demonstrates that alternative indicators would have been useful in predicting the XRI forecast errors, in particular, help wanted advertising, stock prices, money and credit supply measures, and, at longer horizons, oil prices and some measures of investment, orders, consumption, and consumer expectations. These results demonstrate that, over this episode, the XRI forecast errors could have been reduced by using additional indicators and by placing different weights on those that were included. Because the forecast errors in the XRI were large, however, partially explaining these errors does not in the end seem to be a very demanding task. More challenging is seeing whether the alternative indicators might have provided satisfactory forecasts of this and earlier recessions, either alone or as part of an alternative index.

2.4.4   Alternative Indicators: Performance of Single-Indicator Indexes

This subsection presents some initial results analyzing the performance of alternative indicators and indexes since 1988:10. The indexes are of the form (21) and (22). They exploit the cross-covariance among the candidate leading indicators in only a limited way, and they do not readily produce a recession index such as the XRI. However, for the purposes of this section, indexes based on (21) and (22) have two practical advantages over those based on the framework in section 2.1: they are faster to compute, permitting an examination of a much richer initial list of indicators, and, when used in their equally weighted form, the contribution to the composite index of each of the candidate indicators is transparent.

Table 2.13   **Out-of-Sample Regression Tests for Omitted Variables in $P_{t+k|t}$ (p-values of test statistics): OLS Regressions, 1988:10–1991:2 − k**

Variable	0	1	3	6
	\multicolumn{4}{c}{Forecast Horizon (Months)}			
Constant	.096	.022	.000	.000
	\multicolumn{4}{c}{Coincident Indicators}			
IP	.098	.318	.294	.718
GMYXP8	.214	.100	.135	.369
MT82	.223	.910	.917	.269
LPMHUADJ	.346	.703	.390	.219
	\multicolumn{4}{c}{Leading Indicators in the XRI}			
HSBP	.000	.000	.009	.016
MDU82S	.154	.039	.580	.003
EXNWT2FS	.214	.001	.000	.000
LHNAPSS	.121	.500	.048	.978
FYGT10FS	.190	.111	.005	.000
CP6_GM6F	.102	.021	.011	.007
G10_GLF	.444	.291	.142	.561
XLI	.207	.014	.007	.000
	\multicolumn{4}{c}{Leading Indicators in the XRI2}			
LPHRM	.111	.615	.872	.103
IPXMCA	.289	.442	.954	.352
LHEL	.435	.507	.005	.000
IVPAC	.033	.389	.057	.575
	\multicolumn{4}{c}{Financial Indicators}			
FSPCOMF	.174	.006	.000	.000
FM1D82	.008	.088	.012	.000
FM2D82	.235	.535	.327	.033
FMBASE	.183	.381	.627	.131
FYFFF	.179	.142	.353	.002
BAA_G10F	.184	.313	.219	.000
YLD_DUMF	.115	.001	.025	.000
	\multicolumn{4}{c}{Employment Indicators}			
LUINC	.462	.217	.979	.550
LHU5	.620	.798	.093	.950
LHELX	.283	.234	.358	.082
	\multicolumn{4}{c}{Consumption and Retail Sales}			
IPCD	.056	.143	.004	.022
GMCD82	.672	.693	.236	.835
RTR82	.240	.276	.239	.022

Table 2.13   (continued)

Variable	Forecast Horizon (Months)			
	0	1	3	6
	Inventories and Orders			
MPCON8	.579	.366	.633	.528
MOCM82	.641	.667	.764	.012
MDO82	.577	.227	.691	.421
IVMT82	.403	.186	.133	.027
IVM1D8	.495	.018	.114	.845
IVM2D8	.315	.174	.495	.000
IVM3D8	.499	.255	.303	.883
	Additional Indicators			
DLBLNPAP	.095	.000	.027	.010
PMI	.235	.130	.370	.907
PMNO	.297	.440	.467	.492
HHSNTN	.453	.181	.817	.243
HHST	.493	.102	.265	.000
PW561	.829	.851	.209	.002
PW561R	.798	.837	.257	.001
FTM333	.439	.534	.017	.246
FTM333R	.423	.546	.028	.131

Note: The p-values refer to Wald tests of the hypothesis that the coefficients on (z_t, z_{t-1}, z_{t-2}) in the regression of $R_{t+k} - P_{t+k|t}$ on a constant and z_t, z_{t-1}, z_{t-2}, are zero, where k refers to the forecast horizon (months). See the notes to table 2.4. All results were computed using the most recently available data through 1991:2.

Table 2.14 presents RMSEs and MAEs for the "univariate indexes" $\hat{y}_{it}$, which are the forecasts produced by the regression (22) estimated over 1962:1–1988:9. The results over 1988:10–1991:2 provide out-of-sample evidence on each candidate indicator when considered one at a time. The most striking feature of table 2.14 is that, even though the XLI had an MAE of 7.2 percent over the period 1990:5–1990:8, with few exceptions this large forecast error is typical of those for the univariate forecasts. For example, although the stock market declined in August 1990 in anticipation of the economic downturn, this one correct signal was insufficient to provide the XLI with improved forecasting power: its MAE over the final episode was 7.2 percent. Forecasts based on inventories and orders all had larger MAEs than the XLI, and forecasts based on retail sales had MAEs of well over 6 percent. Certain financial variables—a yield curve dummy that performed well in sample and two indicators in the XLI (the public-private spread and the slope of the yield curve)—performed particularly poorly, relative to the other variables. Only five of the indicators in table 2.14—housing starts, help wanted advertising, real M2, the quarterly ratio of the volume of commercial paper to

Table 2.14   **Performance of Single-Indicator Indexes: Six-Month-Ahead Forecast Horizon**

Series	RMSE Computed over:				MAE Computed over:			
	62:1–88:9	88:10–90:8	88:10–90:4	90:5–90:8	62:1–88:9	88:10–90:8	88:10–90:4	90:5–90:8
XLI	2.76	3.42	1.39	7.62	2.20	2.15	1.08	7.24
XLI2	3.80	2.61	1.57	5.24	2.83	1.93	1.35	4.67
Coincident Indicators								
IP	4.31	3.36	1.79	7.04	3.11	2.36	1.39	6.97
GMYXP8	4.27	3.46	1.87	7.24	3.11	2.55	1.57	7.17
MT82	4.27	3.45	1.47	7.63	3.08	2.27	1.17	7.51
LPMHUADJ	4.33	3.47	1.82	7.31	3.11	2.48	1.49	7.18
Leading Indicators in the XLI								
HSBP	3.81	2.40	1.23	5.09	2.87	1.62	.97	4.71
MDU82S	4.25	3.32	1.83	6.89	3.01	2.42	1.48	6.86
EXNWT2FS	4.17	4.15	1.71	9.23	3.08	2.71	1.41	8.89
LHNAPSS	4.22	3.48	1.93	7.21	3.01	2.59	1.64	7.11
FYGT10FS	4.06	3.58	2.07	7.31	2.97	2.67	1.73	7.18
CP6_GM6F	2.97	4.20	1.79	9.30	2.33	2.72	1.35	9.21
G10_GLF	3.68	3.49	1.15	7.99	2.81	2.06	.86	7.79
Leading Indicators in the XLI2								
LPHRM	4.33	3.36	1.59	7.28	3.12	2.26	1.22	7.20
IPXMCA	4.31	3.39	1.71	7.23	3.11	2.34	1.33	7.12
LHEL	3.95	2.59	1.60	5.14	2.83	1.78	1.12	4.90
IVPAC	4.09	4.16	2.10	8.87	3.02	2.93	1.69	8.81
Financial Indicators								
FSPCOMF	3.92	3.99	2.87	7.22	2.92	3.26	2.43	7.16
FM1D82	3.96	3.10	1.57	6.59	2.91	2.14	1.23	6.47
FM2D82	3.54	2.46	1.61	4.74	2.61	1.89	1.32	4.60
FMBASE	4.33	3.50	1.64	7.59	3.08	2.26	1.17	7.45
FCBCUCY	4.33	3.74	1.99	7.84	3.10	2.74	1.68	7.78
FYFFF	3.60	3.18	1.08	7.24	2.49	1.87	.77	7.12
BAA_G10F	4.14	3.60	2.04	7.41	2.94	2.61	1.63	7.29
YLD_DUMF	3.44	4.77	2.65	9.86	2.57	3.55	2.24	9.77
Employment Indicators								
LUINC	4.20	3.57	1.64	7.78	3.01	2.42	1.30	7.71
LHU5	4.27	3.78	1.95	8.00	3.04	2.71	1.61	7.95
LHELX	3.96	2.98	1.35	6.52	2.85	2.01	1.09	6.41

Table 2.14   (continued)

Series	RMSE Computed over:				MAE Computed over:			
	62:1–88:9	88:10–90:8	88:10–90:4	90:5–90:8	62:1–88:9	88:10–90:8	88:10–90:4	90:5–90:8
	Consumption and Retail Sales							
IPCD	4.29	3.79	1.73	8.28	3.08	2.55	1.38	8.11
GMCD82	4.29	3.25	1.61	6.97	3.06	2.22	1.24	6.88
RTR82	4.26	3.09	1.44	6.72	3.04	2.11	1.17	6.58
	Inventories and Orders							
MPCON8	4.34	3.56	1.81	7.58	3.09	2.50	1.46	7.48
MOCM82	4.29	4.00	2.08	8.44	3.05	2.80	1.63	8.32
MDO82	4.30	3.76	2.16	7.68	3.05	2.68	1.67	7.46
IVMT82	4.32	3.99	1.94	8.60	3.08	2.70	1.49	8.47
IVM1D8	4.22	4.28	2.46	8.73	3.10	3.18	2.02	8.68
IVM2D8	4.32	3.80	1.82	8.20	3.13	2.58	1.42	8.08
IVM3D8	4.35	3.62	1.83	7.72	3.12	2.50	1.42	7.64
	Additional Indicators							
DLBLNPAP	4.27	2.80	1.35	6.05	3.08	1.95	1.11	5.98
PMI	4.21	3.46	1.60	7.54	3.08	2.30	1.21	7.49
PMNO	4.05	3.03	1.70	6.24	2.94	2.29	1.48	6.17
HHSNTN	4.00	3.19	2.21	5.95	2.87	2.52	1.86	5.67
HHST	4.08	3.82	2.63	7.14	2.90	3.17	2.36	6.98
PW561	4.22	4.07	2.19	8.51	3.12	2.93	1.82	8.24
PW561R	4.26	4.02	2.19	8.37	3.13	2.84	1.75	8.01
FTM333	4.30	3.45	1.23	7.84	3.05	2.13	.95	7.72
FTM333R	4.28	3.59	1.38	8.06	3.05	2.27	1.07	7.94

Note: All results were computed using the data as revised through 1991:2. See the notes to table 2.12.

bank loans, and the Michigan consumer expectations index—had MAEs less than 6 percent.

Table 2.15 presents results for univariate forecasts of three-month growth, that is, indexes constructed with $c_{t+3|T} - c_{t|T}$ as the dependent variable in (22). The results are broadly similar to those in table 2.15. Each of the univariate indexes substantially misforecast three-month growth during the final episode, typically with forecast errors in the range of 5–7 percent (corresponding to one-quarter-ahead forecast errors of 3–4 percent in the units of annual GNP growth). The four indicators with the smallest MAEs at the six-month horizon have MAEs under 4 percent at the three-month horizon, as do the new orders index (PMNO) and consumer expectations.

In summary, these results suggest that, taken individually, only a handful of indicators would have been useful in predicting the 1990 downturn. During this contraction, consumer expectations, building permits, business expecta-

Table 2.15   **Performance of Single-Variable Indexes: Three-Month-Ahead Forecast Horizon**

Series	RMSE Computed over:				MAE Computed over:			
	62:1–88:9	88:10–90:8	88:10–90:4	90:5–90:8	62:1–88:9	88:10–90:8	88:10–90:4	90:5–90:8
				Coincident Indicators				
IP	4.53	3.06	1.96	4.93	3.28	2.29	1.41	4.67
GMYXP8	4.57	3.39	1.93	5.70	3.30	2.43	1.34	5.38
MT82	4.56	3.21	1.50	5.68	3.27	2.21	1.08	5.30
LPMHUADJ	4.55	3.37	1.84	5.74	3.29	2.40	1.33	5.30
				Leading Indicators in the XLI				
HSBP	4.15	2.53	1.56	4.13	3.07	1.87	1.19	3.72
MDU82S	4.48	3.25	2.01	5.31	3.20	2.28	1.32	4.90
EXNWT2FS	4.42	4.44	2.10	7.83	3.23	3.18	1.74	7.11
LHNAPSS	4.35	3.29	2.03	5.38	3.14	2.57	1.66	5.02
FYGT10FS	4.36	3.40	2.18	5.47	3.17	2.52	1.63	4.95
CP6_GM6F	3.66	4.35	1.51	8.00	2.80	2.98	1.24	7.73
G10_GLF	4.12	3.64	1.38	6.63	3.08	2.41	1.03	6.15
				Leading Indicators in the XLI2				
LPHRM	4.54	3.12	1.88	5.16	3.27	2.23	1.26	4.85
IPXMCA	4.55	3.08	1.86	5.08	3.28	2.23	1.29	4.77
LHEL	4.05	2.68	2.52	3.07	2.89	2.24	2.03	2.82
IVPAC	4.40	3.71	1.73	6.57	3.23	2.51	1.12	6.30
				Financial Indicators				
FSPCOMF	4.30	3.31	2.61	4.72	3.22	2.67	2.03	4.41
FM1D82	4.28	3.10	1.92	5.06	3.09	2.32	1.48	4.62
FM2D82	4.08	2.53	2.02	3.57	2.97	2.06	1.67	3.10
FMBASE	4.51	3.62	1.68	6.40	3.19	2.42	1.22	5.70
FCBCUCY	4.57	3.43	2.10	5.64	3.26	2.67	1.67	5.39
FYFFF	4.09	3.17	1.39	5.67	2.94	2.15	.98	5.30
BAA_G10F	4.25	3.19	2.13	5.05	3.04	2.47	1.69	4.60
YLD_DUMF	4.07	4.52	2.27	7.86	2.97	3.40	1.86	7.58
				Employment Indicators				
LUINC	4.46	3.18	1.83	5.34	3.21	2.28	1.29	4.99
LHU5	4.55	3.57	2.11	5.95	3.25	2.63	1.52	5.65
LHELX	4.29	2.95	1.84	4.81	3.10	2.22	1.40	4.44
				Consumption and Retail Sales				
IPCD	4.57	3.41	1.94	5.74	3.29	2.44	1.34	5.43
GMCD82	4.53	3.26	1.96	5.38	3.26	2.32	1.30	5.06
RTR82	4.53	3.15	1.82	5.27	3.27	2.22	1.25	4.86

Table 2.15 (continued)

	RMSE Computed over:				MAE Computed over:			
Series	62:1–88:9	88:10–90:8	88:10–90:4	90:5–90:8	62:1–88:9	88:10–90:8	88:10–90:4	90:5–90:8
				Inventories and Orders				
MPCON8	4.53	3.55	2.05	5.94	3.22	2.60	1.54	5.50
MOCM82	4.53	3.58	2.02	6.04	3.23	2.63	1.49	5.72
MDO82	4.50	3.64	2.33	5.87	3.17	2.59	1.62	5.24
IVMT82	4.55	3.81	2.37	6.21	3.25	2.78	1.70	5.72
IVM1D8	4.54	3.83	2.17	6.46	3.32	2.82	1.57	6.21
IVM2D8	4.57	3.53	1.93	6.02	3.34	2.56	1.40	5.71
IVM3D8	4.56	3.54	2.04	5.94	3.28	2.57	1.43	5.64
				Additional Indicators				
DLBLNPAP	4.51	2.80	1.71	4.60	3.26	2.17	1.33	4.44
PMI	4.42	3.04	1.84	5.01	3.22	2.30	1.40	4.75
PMNO	4.28	2.68	1.97	4.02	3.08	2.13	1.56	3.70
HHSNTN	4.27	2.32	2.01	3.00	3.10	1.90	1.72	2.41
HHST	4.34	2.75	2.21	3.86	3.12	2.21	1.74	3.48
PW561	4.56	3.94	2.04	6.82	3.29	2.77	1.60	5.95
PW561R	4.58	4.10	2.08	7.13	3.31	2.84	1.60	6.23
FTM333	4.58	2.88	1.61	4.89	3.29	2.05	1.15	4.50
FTM333R	4.57	3.04	1.67	5.18	3.29	2.19	1.20	4.88

Note: All results were computed using the data as revised through 1991:2. See the notes to table 2.12.

tions, help wanted advertising, and oil prices moved in advance of overall economic activity. With the exception of stock prices, indicators of financial market conditions—the slope of the Treasury yield curve, the public-private spreads, exchange rates, and interest rates—exhibited different patterns than they did during the recessions in the 1970s and 1980s. One interpretation of these observations is that, at least since 1969, recessions have been associated with contractionary monetary policy; this was captured by the interest rate indicators, accounting for their strong in-sample performance. The downturn of 1990, however, occurred in the face of monetary policy that, if not expansionary, was far less contractionary than it had been during the recessions of the 1970s and early 1980s. Instead, the contraction was associated with sharp drops in consumer expectations, business expectations, and uncertainty over a possible war in the Gulf.

2.4.5 Construction of Alternative Indexes

The results of the previous section suggest that the key problem in model specification and forecasting over this period was the ability to select those few leading indicators that forecast the 1990 downturn. This indicator selection problem is studied empirically here by constructing composite indexes that forecast six-month growth in the XCI from two shortened lists of the series in tables 2.14 and 2.15. The first list consists of the eleven leading indicators in the XLI and the XLI2, augmented by stock prices, the new orders index, consumer expectations, and oil prices. These four variables were intentionally chosen because of their good performance in the second episode. The second list eliminates from the first exchange rates and all interest rate indicators (EXNWT2FS, G10-G1F, FYGT10FS, CP6-GM6F), which are replaced by measures of sales, orders, new unemployment insurance claims, and manufacturing and trade inventories (RTR82, MPCON8, LUINC, IVMT82).[10]

For each list, all possible indexes of the form (21) and (22) were constructed, subject only to the restriction that the indexes included no more than seven leading indicators. The weights $\{\alpha_j\}$ for each index were estimated by OLS. For each list, this produced 16,383 indexes, which were then ranked by their Schwarz information criterion (evaluated over 1962:1–1988:9), where the number of parameters equaled the number of univariate indexes included in the composite trial indicator. All parameters were estimated over 1962:1–1988:9 (with earlier observations for initial lags) using the most recently available revised data.

The performance of the top fifteen indexes based on the financial list is summarized in panel A of table 2.16. (The individual indexes $\hat{y}_{it}$ were constructed as in table 2.14.) Not surprisingly, the in-sample RMSEs of these fifteen indexes are almost identical and slightly surpass that of the XLI. The out-of-sample RMSEs vary and are somewhat better than the XLI's, reflecting improvements made by the additional included variables—in particular, stock prices, the purchasing managers' index, and help wanted advertising. However, all but one of these top fifteen indexes still have out-of-sample RMSEs exceeding 6 percent, well above the RMSEs achieved by some of the individual indicators in table 2.14.

Indexes constructed using the fifteen non–interest rate and non–exchange rate indicators are examined in panel B of table 2.16. Although the in-sample RMSEs are substantially worse than in panel A (3.1 percent rather than 2.6 percent), the RMSEs in the 1990 episode are cut almost in half. All indexes have out-of-sample RMSEs near—in one case, less than—their in-sample RMSE. The variables that appear in most of the indexes are housing starts, weekly employee hours, help wanted advertising, stock prices, and, to a lesser extent, consumer sentiment. The price of oil appears in only one of these top fifteen indexes, and, significantly, this index exhibits out-of-sample performance typical of the indexes that exclude oil prices.

10. The results in tables 2.14 and 2.15 suggest that real money growth is another plausible indicator to be included. However, we find persuasive Friedman and Kuttner's (in press) evidence that the relation between real money growth and output has been unstable historically—particularly over the 1980s—and therefore excluded monetary aggregates as candidate indicators from these lists.

Table 2.16   Performance of Alternative Composite Indexes: Six-Month Ahead Forecast Horizon

Rank	Included Leading Indicators	RMSE Computed over:				MAE Computed over:			
		62:1–88:9	88:10–90:8	88:10–90:4	90:5–90:8	62:1–88:9	88:10–90:8	88:10–90:4	90:5–90:8
	XLI	2.76	3.42	1.39	7.62	2.20	2.15	1.08	7.24
	XLI2	3.80	2.61	1.57	5.24	2.83	1.93	1.35	4.67
	A. List Including XLI, XLI2, and Selected Alternative Indicators								
1	HSBP, CP6-GM6F, G10-G1F, LPHRM, PMNO, HHSNTN, PW561	2.57	3.04	1.49	6.52	2.07	1.95	.99	6.49
2	HSBP, CP6-GM6F, LPHRM, LHEL, PMNO, HHSNTN, PW561	2.58	2.78	1.39	5.94	2.04	1.86	1.01	5.89
3	HSBP, CP6-GM6F, LPHRM, FSPCOMF, PMNO, HHSNTN, PW561	2.58	3.00	1.52	6.37	2.04	2.02	1.12	6.34
4	HSBP, CP6-GM6F, G10-G1F, LPHRM, LHEL, PMNO, PW561	2.58	3.04	1.30	6.72	2.05	1.93	.94	6.64
5	HSBP, CP6-GM6F, G10-G1F, LPHRM, FSPCOMF, PMNO, PW561	2.59	3.25	1.38	7.20	2.06	2.01	.92	7.16
6	HSBP, CP6-GM6F, G10-G1F, LPHRM, LHEL, FSPCOMF, PMNO	2.59	3.13	1.14	7.09	2.05	1.95	.89	6.99
7	HSBP, FYGT10FS, CP6-GM6F, LPHRM, PMNO, HHSNTN, PW561	2.59	2.97	1.53	6.30	2.06	2.02	1.13	6.26
8	HSBP, CP6-GM6F, G10-G1F, LPHRM, LHEL, PMNO, HHSNTN	2.59	3.04	1.28	6.74	2.06	2.01	1.04	6.63

(continued)

Table 2.16 (continued)

Rank	Included Leading Indicators	RMSE Computed over:				MAE Computed over:			
		62:1–88:9	88:10–90:8	88:10–90:4	90:5–90:8	62:1–88:9	88:10–90:8	88:10–90:4	90:5–90:8
9	HSBP, CP6–GM6F, LPHRM, IVPAC, PMNO, HHSNTN, PW561	2.60	2.93	1.50	6.22	2.06	1.91	1.02	6.18
10	HSBP, MDU82S, CP6–GM6F, LPHRM, PMNO, HHSNTN, PW561	2.60	2.97	1.53	6.28	2.06	1.96	1.06	6.25
11	HSBP, EXNWT2FS, CP6–GM6F, LPHRM, PMNO, HHSNTN, PW561	2.60	2.98	1.52	6.34	2.06	1.96	1.05	6.30
12	HSBP, CP6–GM6F, LPHRM, IPXMCA, PMNO, HHSNTN, PW561	2.60	2.97	1.52	6.29	2.06	1.95	1.05	6.26
13	HSBP, LHNAPSS, CP6–GM6F, LPHRM, PMNO, HHSNTN, PW561	2.60	2.97	1.52	6.29	2.06	1.95	1.05	6.26
14	HSBP, CP6–GM6F, G10–G1F, LPHRM, FSPCOMF, PMNO, HHSNTN	2.60	3.26	1.36	7.24	2.07	2.06	.99	7.18
15	HSBP, CP6–GM6F, LPHRM, LHEL, FSPCOMF, PMNO, HHSNTN	2.60	2.99	1.31	6.57	2.05	2.00	1.05	6.49
B. List Excluding Exchange Rates and All Interest Rate Indicators									
1	HSBP, LPHRM, LHEL, IVPAC, FSPCOMF, PMNO, HHSNTN	3.14	2.43	1.75	4.41	2.38	1.98	1.50	4.27
2	HSBP, LPHRM, LHEL, IVPAC, RTR82, PMNO, HHSNTN	3.14	2.45	1.72	4.52	2.40	1.99	1.49	4.37
3	HSBP, LPHRM, LEHL, IVPAC, MPCON8, PMNO, HHSNTN	3.15	2.17	1.52	4.02	2.39	1.74	1.30	3.86

4	HSBP, LPHRM, LHEL, IVPAC, IVMT82, PMNO, HHSNTN	3.15	2.11	1.60	3.69	2.40	1.68	1.29	3.53
5	HSBP, LPHRM, LHEL, FSPCOMF, MPCON8, PMNO, HHSNTN	3.17	2.00	1.62	3.25	2.41	1.63	1.33	3.09
6	HSBP, LPHRM, LHEL, IVPAC, LUINC, PMNO, HHSNTN	3.17	2.33	1.66	4.26	2.40	1.85	1.38	4.07
7	HSBP, MDU82S, LPHRM, LHEL, IVPAC, PMNO, HHSNTN	3.18	2.36	1.59	4.49	2.41	1.83	1.32	4.28
8	HSBP, LPHRM, LHEL, IVPAC, PMNO, HHSNTN, PW561	3.18	2.26	1.57	4.22	2.40	1.79	1.32	4.04
9	HSBP, LHNAPSS, LPHRM, LHEL, IVPAC, PMNO, HHSNTN	3.18	2.32	1.59	4.34	2.41	1.83	1.34	4.15
10	HSBP, LPHRM, IPXMCA, LHEL, IVPAC, PMNO, HHSNTN	3.18	2.30	1.58	4.31	2.41	1.82	1.34	4.12
11	HSBP, LPHRM, LHEL, FSPCOMF, RTR82, PMNO, HHSNTN	3.19	2.16	1.70	3.61	2.42	1.73	1.38	3.44
12	HSBP, LPHRM, LHEL, FSPCOMF, IVMT82, PMNO, HHSNTN	3.19	2.02	1.70	3.13	2.42	1.70	1.43	2.97
13	HSBP, LPHRM, LHEL, IVPAC, FSPCOMF, MPCON8, HHSNTN	3.20	2.60	2.02	4.42	2.46	2.19	1.77	4.18
14	HSBP, LPHRM, IPXMCA, LHEL, FSPCOMF, PMNO, HHSNTN	3.20	2.12	1.68	3.53	2.41	1.72	1.38	3.35
15	HSBP, LPHRM, LHEL, IVPAC, FSPCOMF, IVMT82, HHSNTN	3.20	2.54	2.05	4.14	2.46	2.12	1.75	3.90

Note: The indexes were selected form all possible indexes of the form (21) and (22) that include at most 7 indicators, selected from lists of 15 indicators. The lists are as follows: panel A: HSBP, MDU82S, EXNWT2FS, LHNAPSS, FYGT10FS, CP6_GM6F, G10_G1F, LPHRM, IPXMCA, LHEL, IVPAC, FSPCOMF, PMNO, HHSNTN, PW561; panel B: HSBP, MDU82S, LHNAPSS, LPHRM, IPXMCA, LHEL, IVPAC, FSPCOMF, LUINC, RTR82, MPCON8, IVMT82, PMNO, HHSNTN, PW561. All results were computed using the data as revised through 1991:2. See the notes to table 2.12.

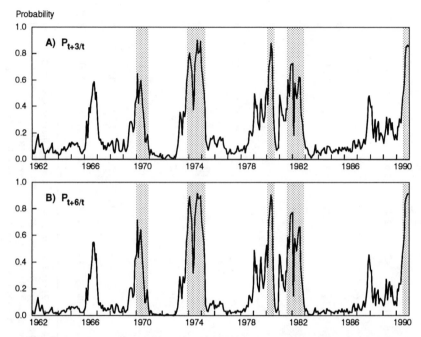

Fig. 2.6   Recession probabilities based on alternative nonfinancial indicators

Note: The dates on the horizontal axes denote t, the date through which the data are available for computing $P_{t+k|t}$. The recession probabilities were computed using the model of sec. 2.1, with the leading indicators: HSBP, LPHRM, LHEL, IVPAC, FSPCOMF, PMNO, HHSNTN. The series are based on data revised through 1991:2. The shaded areas represent NBER data recessions.

As a final exercise, the XLI model of section 2.1 was reestimated, replacing the leading indicators in panel B of table 2.1 with the seven indicators in the top-ranking index from the nonfinancial list (the first row in panel B, table 2.16). (In the notation of sec. 2.1, θ was reestimated, but μ was not.) The resulting recession probabilities $P_{t+k|t}$ are plotted for selected horizons in figure 2.6. The results are striking: the six-month-ahead recession probabilities $P_{t+6|t}$ computed with these indicators over July–October are, respectively, 84, 89, 92, and 91 percent. Evidently, had the short list of fifteen indicators examined in panel B been used over the summer of 1990 to produce recession forecasts, they would have predicted a recession starting in the fall of 1990. At the same time, it must be emphasized that, had they been used during the previous historical recessions, this set of indicators would have done substantially worse than those in the XRI: the index would have provided scant advance indication of recessions in 1969 and 1974 and only ambiguous signals in 1979 and 1981.

The composite indexes in this section put nonzero weight on only a few of the indicators and no weight on most. A natural alternative would be to construct a broadly based index that places weight on many or all of the indicators in table 2.13. One approach, analogous to the method used by the DOC to construct its index, would be to put equal weight on all the included indicators; another, advocated by Sims (1989), would be to impose strong prior restrictions on the weights so that, even though many coefficients would be estimated, these coefficients effectively would be a function of a much smaller number of coefficients that could be estimated more precisely.

Some initial calculations suggest that such broadly based indexes would also have performed poorly in the 1990 episode. For example, a six-month-ahead index of the form (21) and (22), constructed using the forty-one individual leading indicators in table 2.14 with equal weights on each indicator ($\alpha_i = 1/41$), results in an in-sample RMSE of 3.9 percent and an out-of-sample RMSE of 7.4 percent; neither represents a noticeable improvement over a constant forecast. When the weights $\{\sigma_i\}$ are estimated by OLS so that only forty-one parameters are estimated (in addition to the estimated lag coefficients in [22]), the in-sample RMSE drops to a low 2.2 percent, but the out-of-sample RMSE remains very large, 7.0 percent. These broadly based indicators do not exploit correlations across the individual leading indicators, so there might be room for improvement relative to these two crude indexes. Still, the poor performance of the preponderance of individual indicators in this episode, documented in tables 2.14 and 2.15, suggests that other more sophisticated broadly based indexes would also have performed poorly in this episode.

2.5 Discussion and Conclusions

The foregoing analysis has focused on the empirical performance of one particular forecasting tool—the XLI/XRI model—but also has implications that apply more generally to forecasting exercises based on a broad set of leading indicators. Focusing initially on the XRI and the XLI, we draw six conclusions. First, there is only weak evidence for nonlinearities in the data not captured in the linear model sketched in section 2.1. The main exception is the usefulness of the estimated duration of a downturn in predicting when that downturn will end. This duration dependence, however, appears to be restricted to downturns and is significant only at very short forecasting horizons.

Second, forecasts through September 1990 based on the XLI/XRI model performed quite well. For example, the absolute three-month-ahead forecast error in June 1990 was only 0.4 percent at an annual rate. However, the model failed to forecast the precipitous declines that started in October.

Third, there is no compelling evidence that the recession definition or the algorithm for computing recession probabilities was misspecified. Rather, the failure of the model in the fall of 1990 can be attributed to large forecast errors in the conditional means.

Fourth, the forecast errors in the conditional means do not appear to be the result of overparameterization or the imprecise estimation of too many parameters, given the list of included indicators. A key piece of evidence for this conclusion is that simple composite indexes with the same variables as the XLI but fewer parameters and a different, simpler structure exhibit performance comparable to that of the XLI, both in and out of sample. Moreover, these simple alternative indexes that use the same set of indicators make forecast errors as large as or larger than those made by the XLI model during the fall of 1990.

Fifth, the short-horizon recession probabilities produced by the model performed relatively well during this episode. In October, the first month in which there were large declines in the coincident indicators, $P_{t|t}$ was 28 percent; by November, it was 80 percent. Thus, the index can claim the modest success of "forecasting" that the economy was already in a recession, once the downturn had begun in earnest.

Sixth, the key source of difficulty was with the choice of indicators included in the model. The financial variables in the XRI and the XLI behaved quite differently over the summer of 1990 than they had during the preceding recessions in 1973, 1980, and 1981. Prior to those earlier recessions, the Treasury-bill yield curve was sharply inverted, while in June–September 1990 it sloped upward. The corporate paper–Treasury-bill spread in June 1990 was one-third its average value in the month before the previous three recessions. Although these indicators failed to predict the 1990 recession, a few (but not many) alternative indicators would have provided advanced warning had they been incorporated into the XRI. The strongest evidence of this is the performance of the alternative seven-indicator index, constructed from the list of fifteen indicators that excluded the poorly performing interest rate and exchange rate indicators and included selected indicators that, as it turned out, performed well, such as consumer expectations. Had this set of indicators been used as the basis of the XRI, the index would have registered much larger recession probabilities and would have reduced the out-of-sample RMSE by almost half.

These results also suggest some more general conclusions and areas for future research. While the results of sections 2.4.4 and 2.4.5 indicate that the downturn could have been forecast—in the sense that there were composite indexes that, had they been constructed, would have performed well during the summer and fall of 1990—the decisions on which variables to include and which to omit were made with the benefit of hindsight. The challenging, unsolved—and hardly new—problem that this underscores is developing an appropriate methodology for the identification and selection of leading indicators.

Appendix
Variable Definitions

All data were obtained from Citibase, with the exception of those denoted "(AC)," which were calculated by the authors. A single asterisk (*) indicates that log first-differences of the variable were used, a double asterisk (**) that first-differences of the variable were used.

Coincident Indicators

IP*
  Industrial production: total index (1977 = 100; seasonally adjusted).
GMYXP8*
  Personal income: total less transfer payments, 1982$ ($billion, seasonally adjusted at an annual rate).
MT82*
  Manufacturing and trade sales: total, 1982$ ($million, seasonally adjusted).
LPMHUADJ (AC)*
  Citibase series LPMHU (employee-hours in nonagricultural establishments [billion hours, seasonally adjusted at an annual rate]), adjusted for short sampling weeks in 1970:9, 1974:4, 1979:4, 1981:9, and 1982:1. If the sampling week was short in month t, the adjusted series was computed as $\frac{1}{2}$ (LPMHU$_{t+1}$ + LPMHU$_{t-1}$).

Leading Indicators in the XLI

HSBP
  Housing authorized: index of new private housing units (1967 = 100; seasonally adjusted).
MDU82S (AC)
  Manufacturers' unfilled orders: durable goods industries, total ($million, seasonally adjusted) (MDU), deflated by the producer price index: durable manufacturing goods (not seasonally adjusted) (PWDMD): log first-difference, smoothed. PWDMD was seasonally adjusted prior to deflating by removing average monthly growth rates.
EXNWT2FS (AC)
  EXNWT2 is the nominal weighted exchange rate between the United States and France, Italy, Japan, the United Kingdom, and West Germany, constructed using shares of total real imports as weights. EXNWT2FS is the log first-difference, smoothed, led by one month.
LHNAPSS (AC)
  LHNAPS is persons at work: part time for economic reasons—slack work, nonagricultural industries (thousands, seasonally adjusted). LHNAPSS is the log first-difference, smoothed.

FYGT10FS (AC)

FYGT10 is the interest rate: U.S. Treasury constant maturities, 10 year (% per annum, not seasonally adjusted). FYGT10FS is the first-difference, smoothed, led by one month.

CP6_GM6F (AC)

FYCP − FYGM6, led by one month, where FYCP is the interest rate: commercial paper, 6 month (% per annum, not seasonally adjusted), and FYGM6 is the interest rate: U.S. Treasury bills, secondary market, 6 month (% per annum, not seasonally adjusted).

G10_G1F (AC)

FYGT10 − FYGT1, led by one month, where FYGT10 is the interest rate: U.S. Treasury constant maturities, 10 year (% per annum, not seasonally adjusted), and FYGT1 is the interest rate: U.S. Treasury constant maturities, 1 year (% per annum, not seasonally adjusted).

Leading Indicators in the XLI 2

LPHRM

Average weekly hours of production workers: manufacturing (seasonally adjusted).

IPXMCA**

Capacity utilization rate: manufacturing total (% of capacity, seasonally adjusted).

LHEL*

Index of help wanted advertising in newspapers (1967 = 100; seasonally adjusted).

IVPAC

Vendor performance: % of companies reporting slower deliveries (% not seasonally adjusted).

Financial Variables

FSPCOMF (AC)*

S&P'S common stock price index: composite (1941–43 = 10), led by one month.

FM1D82*

Money stock: M1 in 1982$ ($billion, seasonally adjusted).

FM2D82*

Money stock: M2 in 1982$ ($billion, seasonally adjusted).

FMBASE*

Monetary base, adjusted for reserve requirement changes (Federal Reserve Bank of St. Louis) ($billion, seasonally adjusted).

CCI30M*

Consumer installment loans: delinquency rate, 30 days and over (% seasonally adjusted).

FCBCUCY (AC)

Change in business and consumer credit outstanding (%, seasonally adjusted at an annual rate) (FCBCUC) minus the annual percentage growth in total nominal person income (GMPY).

FYFFF

Interest rate: Federal funds (effective) (% per annum, not seasonally adjusted), led by one month.

BAA_G10F (AC)

FYBAAC − FYGT10, led by one month, where FYBAAC is the bond yield: Moody's Baa Corporate (% per annum), and FYGT10 is the interest rate: U.S. Treasury constant maturities, 10 year (% per annum, not seasonally adjusted).

YLD_DUMF (AC)

Inverted yield curve dummy, led by one month. Dummy variable that takes on a value of 1 when G10_G1 is negative.

Employment Variables

LUINC*

Average weekly initial claims, state unemployment insurance, excluding Puerto Rico (thousands, seasonally adjusted).

LHU5*

Unempoyment by duration: persons unemployed less than 5 weeks (thousands, seasonally adjusted).

LHELX

Employment: ratio; help wanted ads: no. unemployed current labor force.

Sales and Consumption Variables

IPCD*

Industrial production: durable consumer goods (1977 = 100; seasonally adjusted).

GMCD82*

Personal consumption expenditures: durable goods, 1982$.

RTR82*

Retail sales: total, 1982$ ($million, seasonally adjusted).

Inventories and Orders

MPCON8*

Contracts and orders for plant and equipment in 1982$ ($billion, seasonally adjusted).

MOCM82*

Manufacturing new orders: consumer goods and material, 1982$ ($billion, seasonally adjusted).

MDO82*

Manufacturing new orders: durable goods industries, 1982$ ($billion, seasonally adjusted).

IVMT82*

Manufacturing and trade inventories: total, 1982$ ($billion, seasonally adjusted).

IVM1D8 (AC)

Log first-difference of IVM1: real manufacturing inventories, materials and supplies: all manufacturing industries (materials and supplies inventories), deflated by the total inventories price deflator, IVMT/IVMT82, where IVMT is total nominal manufacturing inventories. Growth rate in 1982:1 is average of growth rates for 1981:12 and 1982:2 to adjust for accounting change in 1982:1.

IVM2D8 (AC)

Log first-difference of IVM2: real manufacturing and trade inventories: work in process, all manufacturing industries (seasonally adjusted), (work in progress inventories), deflated by the total inventories price deflator, IVMT/IVMT82, where IVMT is total nominal manufacturing inventories. Growth rate in 1982:1 is average of growth rates for 1981:12 and 1982:2 to adjust for accounting change in 1982:1.

IVM3D8 (AC)

Log first-difference of IVM3: real manufacturing inventories: finished goods, all manufacturing industries (finished goods inventories), deflated by the total inventories price deflator, IVMT/IVMT82, where IVMT is total nominal manufacturing inventories. Growth rate in 1982:1 is average of growth rates of 1981:12 and 1982:2 to adjust for accounting change in 1982:1.

Additional Indicators

DLBLNPAP (AC)

Log first-difference of the ratio of the volume of bank loans to the volume of commercial paper, where bank loans are commercial bank loans to the nonfarm corporate business sector and the nonfarm corporate sector, excluding mortgages and bankers' acceptances. The original series is quarterly and was distributed to a monthly basis as follows: the growth rate from QI to QII (say) was used as the data for June, July, and August (because growth from QII to QIII includes lending through September). *Source:* Federal Reserve Board, quarterly flow-of-funds data bank (kindly provided by A. Kashyap, J. Stein, and D. Wilcox).

PMI

Purchasing managers' index (seasonally adjusted).

PMNO

National Association of Purchasing Managers new orders index (%).

HHSNTN

University of Michigan index of consumer expectations.

HHST (AC)

HHSENT interpolated with HHSNTR: 1953–1977:4, HHSENT, University of Michigan index of consumer sentiment, (1966:I = 100; not seasonally adjusted); 1978:1–1990:12, HHSNTR, University of Michigan index of consumer sentiment (February 1966 = 100; not seasonally adjusted).

PW561*

Producer price index: crude petroleum (1982 = 100; not seasonally adjusted).

PW561R (AC)*

PW561/PW, where PW = producer price index: all commodities (1982 = 100; not seasonally adjusted).

FTM333

U.S. merchandise imports: petroleum and petroleum products ($million, seasonally adjusted).

FTM333R

FTM333/PW, where PW = producer price index: all commodities (1982 = 100; not seasonally adjusted).

Aggregate Indexes

XLI (AC)

NBER experimental index of leading indicators.

MTREC (AC)

Expected length of current recession (construction is described in the text).

MTEXP (AC)

Expected length of current expansion (construction is described in the text).

MTTOT (AC)

$(P_{t|t}) \times$ (MTREC) $+ (1 - P_{t|t}) \times$ (MTEXP) (construction is described in the text).

DLEAD*

U.S. Department of Commerce composite index of 11 leading indicators (1982 = 100; seasonally adjusted).

DL3D (AC)

Dummy variable taking on the value of 1 at time t if 3 consecutive downturns of DLEAD have occurred. That is, DL3D$(t) = 1$ if ΔDLEAD$(t) < 0$, ΔDLEAD$(t - 1) < 0$, and ΔDLEAD$(t - 2) < 0$, and DL3D $(t) = 0$ otherwise.

DL3U (AC)

Dummy variable taking on the value of 1 at time t if 3 consecutive upturns of DLEAD have occurred. That is, DL3U$(t) = 1$ if ΔDLEAD$(t) > 0$, ΔDLEAD$(t - 1) > 0$, and ΔDLEAD$(t - 2) > 0$, and DL3U$(t) = 0$ otherwise.

IP3D (AC)

Dummy variable taking on the value of 1 at time t if 3 consecutive downturns of IP have occurred. That is, IP3D$(t) = 1$ if ΔIP$(t) < 0$, ΔIP$(t - 1) < 0$, and ΔIP$(t - 2) < 0$, and IP3D$(t) = 0$ otherwise.

IP3U (AC)

Dummy variable taking on the value of 1 at time t if 3 consecutive upturns of IP have occurred. That is, IP3U(t) = 1 if ΔIP(t) < 0, ΔIP($t - 1$) < 0, and ΔIP($t - 2$) < 0, and IP3D(t) = 0 otherwise.

References

Auerbach, A. J. 1982. The index of leading indicators: "Measurement without theory," thirty-five years later. *Review of Economics and Statistics* 64 (4): 589–95.

Burns, A. F., and W. C. Mitchell. 1946. *Measuring business cycles.* New York: NBER.

Friedman, B. M., and K. N. Kuttner. In press. Another look at the evidence on money-income causality. *Journal of Econometrics.*

Geweke, J. 1977. The dynamic factor analysis of economic time series. In *Latent variables in socio-economic models,* ed. D. J. Aigner and A. S. Goldberger. Amsterdam: North-Holland.

Hamilton, J. D. 1989. A new approach to the economic analysis of nonstationary time series and the business cycle. *Econometrica* 57:357–84.

Harvey, A. C., R. Blake, M. Desai, and C. McKenzie. 1981. Data revisions. In *Applied time series analysis of economic data,* ed. A. Zellner. Economic Research Report no. ER-5. Washington, D.C.: U.S. Department of Commerce.

Hymans, S. 1973. On the use of leading indicators to predict cyclical turning points. *Brookings Papers on Economic Activity* (2), 339–84.

Kling, J. L. 1987. Predicting the turning points of business and economic time series. *Journal of Business* 60, (2): 201–38.

Mankiw, N. G., D. Runkle, and M. D. Shapiro. 1984. Are preliminary announcements of the money supply rational forecasts? *Journal of Monetary economics* 14:15–27.

Mankiw, N. G., and M. D. Shapiro. 1986. News of noise analysis of GNP revisions. *Survey of Current Business* 66 (May): 20–25.

Mitchell, W. C., and A. F. Burns. [1938] 1961. Statistical indicators of cyclical revivals. Reprinted in *Business cycle indicators,* ed. G. H. Moore. Princeton, N.J.: Princeton University Press.

Neftci, S. N. 1982. Optimal prediction of cyclical downturns. *Journal of Economic Dynamics and Control* 4:225–41.

Sargent, T. J., and C. A. Sims. 1977. Business cycle modeling without pretending to have too much *a priori* economic theory. In *New methods in business cycle research,* ed. C. Sims. Minneapolis: Federal Reserve Bank of Minneapolis.

Sims, C. A. 1989. Comment on "New indexes of leading and coincident economic indicators." *NBER Macroeconomics Annual,* 394–97.

Singleton, K. 1980. A latent time series model of the cyclical behavior of interest rates. *International Economic Review* 21 (3): 559–75.

Stekler, H. O., and M. Schepsman. 1973. Forecasting with an index of leading series. *Journal of the American Statistical Association* 68 (342): 291–96.

Stock, J. H., and M. W. Watson. 1988. A new approach to the leading economic indicators. Harvard University, Kennedy School of Government. Typescript.

———. 1989. New indexes of leading and coincident economic indicators. *NBER Macroeconomics Annual,* 351–94.

———. 1991. A probability model of the coincident economic indicators. In *Leading economic indicators: New approaches and forecasting records,* ed. K. Lahiri and G. H. Moore. New York: Cambridge University Press.

Vaccara, B. N., and V. Zarnowitz. 1978. Forecasting with the index of leading indicators. Working Paper no. 244. Cambridge, Mass.: NBER.

Wecker, W. E. 1979. Predicting the turning points of a time series. *Journal of Business* 52 (1): 35–50.

Zarnowitz, V., and C. Boschan. 1975a. Cyclical indicators: An evaluation and new leading indexes. *Business Conditions Digest* (May), v–xxiv.

———. 1975b. New composite indexes of coincident and lagging indicators. *Business Conditions Digest* (November), v–xxii.

Zarnowitz, V., and G. H. Moore. 1982. Sequential signals of recession and recovery. *Journal of Business* 55 (1): 57–85.

Zellner, A., C. Hong, and G. M. Gulati. 1987. Turning points in economic time series, loss structures and Bayesian forecasting. University of Chicago, Graduate School of Business. Typescript.

Comment   Kenneth F. Wallis

Notable among recent work on cyclical indicators is the attempt by James H. Stock and Mark W. Watson (henceforth S–W) to recast the traditional approach in a suitable form for the application of the techniques of modern time-series econometrics. Two previous papers (Stock and Watson 1989, 1991) describe new indexes of coincident and leading indicators, which are based on the dynamic single-index model of Sargent and Sims (1977), and a new recession index, which is an estimate of the probability that the economy will be in recession in six months' time, where a recession is defined as a particular pattern of movements in the unobserved single index or "state of the economy." The publication of probability forecasts in economics is itself a considerable innovation. In the present paper, S–W provide a detailed account of the construction of the recession index and of its forecasting performance both in and out of sample; in the light of its forecast failure in late 1990, they then return to the question of the selection of variables used as indicators in the model.

The evaluation of economic forecasts has a large literature, to which important early contributions came from an NBER project directed by Victor Zarnowitz in the late 1960s. This literature scarcely considers probability forecasts, however, since these have scarcely featured in economics. Rather, the literature on the theory and practice of probability forecasting is largely to be found in the meteorological journals, stimulated by the inclusion of a statement of the probability of precipitation in U.S. weather forecasts over a considerable period of years (for a review, see Dawid 1986). A simple summary indicator of forecast performance is a *reliability diagram* or *calibration curve,*

Kenneth F. Wallis is professor of econometrics at the University of Warwick and director of the ESRC Macroeconomic Modelling Bureau.

in which the observed relative frequency of the event is calculated over subsets of occasions for which the forecast probability was at, or close to, preassigned values and then plotted against those forecast probability values: in the absence of sampling fluctuations, a diagonal line indicates perfect reliability or that the forecaster was "well calibrated" (Dawid 1982). Of course, large samples are always a help, and daily rainfall forecasts are thirty times more frequent than monthly economic forecasts; nevertheless, we can make a start by plotting $\bar{R}$ against $\bar{P}$ within the columns of panel B of S–W's table 2.3. This dramatically illustrates the lack of complete-sample reliability of the recession probability forecasts, which were in general too high. While the criterion of perfect reliability or complete calibration is not by itself a sufficient condition for forecasts to be good—it would be achieved in the present case by a forecaster whose one-month-ahead recession probability forecast was always equal to 0.146—it has often been taken to be a minimum desirable property.

Another useful diagrammatic presentation of probability forecasts is found in an exception to the general comment above about the lack of an economics literature, namely, the contribution to the early NBER project by Fels and Hinshaw (1968). For each turning point during 1948–61, they are concerned with how well it was first forecast and then, ex post, recognized, so for a number of different forecasters they plot $P_{\tau|t}$ for fixed τ, the turning-point date, against t, the date of the forecast, in S–W's notation. (Mention of Fels and Hinshaw is not intended to detract from the originality of S–W's probability forecasts: Fels and Hinshaw's analysis was based on their own subjective assessment of the odds on a turning point implicit in the forecasters' language.) In the present case, this plot amounts to reading the entries in table 2.6 along a diagonal moving upward to the right, setting τ at October 1990 if that is eventually declared to be the turning point. Corresponding plots for previous turning points can be constructed from data shown in the various panels of figure 2.1: although these are within sample, the resulting comparison dramatically illustrates the relative forecast failure of the recession index in the most recent episode.

Attention then turns to the choice of indicator variables to include in the model and the appropriateness of the model itself. The first of these has already been the subject of comment by Sims (1989) and Zarnowitz and Braun (1989), who are now to some extent entitled to say we told you so. Sims questioned the heavy dependence of the new leading index on variables, three out of seven, that are functions of interest rates, while, in comparing the S–W and Department of Commerce (DOC) indexes, Zarnowitz and Braun questioned the inclusion of the nominal exchange rate and the exclusion of the DOC index's vendor performance variable. This criticism is by and large validated by S–W's evidence from the recent past: whereas the financial variables did not perform well, forecasts of the recession could have been improved by a selection of the more traditional indicators, together with a consumer sentiment variable that was added to the DOC set in January 1989. Why, then, were these variables not selected for inclusion in the original model?

The dynamic single-index model is a linear time-invariant model, and the selection and weighting of leading indicator variables is likewise based on linear regression methods. Whereas Sims (1989) expresses disappointment at the use of a model without time-varying coefficients, my reservation concerns its linearity. These are not unrelated, of course, since a linear approximation to a nonlinear model in general has time-varying or, more precisely, state-dependent coefficients. In a forecasting context, however, some model of the time variation is necessary, which requires either a return to the nonlinear model or, if this is unknown, the use of one of the statistical models of time-varying coefficients, which typically rest on underlying constant parameters. In the context of the statistical modeling of the business cycle, features such as its asymmetry are well established, as is the fact that these cannot be adequately accommodated by linear constant-parameter models. See, for example, Hamilton (1989), Pfann (1991), and earlier references given by these authors, whose own work illustrates the distinction drawn by S–W (Stock and Watson 1989, 356–57) between the "intrinsic" and the "extrinsic" views of cycles. In the former view, expansions and recessions are regarded as periods of distinctly different economic behavior, defined by intrinsic shifts in the data-generating process, whereas, in the latter view, expansions and recessions are extrinsic patterns that result from the adaptation of a stable structure to random shocks. Thus, Hamilton (1989) uses a Markov switching regression to characterize changes in the parameters of a linear autoregressive process, whereas Pfann (1991) uses a nonlinear autoregression with constant coefficients to capture asymmetries. Here, as in other areas of economics, competing views need to be tested against one another and, no doubt, against other models yet to be developed. Extension is also required from the univariate to the multivariate setting in which S–W are located, and rightly so, since the business cycle is about comovements in a broad range of macroeconomic aggregates. But the evidence from these different models suggests that S–W should not underestimate the evidence of nonlinearity found in their own rather limited testing and indeed supports their call for further research. If the regime-shift view is upheld, then, at a simple level, the selection of indicators for predicting recessions might be based on weighted rather than ordinary least squares.

Judgment plays an essential part in the selection of indicators, the dating of turning points, and various other aspects of traditional business-cycle analysis, and its elimination is the ultimate target of the modern model-based methods. Judgment, of course, accommodates nonlinearity of unspecified form, but it is not just seat of the pants, Zarnowitz and Braun (1989) noting the reliance of the traditional approach on business-cycle theory and selection criteria that are formally stated, albeit informally weighted; formalization of the former surely requires elements of the structural modeling approach. On the other hand, Sims (1989) notes that S–W have only partially formalized the selection process and that therefore the forecast uncertainty that results from uncertainty about which variables belong in the model is not completely known: "The criteria for [respecifying or adjusting the model] should be more explicit, if we are to have much improvement over the current judgmental DOC procedures" (p. 397). The seasonal adjustment problem provides an interesting parallel. Here, too, the traditional methods were developed in the absence of a formal probability model and formal statistical criteria; subsequently, model-based methods were developed as an alternative and as an aid to understanding the behavior and characteristics of the traditional methods. They have not replaced the traditional methods in the official statistical agencies, however, one objection being the need for skilled judgment in the model-based methods (specifically in the choice of the ARIMA representations used at various points). This might seem a somewhat contrary objection since more generally the traditionalists feel that the modern methods overlook much that is of value in their own use of judgment. Perhaps the same tension will persist in business-cycle analysis, with the result that a probability model that provides a complete rationalization of the traditional methods cannot be attained. Many avenues remain to be explored, however, and, in the meantime, S–W deserve congratulations for having clearly advanced the debate, in particular by establishing a more scientific foundation.

References

Dawid, A. P. 1982. The well-calibrated Bayesian [with discussion]. *Journal of the American Statistical Association* 77:605–13.
———. 1986. Probability forecasting. In *Encyclopedia of statistical sciences,* ed. S. Kotz and N. L. Johnson, vol. 7. New York: Wiley.
Fels, R., and C. E. Hinshaw. 1968. *Forecasting and recognizing business cycle turning points.* Studies in Business Cycles, no. 17. New York: Columbia University Press (for the NBER).
Hamilton, J. D. 1989. A new approach to the economic analysis of nonstationary time series and the business cycle. *Econometrica* 57:357–84.
Pfann, G. A. 1991. Employment and business cycle asymmetries: A data based study. Discussion Paper no. 39. Minneapolis: Federal Reserve Bank of Minneapolis, Institute for Empirical Macroeconomics.
Sargent, T. J., and C. A. Sims. 1977. Business cycle modeling without pretending to have too much *a priori* economic theory. In *New methods in business cycle research,* ed. C. A. Sims. Minneapolis: Federal Reserve Bank of Minneapolis.
Sims, C. A. 1989. Comment on Stock and Watson (1989). *NBER Macroeconomics Annual,* 394–97.
Stock, J. H., and M. W. Watson. 1989. New indexes of coincident and leading economic indicators. *NBER Macroeconomics Annual,* 351–94.
———. 1991. A probability model of the coincident economic indicators. In *Leading economic indicators: New approaches and forecasting records,* ed. K. Lahiri and G. H. Moore. New York: Cambridge University Press.
Zarnowitz, V., and P. Braun. 1989. Comment on Stock and Watson (1989). *NBER Macroeconomics Annual,* 397–408.

3 Estimating Event Probabilities from Macroeconometric Models Using Stochastic Simulation

Ray C. Fair

Government policymakers and business planners are interested in knowing the probabilities of various economic events happening. In 1989 and 1990, for example, there was interest in the probability that a recession would occur in the near future. Model builders who make forecasts typically do not answer probability questions directly. They typically present a "base" forecast and a few alternative "scenarios." If probabilities are assigned to the scenarios, they are subjective ones of the model builders.[1]

Probability questions can, however, be directly answered within the context of macroeconometric models by using stochastic simulation. The first part of this paper (secs. 3.1–3.2) explains how this can be done and gives some examples. An adantage of this procedure is that the probabilities estimated from the stochastic simulation are objective in the sense that they are based on the use of estimated distributions. They are consistent with the probability structure of the model.

Estimated probabilities can also be used in the evaluation of a model. Consider, for example, the event that, in a five-quarter period, there is negative real GNP growth in at least two of the quarters. For any historical five-quarter period, this event either did or did not happen. The actual value or outcome is thus either zero or one. Now, for any five-quarter period for which data exist, one can estimate from a model the probability of the event occurring. If this is done for a number of five-quarter periods, one has a series of probability esti-

Ray C. Fair is professor of economics at Yale University and a research associate of the National Bureau of Economic Research.

The author is indebted to Douglas Hamilton for stimulating his interest in the use of stochastic simulation to estimate probabilities in econometric models. He is also indebted to James Hamilton, James Stock, Mark Watson, and other conference participants for very helpful comments.

1. Within the context of their leading indicator approach, Stock and Watson (1989) do present, however, estimates of the probability that the economy will be in a recession six months hence.

mates that can be compared to the actual (zero or one) values. One can thus evaluate how good the model is at predicting various events. An example of this type of evaluation is presented in the second part of this paper (sec. 3.3).

3.1   The Procedure

3.1.1   The Model

The model considered in this paper can be dynamic, nonlinear, and simultaneous and can have autoregressive errors of any order. Write the model as

$$(1) \qquad f_i(y_t, x_t, \alpha_i) = u_{it}, \quad i = 1, \ldots, n, t = 1, \ldots, T,$$

where y_t is an n-dimensional vector of endogenous variables, x_t is a vector of predetermined variables (both exogenous and lagged endogenous), α_i is a vector of unknown coefficients, and u_{it} is an error term. It is assumed that the first m equations are stochastic, with the remaining $u_{it}(i = m + 1, \ldots, n)$ identically zero for all t.

Each equation in (1) is assumed to have been transformed to eliminate any autoregressive properties of its error term. If the error term in the untransformed version, say, v_{it} in equation i, follows an rth-order autoregressive process,

$$v_{it} = \rho_{1i}v_{it-1} + \ldots + \rho_{ri}v_{it-r} + u_{it},$$

where u_{it} is i.i.d., then equation i is assumed to have been transformed into one with u_{it} on the right-hand side. The autoregressive coefficients $\rho_{1i}, \ldots, \rho_{ri}$ are incorporated into the α_i coefficient vector, and the additional lagged values that are involved in the transformation are incorporated into the x_t vector. This transformation makes the equation nonlinear in coefficients if it were not otherwise, but this adds no further complications to the model because it is already allowed to be nonlinear. It does result in the "loss" of the first r observations, but this has no effect on the asymptotic properties of the estimators. u_{it} in (1) can thus be assumed to be i.i.d. even though the original error term may follow an autoregressive process.

Let u_t be the m-dimensional vector $(u_{it}, \ldots, u_{mt})'$. For the stochastic simulations below, it is assumed that u_t is distributed as multivariate normal $N(0, \Sigma)$, where Σ is $m \times m$. Although the normality assumption is commonly made, the general procedure discussed in this paper does not depend on it. If another distributional assumption were used, this would simply change the way in which the error terms were drawn for the stochastic simulations.

It is assumed that consistent estimates of α_i, denoted $\hat{\alpha}_i$, are available for all i. Given these estimates, consistent estimates of u_{it}, denoted $\hat{u}_{it}$, can be computed as $f_i(y_t, x_t, \hat{\alpha}_i)$. The covariance matrix Σ can then be estimated as $\hat{\Sigma} = (1/T)\hat{U}\hat{U}'$, where $\hat{U}$ is the $m \times T$ matrix of values of $\hat{u}_{it}$.

Let α be the k-dimensional vector $(\alpha_1', \ldots, \alpha_m')'$, where k is the total number of unrestricted coefficients in the model, including any autoregressive coefficients of the original error terms, and let $\hat{\alpha}$ denote the estimate of α. It is also assumed that an estimate of the covariance matrix of $\hat{\alpha}$, denoted $\hat{V}$, is available, where $\hat{V}$ is $k \times k$.

3.1.2   Estimating Standard Errors of Forecasts

It will be useful to consider first the use of stochastic simulation to estimate standard errors of forecasts. A forecast from a model is subject to four main sources of uncertainty—uncertainty from the structural error terms, from the coefficient estimates, from the exogenous-variable forecasts, and from the possible misspecification of the model. Stochastic simulation can easily handle the first three sources, but accounting for possible misspecification is much harder. A method is presented in Fair (1980) that uses stochastic simulation to estimate the degree of misspecification of a model and to adjust the standard errors for the misspecification. This method does not, however, carry over in any straightforward way to the estimation of probabilities, and, in this paper, only the first three sources of uncertainty are considered. The probability estimates are thus based on the assumption that the model is correctly specified.

Given $\hat{\Sigma}$ and $\hat{V}$, the uncertainty from the error terms and coefficient estimates can be estimated. Consider first drawing error terms. Let u_t^* denote a particular draw of the m error terms for period t from the $N(0, \hat{\Sigma})$ distribution. Given u_t^*, $\hat{\alpha}$, and x_t, one can solve the model for period t using a method like the Gauss-Seidel technique. This is merely a deterministic simulation for the given values of the error terms, coefficients, and predetermined variables. Call this simulation a "trial." Another trial can be made by drawing a new set of values of u_t^* and solving again. This can be done as many times as desired. From each trial, one obtains a prediction of each endogenous variable. Let y_{it}^j denote the value on the jth trial of endogenous variable i for period t. For J trials, the stochastic simulation estimate of the expected value of variable i for period t, denoted $\bar{\mu}_{it}$, is

$$(2) \qquad \bar{\mu}_{it} = (1/J)\sum_{j=1}^{J} y_{it}^j.$$

The stochastic simulation estimate of the variance of the forecast error, denoted $\bar{\sigma}_{it}^2$, is

$$(3) \qquad \bar{\sigma}_{it}^2 = (1/J)\sum_{j=1}^{J} (y_{it}^j - \bar{\mu}_{it})^2.$$

If the forecast horizon is more than one period, then each trial is a dynamic simulation over the horizon, with predicted values computed for each endogenous variable for each period. Any lagged endogenous variables in the x_t vector are updated as the simulation proceeds. If, for example, the horizon is eight quarters, then eight vectors u_t^* are drawn ($t = 1, \ldots, 8$), the simulation is over the eight quarters, and eight means and variances are computed for each endogenous variable using formulas (2) and (3).

Consider now drawing coefficients. Let α^* denote a particular draw of the coefficient vector α. Under the assumption that the asymptotic distribution of $\hat{\alpha}$ is multivariate normal with covariance matrix V, α^* can be drawn from the $N(\hat{\alpha}, \hat{V})$ distribution. (Again, the normality assumption is not necessary. Some other distribution could be assumed for $\hat{\alpha}$ and the draws made from it.) Each trial now consists of drawing both error terms and coefficients. If the forecast horizon is more than one period, only one coefficient draw should be done for the entire horizon. This is consistent with the assumption on which the estimation of a model is based, namely, that the coefficients do not change over time.

Accounting for exogenous-variable uncertainty is less straightforward than accounting for uncertainty from the error terms and coefficient estimates. Exogenous variables are by their nature exogenous, and no probability structure has been assumed for them. One might think that exogenous variables should always just be taken to be fixed, but, when comparing forecast-error variances across models, it is important to try to put each model on an equal footing regarding the exogenous variables. Otherwise, the model that takes more important and hard-to-forecast variables as exogenous has an unfair advantage. Therefore, some assumption about exogenous-variable uncertainty has to be made when comparing models.

One approach is to try to estimate variances of the exogenous-variable forecasts from past predictions that model builders and others have made of the exogenous variables. Given these estimates and a distributional assumption, one could then draw exogenous-variable values for each trial. Each trial would then consist of draws of the error terms, coefficients, and exogenous variables. An alternative approach is to estimate autoregressive or vector autoregressive equations for the exogenous variables and add them to the model. One would then have a model with no exogenous variables, and error terms and coefficients could be drawn from the expanded model. Either of these approaches is a way of trying to incorporate exogenous-variable uncertainty into the stochastic simulation estimates of the forecast-error variances.

3.1.3   Estimating Event Probabilities

Estimating event probabilities is straightforward once the stochastic simulation has been set up and the event defined. Consider an eight-quarter prediction period and the event that, within this period, there are two consecutive quarters of negative real GNP growth. Assume that 1,000 trials are taken. For each trial, one can record whether or not this event occurred. If it occurred, say, 150 times out of the 1,000 trials, its estimated probability would be 15 percent. It should be clear that as many events can be considered as desired. Almost no extra work is needed to estimate probabilities beyond what is needed to estimate means and variances, and there is wide latitude in the choice of events. The extra work is simply keeping track of how often each event occurs in the solution for each trial.

3.2   Estimated Probabilities for Three Events

3.2.1   The Model

Estimated probabilities for three events are presented in this section using the model in Fair (1984). There are two contractionary events and one inflationary event.

The model consists of thirty stochastic equations and ninety-eight identities. There are 179 estimated coefficients. The estimation period used for the present results is 1954:I–1989:IV (144 observations). The model is estimated by two-stage least squares with account taken when necessary of the autoregressive properties of the error terms. Ten of the equations are estimated under the assumption of a first-order autoregressive process of the error term, and two of the equations are estimated under the assumption of a third-order process. The autoregressive coefficients are included in the 179 coefficients. The 30×30 covariance matrix of the structural error terms was estimated as $(1/T)\hat{U}\hat{U}'$, where $\hat{U}$ is the $30 \times T$ matrix of estimated residuals (as noted above, T is 144). the 179×179 covariance matrix of the estimated coefficients was estimated using the formula in Fair (1984, 216–17). This matrix is *not* block diagonal even though the correlation of the error terms across equations is not taken into account in the estimation of each equation by two-stage least squares. The correlation affects the covariance matrix, so the matrix is not block diagonal.

There are eighty-two exogenous variables in the model, not counting the constant term, the time trend, and a few dummy variables. For the present results, exogenous-variable uncertainty was handled as follows. Each of the eighty-two exogenous variables was regressed on a constant, time, and its first four lagged values (over the same 1954:I–1989:IV estimation period).[2] The estimator was ordinary least squares. The 82×82 covariance matrix of the error terms was estimated as $(1/T)\hat{E}\hat{E}'$, where $\hat{E}$ is the $82 \times T$ matrix of estimated residuals from the exogenous-variable equations. Denote this estimated matrix as $\hat{S}$.

The eighty-two equations were then added to the model, leaving the expanded model with no exogenous variables except the constant term, the time trend, and a few dummy variables. The expanded model was restricted in two ways. First, the error terms in the thirty structural equations were assumed to be uncorrelated with the error terms in the eighty-two exogenous-variable

---

2. Many of the exogenous-variable equations were estimated in logs. Logs were not used for tax rates and for variables that were sometimes negative or very close to zero.

equations. The 112×112 estimated covariance matrix of all the error terms is thus block diagonal, with one block $\hat{\Sigma}$ and one block $\hat{S}$. This treatment is consistent with one of the assumptions on which the structural equations were estimated, namely, that the exogenous variables are uncorrelated with the structural error terms. Second, the coefficient estimates in the exogenous-variable equations were taken to be fixed in the stochastic simulations. In other words, only coefficients for the thirty structural equations were drawn. This lessens somewhat the uncertainty assumed for the exogenous variables, but it will be seen that the uncertainty from the coefficient estimates is small relative to the uncertainty from the error terms.

The key exogenous variables in the model are government fiscal policy variables, exports, and the price of imports. Monetary policy is endogenous—Fed behavior is explained by an interest rate reaction function, the interest rate reaction function being one of the thirty structural equations.

3.2.2 The Events

From about the beginning of 1989, there was concern that the economy might enter a recession in the near future, a recession generally being considered to be two consecutive quarters of negative real growth. It is thus of interest to examine this period. For the present results, the prediction period was taken to be the five quarters 1990:I–1991:I. Given this period, the following three events were considered:

A. At least two consecutive quarters of negative real GNP growth.
B. At least two quarters of negative real GNP growth.
C. At least two quarters in which inflation (percentage change in the GNP deflator) exceeded 7 percent at an annual rate.

Event A is a recession as generally defined. Event B allows the two or more quarters of negative growth not to be consecutive. Event C is a case in which people would probably start to worry about inflation picking up.

3.2.3 The Stochastic Simulations

Three stochastic simulations were performed, each based on 1,000 trials. For simulations 1 and 2, the exogenous-variable equations were *not* added to the model, and the exogenous-variable values were taken to be the actual values. For simulation 1, only error terms were drawn; for simulation 2, both error terms and coefficients were drawn.[3]

---

3. After the empirical work for this paper was finished, Gregory Chow suggested to me that one may not want to draw coefficients when estimating probabilities. Although coefficient estimates are uncertain, the true coefficients are fixed. In the real world, the reason that economic events are stochastic is because of the stochastic shocks (error terms), not because the coefficients are stochastic. (This is assuming, of course, that the true coefficients are fixed, which is the assumption on which the estimation of the model is based.) As a practical matter, it makes little difference whether or not one draws coefficients because, as will be seen below, most of the uncertainty is from the error terms, not the coefficient estimates. In future work, however, Chow's argument suggests that coefficients should not be drawn when estimating probabilities.

For simulation 3, the eighty-two exogenous-variable equations were added to the model in the manner discussed above. It is important to note that, in order to make this simulation comparable to the other two, the estimated residuals in the exogenous-variable equations were added to the equations and taken to be fixed across all the trials. The draws of the error terms for the exogenous-variable equations were then added to the fixed residuals. Adding the residuals to the exogenous-variable equations means that, when the expanded model is solved deterministically (by setting the error terms in the structural equations equal to zero), the solution is the same as when the non-expanded model is solved using the actual values of the exogenous variables. This treatment of the exogenous-variable equations for simulation 3 means that the base paths of the exogenous variables are the actual paths (just as for simulations 1 and 2). The base paths, for example, are *not* the paths that would be predicted by the exogenous-variable equations if they were solved by setting their error terms equal to zero.

All three simulations are thus based on knowledge of the exogenous-variable values for the period 1990:I–1991:I. The simulations are, however, outside the estimation period since the estimation period ended in 1989:IV. Therefore, the simulations are predictions that could have been made as of the end of 1989:IV had all the exogenous-variable values for the next five quarters been known.

The same draws of the structural error terms were used for all three simulations, and the same draws of the coefficients were used for simulations 2 and 3. This means that the differences across the three simulations are not due to simulation error. There were no cases in which the model failed to solve for the three sets of 1,000 trials.

3.2.4 The Mean Forecasts and Their Standard Errors

It will be useful to present the mean forecasts and the standard errors of the forecasts before presenting the probabilities. The results for the percentage change in real GNP (denoted g) and the percentage change in the GNP deflator (denoted p) are presented in table 3.1. Two of the main features of the results in table 3.1, which are almost always true for stochastic simulations of macroeconometric models, are that the estimated forecast means are close to the predicted values from the deterministic simulation and that drawing coefficients has a small effect on the forecast standard errors. The first result means that the bias in the predicted values from the deterministic simulation, which arises from the nonlinearity of the model, is small. The second result means that the effect of coefficient uncertainty on the forecast standard errors is small—most of the effects come from the structural error terms and the exogenous variables.[4]

---

4. Another common result in this area is that the estimates are not sensitive to the use of more robust measures of central tendency and dispersion than the mean and variance. Forecast means and variances do not necessarily exist, but this does not appear to be a problem in practice. For

Table 3.1   **Forecast Means and Standard Errors**

	1990						1990				
	I	II	III	IV	1991:I		I	II	III	IV	1991:I
Actual[a]	1.73	.40	1.43	−1.59	−2.56	Actual[b]	4.87	4.72	3.86	2.56	5.20
	Forecast Means[a]						Forecast Means[b]				
det.	3.64	1.00	1.37	.98	−.19	det.	4.57	1.31	3.41	3.76	3.38
u	3.58	1.06	1.37	1.02	−.14	u	4.52	1.24	3.46	3.82	3.45
u, c	3.27	.82	1.19	.87	−.23	u, c	4.41	1.43	3.37	3.93	3.40
u, c, e	3.32	.91	1.43	1.02	−.11	u, c, e	4.35	1.60	3.27	3.82	3.39
	Forecast Standard Errors						Forecast Standard Errors				
u	1.84	2.03	2.07	2.01	2.18	u	1.69	1.75	1.63	1.62	1.65
u, c	1.94	2.13	2.23	2.14	2.24	u, c	1.74	1.81	1.69	1.65	1.68
u, c, e	2.84	3.23	3.37	3.24	3.50	u, c, e	2.26	2.33	2.36	2.32	2.45

[a]Percentage change in real GNP (g).

[b]Percentage change in the GNP deflator (p).

Note: All percentage changes are at annual rates. det. = deterministic simulation (error terms in the structural equations set to zero and the model solved once); u = structural error terms drawn; c = coefficients drawn; e = exogenous-variable equations added to the model as discussed in the text.

The actual values for g show that the growth rate was positive but very small in 1990:II and negative in 1990:IV and 1991:I. The forecast means for g are generally larger than the actual values for the five quarters. For 1990:IV, the means are about 1.0, compared to the actual value of −1.59, and, for 1991:I, the means are about −0.2, compared to the actual value of −2.56. Regarding the inflation predictions, 1990:II was underpredicted by about 3 percentage points, 1990:IV was overpredicted by about 1 percentage point, and 1991:I was underpredicted by about 2 percentage points. The predictions for the other two quarters are very close.

The exogenous variables add substantially to the forecast standard errors (compare the u, c rows to the u, c, e rows). It may be that the current treatment of exogenous-variable uncertainty has overestimated this uncertainty. When a model builder makes an actual ex ante forecast based on guesses of the future values of the exogenous variables, it may be that the average errors of the exogenous-variable guesses are less than those implied by adding the exogenous-variable equations to the model. In other words, one may know more in practice about the exogenous variables, particularly government pol-

---

more discussion of this, see Fair (1984, chap. 7). The use of more robust measures in the present case led to very similar results to those reported above.

icy variables, than is implied by the equations. The true forecast standard errors may thus lie somewhere between the u, c and the u, c, e cases above, and the probability estimates reported below may lie somewhere between the two cases.

Given that the predicted values of g are only around 1 percentage point for three of the five quarters and negative for another, and given that the standard errors are generally above 2 percentage points, it seems likely that a fairly large fraction of the trials will have two or more quarters of negative growth. The model is close to predicting negative growth for two or more quarters already, so, given the size of the standard errors, it would not be surprising that a fairly large probability of at least two quarters of negative growth was estimated.

3.2.5   The Estimated Probabilities

The probability estimates are shown in table 3.2. These estimates indicate that the probability of a recession or near recession occurring in the period 1990:I–1990:IV was fairly high according to the model. With the exogenous-variable equations added to the model, the estimated probability is greater than half for event B (two or more quarters of negative growth). The estimated probability of inflation being greater than 7 percent for two or more quarters (event C) is very small—less than 5 percent even with the exogenous-variable equations included.

Two other simulations were run to examine the sensitivity of the results to the exogenous-variable equations. For simulation 4, the error terms in the exogenous-variable equations were assumed to be uncorrelated with each other: $\hat{S}$ was taken to be diagonal. The three estimated probabilities in this case were .397, .529, and .077. Only the last estimate is changed much, where it is now slightly higher. Not accounting for the correlation of the exogenous-variable error terms appears to increase somewhat the variance of the inflation forecasts.

For simulation 5, the exogenous-variable equations were taken to be first-order autoregressive rather than fourth order. This had only a small effect on the results. The three estimated probabilities were .416, .538, and .037. It

Table 3.2   **Probability Estimates for the Three Events**

		Event		
	Simulation	A	B	C
	u	.275	.426	.002
	u, c	.321	.483	.006
	u, c, e	.393	.522	.049

Note: See the note to table 3.1 for the u, c, and e notation.

appears that little is gained in decreasing the estimated uncertainty from the exogenous variables by going from first to fourth order.[5]

Although the probability estimates for events A and B are fairly high, they are perhaps not as high as one might hope given that events A and B actually happened. The use of probability estimates to evaluate models will now be discussed.

3.3   Using Probability Estimates to Evaluate Models

As noted above, it is possible for a given event to compute a series of probability estimates and compare these estimates to the actual outcomes. Consider event A above, the event of at least two consecutive quarters of negative values of g in a five-quarter period. Let A_t denote this event for the five-quarter period that begins with quarter t, and let P_t denote a model's estimate of the probability of A_t occurring. Let R_t denote the actual outcome of A_t—one if A_t occurred, and zero otherwise. As Diebold and Rudebusch (1989) point out, two common measures of the accuracy of probabilities are the quadratic probability score (QPS),

$$(4) \qquad\qquad \text{QPS} = (1/T)\sum_{t=1}^{T} 2(P_t - R_t)^2,$$

and the log probability score (LPS),

$$(5) \qquad \text{LPS} = -(1/T)\sum_{t=1}^{T} [(1 - R_t)\log(1 - P_t) + R_t \log P_t],$$

where T is the total number of observations. It is also possible simply to compute the mean of P_t (say, $\bar{P}$) and the mean of R_t (say $\bar{R}$) and compare the two means. QPS ranges from zero to two, with zero being perfect accuracy, and LPS ranges from zero to infinity, with zero being perfect accuracy. Larger errors are penalized more under LPS than under QPS.

For the empirical work in this section, events A_t and B_t were analyzed for t ranging from 1954:I through 1990:I (145 observations). A_t is the event of at least two consecutive quarters of negative real GNP growth for the five-quarter period beginning with quarter t, and B_t is the event of at least two quarters of negative real GNP growth (not necessarily consecutive) for the five-quarter period beginning with quarter t.

Since t ranges over 145 observations, there are 145 A_t events and 145 B_t events. Estimating the probabilities of these events required 145 stochastic

---

5. Note that estimating, say, a fourth-order autoregressive equation for an exogenous variable with a constant term and time trend included is equivalent to estimating the equation with only a constant term and time trend included under the assumption of a fourth-order autoregressive process for the error term. The equations are simply accounting for the autoregressive properties of the error term once the mean and deterministic trend have been removed. The present results thus show that little is gained in going from a first-order autoregressive process for the error term to a fourth-order process.

simulations. Each stochastic simulation was for a five-quarter period. The beginning quarter for the first simulation was 1954:I, the beginning quarter for the second simulation was 1954:II, and so on through the beginning quarter for the 145th simulation, which was 1990:I. Two sets of 145 stochastic simulations were in fact made. For the first set, the exogenous-variable values were taken to be the actual values—the exogenous-variable equations were not used, and no draws of exogenous-variable errors were made. The model used for this set will be called model (u, c).

For the second set, the exogenous-variable equations were added to the model, and error terms were drawn for these equations. As was done for the results in section 3.2, the error terms in the exogenous-variable equations were assumed to be uncorrelated with the error terms in the structural equations, and no coefficients were drawn for the exogenous-variable equations. Unlike in section 3.2, however, the estimated residuals were not added to the exogenous-variable equations. The base values of the error terms in these equations were assumed to be zero, just as is always done for the structural equations. This means that the model's prediction of the five-quarter period is based only on information available prior to the period. The model used for this set of stochastic simulations will be called model (u, c, e). As noted in section 3.2, the use of the exogenous-variable equations may overestimate exogenous-variable uncertainty, so it is not clear that the structural model should be judged by model (u, c, e) rather than by model (u, c). The truth probably lies somewhere in between.

The number of trials for each stochastic simulation was 100. This means that each set of 145 stochastic simulations required solving the model over a five-quarter period 14,500 times. In some cases, the model failed to solve for the particular draws, and, in these cases, the trial was simply discarded. This means that some of the probability estimates are based on slightly fewer than 100 trials. Most of the failures occurred early in the sample period.

A simple autoregressive model for real GNP was also estimated and stochastically simulated. The model consisted of regressing the log of real GNP on a constant, time, and the first four lagged values of log real GNP. The estimation period was 1954:I–1989:IV, the same as for the structural model, and 145 stochastic simulations were made. In this case, 1,000 trials were made for each simulation. This model will be called model AR.

From this work, one has three sets of values of P_t ($t = 1, \ldots, 145$) for each of the two events, one set for each model. One also has the values of R_t for each event. Given the values of R_t, a fourth model can be considered, which is the model in which P_t is taken to be equal to $\bar{R}$ for each observation, where $\bar{R}$ is the mean of R_t over the 145 observations. This is simply a model in which the estimated probability of the event is constant and equal to the frequency with which the event happened historically. This model will be called model CONSTANT. The results are shown in table 3.3.

Both the structural model and model AR overestimate $\bar{R}$. (Remember that model CONSTANT is constructed so that $\bar{P} = \bar{R}$.) Model AR has somewhat

Table 3.3   **Measures of Probability Accuracy**

	Event A				Event B		
	$\bar{P}$	QPS	LPS		$\bar{P}$	QPS	LPS
Actual ($\bar{P} = \bar{R}$)	.138			Actual ($\bar{P} = \bar{R}$)	.297		
Model (u, c)	.285	.192	.315	Model (u, c,)	.394	.249	.383
Model (u, c, e)	.336	.268	.416	Model (u, c, e)	.445	.322	.481
Model AR	.238	.239	.401	Model AR	.341	.361	.544
Model CONSTANT	.138	.238	.401	Model CONSTANT	.297	.417	.608

less bias than the structural model. Regarding QPS and LPS, model (u, c) is always the best. For event A, model (u, c, e) is the worst, but the results for it, model AR, and model CONSTANT are all fairly close. Model (u, c, e) is noticeably better than model AR and model CONSTANT for event B.

Table 3.4 presents the 145 values of R_t for each event and the 145 values of P_t for each event and each model except model CONSTANT. (P_t for model CONSTANT is simply .138 for all t for event A and .297 for all t for event B.) Figures 3.1–3.3 plot the values of R_t and P_t for event B for models (u, c), (u, c, e), and AR, respectively.

One knows from the QPS and LPS results above that models (u, c) and (u, c, e) do better than model AR, and the three figures provide a helpful way of seeing this. The probability estimates for model AR never get above .64, whereas they are close to 1.0 for models (u, c) and (u, c, e) around a number of the actual occurrences of event B. Remember that model (u, c, e) is based on predicted values of the exogenous variables, and even this version does a reasonable job of having high estimated probabilities when event B occurs and low estimated probabilities when event B does not occur. One of the main times during which the structural model gets penalized in terms of the QPS and LPS criteria is the second half of the 1960s, where the estimated probabilities were fairly high for a number of quarters before event B actually happened.

Note from the figures that the occurrence of event B for the period beginning in 1990:I was not well predicted relative to earlier occurrences. The recession of 1990:IV–1991:I was not an easy one to predict.[6]

6. Note that the values of P_t in the last row of table 3.4 for models (u, c) and (u, c, e)—.350 and .280 for event A and .510 and .340 for event B—are not the same as those presented in table 3.2—.321 and .393 for event A and .483 and .522 for event B—even though the five-quarter period is the same. For model (u, c), the differences are due to the use of 1,000 trials for the results in table 3.2 compared to 100 trials for the results in table 3.4. For model (u, c, e), the differences are further due to the use of predicted values as the base values for the exogenous variables in table 3.4 rather than the actual values in table 3.2. For model (u, c, e), the probability estimates are considerably lower when the predicted values of the exogenous variables are used. The exogenous-variable equations for some of the government spending variables failed to predict the slowdown in the growth rate of these variables that occurred, and this is one of the reasons for the lower probability estimates for model (u, c, e) in table 3.4.

Table 3.4   **Estimated Probabilities from the Three Models**

		Event A				Event B		
Beg. Quar.	Act.	Model $(u, c,)$	Model (u, c, e)	Model AR	Act.	Model $(u, c,)$	Model (u, c, e)	Model AR
1954:I	1.0	.462	.407	.275	1.0	.667	.531	.408
1954:II	.0	.439	.254	.246	.0	.585	.476	.350
1954:III	.0	.200	.188	.171	.0	.345	.266	.264
1954:IV	.0	.215	.170	.122	.0	.557	.318	.180
1955:I	.0	.314	.292	.132	.0	.407	.326	.194
1955:II	.0	.229	.355	.160	.0	.554	.516	.234
1955:III	.0	.337	.394	.190	.0	.584	.564	.276
1955:IV	.0	.363	.474	.200	.0	.758	.684	.290
1956:I	.0	.454	.552	.202	.0	.619	.750	.296
1956:II	.0	.330	.474	.225	.0	.546	.680	.332
1956:III	.0	.418	.474	.195	.0	.622	.680	.294
1956:IV	.0	.280	.408	.178	1.0	.730	.653	.261
1957:I	1.0	.585	.495	.158	1.0	.702	.657	.233
1957:II	1.0	.565	.465	.166	1.0	.765	.636	.241
1957:III	1.0	.442	.434	.183	1.0	.651	.566	.274
1957:IV	1.0	.402	.455	.163	1.0	.644	.646	.241
1958:I	.0	.223	.380	.205	.0	.362	.522	.286
1958:II	.0	.051	.088	.199	.0	.127	.176	.267
1958:III	.0	.063	.068	.082	.0	.125	.136	.132
1958:IV	.0	.156	.110	.085	.0	.200	.154	.116
1959:I	.0	.097	.081	.103	.0	.172	.152	.146
1959:II	.0	.085	.112	.128	1.0	.340	.337	.188
1959:III	.0	.258	.253	.126	1.0	.526	.444	.191
1959:IV	.0	.289	.333	.161	1.0	.495	.455	.230
1960:I	.0	.287	.454	.133	1.0	.468	.546	.214
1960:II	.0	.333	.340	.116	1.0	.548	.515	.169
1960:III	.0	.138	.214	.153	.0	.298	.337	.223
1960:IV	.0	.079	.234	.151	.0	.213	.362	.226
1961:I	.0	.032	.082	.130	.0	.053	.112	.192
1961:II	.0	.021	.051	.088	.0	.031	.071	.135
1961:III	.0	.010	.074	.096	.0	.030	.096	.131
1961:IV	.0	.020	.071	.104	.0	.061	.122	.146
1962:I	.0	.061	.111	.118	.0	.101	.152	.166
1962:II	.0	.091	.131	.136	.0	.131	.192	.195
1962:III	.0	.106	.206	.152	.0	.223	.278	.223
1962:IV	.0	.104	.206	.151	.0	.219	.268	.224
1963:I	.0	.053	.165	.170	.0	.095	.216	.243
1963:II	.0	.040	.122	.132	.0	.070	.184	.204
1963:III	.0	.060	.121	.139	.0	.120	.182	.203
1963:IV	.0	.160	.162	.158	.0	.220	.242	.235
1964:I	.0	.210	.180	.180	.0	.300	.220	.263
1964:II	.0	.160	.232	.172	.0	.230	.333	.263
1964:III	.0	.121	.232	.210	.0	.222	.364	.307
1964:IV	.0	.121	.337	.221	.0	.182	.480	.331
1965:I	.0	.071	.354	.225	.0	.131	.485	.333
1965:II	.0	.081	.480	.210	.0	.212	.653	.309

(*continued*)

Table 3.4   (continued)

Beg. Quar.		Event A				Event B		
	Act.	Model $(u, c,)$	Model (u, c, e)	Model AR	Act.	Model $(u, c,)$	Model (u, c, e)	Model AR
1965:III	.0	.192	.430	.255	.0	.273	.570	.355
1965:IV	.0	.232	.390	.280	.0	.323	.530	.398
1966:I	.0	.276	.500	.315	.0	.357	.640	.428
1966:II	.0	.327	.600	.370	.0	.541	.780	.491
1966:III	.0	.388	.680	.424	.0	.592	.860	.576
1966:IV	.0	.434	.700	.379	.0	.707	.880	.534
1967:I	.0	.500	.670	.380	.0	.630	.850	.530
1967:II	.0	.404	.530	.377	.0	.566	.690	.532
1967:III	.0	.112	.410	.365	.0	.276	.580	.518
1967:IV	.0	.273	.490	.362	.0	.525	.680	.496
1968:I	.0	.354	.400	.393	.0	.455	.590	.540
1968:II	.0	.470	.390	.392	.0	.600	.670	.536
1968:III	.0	.616	.622	.410	.0	.808	.776	.538
1968:IV	.0	.790	.610	.448	1.0	.940	.830	.584
1969:I	1.0	.700	.590	.459	1.0	.830	.750	.627
1969:II	1.0	.850	.910	.408	1.0	.970	.970	.552
1969:III	1.0	.850	.770	.437	1.0	.950	.900	.588
1969:IV	1.0	.780	.690	.418	1.0	.930	.900	.587
1970:I	1.0	.680	.680	.424	1.0	.820	.830	.584
1970:II	.0	.530	.660	.344	1.0	.680	.800	.509
1970:III	.0	.550	.660	.303	1.0	.710	.790	.440
1970:IV	.0	.350	.350	.278	1.0	.600	.490	.401
1971:I	.0	.080	.110	.326	1.0	.110	.200	.459
1971:II	.0	.090	.220	.245	1.0	.230	.360	.383
1971:III	.0	.090	.130	.304	.0	.230	.210	.428
1971:IV	.0	.100	.190	.293	.0	.190	.230	.452
1972:I	.0	.020	.120	.273	.0	.020	.180	.405
1972:II	.0	.020	.180	.247	.0	.020	.260	.371
1972:III	.0	.020	.320	.307	.0	.030	.470	.415
1972:IV	.0	.110	.350	.350	.0	.130	.500	.496
1973:I	.0	.220	.300	.352	1.0	.260	.410	.488
1973:II	.0	.370	.560	.408	1.0	.470	.660	.537
1973:III	.0	.540	.620	.479	1.0	.790	.810	.624
1973:IV	1.0	.720	.710	.451	1.0	.920	.890	.632
1974:I	1.0	.830	.790	.385	1.0	.940	.950	.542
1974:II	1.0	.760	.660	.405	1.0	.900	.840	.562
1974:III	1.0	.870	.630	.366	1.0	.950	.830	.529
1974:IV	1.0	.750	.740	.371	1.0	.800	.860	.514
1975:I	.0	.430	.510	.300	.0	.480	.670	.446
1975:II	.0	.020	.070	.286	.0	.090	.120	.390
1975:III	.0	.050	.000	.148	.0	.070	.000	.252
1975:IV	.0	.090	.050	.159	.0	.130	.060	.227
1976:I	.0	.100	.080	.191	.0	.150	.080	.270
1976:II	.0	.040	.080	.211	.0	.050	.080	.296
1976:III	.0	.040	.090	.242	.0	.050	.100	.344
1976:IV	.0	.030	.100	.236	.0	.140	.120	.360

Table 3.4   (continued)

Beg. Quar.		Event A				Event B		
	Act.	Model $(u, c,)$	Model (u, c, e)	Model AR	Act.	Model $(u, c,)$	Model (u, c, e)	Model AR
1977:I	.0	.100	.090	.210	.0	.120	.090	.314
1977:II	.0	.110	.150	.225	.0	.130	.210	.321
1977:III	.0	.100	.230	.242	.0	.110	.330	.345
1977:IV	.0	.210	.300	.268	.0	.370	.440	.383
1978:I	.0	.110	.370	.332	.0	.190	.520	.464
1978:II	.0	.170	.360	.275	.0	.220	.570	.426
1978:III	.0	.390	.560	.287	.0	.450	.750	.396
1978:IV	.0	.400	.540	.359	1.0	.540	.760	.498
1979:I	.0	.580	.710	.371	1.0	.780	.850	.537
1979:II	.0	.460	.730	.384	1.0	.790	.890	.537
1979:III	.0	.740	.750	.368	1.0	.890	.920	.532
1979:IV	.0	.860	.780	.305	1.0	.950	.900	.448
1980:I	.0	.680	.660	.325	.0	.840	.820	.465
1980:II	.0	.740	.660	.283	1.0	.920	.830	.420
1980:III	.0	.470	.530	.386	.0	.710	.740	.515
1980:IV	.0	.200	.390	.220	1.0	.310	.460	.375
1981:I	1.0	.600	.500	.174	1.0	.750	.640	.258
1981:II	1.0	.950	.610	.213	1.0	.960	.810	.299
1981:III	1.0	.850	.660	.257	1.0	.990	.800	.371
1981:IV	1.0	.980	.830	.230	1.0	1.000	.900	.359
1982:I	.0	.860	.730	.244	1.0	.950	.800	.356
1982:II	.0	.700	.390	.224	.0	.780	.480	.327
1982:III	.0	.580	.220	.112	.0	.660	.330	.174
1982:IV	.0	.180	.080	.113	.0	.270	.080	.170
1983:I	.0	.000	.000	.096	.0	.000	.000	.155
1983:II	.0	.000	.000	.090	.0	.000	.000	.126
1983:III	.0	.000	.010	.091	.0	.000	.010	.127
1983:IV	.0	.000	.020	.112	.0	.010	.020	.153
1984:I	.0	.050	.050	.128	.0	.050	.050	.185
1984:II	.0	.100	.170	.148	.0	.140	.250	.203
1984:III	.0	.320	.250	.179	.0	.480	.300	.251
1984:IV	.0	.400	.260	.204	.0	.520	.410	.293
1985:I	.0	.120	.210	.197	.0	.190	.270	.284
1985:II	.0	.070	.210	.171	.0	.090	.240	.250
1985:III	.0	.030	.110	.185	.0	.060	.140	.262
1985:IV	.0	.040	.160	.183	.0	.080	.180	.263
1986:I	.0	.030	.110	.185	.0	.050	.120	.262
1986:II	.0	.010	.050	.186	.0	.020	.060	.267
1986:III	.0	.000	.000	.220	.0	.000	.000	.317
1986:IV	.0	.010	.030	.201	.0	.010	.050	.300
1987:I	.0	.000	.020	.163	.0	.000	.020	.237
1987:II	.0	.000	.020	.163	.0	.010	.020	.234
1987:III	.0	.010	.110	.181	.0	.010	.150	.254
1987:IV	.0	.070	.160	.185	.0	.070	.190	.263
1988:I	.0	.020	.150	.188	.0	.030	.260	.265
1988:II	.0	.010	.110	.203	.0	.030	.170	.285

(*continued*)

Table 3.4   (continued)

Beg. Quar.		Event A				Event B		
	Act.	Model $(u, c,)$	Model (u, c, e)	Model AR	Act.	Model $(u, c,)$	Model (u, c, e)	Model AR
1988:III	.0	.020	.170	.224	.0	.050	.230	.321
1988:IV	.0	.130	.290	.230	.0	.150	.400	.332
1989:I	.0	.120	.310	.223	.0	.160	.400	.323
1989:II	.0	.170	.300	.213	.0	.370	.470	.307
1989:III	.0	.270	.360	.229	.0	.450	.460	.329
1989:IV	.0	.350	.300	.227	.0	.470	.450	.328
1990:I	1.0	.350	.280	.226	1.0	.510	.340	.321

Note: "Beg. Quar." = beginning quarter. "Act." = actual.

As a final comment, the results in this section are all within sample except for the results for the last five quarters. Even model CONSTANT is within sample because it uses the sample mean over the entire period. In future work, it would be of interest to do rolling regressions and have all the simulations be outside sample. This is expensive because covariance matrices also have to be estimated each time, and it limits the number of observations for which P_t can be computed because observations are needed at the beginning for the initial estimation period. In future work, it would also be useful to do more than one hundred trials per stochastic simulation. There is still considerable stochastic-simulation error with only one hundred trials.

3.4 Conclusion

This paper shows that stochastic simulation can be used to answer probability questions about the economy. The procedure discussed here is flexible in allowing for different models, different assumptions about the underlying probability distributions, different assumptions about exogenous-variable uncertainty, and different events for which probabilities are estimated. The paper also shows that a series of probability estimates can be computed and that these estimates can then be used to evaluate a model's ability to predict the various events.

References

Diebold, Francis X., and Glenn D. Rudebusch. 1989. Scoring the leading indicators. *Journal of Business* 62:369–91.

Fair, Ray C. 1980. Estimating the expected predictive accuracy of econometric models. *International Economic Review* 21 (June): 355–78.

———. 1984. *Specification, estimation, and analysis of macroeconometric models.* Cambridge, Mass.: Harvard University Press.

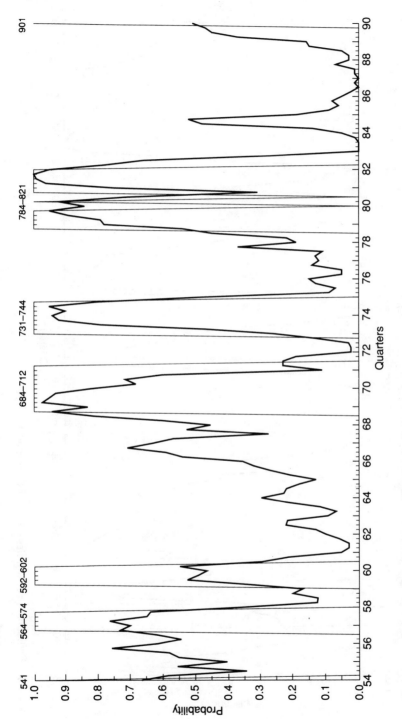

Fig. 3.1 Estimated probabilities for event B for model (*u, c*)

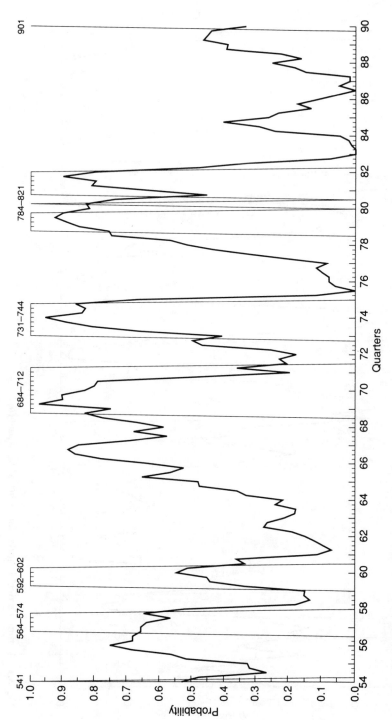

Fig. 3.2 Estimated probabilities for event B for model (*u, c, e*)

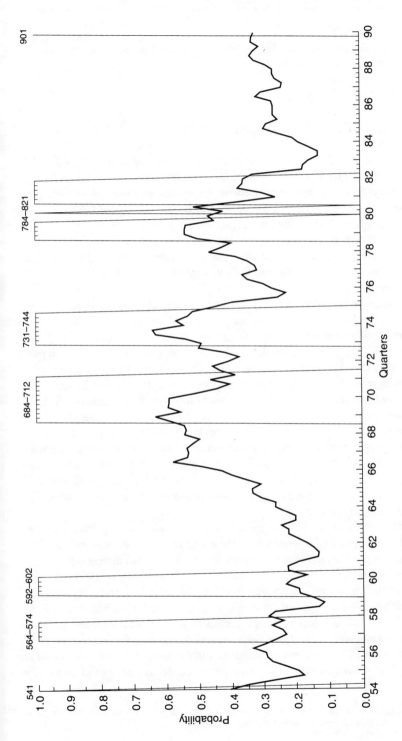

Fig. 3.3 Estimated probabilities for event B for model AR

Stock, James H., and Mark W. Watson. 1989. New indexes of coincident and leading economic indicators. Discussion Paper no. 178D. Harvard University, Kennedy School of Government, April.

Comment   James D. Hamilton

If one has a fully specified econometric model of the economy, as Ray Fair does, and if one has no compunction about torturing a computer, as Fair apparently does not, then one need not be limited to reporting just the point forecast for GNP predicted by the model. By simulating the model, one can in principle calculate the probability distribution of any future economic event. This distribution can reflect both uncertainty about the future course of the economy and uncertainty about the true values of the structural parameters. Fair offers a nice illustration of this method using his model of the U.S. economy.

Although the calculated probabilities of future events provide some of the most interesting insights from Fair's analysis, I would like to begin with the simple point forecasts of real GNP growth, in order to compare Fair's predictions with those of other models. Table 3C.1 compares the results from Fair's simulations with two real-time forecasts. The first forecast is based on a vector autoregression maintained by Christopher Sims at the Federal Reserve Bank of Minneapolis, and the second is based on a survey of alternative forecasts compiled by Victor Zarnowitz for the National Bureau of Economic Research (for sources, see table 3C.1). Between 1954 and 1990, quarterly U.S. real GNP growth averaged 2.9 percent at an annual rate, with a standard deviation of 4 percent. The economy grew unusually slowly during 1990, with a recession beginning in the fourth quarter. Fair's model tracks this outcome fairly well, in contrast to the ex ante forecasts produced by many economists at the beginning of the year.

It is worth emphasizing that Fair's (u, c, e) simulations reported in his table 3.1 are not strictly comparable to these real-time ex ante forecasts. In Fair's simulations, the exogenous variables are not drawn from their conditional distribution based on information available at the beginning of 1990 but are instead drawn from a distribution based on the actual ex post values of these variables. Fair argues that a practical user of his model has better information about the future values of the exogenous variables than is captured by simple autoregressions. Even if one were uncomfortable with this argument, the parameters of his model were estimated without using the 1990 data, with the result that his simulations clearly offer evidence that his model contains an

James D. Hamilton is professor of economics at the University of California, San Diego, and research adviser to the Federal Reserve Bank of Richmond.

Table 3C.1   **Comparison of Forecasts of Real GNP Growth**

	1990				1991:I
	I	II	III	IV	
Actual	1.7	.4	1.4	−1.6	−2.6
Fair	3.3	.9	1.4	1.0	−.1
	(2.8)	(3.2)	(3.4)	(3.2)	(3.5)
Minnesota	2.7	2.9	3.1	3.1	3.1
	(2.5)	(3.3)	(3.0)	(3.1)	(4.5)
NBER	1.2	1.8	2.1	3.0	2.1

Sources: Minnesota: Christopher Sims, "Economic Forecasts from a Vector Autoregression" (Minneapolis: Federal Reserve Bank of Minneapolis, 30 December 1989 [release date]). NBER: Victor Zarnowitz, "Economic Outlook Survey" *NBER Reporter* (Spring 1990).

accurate description of the economy and of the exogenous variables that contributed to the recession of 1990–91.

Although the point estimates in Fair's table 3.1 do not incorporate ex ante uncertainty about the exogenous variables, the standard errors that he calculates are very similar to those that would be calculated from a simulation based solely on historically available information. It is instructive to note that the standard errors for his five-quarter-ahead (u, c, e) simulation for real GNP growth are close to the unconditional standard deviation. This suggests that, in the absence of better information about the values of the exogenous variables than contained in an autoregression, the model does not offer much improvement over a simple forecast that a year from now GNP growth will proceed at its historical average rate. Recall the familiar result that the mean squared error is equal to the variance plus the square of the bias:

$$E_Y[Y - E(Y)]^2 = E_X E_{Y|X}[Y - E(Y|X)]^2 + E_X[E(Y) - E(Y|X)]^2.$$

Let Y in this formula stand for GNP growth; then $E(Y)$ is the unconditional average growth of GNP, and $E_Y[Y - E(Y)]^2$ is the unconditional variance around this mean. Let X represent information on which a forecast of GNP might be based. Then $E_{Y|X}[Y - E(Y|X)]^2$ is the variance of this forecast, the magnitude that would be calculated from Fair's simulations in his equation (3), while $[E(Y) - E(Y|X)]$ is the difference between the forecast and the historical mean. For typical values of X, if the forecast variance $E_{Y|X}[Y - E(Y|X)]^2$ equals the unconditional variance $E_Y[Y - E(Y)]^2$, then the forecast $E(Y|X)$ should be equal to the unconditional mean $E(Y)$.

This suggests another role that simulation might play in model verification. If one finds that the model generates longer-run forecasts that differ significantly from the unconditional mean but that the standard deviations for these forecasts equal or exceed the unconditional standard deviation, then the forecasts might be improved by Bayesian shrinkage toward the unconditional mean. Confidence intervals should also be correspondingly tightened to reflect the value of the prior information, with the result that the distribution of forecast errors converges to the unconditional distribution as the forecast horizon grows larger.

A similar issue may apply to the calculations of probabilities of recessions. Fair's model appears to be helpful in predicting turning points, as measured by both the quadratic probability score and the log probability score. On average, however, the model errs in overpredicting recessions, with the bias most severe for the (u, c, e) simulation. This could result from either the mean GNP growth implied by the model being too low or the standard deviation being too high. Again, Bayesian adjustment so that the distribution of longer-run forecast errors converges to the unconditional distribution of GNP growth might prove helpful. The simpler expedient of shrinking the probabilities of turning points calculated by the model toward the unconditional probabilities would also be interesting to explore.

Overall, Fair has proposed a valuable tool for economic research and practical forecasting, and the results seem quite favorable for his model of the economy.

4   A Nine-Variable
Probabilistic Macroeconomic
Forecasting Model

Christopher A. Sims

Beginning around 1980, Robert Litterman began forecasting aggregate macroeconomic variables using a small Bayesian vector autoregressive (BVAR) model. The model originally used six variables—the Treasury-bill rate, M1, the GNP deflator, real GNP, real business fixed investment, and unemployment. Litterman ceased forecasting with his model and turned the task over to me in 1986. At that time, his model had already changed, and I changed it further in 1987. This paper describes the current form of the model, explains why it changed as it did, and displays some measures of the model's performance since the major 1987 changes.[1]

The model differs in important respects from previous Bayesian VAR models that have been described in the literature (e.g., Litterman 1986, and Doan, Litterman, and Sims 1984). It accounts for nonnormality of forecast errors and allows for time-varying variances as well as time-varying autoregressive coefficients. According to its own likelihood function, it fits much better than the simpler earlier models. It implies much more time variation in autoregressive coefficients than the earlier models. Both within sample and out of sample it produces drastically better forecasts of the price level than the simpler models. For other variables, its advantages over the simpler models are smaller and uncertain.

Christopher A. Sims is professor of economics at Yale University and a research associate of the National Bureau of Economic Research.

This research was supported in part by the Institute for Empirical Macroeconomics at the Minneapolis Federal Reserve Bank and the University of Minnesota and also by National Science Foundation grant SES91–22355.

1. Joint work now under way by Richard Todd and me will provide a much more detailed assessment of the model's forecasting performance and of the contribution of its various components to its behavior.

4.1   A Brief History of These Models

Litterman's model performed remarkably well relative to forecasts prepared by commercial forecasting organizations using much more elaborate models (see Litterman 1986). In particular, as documented by McNees (1986), it performed better than commercial models for real GNP and unemployment but worse for the price level.

The model had not remained static in form from 1980 to 1986. Litterman had adapted the time-varying-parameters framework of Doan, Litterman, and Sims (1984) to his model. Also, it was easy to see in 1986 from graphs or tables of the forecasts that the model was extrapolating inflation at a long-run average rate, despite many quarters in a row of same-signed forecast errors. Thus, it was not surprising that McNees found other models doing better at forecasting inflation. Attempting to rectify this, Litterman added three variables to the original six—the trade-weighted value of the dollar, the Standard and Poors 500 stock price index, and a commodity price index.

With the model in this form, I took over preparing forecasts with it, starting in the fall of 1986. Litterman regularly evaluated his models by calculating measures of their forecast performance based on recursively updating their coefficients through the sample period, generating artificial "out-of-sample" forecasts. He had noted in these exercises a tendency for improvements in the retrospective forecast performance of the BVAR model for inflation to be accompanied by deterioration in its performance for real variables. He had chosen his additional variables aiming to minimize the real-variable deterioration while improving price forecasts. My own analysis suggested, however, that this attempt was not entirely successful. Furthermore, as I took over the model, it had been making a sequence of same-signed errors in forecasting real GNP, which, while not as serious as the earlier sequence of inflation errors, were disturbingly similar in pattern. I decided, therefore, to complicate the specification of the model in several ways, aiming to find a probability model that would track the shifts in trend inflation rates and productivity growth rates while still performing about as well for real variables as Litterman's original simple six-variable model.

The resulting model differs from Litterman's in several respects:

1. It allows for conditional heteroskedasticity (time-varying variances of disturbance terms).
2. It allows for nonnormality of disturbances. Specifically, it allows disturbances to be mixtures of two normal random variables.
3. It takes account of the connection of the constant term to the means of the explanatory variables using a "dummy initial observation," described below.
4. It uses the discrete-time process generated by time averaging of a continuous-time random walk as a prior mean, rather than using a discrete-time random walk.

5. Probably mainly as a result of the first three changes, it fits best with a great deal more implied time variation of parameters than Litterman found optimal with his model.

Likelihood is dramatically higher for this version of the model than for its predecessor. Simulated one- through eight-step-ahead forecasts from the sample period are about as good as or a bit better than with the previous model for real variables, much better for price variables, and slightly worse for interest rates.

4.2   Description of the Model

The data are a time series of $k \times 1$ vectors $X(t)$, determined by a state vector $\beta(t; i, j, s)$ and an equation disturbance $u(t; i)$ according to

$$(1) \quad X_i(t) = \sum_{j=1}^{k} \sum_{s=1}^{m} X_j(t - s)\beta(t; i, j, s) + \beta(t; i, j + 1, 1) + u(t; i).$$

I treat the β's and u's as stochastic processes that generate a distribution, conditional on initial X's, for the other observed X's. In principle, inference on all equations of the system should proceed jointly, as randomness in one equation could be correlated with randomness in other equations.[2] However, because it is computationally convenient, and because some tentative experiments have indicated little advantage from full-system estimation, estimation proceeds equation by equation. What I discuss below, therefore, although I call it the "likelihood," is usually the component of the likelihood corresponding to one equation under the assumption of independence across equations. Likelihood for the full system is then taken as the sum of these equation likelihoods and is the true full-system likelihood only under an assumption of independence of randomness across equations.

4.2   Form of the Distribution of Disturbances

Conditional on prior information, on data observable through date $t - 1$, *and* on $\beta(t - 1; \cdot, \cdot, \cdot)$, the vector $[\beta(t; i, \cdot, \cdot), u(t; i)]$ is taken to be a mixture of two jointly normally distributed random variables, both with mean $[\beta^*(t - 1; i, \cdot, \cdot), 0]'$ and with variance matrices $V(t; i)$ and $\pi_{11}^2 V(t; i)$, respectively; that is, the vector has p.d.f.[3]

---

2. In this model, the algebra of the "seemingly unrelated regressions" of econometric textbooks applies. Thus, even if the randomness is related across equations, if the same X's appear on the right-hand side of each equation and the prior has the same form in each equation, then analysis of the whole system reduces to equation-by-equation analysis. However, the prior that we consider is not symmetrical across equations.

3. Here and below, I will use the abbreviated notation $a(t)$ for $a(t; i, \cdot, \cdot)$ where there can be no ambiguity.

$$
(2) \quad p[\beta(t), u(t; i)|t - 1] = \pi_{10}\phi\left\{\begin{bmatrix} \beta^*(t - 1) \\ 0 \end{bmatrix}, V(t; i)\right\}
$$

$$
+ \left(1 - \pi_{10}\right) \phi\left\{\begin{bmatrix} \beta^*(t - 1) \\ 0 \end{bmatrix}, \pi_{11}^2 V(t; i)\right\},
$$

where $\phi(a, b)$ is the p.d.f. of a normal vector with mean a and variance matrix b.

Conditional on data and prior information observable through $t - 1$ *alone*, $\beta^*(t - 1)$ is taken to be normally distributed with covariance matrix $W(t - 1)$ and mean $B(t - 1)$; that is, it is taken to have p.d.f.

$$
(3) \qquad\qquad q[\beta^*(t - 1)] = \phi[B(t - 1), W(t - 1)].
$$

If π_{10} were zero or one, equations (1)–(3) would justify applying the Kalman filter to an observation on $X_i(t)$ to obtain a posterior distribution for β and u. With other values of π_{10}, the Kalman filter cannot be applied directly since the conditional distribution of $X_i(t)$ is nonnormal. However, the posterior distribution is still easily obtained by two applications of the Kalman filter. One applies it once conditional on the $V(t; i)$ covariance matrix, then again conditional on the $\pi_{11}^2 V(t; i)$ covariance matrix. The posterior p.d.f. on $[\beta(t), u(t; i)]$ is then a weighted sum of the two resulting normal posterior p.d.f.'s, with the weights given by the relative likelihoods of the observed $X_i(t)$ under the two normal prior distributions.

The posterior distribution on $\beta(t)$ generated by this procedure is, of course, itself a mixture of normals, not a normal distribution. If $\beta(t + 1)$ were related to $\beta(t)$ by a linear equation with normal disturbances, the prior distribution on $\beta(t + 1)$ would itself be nonnormal, and the Kalman filter would not be applicable at $t + 1$. Actually, if the prior at $t = 0$ is normal, the prior at $t = 1$ would be a mixture of two normals, so that by conditioning on each normal component of the prior, Kalman filtering twice for each, we could obtain a new posterior that was a mixture of four normals, etc. However, with the number of normal components involved proliferating exponentially, this exact approach would be computationally intractable. A better approximate approach might be continually to keep track of the k most likely of the 2^t branches of the tree of normal components of the mixed posterior distributions, with k set at, say, four or sixteen. Or, instead, at each t one could convert the posterior for $\beta(t - k; i, \cdot, \cdot)$ conditional on data through $t - k$ to the normal distribution with corresponding mean and variance, treating the disturbances from $t - k + 1$ to t exactly. What is actually done for this model is this latter approach with $k = 1$, although a k of two or three would be feasible, at least as an experiment to check the sensitivity of results. One hesitates to work too hard at this since the mixture-of-normals assumption itself is an arbitrary convenience. A matrix t distribution would be more plausible, implying a continuous mixture of normals in place of a mixture of just two normals.

To summarize, the model assumes that $\beta^*(t - 1)$ is a function of $\beta(t - 1)$ such that it has a normal distribution with the same mean and variance as has $\beta(t - 1)$, despite the nonnormality of the latter.

If we could represent this change in distribution by supposing that some sort of random noise were added to $\beta(t - 1)$, it would be natural to think of this as simply nonnormal stochastic time variation in a. However, the nature of the change in distribution precludes its being characterized this way. The assumption is in fact unnatural, justifiable only as a convenient approximation. Note, however, that, because our uncertainty about $\beta(t - 1)$ cumulates the effects of disturbances at many dates, our posterior for it is likely to be much closer to normality than is the conditional distribution for $\beta(t) - \beta^*(t - 1)$. Treating the distribution of the former as approximately normal while carefully accounting for nonnormality in the latter is therefore justifiable as an approximation.

Note that we are in effect assuming that our posterior mean for $\beta(t - 1)$ at $t - 1$ is the same as our prior mean for $\beta(t)$. This makes the $E[\beta(t)|t]$ sequence a martingale. There would be no computational or conceptual difficulty with allowing a more general linear dependence of the prior mean for $\beta(t)$ on $\beta(t - 1)$, and, indeed, in this and other models, Litterman and I have both experimented with specifications where

$$E[\beta(t) - \bar{\beta}|t - 1] = \Theta E[\beta(t - 1) - \bar{\beta}|t - 1],$$

with Θ a scalar and $\bar{\beta}$ the prior mean vector. The best choice of Θ has always turned out to be close to one, however, so that, with sample sizes of the length actually available, there has seemed little advantage to freeing it to differ from one.

4.2.2 Initial Prior Mean

In the model discussed here, m, the lag length, is five—slightly over a year since I am using quarterly data. The vector $B(0; i, j, \cdot)$, the initial prior mean on $\beta(1; i, j, \cdot)$, is set to zero for $i \neq j$. The vector $B(0; i, i, \cdot)$ is given by

$$1.2679, \ -.3397, \ .0910, \ -.0244, \ .00654.$$

These numbers satisfy $B(0; i, i, s) = (1 + \alpha)(-\alpha)^s$, which (if s is allowed to run to infinity instead of being truncated at five) defines the autoregressive coefficients for an ARIMA(0, 1, 1) process with moving average parameters $\alpha = 2 - \sqrt{3}$. It can be shown that this is the form of a unit-averaged Wiener process. Thus, the prior mean makes all elements of X behave like unit-averaged Wiener processes with no lagged cross-relations among components of X.[4]

---

4. Note that, in previous published work, prior means for BVAR models have generally made the components of X discrete-time random walks. The unit-averaged Wiener process prior (at least

4.2.3   The Initial Litterman Prior

The prior covariance matrix is built up by a sequence of modifications of an initial prior. The initial prior makes each scalar component of the $\beta^*(t; i, \cdot, \cdot)$ vector independent of all the others (i.e., it makes the covariance matrix $W[0]$ diagonal) and sets the variance according to

(4)
$$\sqrt{\mathrm{Var}[\beta^* (0; i, j, s)]} = \frac{\sigma(i)}{\sigma(j)} \, \pi_1 \pi_2^{\delta(i,j)} \exp [-\pi_3 \log(s)],$$
$$j = 1, \ldots, k + 1.$$

Here, $\sigma(i)$ is a parameter measuring the scale of fluctuations in variable i, taken in practice as the residual standard error from a univariate fifth-order VAR fit to the entire sample for $i \leq k$. For $j = k + 1$, there is only an $s = 1$ term, as the corresponding a is the "constant term" (here actually not a constant but time varying). For this term, $\sigma(j + 1) = 1/\pi_4$, another unknown parameter. The function $\delta(i, j)$ is the Kronecker delta, one for $i = j$, zero otherwise. Here, as elsewhere in this paper, the parameters π_i are "unknown constants." In principle, we should specify a prior over them to complete a Bayesian framework for inference. However, because doing so would be inconvenient, and because we expect that our prior on them would be uninformative (i.e., we do not know much about them a priori), we integrate over these parameters informally.

4.2.4   The Dummy Initial Observation

The range of differences in observed dynamic behavior for economic time series is fairly large, and, indeed, a reasonable prior specification for the standard error of $\beta^*(0; i, i, 1)$ is about 0.16. But then this component of uncertainty about β^* alone accounts for an implied standard error of forecast for $X_i(1)$ amounting to 16 percent of the initial level of X_i. Since the random components in the other elements of $\beta^*(0)$ are all independent of this one, they all serve only to increase the implied forecast errors. We are not in fact this uncertain about the accuracy of naive random walk forecasts (which is what our initial forecasts, based on prior means for β^*, will be). We are unsure of whether our prior means are exactly right, coefficient by coefficient, but we find it much more likely that the best forecasting model will be one that implies that naive no-change forecasts will be fairly good than that it will be one that implies that great improvements on a no-change forecast are possible. If coefficients deviate from their prior means, we expect that other coefficients

---

where the data have in fact all been collected as unit averages) is a notably more accurate naive standard, however. Observe that the Theil U's (for a definition, see the note to table 4.2 below) obtained by using the correct AR in place of a discrete random walk AR for a process that is actually a unit-averaged Wiener process would be, at forecast horizons 1–4, .933, .9732, .9832, and .9878.

will deviate in an offsetting way, with the result that naive no-change forecasts will still be fairly accurate.

To capture this aspect of prior beliefs, we need to introduce appropriate off-diagonal elements into $W(t; i)$ while leaving the diagonal elements relatively undisturbed. One easy way to do this is to introduce a "dummy observation" in which the prior is modified by feeding it into a Kalman filter that takes as observed data for $X(t - s)$, $s = 1, \ldots, m$, the actual m initial values of X from the sample and for $X_i(t)$, not the actual $X_i(m + 1)$, but instead the model's own forecast, based on the prior mean for β^*, of $X_i(m)$. The data in this dummy observation are weighted by a parameter π_s, which can be expected to be best taken to be near one if the variances of the $u(t; i)$ disturbances have been specified as near to the variance of forecasts from a naive random walk model. Because the Kalman filter finds that, with these artificial data, the prior mean generates perfect forecasts, the Kalman filter makes the posterior mean the prior mean. Only the variance matrix of the prior mean is changed. The change is of rank one and in practice turns out to have only modest effects on diagonal elements of W.

In most previous published work with BVARs, there has been a "sum-of-coefficients" modification to the prior. That modification can be characterized as a sequence of Kalman filtering operations indexed by $j = 1, \ldots, k$, in each of which $X(t - s)$ is set to zero for $s = 1, \ldots, m$, except for $X_j(t - s)$, $s = 1, \ldots, m$, all of which are set to one, while $X_i(t)$, the dependent variable, is set to one if and only if $j = i$. Because most economic time series are smooth, $X(t - s)$ and $X(t - s - 1)$ have similar values. Thus, the dummy initial observation used here is approximately a linear combination of the dummy observations used in imposing the sum-of-coefficients modifications. In practice, the dummy initial observation seems to reduce or eliminate the usefulness of sum-of-coefficients dummy observations. This point is substantively important because heavily weighted sum-of-coefficients dummy observations push the model toward a limiting form written entirely in terms of differences, which eliminates all long-run relations across variables. Putting the same point another way, the old sum-of-coefficients dummy observations pulled the model toward a form with as many unit roots as variables and no cointegration, while the current dummy initial observation pulls the model toward a form with unit-root nonstationarity in all variables without down-weighting the possibility of cointegration.

This dummy-initial-observation idea was discovered in the process of adapting BVAR methodology to a context where the number of series available for a model increases at several dates scattered through a historical sample. A natural approach to such a situation is to begin with a prior for a model with all the variables that will eventually be available, padding the data for variables that are initially unavailable with zeros. Applying the Kalman filter to the padded data is equivalent to applying it to a smaller model. The prior means and variance matrix of the coefficients on unavailable variables are left unaltered by the Kalman filter when the data for them is set at zero. However, at the time when data on a series do become available, the prior shows an exaggerated version of the problem described above as motivating the dummy initial observation. The new data multiply large prior variances on individual coefficients to imply large forecast errors, and the uncertainty about coefficients on the newly entering variable shows no correlation with uncertainty about coefficients on the variables already in the model. We know in fact that the small model estimated up to this point is a good forecasting model, and the availability of data on a new variable has not made its forecast accuracy worse. To make the prior reflect this knowledge, a dummy observation, in which the prior mean coefficients at t are presented to the Kalman filter as making perfect forecasts for $t + 1$, is appropriate. The prior mean coefficients are all zero for the newly introduced variable, so the dummy observation expresses confidence in the small model estimated without the new variable. Covariances between coefficients are created by the dummy observation, so that deviations from zero in coefficients on the new variable imply likely offsetting changes in other coefficients to leave forecasts from the previously estimated small model fairly close to those of the expanded model.

4.2.5   Relative Tightness on Durable Goods Prices

There is an a priori basis for expecting that prices of durable goods frequently traded in open markets will follow stochastic processes well approximated as Wiener processes over short time spans. Thus, our prior mean is inherently more attractive for such variables than, for example, for GNP or unemployment. I therefore introduce into (4) an additional multiplicative factor

(5) $$\pi_9 IDGP(j),$$

where $IDGP(j)$ is zero for variables that are not durable goods prices and one for variables that are. The latter are taken to be the value of the dollar, stock prices, and commodity prices. A case could be made for including three-month Treasury-bill rates and M1 in this list, but they were left out as not actually being prices of durable goods.

4.2.6   Inflation Neutrality

In theoretical models without money illusion, the price level can change without any effect on real variables. If the data show persistent changes in the price level, price-level neutrality implies certain restrictions on the coefficients of the model. In particular in a log-linear model, coefficients on the right-hand-side nominal variables should sum to one in equations with nominal dependent variables and to zero in equations with real dependent variables. The prior mean for the coefficients in this model already almost satisfies this restriction since only coefficients on own lags have nonzero means and these sum almost exactly to one. To pull the prior in the direction of sticking with price-level neutrality, we can perturb it with a dummy observation in which current values and all lags of nominal variables are set at one while all other variables are set at zero. For the nine variables in this model, the nominal variables are the money stock, the price level, stock prices, and commodity prices.[5] The model uses such a dummy observation, scaled up by a factor of 2.0. The use of this dummy observation has little effect on the likelihood or the estimated coefficients, but, as with δ in the next section, there has been no systematic exploration of the parameter space allowing variation in this parameter.

4.2.7   Covariance Matrix of Disturbances

The upper-left diagonal component of the matrix $V(1; i)$ corresponding to all the β's is taken to be $\pi_6^2 W(0; i)$, that is, just a scaled version of the initial prior covariance matrix. However, the scale of this matrix is allowed to adapt over time to the observed squared errors in the model. The idea here is very close to that of the ARCH models pioneered by Engle (1982), but it differs in that, instead of variances being adapted to the sizes of past unobservable true disturbances (u and $\beta - \beta^*$ in our notation), they are adapted to the sizes of past actual forecast errors, that is, in our notation to sizes of

$$v(t; i) = X_i(t) - \sum_{j=1}^{k} \sum_{s=1}^{m} X_j(t - s)B(t - 1; i, j, s)$$
$$+ B(t; i, j + 1, 1).$$

The specification adopted here has the advantage that it makes the variance of disturbances at $t + 1$ known at t, allowing a single pass of the Kalman filter through the data to evaluate the sample likelihood function. More specifically, the scales of the $V(t; i)$ matrices are adapted to the recent history of forecast errors in all equations of the system according to the following scheme. Let $v^*(t; i; 0)$ be $v(t; i)$ divided by the model's implied variance for $v(t; i)$ conditional on the true disturbance matrix being $V(t; i)$, while $v^*(t; i; 1)$ is $v(t; i)$ divided by the model's implied variance for $v(t; i)$ conditional on the true disturbance matrix being $\pi_{11}^2 V(t; i)$. Then let

(6) $$v^{**}(t; i)^2 = p_0 v^*(t; i; 0)^2 + p_1 v^*(t; i; 1)^2,$$

where p_0 is the posterior probability, given data at t, of the smaller variance normal component of the mixed distribution for the disturbance at t, and $p_1 = 1 - p_0$ is the posterior probability of the other component. If the model is correct, v^{**} should average out to about one.

Let

---

5. There could be some dispute over whether to treat the value of the dollar also as a nominal variable. It could behave either way, depending on how price-level changes are related across countries.

(7) $\tau(t; i) = 1 + \pi_7 \left[\pi_8 v^{**}(t; i)^2 + (1 - \pi_8) \sum_{i=1}^{k} \frac{v^{**}(t; i)^2}{k} - 1 \right] + \delta.$

Then we take

(8) $V(t + 1; i) = \tau(t; i)V(t; i).$

Thus, π_7 measures the overall responsiveness of forecast error variance to the magnitude of the current errors, and π_8 measures the relative weight on own errors versus system-wide average errors in making the adjustment. If $\delta = 0$ in this specification, each $v(t; i)^2$ is a martingale, but, since these terms are necessarily positive, they form martingales bounded below. Thus, with $\delta = 0$, the model implies that $v(t; i)$ converges almost surely to a constant. While this implication is perhaps no more unreasonable than the implications of martingale behavior for β itself (which we have imposed), experimentation with δ nonzero seems warranted. The current version of the model takes $\delta = 0.01$, which slightly improves fit over $\delta = 0$, but there has been no systematic exploration of the likelihood surface in δ as there has been for the π vector.

4.3   Model Fitting

What I have described above is an eleven-parameter[6] probability model for the nine quarterly observed time series in the model. A classically oriented statistician can ignore the Bayesian jargon in the model description, treat the β's as well as the u's as unobserved random disturbances, and interpret the π's as the model parameters. From this perspective, our estimation procedure is simply maximum likelihood (although, as mentioned above, since we add up individual equation log likelihoods to form the system likelihood used as the fit criterion, we are in effect assuming independence of all random disturbances across equations, a potentially unrealistic assumption).

My own view is that maximum likelihood is justifiable only as an approximation to a Bayesian procedure or as a device for summarizing a likelihood function. The most important single aspect of a likelihood function, at least if it has a well-defined peak, is its maximum. Nonetheless, we must bear in mind that the peak might not be well defined or that the shape of the likelihood may otherwise turn out to differ from the usual Gaussian shape. In practice, this means that, if likelihood turns out to be insensitive to some dimension of variation in β, we ought to verify that the implications of the model that are important to us—forecasts and policy analysis—are also insensitive to this dimension of variation. If not, results from several parameter settings should be studied.

---

6. This counts only the parameters π_1–π_{11}, not δ, the drift in the variance process, or the weight on the price-neutrality dummy observation. There has been no systematic exploration of the parameter space along these latter two dimensions, so eleven is probably the right measure for assessing how much overfitting is likely to have occurred.

The derivation and interpretation of the likelihood function for this type of model have been described in Doan, Litterman, and Sims (1984). The mechanics of likelihood maximization have been handled with a nonstandard hill-climbing routine, described in Sims (1986b). Because each function maximization is relatively expensive (involving a pass through the data with two Kalman filter applications at each sample point), it seemed important to use global information about the shape of the likelihood in deciding on each function evaluation. The program used, BAYESMTH, fits a surface to the observed likelihood values to generate a guess for the location of the function's peak. It is applied iteratively, with fifty to one hundred function evaluations used to obtain very rough convergence.[7] An advantage of the Bayesian hill-climbing routine is that it can be used at any iteration to generate a best guess at the shape of the likelihood, which is more important for inference than the precise location of the peak.

It is worth noting that, in 1986, when this form of the model was arrived at, the nine-variable version of the model could not be estimated on a PC. Programs were developed on a PC in a six-variable version of the model that took forty minutes to complete a single evaluation of the likelihood. Iterative maximization of the likelihood was carried out with likelihood evaluations on a Cray supercomputer, which could complete a likelihood function evaluation for the nine-variable model in about twenty seconds. Now, a 33MHz 486 PC can evaluate the likelihood for a full nine-variable version of the model in about ninety seconds.

4.4   Characteristics of the Fitted Model

In the rows labeled "87," table 4.1 shows the π vector that achieved the highest level of the likelihood function when the model was fit to data for 1949:III–1987:III in 1987:IV. (The data used are described in the appendix.) Observe that, with $\pi_{11} = 3.8$ and $\pi_{10} = 0.31$, the mixed distribution is notably nonnormal, with a fourth moment 2.43 times as large as that of a normal distribution with the same variance. This is about the same kurtosis as for a t-distribution with five degrees of freedom. Geweke (1992) finds similar kurtosis using a different form of nonnormality in modeling macroeconomic time-series data.

Parameter 7, at 0.25, is small enough to imply significant delay in the reaction of forecast error variances to the previous history of errors, but large enough to imply substantial adaptation within a year. Parameter 8, at 0.34, implies that more weight is given to system-wide average error than to an individual equation's own error in adapting forecast error variances to historical experience.

---

7. Iteration is ordinarily halted when, say, ten or twelve successive function evaluations produce cumulated change in the log likelihood of less than 0.5.

Table 4.1   **Likelihood-Maximizing π Vectors**

π Subscript	Model Version	π Value	Description of π
1	87	.17	Overall tightness
	6	.10	
	11	.24	
2	87	.19	Relative tightness on other variables
	6	.11	
	11	.17	
3	87	.90	Exponent for increase in tightness with lag
	6	.14	
	11	.92	
4	87	3.41	Standard error of constant term relative to $\sigma\,(i)$
	6	5.31	
	11	1.71	
5	87	.89	Weight on initial dummy observation
	6	3.03	
	11	2.21	
6	87	.09	Ratio of initial standard error of time variation
	6	.00	to initial prior standard error
	11	.10	
7	87	.25	Overall sensitivity of forecast error variance to
	6	.00	current error magnitudes
	11	.21	
8	87	.34	Relative weight on equation's own error size
	6	.00	vs. average of system error sizes in setting
	11	.32	variance evolution
9	87	.27	Relative tightness of the prior on durable
	6	1.28	goods price equations
	11	.12	
10	87	.31	Probability that the disturbance is drawn from
	6	.00	the normal component with larger variance
	11	.35	
11	87	3.76	Standard deviation of the more diffuse of the
	6	1.00	two components of the disturbance
	11	3.66	distribution, as a multiple of the standard
			deviation of the less diffuse

Note: A vector of 11 hyperparameters is displayed for each of three versions of the model. In each group of three numbers, the top one refers to a model fit in 1987:IV to data available then for 1949:III–1987:III, and the lower two refer to models fit in 1992:II to data available then for 1949:III–1992:I. The middle one was fit while parameters 7, 8, 10, and 11 were held fixed at the displayed values.

From parameters 1 and 2, we see that the prior standard deviation of the coefficient on the first own lag in each equation is about 0.2 and that coefficients on other variables are given prior standard deviations about 20 percent of the prior standard deviations on own lags. Parameter 3, close to one, implies that prior standard deviations on coefficients for lag s decline approximately as $1/s$. Parameter 6, at about 0.1, implies that the variance of a one-period change in the coefficient vector is about 1 percent of its initial prior variance. The prior uncertainty about the coefficients is thus about the same as prior uncertainty about the parameter change over one hundred quarters.

The parameters that we have discussed to this point are all about the same in both the model fit in 1987 and the current update of that model. The remaining ones, parameters 9, 5, and 4, showed substantial changes with the update. As it stands, the model simply scales the prior covariance matrix by π_6 to obtain the covariance matrix of coefficient changes. Along these dimensions in which refitting has resulted in large changes, it is possible that the model should allow differences between the prior covariance matrix and the coefficient-change covariance matrix. Of course, it is also possible that these results simply reflect sample information. Note that, while the October 1987 stock market crash had occurred at the time of the 1987:IV model fitting, it was not in the data set on which the model was fit.

The biggest change is in parameter 9, which, in going from 0.27 to 0.12, implies a much tighter prejudice in favor of the random walk model for the durable goods price variables after refitting. This is in line with the fact, documented below, that the model's forecasts for these variables have shown little if any margin of superiority over those of a naive continuous-time random walk model. Parameters 5 and 6 show increased weight on the initial dummy observation and decreased prior variance for the constant term with refitting.

The differences in parameters between the 1987 version and the updated version of the model are enough to make modest but noticeable changes in model forecasts. For the 1982:II forecast, for example, the general shape of forecast paths for variables is little affected, but the level of long-run growth to which the forecast paths gravitate is affected. For variables not hit by parameter 9, these differences are on the order of 0.1–0.3 percentage points in the forecast annualized growth rates (and about the same magnitude in the forecast levels of interest rates). For the value of the dollar, stock prices, and commodity prices—the three variables hit by π_9—the forecast long-run annualized growth rates are affected by 1 or 2 percentage points.

The model with coefficient variation, nonnormality, and time-varying variances suppressed, reported in the middle rows of table 4.1, fits best with a tighter overall prior, relatively stronger prior restriction on cross-variable relations, weakly damped prior variances on longer lags, and small weight on the durable goods price restriction. The increased tightness in parameters 1 and 2, pulling all variables closer to the random walk model, roughly offsets the increased looseness in parameters 9, 3, and 4.

Imposition of these simplifying restrictions reduces likelihood for each equation, and the sum of the reductions in twice the log likelihood (which can be interpreted as measured in "chi-squared" units) is 1,146. This is a very large likelihood reduction, corresponding roughly to what would be produced by increasing forecast RMSE by 30 percent in every equation. Since the RMSE differences between the six-parameter and the eleven-parameter model

Table 4.2   **Theil U Statistics, 1949:III–1992:I**

		Quarters Ahead			
	Model Version	1	2	4	8
Treasury-bill rate	87	.9493	1.0295	.9786	.9845
	6	.9746	1.0362	1.0002	.9387
	11	.9682	1.0570	.9858	.9928
M1	87	.4546	.4354	.4252	.4265
	6	.4645	.4410	.4178	.3920
	11	.4489	.4305	.4185	.4203
GNP deflator	87	.3799	.3169	.2906	.2737
	6	.4350	.4053	.4184	.4347
	11	.3787	.3143	.2857	.2679
Real GNP	87		.6857	.6937	.6693
	6	.7388		.6557	.6047
	11	.7290	.6675		.6653
Business fixed in-	87	.8686	.8989	.9782	1.1132
vestment	6	.8847	.9165	.9231	.8961
	11	.8533	.8655	.9272	1.0720
Unemployment	87	.7936	.8510	.9238	.9835
	6	.8110	.8827	.9612	.9615
	11	.7910	.8443	.9133	.9516
Trade-weighted	87				1.2309
value of dollar	6		1.0203	1.0585	1.1613
	11		1.0185	1.0664	1.1932
S&P 500 stock	87	.9126	.9197	.9217	.9470
price index	6	.9243	.9499	.9645	.9969
	11	.9234	.9444	.9593	.9932
Commodity price	87	.8517	.9217	1.0308	1.2121
index	6	.8128	.8951	1.0682	1.2043
	11	.8578	.9227	1.0021	1.0967

Note: In each group of three numbers, the figures shown correspond to the three parameter settings displayed in the corresponding groups of three numbers in table 4.1: an 11-hyperparameter model fit in 1987, a 6-hyperparameter model fit in 1992, and the 11-hyperparameter model fit in 1992. The Theil U is the ratio of root mean squared error (RMSE) of model forecasts to the RMSE of naive no-change forecasts for the same period.

shown in table 4.2 are not nearly this large, it is clear that much of the likelihood improvement comes from more accurate modeling of the evolution of forecast error variances in the eleven-parameter model.

4.5   Measures of Forecasting Performance

Table 4.2 shows how these differences in parameters affect model forecast performance. All the numbers in this table are Theil U statistics, meaning ratios of model RMSEs to naive no-change RMSEs. All the errors entering into these calculations come from using the model, with VAR coefficients recursively updated each quarter, to prepare forecasts through the sample. A single consistent time series, constructed in 1992:II, is used for each variable, so that forecast errors measured here do not correspond exactly to the actual historical forecast errors. Data for periods after the forecast date affect the forecast for that date only insofar as they have influenced selection of parameters. The rows labeled 6 and 11 had parameters (π_j's, not VAR coefficients) fit to the full sample through 1992:I, while the rows labeled 87 had parameters fit to data through 1987:III only. Forecasts made and circulated regularly from this model from 1987:IV through 1992:II have all used the same set of parameter values, that corresponding to the "87" rows of table 4.2.

The 1987:IV–1992:I postsample period for the 1987 model is about 10 percent of the full sample. A 20 percent improvement in forecast accuracy over this period, with no deterioration in performance for the sample period, would improve the Theil U for the full period by about 2 percent. In column 1 of table 4.2, there are no improvements of this magnitude in the Theil U from the updated fit. As we move rightward along the columns, the forecasts whose accuracy is being measured overlap in time more and more, with the result that the sampling variation in the forecast accuracy measure, particularly over the short postsample period, increases substantially. The update of parameter estimates produces improvements in two-quarter forecasts of 2.7 percent in real GDP/GNP and 3.9 percent in investment. At the four-quarter horizon, there are improvements of 2 percent or more in these same two variables and also in commodity prices. At the eight-quarter horizon, GNP/GDP drops off the list, and the GNP/GDP deflator, unemployment, and the trade-weighted dollar are added. The only differences of 4 percent or more are for investment at the four-quarter horizon (5.5 percent), commodity prices at the eight-quarter horizon (10.5 percent), and stock prices at the eight-quarter horizon (4.9 percent) in favor of the 1987 version of the model). On the whole, it is clear that there is some gain from updating the fit, as would be expected, but that the model's out-of-sample forecast performance does not drastically contradict the 1987 parameter estimates.

The U statistics for the simplified six-parameter model show that, for most variables and time horizons, the eleven-parameter model performs better, but not by very much. The sharpest exception is for the GNP/GDP deflator. The smaller model is worse there by a large margin. At the eight-quarter horizon, the smaller model is 10 percent better for real GNP/GDP and 20 percent better for investment. Since this better performance for the smaller model is not matched at the shorter time horizons for these variables, it is hard to know what to make of it. It could be sampling variation, but it might also indicate a weakness in the larger model at long horizons for these variables.

Table 4.3 focuses on the performance of the 1987 version of the model for the postsample period, again using a single 1982:II data set rather than the historical sequence of regularly revised data series. The first three rows in each horizontal block of four rows compare the RMSE over 1988:I–1992:I for the 1987 model to the RMSE of alternative forecasting schemes: a naive no-

Table 4.3   **Performance in 1988:I–1992:I**

		Quarters Ahead			
		1	2	4	8
Treasury-bill rate	F/N	.8097	.9620	1.0444	1.1633
	F/S	.5890	.7660	1.0898	1.1497
	F/6	.7667	.8238	.8826	.8867
	F		.9686		
M1	F/N	.4702	.5165	.6272	.6527
	F/S	1.0676	1.1407	1.2289	1.1253
	F/6	.8387	.8283	.8414	.7093
	F	.0077	.0152	.0306	.0542
GNP deflator	F/N	.2246	.2140	.2063	.1157
	F/S	.4532	.5307	.5676	.3448
	F/6	.3983	.3342	.2793	.1298
	F	.0022	.0042	.0081	.0091
Real GNP	F/N	.7257	.7925	.7958	.9917
	F/S	.4456	.5407	.5065	.5734
	F/6	1.0236	1.0736	1.0230	1.0831
	F	.0043	.0087	.0147	.0278
Business fixed	F/N	.9077	.9019	.9840	1.5563
investment	F/S	.6251	.5606	.5374	.6133
	F/6	.8263	.7197	.6520	.8139
	F	.0153	.0245	.0426	.0844
Unemployment	F/N	.9419	1.0043	1.0177	.8768
	F/S	.5976	.5972	.6121	.5732
	F/6	1.1643	1.2738	1.4563	1.7785
	F	.0364	.6099	.1280	.1692
Trade-weighted	F/N	1.0662	1.1994	1.4599	1.8827
value of dollar	F/S	1.6418	1.5944	1.4049	1.0495
	F/6	1.0154	1.0362	1.1170	1.3192
	F	.0473	.0798	.1161	.1570
S&P 500 stock	F/N	1.0065	1.0050	.9396	.8444
price index	F/S	.9319	.9321	.9343	.8234
	F/6	.9958	.9000	.7980	.5859
	F	.0523	.0874	.1366	.1805
Commodity price	F/N	1.0679	1.2901	1.5340	2.7498
index	F/S	.4230	.3700	.3377	.4666
	F/6	.4600	.3388	.2599	.2875
	F	.0145	.0247	.0428	.0909

Note: In each horizontal block, F/N is the ratio of root mean squared error (RMSE) for the model to that for a naive no-change forecast, both for the forecast period 1988:I–1992:I. F/S is the ratio of RMSE for the model over 1988:I–1992:I to that for the model over 1949:III–1992:I. F/6 is the ratio of model RMSE to the RMSE for the 6-hyperparameter model displayed as the middle numbers in table 4.1. The row labeled F is the RMSE for the model over 1988:I–1992:I. The model is the version using hyperparameters chosen in 1987:IV to fit data for 1948:III–1987:III, except for the 6-parameter model used for comparison in the third rows. The 6-parameter model was fit to 1992:I data.

change model over 1988:I–1992:I, the 1987 model over 1949:III–1992:I, and the simplified six-parameter model (fit to data through 1992:I) 1988:I–1992:I. The fourth row shows the RMSE for the 1987 model over 1988:I–1992:I.

In certain senses, this period was unusually easy to forecast. Note that, for seven of the nine variables, the F/S rows are uniformly less than one. This means that, for these variables, RMSE was smaller in the postsample period than in the sample period. Yet, for most variables, comparison of the F/N row with the corresponding 87 row in table 4.2 shows little improvement, or even deterioration, in the model's performance relative to that of naive no-change forecasts. In other words, forecasting in this period was easy, by historical standards, for both the model and the no-change alternative, with the proportional improvement generally stronger for the naive models. This leaves the implications for evaluating the model ambiguous. The model has done "well" by historical standards, but such performance in a period when naive models are also doing "well" is weak support at best for the model.

There are two strong exceptions to this general conclusion. The GNP/GDP deflator forecasts for this period were better than their historical average, and they also improved relative to naive forecasts. This positive picture must be qualified by the fact that nothing within the model suggests that such a dramatically good performance is likely to be anything more than a random piece of good luck. The value of the dollar, on the other hand, was forecast with RMSE 60 percent worse than its historical average, in a period when naive forecasts at long horizons were getting better. The six-parameter model performed much better for this variable and this period.

For commodity prices, the naive model was much better than the model at forecasting horizons beyond one quarter. But this seems likely to reflect an unusual spate of good luck for the naive model since the 1987 model had better RMSE than its historical average and moving in the direction of the naive model by going to the six-parameter model produced drastically worse RMSE for this variable. A similar argument suggests that not too much should be made of the strong advantage of the naive model over the 1987 model at the eight-quarter horizon for investment.

The substantial advantage of the six-parameter model over the 1987 model at all horizons for unemployment is worrisome. The facts that the 87 model nonetheless showed substantial absolute improvement in RMSE over the sample period and that there is no correspondingly strong advantage of the six-parameter over the eleven-parameter model for the full sample in table 4.2 suggest that this, too, may well be a random fluctuation in the relative performance of the models.

4.6 Tracking the 1990–91 Recession

The model did not perform brilliantly in tracking the 1990–91 recession, but this may make it all the more useful to examine graphically how it behaved. This recession was mild, with no annualized growth rate for GNP/GDP much outside the ±3 percent range. Since the model's historical RMSE for GNP/GDP is about 0.5 percent in levels, and therefore 2 percent at an annual rate, it cannot be expected that the model would precisely track the path of GNP over such a mild fluctuation. On the other hand, the two quarters of negative GNP growth in 1990:IV and 1991:I were almost completely unanticipated by the model.

The pattern of changing forecasts over this period is largely explained by two factors: the forecast path for each variable adapts to the new initial conditions as errors are accounted for, and the steady drop in interest rates, largely unanticipated by the model, affects predictions for other variables over a two- to three-year horizon. Before looking at the data for actual forecasts over the span of the recession, I document the cross-variable effects of interest rate disturbances.

Figure 4.1 displays interest rate forecasts made in June 1992, using data on national accounts through 1992:I and some contemporaneous data on other variables. One forecast uses a 1992:II Treasury-bill rate of 3.687 percent, which is a guess, based on actual monthly data for April and May of the likely actual 1992:II value. The other two forecasts condition on 1992:II bill rates lower by 0.25 and 0.5 percent. The forecast is made by updating coefficients based on data through 1992:I for all variables, forecasting 1992:II using these

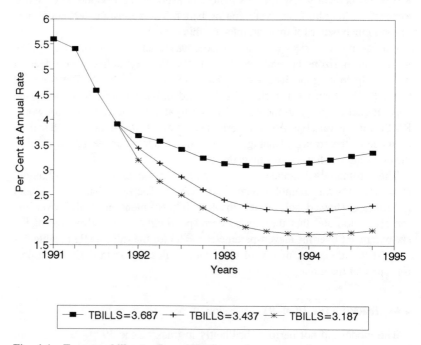

Fig. 4.1   Treasury-bill rate, June 1992 forecast

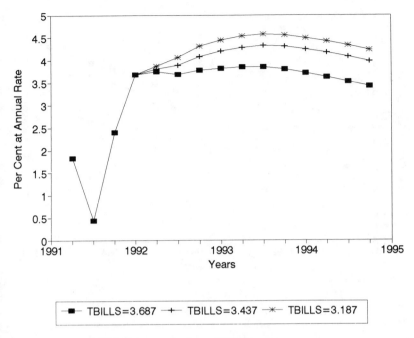

Fig. 4.2   Real GDP/GNP growth, June 1992 forecast

coefficients, replacing the forecast values for 1992:II for the bill rate, M1, the unemployment rate, the value of the dollar, and stock prices with "actual" values based on monthly data for the first two months of the model, updating the coefficients again, treating this mixed vector of forecast and actual values for 1992:II as if it were a new data point, then projecting from 1992:III onward with this final set of updated coefficients. The parameters of the model are those obtained from 1992 updates of the likelihood (the "11" rows in tables 4.1 and 4.2), not those of the 1987 model. Note that these interest rate forecasts diverge and that the paths are spread apart by much more than their original 0.5 percent dispersion after a year or two. Note also that nonlinearity shows itself clearly—since the Treasury-bill rate enters the model untransformed, an initial 0.25 percent perturbation in its path would in a linear model produce exactly half the perturbation in the remaining forecast path that an initial 0.5 percent would. Here instead the 0.5 percent initial perturbation produces considerably less than double the effect of a 0.25 percent perturbation after the initial period.

   Figure 4.2 shows that the lower interest rates imply a forecast of more rapid output growth. Fig. 4.3 shows that the lower interest rates imply only slightly different GDP deflator inflation forecasts. The forecast inflation is lower with lower interest rates, but by a small enough amount that most of the drop in nominal rates still translates into a lower real rate. Fig. 4.4 shows that the sign

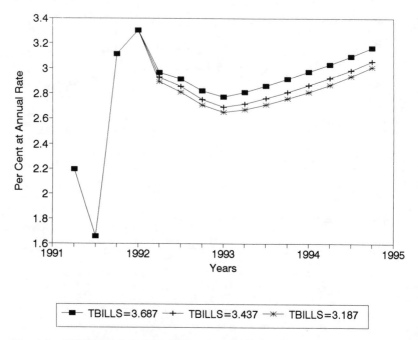

Fig. 4.3   GNP/GDP deflator inflation, June 1992 forecast

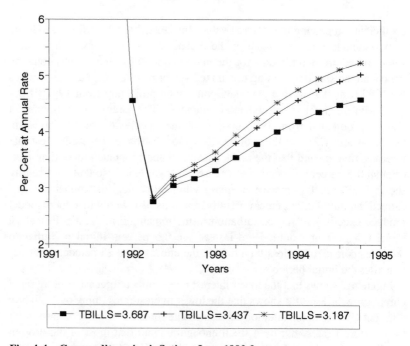

Fig. 4.4   Commodity price inflation, June 1992 forecast

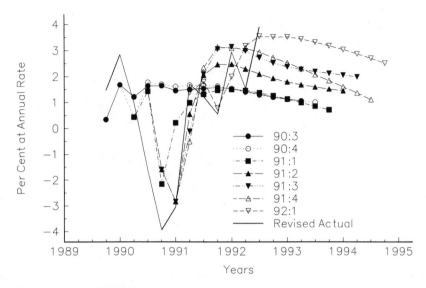

Fig. 4.5   Real GNP/GDP growth forecasts

of the effect on inflation in commodity prices is the opposite of that on inflation in the GDP deflator and that the magnitude is larger. (Note, however, that
the commodity price index is much more volatile than the GDP deflator.)

This pattern of results is similar to the pattern that I noted in an earlier paper
(Sims, in press) analyzing data across several countries with simpler VAR
models. It raises interesting questions of interpretation, discussed in the earlier paper, that I leave aside here.

Figure 4.5 shows successive forecasts of GNP/GDP growth rates over the
recession period, together with the actual growth rates for the period as shown
in the revised GDP data available in December 1992. Unlike the forecast errors reported in the tables, these are actual historical forecasts, so the effects
of data revisions can be seen in the plots. Each plotted line shows actual data
for three quarters before the first quarter for which there were no data on GNP
at the time of forecast, together with forecast values for the twelve subsequent
quarters. In 1990:IV, the forecast (which used data through 1990:III for national accounts but some current data on interest rates, unemployment,
money, the exchange rate, and stock prices) still showed no negative growth,
although the projected positive growth rate of about 1.5 percent was low by
historical standards. The 1990:IV GNP data were enough to pull the forecast
growth for 1991:I down to less than 1 percent at an annual rate, but this left
an error, compared to the actual negative growth of nearly 3 percent, nearly
as large as for 1990:IV. The 1991:II and later forecasts, however, have been
fairly well on track for the pattern of slow recovery since then.

Figure 4.6 shows how these patterns appear on a graph in levels. The fact

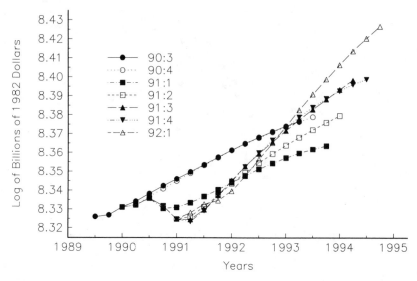

Fig. 4.6   Real GNP/GDP level forecasts

that the prerecession forecasts were for slow growth did not prevent them from being substantially mistaken about the 1991–92 levels of GNP. If growth proceeds as the model projects through 1992, GDP will be back up to its 1990:IV projected path around the end of 1992.

Figure 4.7 shows the sequence of interest rate forecasts. In every quarter except 1991:III, the interest rate fell by substantially more than the model had anticipated. On the basis of figures 4.1–4.4, we should expect that these interest rate shocks should increase forecast growth rates for output, slightly decrease forecast GDP deflator inflation, and increase forecast commodity price inflation over a two- to three-year horizon. We can see the corresponding increasingly optimistic long-run output growth forecasts in figures 4.5 and 4.6. Figures 4.8 and 4.9 show that, indeed, long-run GDP deflator inflation forecasts shifted downward and long-run commodity price inflation forecasts shifted upward. Note also the substantial effect of the data revision and switch to GDP rather than GNP accounting between the 1991:IV and the 1992:I forecasts. From figure 4.8, the "actual" inflation rate for 1991:III used in forming the 1991:IV forecast can be seen to be more than a percentage point above that used in forming the 1992:I forecast.

4.7   Conclusion

This model represents a further step in a research program attempting to bring into the realm of explicit probabilistic theory more of our uncertainty about the way the economy works. The model has been used for forecasts

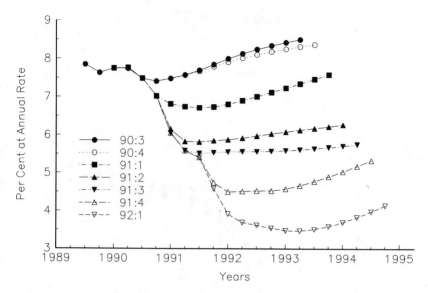

Fig. 4.7   Treasury-bill rate forecasts

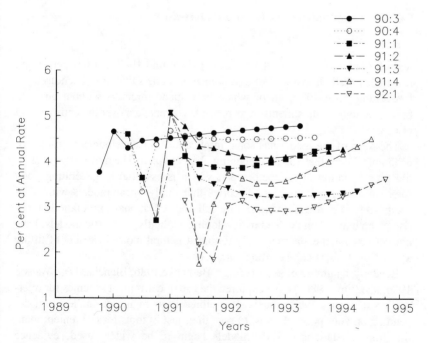

Fig. 4.8   GNP/GDP deflator inflation forecasts

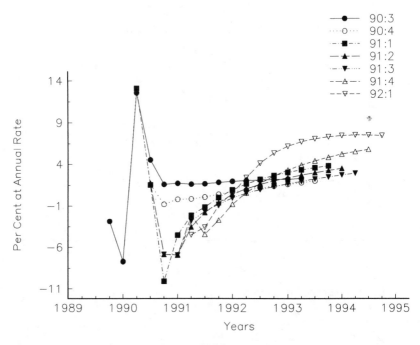

Fig. 4.9   Commodity price inflation 1992 forecasts

with the same parameters (the π vector) since mid-1987 and has performed reasonably well. It is a part of a sequence of models that have been used for forecasting since 1980, all of which have made forecasts without any add factors or ad hoc adjustments in response to current data over the entire period of record.

The form of the model has some implications for developments in macro-economic theory that aim at explaining observed data. The model has substantial time variation in its coefficients, which is essential to generating good forecasts for some variables. Theories that imply linear models with fixed coefficients will therefore inevitably fall short. Rational expectations theorists, who have taken the lead in developing explicitly stochastic models, have not yet generated econometrically usable structural models capable of fitting a world of stochastically drifting parameters.

Recently, a number of authors (e.g., Bernanke 1986; Blanchard and Watson 1986; and Sims 1986a) have explored the use of convenient schemes for interpreting stationary VAR models. It is either discouraging or challenging, depending on your point of view, to note that, just as tools for convenient identification of stationary VAR models begin to be widely used, evidence emerges that stationary VAR models are inadequate. The problem of generating convenient identification schemes for the nonlinear, nonnormal model laid out in this paper appears quite difficult.

Appendix
Data Description

Treasury-bill rate. Three-month Treasury-bill rate, auction average.

M1. Pre-1959 data on M1, spliced together with more recent official data. For this series as for others described below as spliced, the splicing is done simply by scaling the earlier data to match the level of the more recent data at the date of switch.

PGDP. GDP deflator, 1987 = 100, seasonally adjusted. Spliced to earlier data on the GNP deflator at 1959:I.

GDP87. GDP, 1987 prices, seasonally adjusted. Spliced to earlier data on real GNP at 1959:I.

BFI87. Business fixed investment in 1987 prices, seasonally adjusted, from the GDP accounts. Spliced to earlier data from the GNP accounts at 1959:I.

UNEMP. Unemployment rate, civilians aged twenty and over, seasonally adjusted.

DOLLAR. Federal Reserve Board trade-weighted index of the value of the U.S. dollar, 1973 = 100.

STOCKS. The Standard and Poors 500 stock index, 1941–43 = 10.

PCOMM. Sensitive intermediate and crude producer prices index, January 1948 = 100 (U.S. Department of Commerce, *Business Conditions Digest,* ser. A0M098).

References

Bernanke, B. 1986. *Alternative explanations of the money-income correlation.* Carnegie-Rochester Policy Series on Public Policy. Amsterdam: North-Holland.

Blanchard, Olivier, and Mark Watson. 1986. Are all business cycles alike? In *The American business cycle,* ed. R. J. Gordon. Chicago: University of Chicago Press.

Doan, T., R. Litterman, and C. Sims. 1984. Forecasting and policy analysis using realistic prior distributions. *Econometric Reviews* 3 (1): 1–100.

Engle, Robert F. 1982. Autoregressive conditional heteroskedasticity with estimates of the variance of U.K. inflation. *Econometrica* 50: 987–1008.

Geweke, John. 1992. Priors for macroeconomic time series and their application. Institute for Empirical Macroeconomics Discussion Paper no. 64. Minneapolis: Federal Reserve Bank of Minneapolis.

Litterman, Robert B. 1986. Forecasting with Bayesian vector autoregressions—five years of experience. *Journal of Business and Economic Statistics* 4 (1): 25–38.

McNees, Stephen K. 1986. Forecasting accuracy of alternative techniques: A comparison of U.S. macroeconomic forecasts. *Journal of Business and Economic Statistics* 4 (1): 5–24.

Sims, Christopher. 1986a. Are forecasting models usable for policy analysis. *Quarterly Review of the Federal Reserve Bank of Minneapolis* 10 (Winter): 2–16.

———. 1986b. BAYESMTH: A program for multivariate Bayesian interpolation. Center for Economic Research Discussion Paper no. 234. University of Minnesota.

———. In press. Interpreting the macroeconomic time series facts: The effects of monetary policy. *European Economic Review.*

Comment   Pierre Perron

It is a humbling experience to be asked to comment on such a paper. Forecasting economic time is surely not an easy task, and relatively few succeed at providing a useful product that is based on scientific principles and is free of the so-called add factors. Christopher Sims has been the intellectual leader of a class of forecasting models that, indeed, can claim such success. This paper provides an overview of the main features of the model as it now stands as well as several assessments of the quality of recent forecasts. Being neither an expert on the topic of forecasting nor particularly well trained in the Bayesian tradition, I will restrain myself to some general remarks that I hope will help the reader better understand and appreciate some issues underlying this methodology. These comments pertain to the following topics: the Bayesian interpretation, the treatment of trends, and the use of the mixture of normal distribution and its implications.

The Bayesian Interpretation

When reading a discussion of a paper that uses Bayesian tools, the reader often expects the discussant to probe or question the priors. I will refrain from doing so. In a sense, I am inclined to think that little can be gained from discussing whether one prior is better than another. What appears more important is to question the robustness of the results to reasonable changes in the prior specifications. This is, in principle, desirable, but in a project of this magnitude it appears difficult to ask the investigator for a full sensitivity analysis. In effect, I have nothing against the priors; none seem particularly unreasonable or, again, particularly undebatable. Many are imposed explicitly to make the model tractable. This is, however, fair game and does not appear any less a flaw than other simplifications found in alternative methodologies.

Pierre Perron is associate professor of economics at the University of Montreal and a research associate at the Centre de Recherche et Développement en Economique.

What strikes me, however, is that the model and the way in which it is estimated can hardly be said to be more Bayesian than any other popular approaches such as the standard VAR, the structural VAR (e.g., Blanchard and Watson 1986), the error correction type model of Stock and Watson (1991), or even, if I dare say so, the traditional simultaneous equations models of the Cowles Commission type (e.g., Fair 1984).

The basic starting point of the model is a data-generating process (DGP) of the general form

$$(1) \qquad x(t) = f[x(t - 1), \ldots, x(t - m); \theta(t)],$$

where $x(t)$ is the $k \times 1$ vector of variables in the system (the nine macroeconomic time series). In application, f is specified as a VAR of order m with time-varying parameters:

$$(2) \qquad \begin{aligned} x_i = & \sum_{j=1}^{k} \sum_{s=1}^{m} x_j(t - s)\beta(t; i, j, s) \\ & + \beta(t; i, j + 1, 1) + u(t; i), \quad i = 1, \ldots, k. \end{aligned}$$

So $\theta(t)$ contains here all the β's. The parameters $\theta(t)$ are specified to evolve according to a general function of the form

$$(3) \qquad g[\theta(t)|\Phi(t - 1)] = g\{\theta(t); \theta(t - 1); [x(t - s), s \geq 1]; \mu\},$$

where $\Phi(t - 1)$ is the information set dated time $t - 1$. Here the vector μ are some "hyperparameters" that govern the evolution of the parameters of the model. The vector of parameters $\theta(0)$ is also treated as a random variable with a marginal probability density function of the form $h[\theta(0), \gamma]$. Here μ and γ are the π's in the notation of the paper (eleven of them in all). Hence, the likelihood of the data is

$$(4) \qquad p[x(t); t = 1, \ldots, T | x(-m - 1), \ldots, x(0); \mu, \gamma].$$

The model is estimated by maximizing the likelihood function with respect to μ and γ (more precisely, the method of estimation is quasi maximum likelihood since all k equations are estimated separately; as stated, it would be maximum likelihood estimation with no correlation across errors in the different equations). I see very little that is explicitly Bayesian in this approach; no priors are imposed over the π's to obtain the posterior distribution.

Sims (1991) argues that what makes this modeling approach explicitly Bayesian is the presence of the probability density function $h[\theta(0), \gamma]$ for the vector of initial conditions for the time paths of the parameters $\theta(t)$. The argument is that maximum likelihood estimation of γ will not yield a consistent estimate, thereby invalidating the standard justification for the classical approach (essentially because the accumulation of information as additional data become available does not add information about γ given that the initial conditions have transient effects). I think that such an argument is open to debate.

This point can be illustrated as follows. In a state space model with stationary variables, one can use the ergodic distribution of the parameters to initialize the system. When the time paths of the variables are nonstationary, this is no longer feasible, and one must either condition on some initial values or specify probability distributions for them. Sims's (1991) arguments imply that doing the latter necessarily makes the model Bayesian. I do not think that a classical interpretation of this modeling is strained. The initial distribution need not be viewed as imposing some priors; rather, it can be viewed simply as a convenient way to allow for randomness in the initial condition. The fact the maximum likelihood estimation on these parameters is inconsistent is also not much of a problem in a classical approach given that these initial conditions are often viewed as nuisance parameters, that is, parameters that are not the object of direct inference. In any event, it appears less strained to give a classical interpretation to the imposition of a probability distribution on the initial conditions than it is to give a Bayesian interpretation of the estimation method obtained without specifying prior distributions on μ.

The many priors imposed and discussed at length to justify them are ways to impose restrictions on the unrestricted time-varying parameters VAR given by (2). After all, this VAR is much too general, and some restrictions need to be imposed. This is no different than for any other forecasting model.

The final product is basically a constrained VAR where the constraints are highly nonlinear. Hence, the priors can be viewed as simply imposing a priori restrictions as in any other more "structural" model. The basic difference here from, say, the Cowles Commission approach is that the restrictions are "justified" using prior distributions that are themselves justified by extraneous empirical results (e.g., the plausibility of unit roots characterizing the time series) instead of being based primarily on theoretical arguments.

Let me stress that none of the comments above are meant to carry any negative connotations. On the contrary, I view it as quite an achievement when one is able to end up with a successful model with only some eleven free parameters by imposing restrictions that do not appear unbelievable. My view is basically that the priors act as alternative justifications for parameter reduction efforts that are present in all methods. The advantage here may lie in the highly nonlinear aspects of the restrictions that are eventually achieved.

The Treatment of Trends

One of the priors imposed is that the parameters are such that the data series have a prior mean of independent integrated processes. Some have argued that this is basically equivalent to first-differencing the data prior to the analysis. This implication is false, as argued in Sims (1991), because only the mean of the prior is centered on the unit root but variability is allowed. Note, however, that such centering on the unit root creates potential problems associated with the probability mass put on explosive processes. It might be more appropriate to truncate or downweight the possibility of explosive roots relative to stationary ones.

The main point that I wish to convey, however, is that there is a more subtle way in which the structure of the model implies *fitted* unit root processes for any series that seems to be characterized by a nonstationary mean (e.g., real GNP, M1, the GNP deflator, stock prices, etc.). This is linked to the treatment of trends or, indeed, their absence. The basic fact to recognize is that no time trends are included as regressors in the estimated VAR as described (prior to the imposition of restrictions) by (2). My argument is that leaving out time trends (of any variety, linear or segmented, with constant or random coefficients) implies fitted series with unit roots. As much as Sims does not appear particularly to be a proponent of unit roots—see, for example, Sims (1988) (and I am not either; see Perron [1989])—the absence of trends in the estimated model precludes having series estimated to be characterized by "trend-stationary" processes (which we may view as equivalent to using differenced data).

To see how the argument goes, it is useful to consider a standard VAR with time-invariant parameters (for a more detailed treatment, see also Campbell and Perron [1991]). Consider a DGP of the form

$$(5) \qquad x_t = \mu + \delta t + Z_t, \quad A(L)Z_t = e_t \sim N(0, \Sigma),$$

with $A(L)$ a matrix polynomial of order m in the lag operator L. We can write (5) as

$$(6) \qquad A(L)x_t = A(1)\mu + \Phi\delta + A(1)\delta t + e_t,$$

where $\Phi = \sum_{i=1}^m iA_i$ is the mean lag matrix. Alternatively, denote $A(1) = \Pi$ following Johansen's (1988) notation for cointegrated systems:

$$(7) \qquad \Delta x_t = \mu^* + \Pi x_{t-1} - \Pi\delta(t-1) + \text{lags}(\Delta x_t) + e_t$$

or

$$(8) \qquad \Delta x_t = \mu^* + \Pi Z_{t-1} + \text{lags}(\Delta x_t) + e_t.$$

Note that, in general, the vector Z_t may contain elements with unit roots as well as stationary processes. It depends on the values of the matrices in the lag polynomial $A(L)$. To see that the fitted series will behave as unit root processes if the estimated model does not contain trend regressors, consider the following. A VAR with no time trends will be misspecified unless $\Pi\delta = 0$. In general, with a cointegrated system, $\Pi = \alpha\beta'$, where α and β are $k \times r$ matrices, r being the number of cointegrating vectors present and β being the matrix whose columns are the cointegrating vectors. Hence, $\Pi\delta = 0$ if and only if $\beta'\delta = 0$; that is, the cointegrating vectors that annihilate the nonstationarity in the noise component ($\beta'Z_t \sim I[0]$) also annihilate the nonstationarity in the trend component. Such a condition is often referred to as "deterministic cointegration."

The condition $\beta'\delta = 0$ may be one that is natural to impose, but it precludes the possibility of variables with a stationary noise component. Suppose that one of the variables (say the jth) is trend stationary, that is, $\delta_j \neq 0$ and $Z_{j,t} \sim I(0)$; then one of the rows of β' is $e_j = (0, \ldots, 1, 0, \ldots, 0)$ (with a one in the jth position). Here, the unit vector is a (trivial) cointegrating vector. However, one of the conditions for the nonmisspecification of a VAR with no trends as regressors is that $e_j'\delta = \delta_j = 0$, that is, that the series is trendless. Accordingly, the model is misspecified if there is a series with a nonzero trend and a stationary noise component. The effect of this possible misspecification is to bias the parameters in such a way that the fitted values imply the presence of a unit root, and this bias does not vanish in large samples (for a proof in the univariate case, see Perron [1988]).

The example given above shows the importance of the treatment of trends. While I considered only simple linear time trends in the context of VAR with constant coefficients, the same principle applies in a more general context. The presence of trend regressors is necessary if trending series with stationary noise components are to be entertained as a possibility. I do not suggest the inclusion of linear time trends with constant coefficients in each equation. An interesting extension would involve the inclusion of time trends in the general VAR (2) with time-varying coefficients as well. The changes in these coefficients may be infrequent, and the prior distribution of mixed normality for the coefficients is particularly well suited for this purpose (I discuss this further below).

This increased generality would not come without drawbacks, however. It has been documented that the presence of time trends in estimated autoregressions creates, in general, a large downward bias on the sum of the autoregressive coefficients (see, e.g., Andrews 1991). Note, however, that this bias, unlike the ones created without trends, vanishes in large samples. In any event, asymmetrical priors could correct this bias. Such an extension may also introduce complexities in the specification of the priors. For example, flat priors on the trend coefficients and the autoregressive parameters are no longer adequate. Consider, for example, a simple univariate AR(1) such that $x_t = \mu + \delta t + Z_t$ with $Z_t = \alpha Z_{t-1} + e_t$. Such a process can be written as

$$(9) \qquad x_t = (1 - \alpha)\mu + \delta\alpha + (1 - \alpha)\delta t + \alpha x_{t-1} + e_t$$

or

$$(10) \qquad x_t = \mu^* + \beta t + \alpha x_{t-1} + e_t,$$

where $\mu^* = (1 - \alpha)\mu + \delta\alpha$, and $\beta = (1 - \alpha)\delta$. Note that, when $\alpha = 1$, $\beta = 0$, and a good prior should reflect this relation. Accordingly, priors should not be imposed on α, β, and μ^* but directly on α, δ, and μ. This may be more difficult to implement in practice. For similar arguments cast explicitly in a Bayesian framework, see Uhlig (1991).

The Mixture of Normals Prior

In his concluding comments, Sims argues that "the model has substantial time variation in its coefficients, which is essential to generating good forecasts for some variables." The importance of time variation in the coefficients is indeed highlighted throughout the paper. I certainly agree with this interpretation and the fact that the introduction of time variation in the parameters is a major step forward. However, in this model, time variation is associated with another modeling device, namely, specifying the form of the distribution of disturbances as a mixture of two normals. I think that such an assumption (or prior) is not simply "an arbitrary convenience" but rather a potentially equally important feature of the model.

The mixture of normal assumption for the distribution of the disturbances has the following form for the vector $[\beta(t), u(t; i)]$:

$$
(11) \quad p[\beta(t), u(t; i)|t - 1] = \pi_{10}\phi\left\{\begin{bmatrix} \beta^*(t - 1) \\ 0 \end{bmatrix}, V(t; i)\right\}
$$
$$
+ (1 - \pi_{10})\phi\left\{\begin{bmatrix} \beta^*(t - 1) \\ 0 \end{bmatrix}, \pi_{11}^2 V(t; i)\right\},
$$

where $\phi(a, b)$ is the normal density function with mean a and variance b. This specification states that $[\beta(t), u(t: i)]$ has mean $[\beta^*(t - 1), 0]$, where $\beta^*(t - 1)$ is also specified to follow a specific distribution. Its variance, however, is $V(t; i)$ with probability π_{10} and $\pi_{11}^2 V(t; i)$ with probability $(1 - \pi_{10})$.

While the use of mixtures of normal distribution, and other non-Gaussian distributions in general, for disturbances is rather new in econometric modeling, it has some history in the statistics literature (see, in particular, Kitagawa [1987] and the comments related to that paper, esp. Martin and Raftery [1987]). The main motivation for its use is the modeling of structural changes (and outliers) in a time series of data. To see why this is so, consider the case where, in (11), π_{10} is small and π_{11} is large (substantially larger than one). In this case, the disturbances are drawn from the low-variance normal distribution most of the time, but, occasionally, a disturbance is drawn from the normal distribution with high variance. This effectively introduces a fat-tailed type behavior for the disturbances. To see why this can be useful in the analysis of structural change, note first that the β's follow martingale-like paths and that the x's are, in general, integrated as well (in the sense that the errors $u[t: i]$ have a permanent effect on the level of the series $x[t]$). In this case, a disturbance $u(t; i)$ drawn from the high-variance component will create a pattern similar to a structural change in the level of the x's (since the event is relatively rare and of a different order of magnitude than the disturbances that are drawn most of the time). Similarly, a disturbance to the coefficients $\beta(t; i, j + 1, 1)$ (in the notation of [2]), that is, in the constants of each equation, will create a pattern similar to a structural change in the rate of growth of the series. Disturbances from the high-variance component to other coefficients create major changes in the autoregressive coefficients that are more difficult to interpret but that could include structural changes in cointegrating vectors. Note that, if trends are included in the specifications to allow "trend-stationary" series, similar disturbances to the u's and the constants become, respectively, outliers and changes in level while structural changes in slopes would be associated with draws from the high-variance component for the coefficients on the time trends.

Many recent papers have argued that structural changes of the type described above are likely to be important ingredients in the characterization of many economic time series (e.g., Perron 1989, 1990; Hamilton 1989; Chen and Tiao 1990; Gregory and Hansen 1992; and others). A recent study by Park (1992) also extends Kitagawa's (1987) framework explicitly allowing mixtures of normals and shows its relevance in characterizing some aggregate economic time series involving a one-time change in slope. For these reasons, I think that the mixture of normals specification is likely to be a key ingredient in the success of this methodology. It would indeed be of substantial interest to report in some future work the time path of the coefficients and the implied decomposition into trend and noise components.

Several comments stand out from the structural change interpretation discussed above. First, let me reiterate the point made in the last section about the potential importance of including trend regressors to allow for the presence of series with a noise component that is stationary (in the sense of having no unit root but not excluding possible changes in the autoregressive coefficients). When allowance is made for the possibility of structural changes in slope and/or intercept, such a generalization becomes even more relevant (see Perron 1989).

A comment specifically directed to the specification of the mixture of normals (11) is the following. Note that there is only one parameter, π_{10}, measuring the probabilities associated with each component of the mixture; accordingly, the probability of drawing a disturbance from the high-variance component is the same for all elements of the vector $\beta(t)$ (i.e., the drift and the autoregressive coefficients) and for the errors $u(t; i)$. Under the interpretation discussed above, this implies the same probability of occurrences for changes in level, in slope, or in the autoregressive coefficients (e.g., in the cointegrating vectors). Similarly, the coefficient π_{11} is unique; hence, the relative difference in the magnitude of the variances in the mixture is the same for all coefficients. These constraints appear overly stringent. I do not see why one should expect the same probability of changes for all coefficients (or for changes in different components of the trend function of the noise function). I believe that substantial gains could be achieved by relaxing this constraint.

Concluding Comments

The main lesson that I have learned from having to study the issues behind the forecasting methodology proposed by Sims, to write these comments, is that I came to appreciate its qualities better. I expressed some divergence of opinion as to its Bayesian interpretation, but such issues are mainly ones of semantics and in no way question the fact that this forecasting model is well grounded and a very useful development in this line of research. My other comments are merely suggestions for possible extensions that could improve what is already a successful model.

While the model presented here appears relatively successful at providing unconditional predictions, it falls short when considering conditional predictions to analyze policy interventions and interpret the more structural aspects of the model. These issues can be analyzed only in a carefully identified system. Such identification issues have been studied in the context of VAR models with time-invariant parameters (see, e.g., Blanchard and Watson 1986; and Sims 1986) but are still open questions in the present, more general framework with time-varying parameters. Analyses pertaining to these identification issues indeed appear to be important avenues for future research.

References

Andrews, D. W. K. 1991. Exactly unbiased estimation of first order autoregressive/ unit root models. Discussion Paper no. 975. New Haven, Conn.: Cowles Foundation.

Blanchard, O. J., and M. W. Watson. 1986. Are all business cycles alike? In *The American business cycle,* ed. R. J. Gordon. Chicago: University of Chicago Press.

Campbell, J. Y., and P. Perron. 1991. Pitfalls and opportunities: What macroeconomists should know about unit roots. *NBER Macroeconomics Annual,* 141–201.

Chen, C., and G. C. Tiao. 1990. Random level-shift time series models, ARIMA approximations, and level-shift detection. *Journal of Business and Economic Statistics* 8:83–98.

Fair, R. C. 1984. *Specification, estimation and analysis of macroeconometric models.* Cambridge, Mass.: Harvard University Press.

Gregory, A. W., and B. E. Hansen. 1992. Residual-based tests for cointegration in models with regime shifts. Working Paper no. 335. University of Rochester Center for Economic Research.

Hamilton, J. D. 1989. A new approach to the economic analysis of nonstationary time series and the business cycle. *Econometrica* 57:357–84.

Johansen, S. 1988. Statistical analysis of cointegrating vectors. *Journal of Economic Dynamics and Control* 12:231–54.

Kitagawa, G. 1987. Non-Gaussian state space modeling of nonstationary time series. *Journal of the American Statistical Association* 82:1032–41.

Martin, R. D., and A. E. Raftery. 1987. Comments: Robustness, computation and non-Euclidean models. *Journal of the American Statistical Association* 82:1044–50.

Park, J. 1992. E-M estimation of nonstationary state-space models with mixture Gaussian long-run errors: A structural change estimation. Princeton University. Mimeo.

Perron, P. 1988. Trends and random walks in macroeconomic time series: Further evidence from a new approach. *Journal of Economic Dynamics and Control* 12:297–332.

———. 1989. The Great Crash, the oil price shock and the unit root hypothesis. *Econometrica* 57:1361–1401.

———. 1990. Testing for a unit root in a time series with a changing mean. *Journal of Business and Economic Statistics* 8:153–62.

Sims, C. A. 1986. Are forecasting models usable for policy analysis? *Quarterly Review of the Federal Reserve Bank of Minneapolis* 10 (1): 2–16.

———. 1988. Bayesian skepticism on unit root econometrics. *Journal of Economic Dynamics and Control* 12:463–74.

———. 1991. VAR econometrics: An update. Yale University. Mimeo.

Stock, J. H., and M. W. Watson. 1991. A probability model of the coincident economic indicators. In *Leading economic indicators: New approaches and forecasting records*, ed. K. Lahiri and G. H. Moore. Cambridge: Cambridge University Press.

Uhlig, H. 1991. What macroeconomists should know about unit roots as well: The Bayesian perspective. Princeton University. Mimeo.

5   Why Does the Paper-Bill Spread Predict Real Economic Activity?

Benjamin M. Friedman and Kenneth N. Kuttner

People have always sought reliable ways to predict the future, and economic fluctuations are no exception. Public policymakers, charged with the responsibility of maintaining full but not overfull employment of the economy's productive resources, want to know when to take actions that will either stimulate or retard economic activity. Business executives who plan to build new factories or modernize old ones, or who consider the introduction of new products, want to know when the markets for what their companies make will be strong. Both individual and institutional investors, allocating their portfolios across major asset categories like equities and fixed-income securities, and in some cases picking specific corporations' stocks, want to know whether recession or economic expansion will prevail over the relevant investment horizon.

A series of recent papers—Stock and Watson (1989b), Friedman and Kuttner (1992), Bernanke (1990), and Kashyap, Stein, and Wilcox (1993)—has shown that, for the past three decades or so, the difference between the respective interest rates on commercial paper and Treasury bills has borne a systematic relation to subsequent fluctuations of nonfinancial economic activity in the United States. As such relations go, this one has been fairly robust. The paper-bill spread easily outperforms any single interest rate, either nominal or real, as well as any of the monetary aggregates, as a predictor of real economic activity. The spread bears a statistically significant relation not just to

Benjamin M. Friedman is the William Joseph Maier Professor of Political Economy at Harvard University. He is also the director of the monetary economics program and a research associate of the National Bureau of Economic Research. Kenneth N. Kuttner is a senior research economist and research officer at the Federal Reserve Bank of Chicago.

The ideas presented in this paper are the authors'. They do not necessarily reflect the official stance of the Federal Reserve Bank of Chicago. The authors are grateful to Ben Bernanke, Timothy Cook, Mark Watson, Jeff Wooldridge, and an anonymous referee for helpful comments on a preliminary draft and to the General Electric Foundation and the Harvard Program for Financial Research for research support.

future movements of aggregate output and spending but to almost all the familiar components of real activity as well. Finally, in contrast to the monetary aggregates (the subject of an earlier literature along these lines, which ended in disappointment), there is no ambiguity about whether the paper-bill spread is related to the real or the price side of nominal income fluctuations. (On the latest evidence, money is related to neither.) The spread is a predictor of real economic activity, not prices, and of nominal magnitudes only to the extent that they reflect real ones.

Why is all this so? And is there any ground for confidence that the relations that have connected the paper-bill spread to subsequent business fluctuations in the past will continue to prevail for at least some time into the future? These questions motivate the analysis presented in this paper.

Section 5.1 briefly reviews and expands the evidence from previous work documenting the relations between the paper-bill spread and real economic activity in the United States. Section 5.2 details some of the practical differences between commercial paper and Treasury bills that plausibly account for the spread between the respective interest rates on these two instruments. An important product of this part of the analysis is a decomposition of the observed spread into a component that covaries directly with the general level of interest rates, a component directly representing the variation over time in the perceived risk of default on commercial paper, and a component capturing other influences that vary over time in a way that may or may not be related to the business cycle. Section 5.3 uses a simple model of the behavior of borrowers and lenders in the short-term credit markets to develop three distinct (albeit not mutually exclusive) hypotheses to account for the relation between the paper-bill spread and fluctuations in business activity. Section 5.4 applies a variety of statistical tests to provide evidence bearing on the validity of any or all of these three hypotheses. Section 5.5 brings together the principal conclusions developed throughout the paper.

To anticipate, the evidence presented in this paper suggests, at the least, a twofold explanation for the predictive power of the paper-bill spread with respect to real economic activity, an explanation based on both default risk and monetary policy. First, changing perceptions of default risk, as business prospects alternately strengthen and ebb, exert a clearly recognizable influence on the spread and also account for part of the spread's relation to subsequent movements of real output. Second, in a world in which investors view commercial paper as an imperfect substitute for Treasury bills—a key assumption, for which the relations estimated in section 5.4 provide some supporting evidence—a widening paper-bill spread is also a symptom of the contraction in bank lending due to tighter monetary policy. Finally, independent changes in the behavior of borrowers in the commercial paper market, due to their changing cash requirements over the course of the business cycle, also influence the paper-bill spread in ways that connect it to subsequent economic fluctuations.

5.1 The Basic Relation

The upper panel of figure 5.1 shows monthly average values of the respective interest rates on six-month prime-rated commercial paper and 180-day U.S. Treasury bills, for 1959–90.[1] Both series display the basic features characteristic of practically all U.S. interest rates during this period: a generally rising overall trend from the 1950s until the early 1980s, increasing volatility beginning in the early 1970s, a downward trend and reduced volatility in the mid- to late 1980s, and the familiar cyclicality throughout. (The shaded areas in the figure represent recessions as designated by the National Bureau of Economic Research.) The commercial paper rate has, almost always, exceeded the Treasury bill rate.[2] While the covariation of the two series is hardly perfect, the dominant visual impression offered by these data is that the two interest rates tend to move roughly together over time.

The covariation of the two rates is not perfect, however, and the focus of this paper is on the movement over time of the difference between them. The lower panel of figure 5.1 (with magnified scale compared to that of the upper panel) plots the monthly average difference between the six-month commercial paper rate and the 180-day Treasury bill rate for the same period. Over the entire thirty-two-year sample, the mean spread was 0.57 percent per annum (i.e., fifty-seven basis points), with a standard deviation of 0.49 percent. In contrast to the upper panel, here there is little evidence of persistent time trends. But like the two interest rates themselves, the spread between them does display a distinct cyclicality. As table 5.1 shows, the spread is typically wider not just during but also immediately prior to recessions (although the 1990 experience—in which the spread widened much longer in advance of the recession, only then to narrow again before the recession began—is an obvious counterexample).

Table 5.2, updated from Friedman and Kuttner (1992), shows that the widening of the paper-bill spread in anticipation of downturns in real economic activity represents information beyond that already contained in the serial correlation of real activity itself or in fluctuations of either price inflation or federal government expenditures. The table also shows that other familiar financial variables, like interest rates or growth of the monetary aggregates, either do not contain such incremental information at all or do so to a lesser extent.

---

1. Here, as well as elsewhere throughout this paper, the interest rates shown are discounts calculated on a 360-day basis. Data are from the Federal Reserve Board's H.15 release.

2. The only exceptions in this 384-month series are 1975:7–9, 1976:3, 1976:5, and 1977:1–3. Prior to November 1979, the "six-month" commercial paper rate recorded by the Federal Reserve Board actually corresponded to paper with maturities of 120–79 days. The few anomalous negative values of the paper-bill spread may therefore reflect a steep, upward-sloping term structure for commercial paper in specific months during that period (see *Federal Reserve Bulletin* 65 [December 1979], A-27, no. 2).

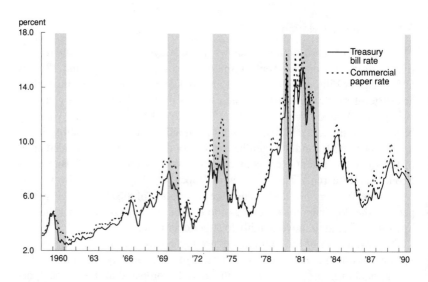

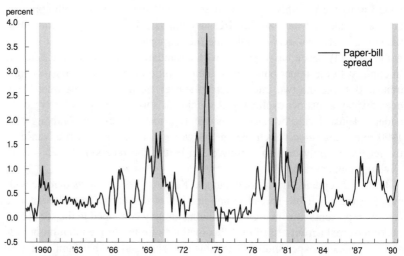

Fig. 5.1   Six-month commercial paper and Treasury bill rates and the paper-bill spread, 1959–1990

Table 5.1   **Cyclical Behavior of the Paper-Bill Spread**

	Spread (%)	Observations
Mean over entire 1959:1–1990:12 sample	.57	384
Mean during recessions	1.10	66
Mean excluding recessions	.46	318
Mean 1–6 months prior to recessions	.88	36
Mean 7–12 months prior to recessions	.50	36

Source: Board of Governors of the Federal Reserve System.

Note: Observations are monthly averages of daily data. Underlying interest rates are for 6-month commercial paper and 6-month Treasury bills.

Table 5.2   **F-Statistics for Financial Variables in Quarterly Real Output Equations**

	1960:2–1990:4	1960:2–1979:3	1970:3–1990:4
	Three-Variable System (real output, price index, financial variable)		
$r_P - r_B$	7.70***	8.12***	5.32***
$\Delta\ln(M1)$	2.65**	2.59**	1.77
$\Delta\ln(M2)$	4.66***	3.78***	2.19*
$\Delta\ln(\text{credit})$	1.21	1.97	.34
Δr_P	5.80***	1.95	4.14***
Δr_B	4.76***	2.21*	3.62***
$r_{10} - r_{FF}$	7.34***	4.44***	6.70***
	Four-Variable System (also including mid-expansion government expenditures)		
$r_P - r_B$	7.16***	7.10***	4.68***
$\Delta\ln(M1)$	2.85**	2.71**	1.81
$\Delta\ln(M2)$	4.32***	3.63***	1.81
$\Delta\ln(\text{credit})$	1.02	2.34*	.16
Δr_P	5.61***	1.55	3.94***
Δr_B	4.52***	1.81	3.44**
$r_{10} - r_{FF}$	7.23***	3.82***	6.41***

Note: Regressions include four lags of each included variable. Real output variable is gross national product in 1982 dollars. Price index is the implicit GNP deflator. r_P is the rate on 6-month prime commercial paper. r_B is the rate on 6-month Treasury bills. Credit is total domestic nonfinancial debt. r_{10} is the 10-year Treasury-bond yield. r_{FF} is the Federal funds rate.

*   Significant at the 10% level.

**   Significant at the 5% level.

***   Significant at the 1% level.

The upper panel of the table presents F-statistics for the null hypothesis that all coefficients δ_i are zero in regressions of the form

$$(1) \qquad \Delta X_t = \alpha + \sum_{i=1}^{4} \beta_i \Delta X_{t-i} + \sum_{i=1}^{4} \gamma_i \Delta P_{t-i} + \sum_{i=1}^{4} \delta_i Z_{t-i} + u_t,$$

where X and P are the natural logarithms of real gross national product and the corresponding price deflator, respectively; Z is, first, the difference between the six-month prime commercial paper rate and the 180-day Treasury bill rate and then, in sequence, a series of other familiar financial variables as indicated in the table; u is a disturbance term; and α, β_i, γ_i, and δ_i are all coefficients to be estimated. The lower panel presents analogous F-statistics based on equations that are identical to (1) except that they also include, as an additional set of regressors, a distributed lag on the (log) change in "mid-expansion" federal expenditures. The table presents results separately for the full 1960:II–1990:IV sample and for two subsamples: 1960:II–1979:III (i.e., until the Federal Reserve System's adoption of new monetary policy procedures in October 1979) and 1970:III–1990:IV (i.e., since the elimination of Regulation Q interest ceilings on large certificates of deposit in June 1970).[3]

Among the seven financial variables considered, the paper-bill spread is one of only two—the other being the long-short spread—that contain incremental information about subsequent movements of real output that is significant at the .01 level in the full 1960–90 sample and in both subsamples separately, regardless of whether the fiscal variable is included. Indeed, none of the other five financial variables considered meets this criterion even at the .10 significance level.

Table 5.3 presents an analogous set of results based on monthly data. Here industrial production takes the place of real gross national product, the producer price index takes the place of the GNP deflator, each distributed lag is of length 6, and the results shown correspond only to the upper panel of table 5.2—that is, without the fiscal variable.[4] Here the paper-bill spread is alone among the seven variables tested in containing incremental information about subsequent movements of industrial production that is significant at the .01 level in the full 1960–90 sample as well as in both subsamples separately. The growth rate of the M2 money stock, the change in the commercial paper rate, and the long-short spread satisfy this criterion at the .05 level. None of the other financial variables does so even at the .10 level.

Table 5.4 presents results for an alternative form of test, suggested by Stock and Watson (1989a), again based on monthly data. The Stock-Watson regression includes twelve lags each of the respective log changes in industrial pro-

---

3. Data for gross national product, the deflator, mid-expansion federal spending, and the monetary aggregates are seasonally adjusted. Data for interest rates and the paper-bill spread are not.
4. There is no readily available monthly series corresponding to mid-expansion federal government expenditures.

Table 5.3   ***F*-Statistics for Financial Variables in Monthly Real Output Equations**

	1960:2–1990:12	1960:2–1979:9	1970:7–1990:12
	Three-Variable System (real output, price index, financial variable)		
$r_P - r_B$	8.47***	6.33***	6.10***
$\Delta\ln(M1)$	2.27**	2.23**	.95
$\Delta\ln(M2)$	4.70***	3.69***	2.12**
$\Delta\ln(\text{credit})$	1.45	1.44	1.46
Δr_P	2.89***	3.40***	2.09*
Δr_B	2.03*	1.17	1.61
$r_{10} - r_{FF}$	3.99***	4.73***	2.49**

Note: Regressions include six lags of each included variable. Real output variable is industrial production. Price index is the producer price index. For definitions of the other variables, see table 5.2.
*   Significant at the 10% level.
**   Significant at the 5% level.
***   Significant at the 1% level.

Table 5.4   ***F*-Statistics for Financial Variables in Monthly Real Output Equations (Stock-Watson specification)**

	1960:2–1990:12	1960:2–1979:9	1970:7–1990:12
	Four-Variable System (real output, price index, commercial paper rate, financial variable)		
$r_P - r_B$	6.04***	2.85***	4.24***
$\Delta\ln(M1)$	.83	.77	.59
$\Delta\ln(M2)$	3.08***	2.25**	1.47
$\Delta\ln(\text{credit})$	1.10	.93	1.29
$r_{10} - r_{FF}$	2.11*	1.16	1.62

Note: Regressions include six lags of the financial variable, twelve lags of each of the other three variables, and a linear time trend. Variables are defined as in tables 5.2 and 5.3
*   Significant at the 10% level.
**   Significant at the 5% level.
***   Significant at the 1% level.

duction and the producer price index, twelve lags of the change in the commercial paper rate (so that the list of variables corresponding to Z now excludes the paper rate change and the bill rate change), six lags on the designated financial variable, and a linear time trend. Here the paper-bill spread is again the only financial variable tested that contains incremental information about subsequent movements in industrial production that is significant at the .01 level regardless of sample. None of the others—including the long-short spread—does so even at the .10 level.

Finally, table 5.5 presents both F-statistics and variance decompositions based on a series of vector autoregression systems including, in each case, the respective log changes in real output and the corresponding price deflator, the paper-bill spread, and, one at a time in succession, each of the other financial variables considered in tables 5.2 and 5.3 above. The estimation is based on quarterly data, with variables and lag specification corresponding to those underlying the upper panel of table 5.2. For each system, the table presents the F-statistics for the distributed lags on the paper-bill spread and the other financial variable in the equation for real output, then the respective share of the variance of real output accounted for by the paper-bill spread and by the other financial variable (together with the corresponding 95 percent confidence intervals), measured at both four- and eight-quarter horizons. For purposes of these variance decompositions, the real output variable is ordered first, the price variable second, the other financial variable third, and the paper-bill spread last.

When the measure of output used is real gross national product (the upper panel), the F-statistics presented in table 5.5 indicate that the paper-bill spread contains incremental information about subsequent movements in real output that is significant at the .01 level in the presence of any of the additional financial variables except M2 and the long-short spread, in which case the relevant information is significant at the .05 level and the .10 level, respectively. Among the other financial variables considered, only the long-short spread and the bill rate change are significant here at the .10 level or better in the presence of the paper-bill spread.

When the output measure is real domestic absorption (the middle panel), however, the paper-bill spread contains information that is significant at the .01 level in the presence of *any* of the other financial variables. Among the others, here only the paper rate change and the bill rate change (separately) contain significant incremental information in the presence of the paper-bill spread. Similarly, when the output measure is real investment in plant and equipment (the lower panel), the paper-bill spread again contains information that is significant at the .01 level in the presence of *any* of the other financial variables. Here the bill rate change is the only other variable to contain significant incremental information in the presence of the paper-bill spread.[5]

The variance decomposition results presented in table 5.5 largely support these findings from significance tests based on the output equation alone. In most of the vector autoregression systems estimated, the paper-bill spread accounts for a percentage of the variance of the relevant real output measure, either four or eight quarters ahead, that is both economically important (typically between 10 and 20 percent) and statistically significant (at the .05 level). Further, in most cases the paper-bill spread dominates whatever is the other financial variable in the system despite the ordering of the paper-bill spread

---

5. In related work, Wizman (1990) has shown that results like those presented in table 5.5 carry over to systems simultaneously containing many more variables.

Table 5.5   **Performance of Alternative Financial Indicators in Quarterly Real Output VARs**

	Output = Real Gross National Product					
	$\Delta\ln(M1)$	$r_P - r_B$	$\Delta\ln(M2)$	$r_P - r_B$	$\Delta\ln(\text{credit})$	$r_P - r_B$
F-statistic	1.59	6.29***	.76	3.33**	.92	7.11***
% of variance:						
@ 4Q	9 ± 9	18 ± 12	12 ± 10	9 ± 9	4 ± 5	22 ± 12
@ 8Q	11 ± 9	18 ± 12	15 ± 11	10 ± 8	5 ± 5	22 ± 12
	Δr_B	$r_P - r_B$	Δr_P	$r_P - r_B$	$r_{10} - r_{FF}$	$r_P - r_B$
F-statistic	2.19*	4.81***	1.89	3.51***	2.09*	2.39*
% of variance:						
@ 4Q	12 ± 10	14 ± 10	16 ± 11	9 ± 8	15 ± 11	7 ± 7
@ 8Q	16 ± 11	14 ± 10	18 ± 12	10 ± 8	17 ± 11	13 ± 11

	Output = Real Domestic Absorption					
	$\Delta\ln(M1)$	$r_P - r_B$	$\Delta\ln(M2)$	$r_P - r_B$	$\Delta\ln(\text{credit})$	$r_P - r_B$
F-statistic	1.44	8.57***	1.81	5.26***	1.34	10.30***
% of variance:						
@ 4Q	10 ± 10	19 ± 12	15 ± 11	10 ± 9	3 ± 5	27 ± 14
@ 8Q	12 ± 10	20 ± 12	17 ± 12	13 ± 9	4 ± 5	27 ± 14
	Δr_B	$r_P - r_B$	Δr_P	$r_P - r_B$	$r_{10} - r_{FF}$	$r_P - r_B$
F-statistic	3.45*	6.79***	2.88**	4.06***	1.48	3.96***
% of variance:						
@ 4Q	16 ± 11	15 ± 11	22 ± 12	8 ± 8	18 ± 12	8 ± 8
@ 8Q	22 ± 13	17 ± 11	23 ± 12	14 ± 10	19 ± 12	18 ± 12

	Output = Real Business Fixed Investment					
	$\Delta\ln(M1)$	$r_P - r_B$	$\Delta\ln(M2)$	$r_P - r_B$	$\Delta\ln(\text{credit})$	$r_P - r_B$
F-statistic	.32	4.07***	.68	2.14*	.17	4.66***
% of variance:						
@ 4Q	7 ± 9	17 ± 12	14 ± 12	9 ± 10	2 ± 4	21 ± 14
@ 8Q	8 ± 9	20 ± 14	17 ± 14	10 ± 10	3 ± 4	24 ± 16
	Δr_B	$r_P - r_B$	Δr_P	$r_P - r_B$	$r_{10} - r_{FF}$	$r_P - r_B$
F-statistic	2.26*	4.71***	1.60	4.32***	.89	3.54***
% of variance:						
@ 4Q	4 ± 5	20 ± 14	8 ± 9	17 ± 13	6 ± 8	13 ± 12
@ 8Q	12 ± 11	19 ± 14	15 ± 14	16 ± 12	14 ± 12	14 ± 11

Note: Sample in each case is 1960:2–1990:4. Equations include four lags of each variable. The mean variance decomposition and its confidence interval were computed via Monte-Carlo simulations with 1,000 draws. Variables are defined as in table 5.2. The ordering for the decompositions is as follows: output, prices, financial variable, paper-bill spread.

*   Significant at the 10% level.

**   Significant at the 5% level.

***   Significant at the 1% level.

last in the underlying orthogonalization. Table 5.6 highlights the relevance of this ordering by presenting alternative variance decomposition results for those three financial variables that, for at least some output measures, account for a greater share of output in the decompositions shown in table 5.5. In these alternative results, in which the paper-bill spread is ordered third and the other financial variable fourth, the dominance of the paper-bill spread is pervasive.

In sum, both single-equation significance tests and multiple-equation variance decompositions based on the last three decades of U.S. experience consistently point to a statistically significant relation between movements of the paper-bill spread and subsequent fluctuations in real economic activity, even in the presence of other financial variables that previous researchers have often advanced as potential business-cycle predictors.

5.2   Accounting for the Spread

Commercial paper represents the unsecured, discounted short-term (up to 270 days) liability of either nonfinancial business corporations or financial intermediaries. As of year-end 1990, the volume of such claims outstanding in the United States totaled $610 billion, of which approximately 19 percent was the liability of U.S. nonfinancial businesses, 5 percent of U.S. bank holding companies, 55 percent of U.S. nonbank financial intermediaries, and 12 percent of foreign obligors. Roughly one-third of the $610 billion had been originally issued directly by the obligors (in practically all cases financial institutions) and the remaining two-thirds through commercial paper dealers acting in the obligors' behalf. Although commercial paper in some form or other has existed in the United States for over a century, the commercial paper market in its current form is largely a post–World War II phenomenon, and the market's growth in recent decades has been rapid. As recently as 1960, for example, the total volume outstanding was just $6.5 billion (13 percent issued by U.S. nonfinancial businesses, 57 percent by U.S. nonbank financial intermediaries, and 18 percent by foreign obligors).[6]

Treasury bills represent the short-term (up to one year) discount obligations of the U.S. Treasury, backed by the full faith and credit of the U.S. government. The Treasury first issued discounted instruments resembling today's Treasury bills in 1929. Since then, the volume outstanding has fluctuated with the level of the government's debt and also with the varying maturity patterns used to finance that debt. Given the enormous volume of debt of all maturities used to finance the U.S. military effort in World War II, the Treasury bill market has been large and well developed throughout the postwar period. The volume of Treasury bills outstanding in 1946 was $17 billion. At year-end 1990, it was $482 billion.

Three factors appear most important in accounting for the typically greater

---

6. Data are from the Federal Reserve System's flow-of-funds accounts. Useful descriptive accounts of the development and functioning of the commercial paper market include Selden (1963), Baxter (1966), Hurley (1977, 1982), and Stigum (1990).

Table 5.6   **Performance of Alternative Financial Indicators in Quarterly Real Output VARs, Orthogonalization Order Reversed**

	$r_P - r_B$	$\Delta\ln(M2)$	$r_P - r_B$	$r_{10} - r_{FF}$	$r_P - r_B$	Δr_P
			Output = Real Gross National Product			
F-statistic	3.33***	.76	2.39*	2.09*	3.51***	1.89
% of variance:						
@ 4Q	17 ± 12	4 ± 5	16 ± 11	6 ± 7	18 ± 12	7 ± 7
@ 8Q	16 ± 11	8 ± 8	15 ± 10	15 ± 11	17 ± 11	12 ± 9
			Output = Real Domestic Absorption			
F-statistic	5.26***	1.81	3.96***	1.48	4.06***	2.88**
% of variance:						
@ 4Q	21 ± 13	5 ± 6	21 ± 13	4 ± 7	21 ± 12	10 ± 8
@ 8Q	20 ± 12	11 ± 10	21 ± 12	17 ± 13	21 ± 11	17 ± 11
			Output = Real Business Fixed Investment			
F-statistic	2.14*	.68	3.54***	.89	4.32***	1.60
% of variance:						
@ 4Q	18 ± 14	5 ± 7	17 ± 14	3 ± 4	21 ± 14	3 ± 4
@ 8Q	19 ± 14	8 ± 9	16 ± 13	12 ± 12	23 ± 14	7 ± 7

Note: The ordering for the decompositions is as follows: output, prices, paper-bill spread, financial variable. See also note to table 5.5.

observed interest rate on commercial paper than on Treasury bills. First, federal statute precludes states or municipalities from taxing income earned as interest on any U.S. Treasury obligations, bills included, except for those states that employ the franchise tax on business income or impose an excise tax on bank income. By contrast, interest earned on privately issued obligations, like commercial paper, is typically taxable at the state or municipal level. As of 1990, forty-three states (plus the District of Columbia) had individual income taxes, with rates applicable to interest income varying up to a high of 14 percent in Connecticut. Similarly, twenty-eight states (plus the District of Columbia) had corporate income taxes.[7] In addition, some municipalities have income taxes applicable to interest income. In 1990, New York City taxed income earned by residents at a maximum rate of 3.95 percent.[8]

To the extent that an investor choosing between commercial paper and Treasury bills is a taxable entity domiciled in a state and/or municipality with an income tax, therefore, some positive interest rate spread between paper and bills is necessary to render the two instruments' respective returns identical on an after-tax basis—that is, to achieve

7. In addition, seventeen states had a franchise tax on business income, and eighteen states levied an excise tax on bank income (see *State Tax Handbook* 1990).

8. Cook and Lawler (1983) provided a highly useful discussion of the role of taxes in accounting for the paper-bill spread.

(2) $$(1 - \tau)r_P = r_B,$$

where r_P and r_B are the nominal interest rates paid on commercial paper and Treasury bills, respectively, and τ is the effective state/municipal tax rate. Moreover, the spread required for this purpose varies directly with the level of the tax-exempt rate, according to

(3) $$r_P - r_B = \left(\frac{\tau}{1 - \tau}\right)r_B.$$

Given values of 0.57 percent for the spread and 6.48 percent for the bill rate, on average for the 1959–90 sample period spanned in figure 5.1 above, the implied effective tax rate would be 8.1 percent (i.e., 0.081) if differential taxability were the sole factor accounting for a nonzero average spread over time. (A 9.7 percent tax rate would be required to explain in full the average spread between commercial paper and Treasury bills at three months' maturity.)

A second factor clearly differentiating Treasury bills from commercial paper is that payment on the paper is subject to potential default by private obligors. Moreover, in the event of bankruptcy, the unsecured status of commercial paper typically places it low on the scale in the application of the conventional "me-first" rules. Given any nonzero probability of default, even a risk-neutral investor would require a positive paper-bill spread to want to hold commercial paper instead of Treasury bills. The expected after-tax returns on the two assets are identical when

(4) $$(1 - \pi\phi)(1 - \tau)r_P - \pi\phi = r_B,$$

where r_P is now the *promised* interest rate on the commercial paper, π is the probability that a default on the paper will occur within the time horizon that is relevant for this investment, ϕ is the fraction ($0 \le \phi \le 1$) of the stated principal amount that the investor will lose in the event of default, and τ is again the state/municipal tax rate.

If investors are risk averse, however, mere equality of expected returns is insufficient to make an investor willing to hold a risky rather than a risk-free asset, so the required spread is correspondingly greater. To take a simple example, suppose that an investor's portfolio consists entirely of Treasury bills and commercial paper and that the investor's choice between them is governed by maximization of expected utility of nominal end-of-period wealth, where the "period" is identical to the stated maturity of the bills and the paper (so that the bills are genuinely riskless) and utility is characterized by constant relative risk aversion. Then the relation between the two (promised) interest rates that leaves the investor just indifferent between the two assets at the margin is

(5) $$[1 - \pi\phi - 2\alpha\rho\pi(1 - \pi)\phi^2] (1 - \tau)r_P$$
$$- \alpha\rho\pi(1 - \pi)\phi^2 (1 - \tau)^2 r_P^2 - \pi\phi[1 + \alpha\rho(1 - \pi)\phi] = r_B,$$

where α is the fraction of the investor's portfolio invested in commercial paper, and ρ is the coefficient of relative risk aversion.

In contrast to the experience of the interwar period, which included 171 separate default episodes, few issuers have defaulted on their outstanding commercial paper since World War II.[9] By far the most significant postwar default was Penn Central's failure to meet payment on $82 million of paper due in June 1970. Following the Penn Central default, the major credit rating agencies introduced new systems of rating commercial paper, not only distinguishing prime-rated from non-prime-rated paper, but also designating three separate categories of prime-rated paper (P1, P2, and P3 by Moody's; A1, A2, and A3 by Standard and Poor's). Since the introduction of these ratings, only six rated issuers had experienced defaults by the end of 1991, and four of these had lost their prime ratings before their respective defaults occurred.[10]

Some authors have pointed to the scant experience of actual defaults to argue that default risk must play a small if not negligible role in accounting for the observed positive spread between the promised interest rate on commercial paper and the Treasury bill rate (see, e.g., Bernanke 1990). To be sure, this argument is plausible if the question at hand is whether default risk *alone* can explain the spread. As with the two instruments' differing tax status, however, the relevant issue is the potential role played by default risk in conjunction with other factors.

Gauging the relevant default rate π and loss rate ϕ to employ in an expression like (5) is problematic for several reasons. One is just the distinction between event frequencies observed within any (finite) sample and the corresponding subjective probabilities as assessed by rational agents—in other words, the familiar "peso problem" (see, e.g., Krasker 1980). A second is that there is no guarantee that the relevant agents whose subjective probabilities have mattered for the relative pricing of commercial paper and Treasury bills were in fact "rational" in the usual technical sense. Yet a third is that many of these agents—those acting in a fiduciary capacity, for example— may have been responding to incentives not encompassed within the usual risk-return utility calculus. (The manager's embarrassment in the event of a client's holding defaulted paper may matter, in addition to the pecuniary loss to the account.) Finally, many investors in commercial paper either cannot or do not diversify their holdings sufficiently to render their own potential loss rates equivalent to those of the commercial paper universe outstanding. Such investors therefore plausibly perceive a potential default as a more catastrophic event than the aggregate data would suggest.

Figure 5.2 plots combinations of default probability π (for values up to a maximum of .1) and state tax rate τ (for values up to .09) that satisfy the

9. For an account of the interwar experience, see Selden (1963).
10. For a detailed history of experience under the rating system, see Moody's Investors Service (1992).

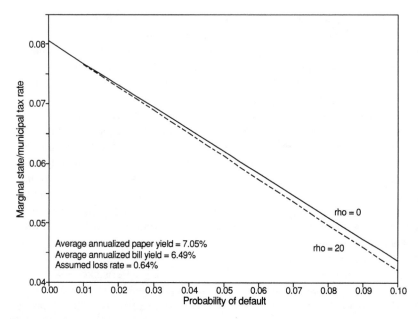

Fig. 5.2   Tax rates and default probabilities consistent with the observed 1959–90 average paper-bill spread

relation in (5) for the average values of r_P and r_B observed over 1959–90, given the default-state loss rate $\phi = .0064$, portfolio proportion $\alpha = .37$ (the most recent actual paper/[paper + bill] ratio as measured in the Federal Reserve's flow-of-funds accounts), and two separate values of the coefficient of relative risk aversion ρ: zero (i.e., risk neutrality) and twenty. A loss rate of .0064 corresponds to the worst-recorded experience for the commercial paper market in any given year since World War I, when 0.64 percent of the outstanding paper was lost in defaults in 1931. Parameter π therefore represents the probability that investors associate with a given year's replicating the 1931 default experience.

As the discussion of equations (2) and (3) above indicates, a state tax rate of .081 would be sufficient to account fully for the observed mean paper-bill spread in the absence of any possibility at all of default. A nonzero probability of default makes the observed mean spread consistent with a lower tax rate. For example, if investors believe that there is a one-in-twenty chance of default on 0.64 percent of their commercial paper holdings (i.e., $\pi = .05$), this default probability, together with a state tax rate of approximately .06, would be sufficient to account for the entire observed mean spread. As the figure makes clear, these results are not very sensitive to the assumed risk aversion.

Finally, a third factor potentially also underlying the positive average paper-bill spread is the greater liquidity of Treasury bills compared to commercial paper.[11] The market for U.S. Treasury bills has traditionally been the most liquid of any asset market in the United States (in recent decades, in the entire world) in terms of an investor's ability to buy or sell large amounts of securities with minimum transactions costs, minimum effect of the investor's own action on the market price, maximum availability of agents willing to act in the investor's behalf, and maximum availability of either financing for margined long positions or securities to borrow against short positions. Despite substantial advances in the last decade or two, the commercial paper market has never met this standard. Firms issuing commercial paper or dealers acting in their behalf are usually willing to take back paper presented by investors before the stated maturity date, but they bear no legal obligation to do so. Finding third-party buyers is also problematic.

Various legal restrictions also contribute to making Treasury bills a more liquid asset than commercial paper for the specific categories of investors to which they apply. Commercial banks and other depository institutions, for example, can use Treasury bills as collateral when they borrow from the Federal Reserve discount window. Commercial paper is not eligible collateral for this purpose. Similarly, under current federal tax law, state governments undertaking advance refunding of outstanding obligations must invest the proceeds in Treasury securities to avoid sacrificing the exemption of the interest that they pay from taxability at the federal level. Here too, commercial paper does not qualify.

Differential liquidity therefore presumably accounts for at least some part of the positive paper-bill spread on average over time. In analytic terms, a liquidity value of bills over paper might simply take the form of a constant subtracted from the left-hand side of (5), which in turn would shift both curves in figure 5.2. But differential liquidity could also account for either cyclical variation of the paper-bill spread (e.g., if investors value liquidity more highly when a recession increases the uncertainty surrounding their own cash flows) or a time trend in the spread (presumably negative, to reflect the gradually increasing efficiency of the commercial paper market during the past few decades).

In the end, what is most interesting about the paper-bill spread is neither the mean spread over time nor the presence or absence of a time trend but the way in which variation of the spread through time corresponds, with some lead period, to fluctuations in real economic activity. There is little reason to think that state or municipal income tax rates vary systematically with the business cycle. By contrast, there is some ground for suspecting that the value that investors place on the greater liquidity of bills over paper does so. Further, as figure 5.3 shows, both the frequency of business failures and the vol-

11. The classic discussion of liquidity in this context is that of Kessel (1965). An aspect of Kessel's treatment that is especially relevant to some of the results presented below is his argument that the premium placed on liquidity would (like the tax effect and the default risk effect discussed above) vary directly with the level of interest rates.

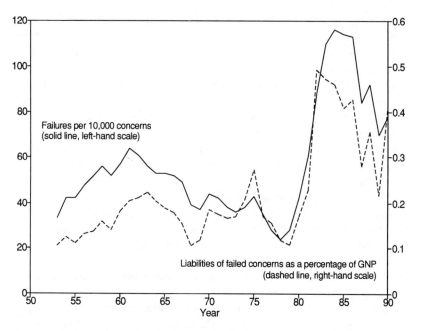

Fig. 5.3   Bankruptcy and default rates, 1953–90
Source: Dun and Bradstreet.
Note: Coverage does not include all industry sectors.

ume of defaulted business liabilities (scaled by gross national product) vary inversely with the pace of real economic activity.[12] As a result, it is also plausible to suppose that rational investors increase their subjective assessment of default rate π (and perhaps also their assessment of loss rate ϕ) if they have independent information indicating that a business recession is imminent. If they do, then arbitrage behavior like that underlying the relation in (5) would, in turn, deliver time variation in the paper-bill spread that would anticipate business fluctuations.

In addition, given that such features as the favorable tax treatment of bills, the default risk on paper, and the superior liquidity of bills render these two instruments imperfect portfolio substitutes, fluctuations in their relative market supplies will also lead to fluctuations in the spread along the lines illustrated in (5). As the discussion in section 5.3 below explains, some of these supply movements, and hence some of the resulting fluctuations in the spread, are plausibly related to the business cycle. Others, however, may merely reflect institutional technicalities of the Treasury bill market. Short-term fluctuations in the Treasury's cash flow alternatively swell the supply of bills or

---

12. For discussions of the increase in the failure rate and the default rate as a result of increased financial fragility in the 1980s, see Friedman (1986, 1990).

increase the demand (by forcing banks to present eligible collateral against enlarged tax and loan account balances). These fluctuations occur in part on a seasonal basis but also in part irregularly. Fluctuations in the volume of advance debt refundings by state and local governments, as sometimes occur in anticipation of changes in tax legislation, also affect the demand for Treasury bills (because of legal restrictions on these borrowers' options for temporarily reinvesting the proceeds of advance refundings). So do fluctuations in the Federal Reserve's open market operations (because most open market purchases and sales take place in Treasury securities). So do most exchange market interventions by foreign central banks (because most central banks, although nowadays not all, hold a disproportionately large share of their dollar portfolios in Treasury bills compared to the portfolio of the typical private market participant). So do the "window dressing" activities of banks and other private investors that choose to sacrifice a few days' interest differential in order to show atypically large Treasury bill holdings on their year- or even quarter-end financial statements. The effect of each of these institutional distortions is presumably to introduce "noise" in the paper-bill spread, in the sense of movement unlikely to correspond to what matters in financial markets for nonfinancial economic activity.

Table 5.7 presents estimation results for a series of regressions intended to capture some of the main elements in the discussion above of the determinants of the paper-bill spread. The coefficient values in the first row of the table, based on monthly data spanning 1974:1–1990:12, show that the paper-bill spread is positively (and strongly) related to the level of the bill rate, as the tax argument and the default-risk argument presented above both suggest.[13] The results in the second row show that the spread is also positively (and strongly) related to the perceived commercial paper default risk, measured here by the differential between the respective interest rates on P2- and P1-rated paper. The results in the third row show that both findings hold up, to at least a marginally significant degree, when the regression includes the two variables together. Finally, the results in the fourth row show that, even in the presence of these two variables, there is again no statistically significant evidence of a time trend in the spread. (A negative time trend, e.g., might represent a declining liquidity value of bills over paper as the commercial paper market has developed over time.)

The lower panel of table 5.7 shows the results of an attempt to replicate, for the longer sample spanning 1959:1–1990:12, the four regressions shown just above. Because published commercial paper ratings were not introduced until

---

13. Although augmented Dickey-Fuller tests for stationarity of the paper-bill spread reject the nonstationarity null at the .01 level, the fact that analogous tests for the interest rate level do not reject at the .10 level warrants care in interpreting the standard errors on the interest rate in these regressions, which may have nonstandard asymptotic distributions. Indeed, the observation that the spread is I(0) while the interest rate is I(1) is inconsistent with any hypothesis that the spread merely captures the effect of the interest rate level (via, e.g., differential taxation).

Table 5.7   **Decompositions of the Paper-Bill Spread**

	Constant	Interest Rate Level	Quality Differential	Trend	$\bar{R}^2$	SE	D-W
	Using the Commercial Paper Quality Differential (sample 1974:1–1990:12)						
1	.12	.09			.16	.50	.30
	(.23)	(.02)					
2	.25		.70		.22	.48	.33
	(.15)		(.20)				
3	−.11	.05	.54		.30	.47	.32
	(.27)	(.03)	(.27)				
4	−.76	.05	.68	−.0015	.28	.46	.33
	(.83)	(.02)	(.15)	(.0018)			
	Using the Corporate Bond Quality Differential (sample 1959:1–1990:12)						
1	.12	.07			.16	.44	.31
	(.09)	(.02)					
2	.43		.13		.01	.48	.28
	(.13)		(.11)				
3	.19	.09	−.20		.18	.44	.33
	(.09)	(.03)	(.13)				
4	.31	.11	−.15	−.0008	.19	.43	.34
	(.15)	(.03)	(.12)	(.0007)			

Note: Numbers in parentheses are robust standard errors, corrected for 12th-order moving-average serial correlation.

after the Penn Central default, however—hence the 1974 starting date of the sample used for the regressions in the upper panel—here the spread between the respective interest rates on Baa- and Aaa-rated corporate *bonds* is used as a proxy for perceived commercial paper default risk. Risk of default over the coming six months need not be the same as risk of default over the life of a twenty- or thirty-year bond, however, so the default-risk aspect of the attempt to extend these results backward to the longer sample does not deliver significant results.[14] (Indeed, in equations combining the bill rate level and the bond quality spread, the point estimates for the spread variable's coefficient are, nonsensically, negative). By contrast, the strongly positive relation between the paper-bill spread and the level of the bill rate corresponds well to the result found in the shorter sample. So does the absence of any evidence of a time trend.

14. An additional symptom of the weak link between the paper-bill spread and the Baa-Aaa bond spread is that, while the paper-bill spread is I(0), the bond quality differential appears to be I(1) over the 1959–90 sample. (Augmented Dickey-Fuller tests are unable to reject the null hypothesis of nonstationarity of the bond quality differential even at the .10 level, while analogous tests for the paper-bill spread over the shorter 1974–90 sample do reject the null at the .05 level.) In other words, the bond quality differential appears to contain an integrated component that is not shared by the paper-bill spread.

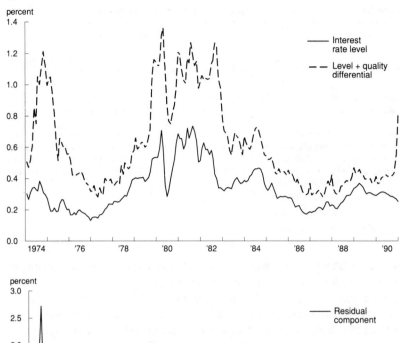

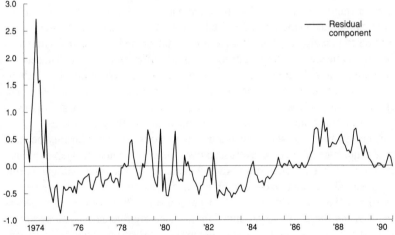

Fig. 5.4   Interest rate level, default risk, and residual components of the paper-bill spread, 1974–90

Figure 5.4, based on the regression in the third row of the upper panel of table 5.7, shows a decomposition of the monthly variation of the paper-bill spread during 1974–90 into three components: a part attributed to variation in the bill rate; a part attributed to perceived default risk, as measured by the P2-P1 differential; and the regression residual (augmented by the constant term). Table 5.8 presents summary statistics for these three components, including their respective simple correlations with changes in real output, as

Table 5.8   Analysis of Components of the Paper-Bill Spread

	Mean	SD	$\Delta\ln(IP_t)$	$\Delta\ln(IP_{t+1})$	F-Statistic
			Correlation with:		
Constant	−.12	. . .	. . .	. . .	. . .
Interest rate level	.45	.14	−.11	−.21***	2.65**
Quality differential	.28	.20	−.43***	−.42***	4.00***
Residual	. . .	.47	−.13*	−.24***	2.60**

Note: Results for the residual are based on the regression in the top panel of table 5.7, row 3. The correlations use data from 1974:1–1990:12. The F-statistics are from reduced-form real output regressions analogous to those in table 5.3, for the 1974:7–1990:12 sample. IP is the index of industrial production.
*   Significant at the 10% level.
**   Significant at the 5% level.
*** Significant at the 1% level.

well as F-statistics for the significance of distributed lags on these components in equations for real output analogous to (1) above.

What stands out in these results is that *each of the three components* of the paper-bill spread—the part attributed to variation in the bill rate, the part attributed to perceived default risk, and the unattributed residual component—contain statistically significant incremental information about subsequent fluctuations in real output. The simple correlation of each component with the change in real output one month ahead is significant at the .01 level. The distributed lag on each component in equations for real output analogous to those reported in table 5.3 above is significant at the .05 level or better.

Hence factors like state and municipal taxation, which plausibly account for a major part of the *average* spread over time but do not themselves plausibly fluctuate in a systematic way over the business cycle, may still play a role in the spread's predictive content by virtue of the way in which their effect on the spread interacts with the level of the bill rate. Perceived default risk (as measured by the P2-P1 differential) more plausibly fluctuates with prospects for business activity, and it is also apparently part of the story.[15] Finally, the significance of the residual component may represent a role for either variation in the liquidity value of bills over paper or variation in perceived default risk not captured by the P2-P1 differential, or both.

5.3   Borrowers and Lenders in the Short-Term Credit Markets

The analysis presented in section 5.2 suggests a role for both time-varying default risk and a time-varying liquidity premium as explanations of the pre-

15. As the analysis above indicates, default risk may also explain why the level of the bill rate would influence the spread. (The relation in [4], e.g., implies that the spread is proportional to the bill rate, with coefficient determined in part by the default probability.)

dictive power of the paper-bill spread with respect to real output. Based as it is entirely on the observed spread and on inferred components of the spread, that analysis has little to say about how variations over time in either default risk or the liquidity value of bills over paper arise or why these variations are related to fluctuations in real output. Given the nature of recorded bankruptcies, it is straightforward to see why perceived default risk might covary with the business cycle. Why the liquidity value of bills over paper might do so bears further investigation. In both cases, however, developing hypotheses about financial behavior that facilitate bringing to bear data on debt quantities as well as interest rates is likely to be helpful as a way of distinguishing empirically among competing explanations for the predictive properties of the spread.

Three such hypotheses are especially interesting in this context.

5.3.1   Changes in Perceptions of Default Risk

First, a widening of the paper-bill spread in advance of business downturns may reflect anticipations, on the part of investors, that a downturn is likely to occur and hence that default by private borrowers with cyclically sensitive cash flows has become more likely. To the extent that these anticipations tend on average to be correct, fluctuations in the spread will predict fluctuations in the growth of real output. Further, if investors' anticipations in this regard embody information from disparate sources or information that is otherwise difficult to quantify or to summarize in a compact way, the paper-bill spread will have predictive content that is significant even in the presence of other standard predictors of output fluctuations like those included in the regressions presented in section 5.1 above.

Figure 5.5 shows schematically the implications, for the bank loan market (left) and the commercial paper market (right), of an increase in the default risk that lenders in the short-term credit markets associate with private obligations, on the assumption that the interest rate on (default-free) Treasury bills remains unchanged. As is consistent with the effect of an increase in π in equation (4) above, the upward-sloping curves representing lenders' portfolio demands (alternatively, their supply of credit) in both markets shift inward.[16] As a result, the new equilibrium in each market exhibits a smaller quantity of credit extended and a higher interest rate (relative to default-free bills) than before the increase in perceived default risk. Hence the implied covariation between the observed spread to bills and the relevant credit quantity is negative in each market.

In principle, therefore, the loan-bill spread and the paper-bill spread might equally predict fluctuations in real output. No one has forcefully argued this

16. Here and below, the curve representing banks' demand for loans (supply of credit) is drawn with positive but finite slope. Making the curve vertical—i.e., assuming that banks in the aggregate have no flexibility to expand credit for a given quantity of reserves supplied by the central bank—would not materially change the analysis.

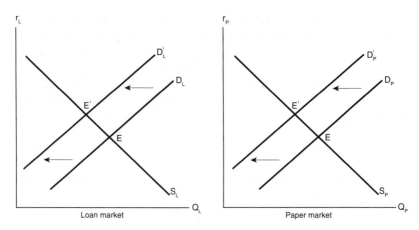

Fig. 5.5   The default risk hypothesis

case empirically for the loan spread, however.[17] One reason is probably that bank loans have many implicit (i.e., noninterest) price elements, so that changes in observed loan interest rates are not a good measure of changes in the cost of loans over short time horizons. Another likely reason is that bank lending often involves long-term customer relationships in which what may appear to be short-term departures from market-clearing price behavior may be perfectly rational. On both counts, it is not surprising that the paper-bill spread is superior as a short-run predictor of fluctuations in real output. (As table 5.1 above shows, the widening of the paper-bill spread before recessions is a matter of at most six months.)

5.3.2   Changes in Monetary Policy

A second explanation of the predictive power of the paper-bill spread, emphasized by Bernanke (1990) and implicit in the work of Kashyap, Stein, and Wilcox (1993), points to monetary policy. Figure 5.6 illustrates the basic mechanics at work here, again focusing on the respective markets for bank loans and commercial paper. A tightening of monetary policy (smaller growth of bank reserves) causes banks' demand for loans to shift inward. As in figure 5.5 above, the result is a higher loan rate and a smaller loan quantity. Here, however, nonbank investors' demand for commercial paper has not changed. As would-be borrowers who do not receive bank loans seek credit elsewhere, supply in the paper market shifts outward.[18] Hence the quantity of paper issued rises, as does the commercial paper interest rate.

17. In regressions analogous to those summarized in table 5.3 above, e.g., the loan-bill spread is significant at the .05 level in the second subsample but not in the first and not for the full sample. In the context represented by table 5.5 above, the loan-bill spread is not significant, even at the .10 level, in regressions also including the paper-bill spread. (Kashyap, Stein, and Wilcox (1993) have advanced an argument for what amounts to the loan-to-paper *quantity* ratio.)

18. An alternative way to express the same relation is to note that demand in the paper market depends on the loan rate.

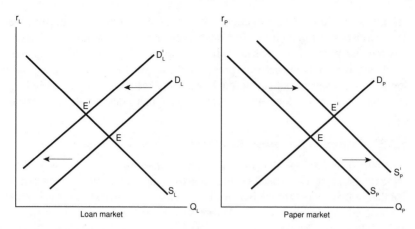

Fig. 5.6   The monetary policy hypothesis

What is missing in the argument thus far is a reason why this increase in the paper rate would also represent an increase in the paper-bill spread. Tighter monetary policy presumably raises the bill rate too. If the predictive content of the paper-bill spread arises because changes in the spread reflect changes in monetary policy, which in turn affects output for any or all of the standard reasons, tighter monetary policy must raise the paper rate not just absolutely but also relative to the bill rate.

One answer to this question, following the analysis in section 5.2 above, is that both the tax component of the spread (for given state/municipal tax rates) and the default risk component (for given default probability and expected loss rate) depend directly on the level of the bill rate. To the extent that tight monetary policy raises the bill rate, therefore, it also widens the paper-bill spread. This line of argument is satisfactory as far as it goes, but ultimately insufficient. As the correlations and F-statistics presented in table 5.8 show, the predictive content of the paper-bill spread is not simply a matter of the spread's proportional covariation with the bill rate.

An alternative (albeit not mutually exclusive) explanation offered by Bernanke and by Kashyap et al. emphasizes, in part, heterogeneity among borrowers. If the obligations of borrowers who shift from the bank loan market to the commercial paper market when monetary policy tightens are systematically less attractive to commercial paper investors than the obligations of borrowers whose paper is already outstanding—either because these new borrowers are less creditworthy or because they deal in smaller volume so that their paper is less liquid—then the resulting rise in default risk or loss of liquidity for the representative issuer's paper will lead the market-average commercial paper rate to rise relative to the rate on Treasury bills (or any other instrument the risk and liquidity of which remain unchanged).

Yet a third potential explanation (again not mutually exclusive of the other two) reflects the behavior of investors allocating their portfolios among different assets, as captured in equation (5). Even apart from changing objective characteristics like default risk or liquidity, the mere fact that investors regard commercial paper and Treasury bills as imperfect substitutes implies that some widening of the paper-bill spread is necessary, when tight monetary policy forces borrowers out of the banks and into the open market, to induce investors to increase the share of their assets that consists of commercial paper.

5.3.3 Changes in Borrowers' Cash Flows

Finally, it is also possible that the behavior that shifts in such a way as to increase the paper-bill spread when real economic activity turns downward is not that of lenders but that of borrowers. As table 5.1 above shows, the spread is especially wide not only just before recessions but during recessions as well. Influences like tight monetary policy, by contrast, might well be expected to change direction during the course of a recession, leading the spread to decrease.[19] (The analogous point does not apply to hypotheses based on time-varying default risk since, as is clear from fig. 5.3 above, bankruptcy and default rates typically remain high for at least a year after a recession ends.)

One major influence on borrowers' behavior that could plausibly account for movements of the paper-bill spread in this context is the cyclical variation of firms' cash flows. As revenue growth ebbs and both inventory accumulation and operating costs continue to rise, in the final stages of a business expansion, firms' credit requirements increase. Figure 5.7 shows such an increase as an outward shift in the supply of both bank loans and commercial paper. As in the case of the default risk hypothesis, shown in figure 5.5 above, the underlying mechanics are the same in both markets, at least in principle. The cash flows hypothesis, however, implies a positive correlation between changes in the paper rate and changes in the paper quantity.

As in the case of the monetary policy hypothesis, here too some further argument is necessary to render the implied absolute increase in the paper rate an increase also relative to the bill rate. Once again, either the borrower-heterogeneity argument or the imperfect-substitutes argument, or both, will suffice.

5.4 Some Evidence on Competing Hypotheses

The results presented in tables 5.7 and 5.8 above indicate that such factors as taxes, default risk, and liquidity, which plausibly explain much of the positive *average* paper-bill spread, also play some role in accounting for the *movement* of the spread over time (table 5.7) as well as the spread's predictive power with respect to fluctuations of real output (table 5.8). In terms of the more structural analysis of section 5.3 above, an increase in perceived default

---

19. As fig. 5.1 above shows, the spread does in fact tend to decrease before the recession ends.

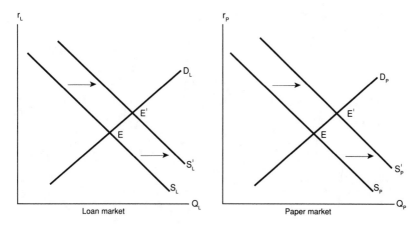

Fig. 5.7   The cash flows hypothesis

risk represents a straightforward influence on the behavior of lenders. A widening of the paper-bill spread due to the increasing importance of differential taxation, as the general level of interest rates rises, likewise represents an influence on lenders' behavior, but the reason why interest rates rose in the first instance may reflect tighter monetary policy or still other influences on either borrowers' or lenders' behavior. The same is true of arguments based on liquidity. A shift in the composition of the "market portfolio" toward a greater weight on commercial paper may well cause the spread between the respective returns to paper and other assets (including bills) to widen, but the question once again is why the outstanding volume in the paper market grew so rapidly in the first place. Answering questions like these on the basis of information about interest rates alone is clearly impossible.

Figures 5.8 and 5.9 present the basic data corresponding to the *quantities* at issue in the discussion of competing hypotheses in section 5.3. The top panel of figure 5.8 shows that the four-quarter growth rate in the outstanding volume of bank loans (commercial and industrial loans) typically peaks in advance of the onset of recessions—very slightly in advance in most episodes, although much more so in 1957. The figure's bottom panel (with greatly reduced scale) plots analogous four-quarter growth rates for the total volume of non-bank-related domestic commercial paper outstanding as well as for the components of this total representing the obligations of nonfinancial corporations and finance companies, respectively. In contrast to bank loan growth, the growth of *nonfinancial* paper tends to surge during recessions (1953, 1957, 1960, 1973, 1981) more often than it tends to peak beforehand (1970 and 1980). Growth of *finance company* paper, however—and therefore of the total, too, since finance companies typically have nearly three times as much in outstandings as nonfinancial issuers—is more like that of bank loans.[20]

---

20. Data are from the flow-of-funds accounts.

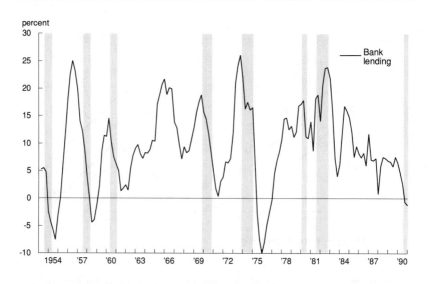

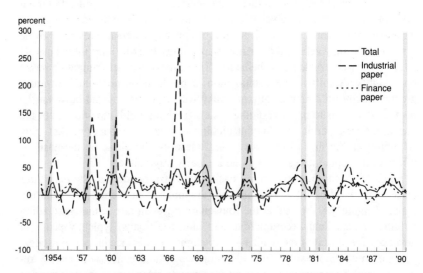

Fig. 5.8   Nominal four-quarter bank loan and commercial paper growth, 1953–90

Figure 5.9 draws the same comparisons in a different way by plotting the respective changes in outstanding bank loans, commercial paper issued by nonfinancial corporations, and finance company lending to nonfinancial corporations (all deflated by the gross national product deflator) during ten-quarter intervals surrounding business-cycle peaks. Each (deflated) series is expressed as the log deviation from the corresponding Hodrick-Prescott trend, normalized to equal zero in the peak quarter. Here again, the tendency for the

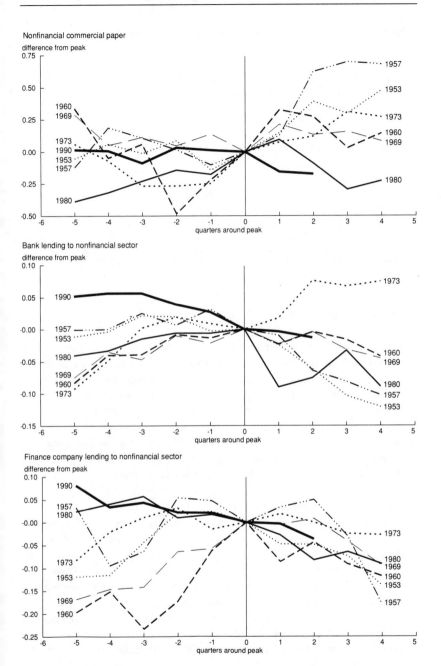

Fig. 5.9   Nonfinancial sector commercial paper issuance, borrowing from banks, and borrowing from finance companies around cyclical peaks

Table 5.9   Correlation Coefficients between the Paper-Bill Spread and Selected
                   Variables

	Real	Nominal
% change in commercial paper issued by the nonfinancial corporate sector	.32***	.33***
% change in bank loans to the nonfinancial corporate sector	.17*	.17*
Nonfinancial sector financing deficit	.35***	.24***
GNP, leading 2 quarters	−.47***	−.23***
GNP, leading 1 quarter	−.51***	−.23***
GNP, current	−.46***	−.15*
GNP, lagging 1 quarter	−.29***	−.03
GNP, lagging 2 quarters	−.24***	−.001

Note: Observations are quarterly; the sample is 1952:2–1990:3. Financial flow variables are from the flow-of-funds data base. Real variables are deflated by the implicit GNP deflator. The financing deficit is the difference between capital expenditures and after-tax cash flow for the nonfarm, nonfinancial corporate sector.
*   Significant at the 10% level.
**   Significant at the 5% level.
*** Significant at the 1% level.

growth of bank loans and finance company paper to peak in advance of the recession, and for the growth of nonfinancial-issuer commercial paper to continue—in some episodes, to accelerate—on into the recession, is apparent.[21]

Given the tendency of the paper-bill spread to widen in advance of recessions and to remain wide during recessions, these observed quantity movements provide support for either the monetary policy hypothesis or the cash flows hypothesis as outlined in section 5.3. Declining growth of bank loan volume, triggered by tighter monetary policy, leads to increases both in the growth of commercial paper volume and in the paper-bill spread, as either of these two hypotheses (but not the default risk hypothesis) implies.

The simple correlations shown in the first two rows of table 5.9 provide further support, especially for the cash flows hypothesis. The paper-bill spread is positively correlated with the contemporaneous real growth rates of commercial paper volume and bank loan volume, but the correlation with paper volume growth is far greater. Under the cash flows hypothesis, both correlations would be positive, while, under the monetary policy hypothesis, the spread–to–paper growth correlation would be positive and the spread–to–loan growth correlation would be negative. By contrast, under the default risk hypothesis, both correlations would be negative.

Two further elements of this price-quantity interaction give still further

21. Kashyap, Stein, and Wilcox (in press) examined similar plots, but ones based on the dates identified by Romer and Romer (1989) with changes in monetary policy rather than on actual business-cycle peaks. Kashyap et al. also did not incorporate finance company paper in their analysis.

weight to the cash flows hypothesis in preference to the monetary policy hypothesis. First, as the third row of table 5.9 shows, the paper-bill spread is also strongly correlated with contemporaneous growth of the cash deficit that nonfinancial corporations need to finance.[22] Second, the role of the finance companies presents a particular puzzle for the monetary policy hypothesis. Tighter monetary policy would, in the first instance, restrict the lending of banks but not finance companies. Would-be borrowers not accommodated by banks would then turn to finance companies, with the result that these institutions' lending (and hence their borrowing to fund that lending) would rise along with that of nonfinancial issuers of commercial paper. As figures 5.8 and 5.9 show, however, growth of finance paper fluctuates more in step with growth of bank loans than with growth of paper issued by nonfinancial corporations.

Especially when they relate prices and quantities, simple correlations can often be misleading. Table 5.10 therefore presents the results of estimating several variations of a regression relating the paper-bill spread to contemporaneous and lagged growth in the total volume of non-bank-related domestic commercial paper outstanding (including issues of both nonfinancial firms and finance companies) and to a direct measure of perceived default risk.

The ordinary least squares regression reported in row 1 of the table shows that the spread is related positively both to lagged paper volume growth (expressed relative to the total amount of paper and bills outstanding) and to perceived default risk as measured by the P2-P1 differential and negatively to the relative quantity of Treasury bills outstanding. It also shows that the time trend is not only negative (as usual) but statistically significant along with the other three variables. The relation of the paper-bill spread to paper volume growth and the bill quantity provides evidence supporting the assumption that investors regard commercial paper and Treasury bills as imperfect portfolio substitutes, which is an important element in either the monetary policy hypothesis or the cash flows hypothesis. The relation of the spread to the P2-P1 differential, even in the presence of growth in paper volume, provides evidence in favor of the default risk hypothesis. The significance here of the negative time trend—indicating a declining spread on average over time, as the commercial paper market has become more fully developed—presumably reflects the advantage of using a relation that makes at least some allowance for supply effects on the relative yields of commercial paper and Treasury bills (in contrast to, e.g., the insignificant time trends shown in table 5.7 above).

Allowing for the simultaneity of supply and demand renders this evidence in favor of imperfect substitutability and the role of perceived default risk even more persuasive. Row 2 of table 5.10 reports two-stage least squares estimates of the same regression, using as instruments the log change in the real

---

22. The deficit is the difference between internally generated funds (gross of depreciation) and investment outlays. Data are from the flow-of-funds accounts.

Table 5.10   Structural Equations for the Paper-Bill Spread

	Dependent Variable	Method	Sample	CPFLOW (t)	TBSHARE (t − 1)	CPQ (t)	BONDQ (t)	r_{B6} (t)	Constant	Trend	PENN	SE	D-W
1	$r_{P6} - r_{B6}$	OLS	74:2–90:4	10.99 (4.90)	−6.78 (1.64)	.61 (.10)			5.10 (1.34)	−.027 (.010)		.36	.87
2	$r_{P6} - r_{B6}$	2SLS	74:2–90:4	25.31 (10.49)	−6.04 (1.87)	.77 (.15)			4.26 (1.52)	−.024 (.012)		.40	1.20
3	$r_{P3} - r_{B3}$	2SLS	74:2–90:4	25.26 (9.67)	−6.36 (2.32)	.94 (.17)			4.63 (1.90)	−.026 (.014)		.46	1.30
4	r_{P6}	2SLS	74:2–90:4	18.36 (8.82)	−6.58 (1.72)	.80 (.18)		.97 (.01)	4.95 (1.43)	−.025 (.011)		.37	1.09
5	$r_{P6} - r_{B6}$	OLS	67:3–90:4	11.83 (3.04)	−6.32 (.70)		.23 (.12)		4.69 (.62)	−.024 (.003)	.45 (.19)	.41	.87
6	$r_{P6} - r_{B6}$	2SLS	67:3–90:4	40.11 (17.74)	−6.23 (1.17)		.55 (.18)		3.93 (.96)	−.028 (.007)	1.57 (.64)	.55	1.35
7	r_{P6}	2SLS	67:3–90:4	23.33 (13.52)	−6.14 (.84)		.33 (.13)	1.01 (.03)	4.22 (.65)	−.026 (.005)	.92 (.46)	.44	1.10

Note: Variable definitions: r_{P6} = 6-month commercial paper rate (%); r_{B6} = 6-month Treasury bill rate (%); r_{P3} = 3-month commercial paper rate (%); r_{B3} = 3-month Treasury bill rate (%); BONDQ = Baa-Aaa corporate bond quality differential (%); CPQ = P2-P1 paper quality differential (%); CPFLOW = change in total commercial paper ÷ total stock of commercial paper and Treasury bills; TBSHARE = Treasury bill outstandings ÷ total stock of commercial paper and Treasury bills; PENN = dummy variable equal to 1 in 1970:3, the date of the Penn Central default. Estimates are based on quarterly observations, for the sample indicated. Numbers in parentheses are robust standard errors, corrected for 4th-order moving-average serial correlation. In the 2SLS regressions, CPFLOW is replaced by the instrument formed by its projection onto a constant, the lagged dependent variable, and the current value and one lag of the following: real monetary base growth, real nonborrowed reserve growth, and the difference between nonfinancial firms' investment expenditures and their after-tax cash flow.

monetary base, current and lagged once; the log change in real nonborrowed reserves (augmented to include "extended credit"), current and lagged once; and the financing deficit of nonfinancial corporations (as a share of the amount of paper and bills outstanding), current and lagged once—all variables that are plausibly related to either monetary policy or borrowers' financing needs.[23] Two-stage least squares estimation based on these variables as instruments for the change in the volume of commercial paper outstanding increases the coefficients on paper volume growth and on the pure default risk variable.[24] The regression reported in row 3 shows that comparable results also follow from measuring the respective interest rates on commercial paper and Treasury bills at three- rather than six-months' maturity.[25]

The regression reported in row 4 of table 5.10, again using six-month rates, further confirms these findings and indicates once more the importance of simultaneity in this context. If the correct dependent variable for studying investors' willingness to buy commercial paper versus Treasury bills is the paper-bill spread, then adding the bill rate to both sides of the equation (so that the dependent variable is simply the paper rate) should result in a coefficient of unity on the bill rate as an independent variable and unchanged coefficients elsewhere. Comparison of rows 4 and 2 shows that the bill rate does indeed have a coefficient of approximately unity and that, in other respects, the new regression corresponds quite closely to its earlier equivalent.[26] Once again, the conclusions to be drawn are that investors regard commercial paper and Treasury bills as imperfect substitutes in a way that matters for the paper-bill spread, that the spread is related to fluctuations in paper volume growth that correspond to variables plausibly reflecting changes in either monetary policy or business financing needs, and that there is a further, independent role for changes in perceived default risk.

The results shown in rows 5–7 of table 5.10 indicate that using the Baa-Aaa bond rate differential in place of the P2-P1 paper rate differential (which, following the discussion above, permits lengthening the sample) preserves the overall flavor of the evidence. The coefficient on the quality variable is much smaller (albeit still statistically significant), as is consistent with the bond differential's measuring much less accurately the default probabilities that are relevant to commercial paper investors, but in other respects the results for the longer sample are highly similar to those shown above.

---

23. The P2-P1 spread and the lagged bill share are also included as instruments because they are treated as exogenous in the regression.

24. These results are robust to such changes in the instrument list as dropping the financing deficit or including instruments constructed from interest rates.

25. The increase in the estimated coefficient on the quality differential in this regression is reassuring, in that the P2-P1 differential is actually measured for one-month maturities.

26. Because the commercial paper rate and the Treasury bill rate are each I(1), the limiting distribution of the coefficient on the bill rate in row 4 is nonnormal, so its t-statistic overstates the precision of the parameter estimate. The coefficients on the remaining stationary regressors will have normal limiting distributions, however.

Table 5.11   **F-Statistics for Financial Variables in Augmented Monthly Real Output Equations**

	1960:1–1990:12	1974:7–1990:12
$\Delta\ln(M1)$	.56	.65
Δr_B	.87	1.84*
Baa-Aaa bond quality differential	3.94***	
P2-P1 paper quality differential		2.25**
$r_P - r_B$	5.26***	4.08***

Note: The estimated six-variable system includes the first-differences of the logs of industrial production, the producer price index, and M1; the first-difference of the 6-month Treasury bill rate; the quality differential in levels; and the paper-bill spread in levels. Six lags are included for each regressor.

*   Significant at the 10% level.
**   Significant at the 5% level.
*** Significant at the 1% level.

Finally, the question remains whether the information about real output contained in the paper-bill spread cannot be just as easily (or almost as easily) represented with more standard variables, including variables corresponding conceptually to the several hypotheses developed in section 5.3. On the evidence, the answer is no. The results summarized in table 5.11 and in figures 5.10 and 5.11 show that, even after allowing for such variables as money growth and perceived default risk and the general level of interest rates, there is still a further element of the paper-bill spread that contains predictive content with respect to fluctuations in real output that is both statistically significant and economically important.

The first column of table 5.11 shows F-statistics for the real output equation of a six-variable vector autoregression including the respective log changes in industrial production, the producer price index, and M1; the change in the bill rate; the Baa-Aaa differential; and the paper-bill spread. The estimation uses monthly data spanning 1960:1–1990:12, with a lag length of six. Even in the presence of these five other variables, representing so many of the hypotheses considered in this paper, the distributed lag on the paper-bill rate is still significant at the .01 level. The table's second column shows F-statistics for an analogous system with the P2-P1 differential in place of the Baa-Aaa differential, and sample 1974:7–1990:12. Here the paper-bill spread is again significant at the .01 level.

Moreover, this "residual" explanatory power of the paper-bill spread is not just statistically significant but quantitatively important. Figures 5.10 and 5.11 show the respective sets of impulse response functions indicating the effects on real output (estimated responses, bounded by 95 percent confidence intervals) due to the financial variables in these two systems, orthogonalized in the order that the variables are listed above—that is, with the paper-bill spread placed last. In the system estimated for the longer sample, the "resid-

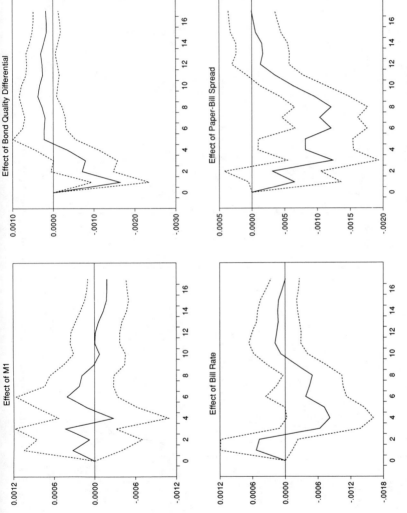

Fig. 5.10 Impulse response functions for real output (using the Baa-Aaa bond quality differential)

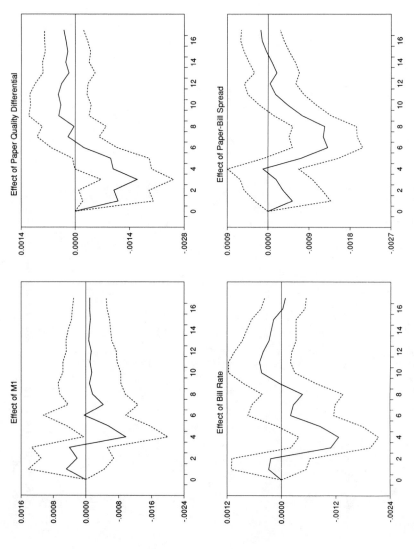

Fig. 5.11 Impulse response functions for real output (using the P2-P1 paper quality differential)

ual" effect of the spread on real output is immediate, large, and prolonged. In the system estimated for the shorter sample, the effect is less regular but clearly visible nonetheless and statistically significant at the familiar six-month horizon by which a widening of the spread usually anticipates recessions.

Even if it were true, therefore, that changes in monetary policy or changes in perceived default risk in principle account fully for the fluctuation of the paper-bill spread and for its relation to fluctuations in real output, the spread would remain a potentially useful predictor because of its ability to embody relevant aspects of those influences that are not captured by standard variables like money growth and observed debt quality differentials.

5.5 Summary of Conclusions

The empirical evidence assembled in this paper supports several specific conclusions about the relation between the paper-bill spread and real economic activity in the United States. To begin, regression-based evidence for the last three decades of U.S. experience—including two subperiods delineated by key structural changes in financial institutions—consistently points to a statistically significant relation between movements of the paper-bill spread and subsequent fluctuations in real output, even in the presence of other financial variables that previous researchers have often advanced as potential business-cycle predictors. This evidence includes not only significant explanatory power of the spread in equations for real output movements but also significant ability of the spread to account for the variance of real output at forecast horizons relevant in a business-cycle context.

Next, readily identifiable features of commercial paper and Treasury bills—including the favorable tax treatment of bills at the state and municipal level, the default risk on paper, and the superior liquidity of bills—distinguish these two instruments in such a way that rational investors would not plausibly treat them as perfect substitutes. These factors can reasonably account for the *average* spread observed over time between the two instruments' respective interest rates. The central focus of this paper, however, is not the mean paper-bill spread but the spread's *variation* over time and, in particular, the predictive power of that variation with respect to real output. In this context, an important finding of this paper is that a decomposition of the spread into components reflecting the interest rate level, a time-varying measure of default risk, and a residual delivers three components, each of which bears a significant relation to subsequent movements in real output.

Finally, evidence based on a more structural approach exploiting the presumed imperfect portfolio substitutability of commercial paper and Treasury bills provides support for each of three hypotheses about why movements of the spread anticipate movements in real output. First, changing perceptions of default risk exert a clearly recognizable influence on the spread, an influence that is all the more discernible after allowance for supply effects associated with imperfect substitutability. In this respect, the spread serves as a useful "indicator" variable, compactly summarizing information available to investors from a variety of disparate sources, but the underlying relations play no directly causal role in affecting economic activity. Second, given imperfect substitutability, a widening paper-bill spread is also a symptom of the contraction in bank lending due to tighter monetary policy. In this respect, the spread does in part reflect a causal influence on economic activity. Third, there is also some evidence of a further role for independent changes in the behavior of borrowers in the commercial paper market due to their changing cash requirements over the course of the business cycle, but for the most part this third channel remains a potential object of further research.

These findings are subject to numerous caveats, of course, and in most cases there is no need to reiterate them here. The one reservation that does perhaps deserve explicit attention in conclusion is that the ability to sort out these three competing hypotheses (or, for that matter, still others) with time-series data relies crucially on the presence of multiple independent shocks generating movements in economic activity. For example, if changes in monetary policy were the only factor determining whether the economy were to be in a boom or a recession, then the effect associated above with changing perceptions of default probabilities and the effect associated with changing business cash flows would both be merely subsidiary reflections of monetary policy. In this respect, investigation of the relation between the paper-bill spread and real economic activity is little different from much of empirical macroeconomics. Given the rich data potentially available on commercial paper transactions by individual borrowers and lenders, however, in this case a useful supplement to research based on the aggregate time series would be parallel exploitation of micro-level data.

References

Baxter, Nevins D. 1966. *The commercial paper market*. Boston: Bankers Publishing Co.
Bernanke, Ben S. 1990. On the predictive power of interest rates and interest rate spreads. *New England Economic Review* (November/December), 51–68.
Cook, Timothy Q., and Thomas A. Lawler. 1983. The behavior of the spread between Treasury bill rates and private money market rates since 1978. *Federal Reserve Bank of Richmond Economic Review* 69 (November/December): 3–15.
Friedman, Benjamin M. 1986. Increasing indebtedness and financial fragility in the United States. In *Debt, financial stability and public policy*. Kansas City: Federal Reserve Bank of Kansas City.
———. 1990. *Implications of increasing corporate indebtedness for monetary policy*. London: Group of Thirty.
Friedman, Benjamin M., and Kenneth N. Kuttner. 1992. Money, income, prices and interest rates. *American Economic Review* 82 (June): 472–92.

Hurley, Evelyn. 1977. The commercial paper market. *Federal Reserve Bulletin* 63 (June): 525–36.

———. 1982. The commercial paper market since the mid-seventies. *Federal Reserve Bulletin* 68 (June): 327–33.

Kashyap, Anil, Jeremy C. Stein, and David Wilcox. 1993. Monetary policy and credit conditions: Evidence from the composition of external finance. *American Economic Review* 83:79–98.

Kessel, Reuben A. 1965. The cyclical behavior of the term structure of interest rates. Occasional Paper no. 91. New York: NBER.

Krasker, William S. 1980. The "peso problem" in testing the efficiency of forward exchange markets. *Journal of Monetary Economics* 6 (April): 269–76.

Moody's Investors Service. 1992. *Defaults and orderly exits of commercial paper issuers.* New York: Moody's, February.

Romer, Christina D., and David H. Romer. 1989. Does monetary policy matter? A new test in the spirit of Friedman and Schwartz. *NBER Macroeconomics Annual,* 121–69.

Selden, Richard T. 1963. Trends and cycles in the commercial paper market. Occasional Paper no. 85. New York: NBER.

State tax handbook. 1990. Chicago: Commerce Clearing House.

Stigum, Marcia. 1990. *The money market.* Homewood, Ill.: Dow Jones Irwin.

Stock, James, and Mark W. Watson. 1989a. Interpreting the evidence on money-income causality. *Journal of Econometrics* 40 (January): 161–82.

———. 1989b. New indexes of coincident and leading economic indicators. *NBER Macroeconomics Annual,* 351–94.

Wizman, Thierry. 1992. The role of monetary shocks: Evidence from tests of the relation between interest-rate spreads and economic activity. In Essays in empirical macroeconomics and finance. Ph.D. diss., Harvard University.

Comment   Ben S. Bernanke

The classic challenge to economic researchers is to make a statement about the economy that is both true and surprising. The observation that the spread between the commercial paper and the Treasury-bill interest rates has remarkable predictive power for the economy, documented in earlier work by Friedman and Kuttner (1990) and by Stock and Watson (1989), appears to satisfy both conditions. In this interesting and nicely executed contribution, Friedman and Kuttner build on their previous analysis of the paper-bill spread to try to explain *why* the spread appears to predict so well. Understanding why the spread predicts is important, both for the light it sheds on the workings of the economy and for helping us assess whether this spread will continue to be informative in the future.

In tackling the question of why the paper-bill spread predicts economic

Ben S. Bernanke is professor of economics at Princeton University and a research associate of the National Bureau of Economic Research.

activity, Friedman and Kuttner follow the most obvious leads (differential taxation of interest on the two instruments, default risk, and monetary policy effects) and add a new explanation (changing cash requirements of borrowers over the cycle). I generally agree with their approach and their list of suspects; my comments consist primarily of reactions to some details of the paper.

Friedman and Kuttner begin in section 5.1 by documenting the strong predictive power of the paper-bill spread. While this is by now fairly familiar ground, several points are worth highlighting.

First, as a general rule, the most striking results for the paper-bill spread are found when predictive power is assessed by a Granger-causality metric. Indeed, while Friedman and Kuttner in most cases trace the paper-bill spread against only one or two other financial variables at a time, Bernanke and Blinder (1992) show that the spread retains its strong Granger-causality properties even in kitchen-sink VARs with a number of other financial variables included simultaneously. For example, in a forecasting equation for industrial production that also included six monthly lags each of industrial production, the CPI, M1, M2, the term structure premium, and the Federal funds rate, Bernanke and Blinder found that the marginal probability that the paper-bill spread can be excluded from the equation was .0049, while none of the other monetary or financial variables was significant even at the .20 level. Similarly, Bernanke (1990) showed that the paper-bill spread is an effective predictor in the Granger sense even when the official index of leading indicators is included in the prediction equation.

On the other hand, when the metric of forecasting power is the percentage of forecast variance explained at various horizons, the performance of the paper-bill spread is good but somewhat less dominant (see Friedman and Kuttner's tables 5.5 and 5.6). Bernanke and Blinder (1992) found that, on the variance decomposition metric, the Federal funds rate (or the spread between the funds rate and the Treasury-bond rate) does somewhat better than the paper-bill spread in predicting a variety of macro variables at monthly frequencies (Friedman and Kuttner still give the edge to the paper-bill spread). Bernanke and Blinder argue that the contrast between the Granger-causality and the variance decomposition findings is consistent with the joint hypothesis that (1) monetary policy is an important source of fluctuations, (2) the funds rate is the best financial indicator of the stance of monetary policy, but (3) the paper-bill spread is the best indicator of overall conditions in credit markets, as determined by both monetary policy and other factors.

Second, while it may be true that the paper-bill spread is the overall winner in the forecasting derby (a result also found for a long list of macro variables by Bernanke [1990]), there really is quite a bit of independent information in some other interest rate indicators as well, including the aforementioned funds rate and the funds rate–bond spread, the spread between one-year and ten-year government bonds, the CD-bill spread, quality spreads (such as the Baa-Aaa corporate spread or the P1-P2 paper spread), and others. An alternative to Friedman and Kuttner's approach of focusing on the single best indicator (the paper-bill spread) would have been to undertake a more multivariate analysis. For example, one might apply factor-analysis techniques to try to extract the best-predicting factors from a list of interest rate indicators and then attempt to interpret these factors economically (e.g., as indicators of monetary policy, default risk, etc.). This is not an easy exercise, but it seems to me to be a useful direction for future research.

A final point on section 5.1 is that Friedman and Kuttner's results do not directly address the question of whether the predictive power of the paper-bill spread has survived into the 1980s. Bernanke (1990) suggested that the forecasting power of the spread significantly weakened in the last decade, and, as Friedman and Kuttner note, the spread did not do well in forecasting the 1990 recession. True, it is not easy to assess the extent to which the paper-bill spread's predictive power has recently declined, as we have only eight or nine years of data since the Volcker experiment ended in 1982. However, the issue is an important one, not only for forecasting reasons, but also for trying to understand the economic reasons for the spread's predictive power. For example, if the spread predicts the course of the real economy because it measures default risk, its forecasting power should not have deteriorated in the last decade; but, if the relative illiquidity of the commercial paper market is a key factor, then the spread's forecasting power might have declined over time as that market has gotten deeper.

Section 5.2 of the paper discusses factors that account for the average size of the paper-bill spread, particularly differences in taxability and differences in default risk of the two types of assets. I found the authors' discussion of the role of default risk to be very helpful, but I still disagree somewhat with their implied conclusion that default risk is quantitatively an equal partner in explaining the level and movements of the spread. Even admitting factors such as imperfect diversification and differences between objective and subjective assessments of default risk, it is hard to see how default risk could account for more than ten to twenty basis points of the level of the spread given actual loss experience in the postwar period. Perhaps more important, *changes* in default risk over time seem unlikely to account for a major part of the rather large observed changes in the spread. On the other hand, changes in the spread due to changes in default risk could be informative about the economy even if they are quantitatively small.

The principal empirical exercise of section 5.2 is an attempt to break down movements in the spread to parts attributed to (1) movements in the level of interest rates, (2) changes in default risk (as measured by the commercial paper and corporate-bond quality spreads), and (3) the residual. I am not quite clear as to the motivation for this decomposition since (as the authors discuss later in the paper) the economic interpretation of this decomposition is not unambiguous. Changes in the level of interest rates in particular could be the result of a number of factors, such as monetary policy, for example. Similarly, the "quality spread" in the commercial paper market could conceivably reflect changing liquidity differentials between the thick P1 market and the thin P2 market as well as default risk. For this reason, I prefer the more explicitly structural analysis that is performed later in the paper.

Section 5.3 discusses major candidate explanations for the predictive power of the spread using a simple but instructive supply-demand framework, and section 5.4 presents some evidence on these competing hypotheses. An important contribution of section 5.4 is the use of data on both interest rates and asset quantities to help discriminate between the various hypotheses. The evidence seems very clear that the assumption of imperfect substitutability between paper and other assets is essential for explaining why the paper-bill spread is predictive; imperfect substitutability is a key element in stories that link the behavior of the spread to monetary policy actions. There also seems to be some support for Friedman and Kuttner's hypothesis that changing borrower needs for liquidity help drive the spread. A perhaps naive question about this hypothesis is why shortages of borrower liquidity (as signaled by an increase in the spread) necessarily foretell recessions. It seems that an expanded demand for external finance by borrowers might as easily signal an anticipated boom as the end of an expansion.

The results of this section cast some light on the work by Kashyap, Stein, and Wilcox (in press), who interpreted the tendency of commercial paper outstanding to expand during periods of loan contraction as evidence for the idea that monetary policy works by affecting bank loan supply. The argument of Kashyap et al. was that the negative correlation of loan growth and commercial paper growth implies that borrowers are being forced to substitute away from loans when monetary stringency reduces loan supply; if bank loan growth were driven instead by changes in credit demand, then the growth rates of loans and commercial paper would be positively correlated. Friedman and Kuttner note that finance company lending to business, which may be an even closer substitute for bank loans than commercial paper, does not generally expand during periods of loan contraction—which, from the point of view of the thesis of Kashyap et al., is a puzzle. In this respect, the recent behavior of these credit quantities is interesting: as Bernanke and Lown (1991) have noted, during the initial phases of the current "credit crunch," for example, during the year before the beginning of the current (1990) recession, slowdowns in bank lending *were* accompanied by expansions in both commercial paper and finance company lending, which is consistent with the idea that there was a constraint on loan supply during that period. During the recession itself (1990:II–1991:I), however, commercial paper and finance company lending both weakened along with bank lending. The failure of commercial paper issuance to expand in particular suggests either that the 1990 recession is the first not to have been associated with a contraction in the supply of alternatives to commercial paper or, alternatively, that some force has restricted the supply of funds to the commercial paper market as well as the supply of bank and finance company loans.

In the end, Friedman and Kuttner reject monocausal explanations and conclude that several factors contribute to the predictive power of the paper-bill spread. However, even when one attempts to control for these various factors, it seems impossible to wipe out the residual predictive power of the paper-bill spread. I think that, despite the excellent start made by this paper, there may still be more to learn about why the paper-bill spread contains so much information about the future.

References

Bernanke, Ben S. 1990. On the predictive power of interest rates and interest rate spreads. *New England Economic Review* (November/December), 51–68.

Bernanke, Ben S., and Alan S. Blinder. 1992. The Federal funds rate and the channels of monetary transmission. *American Economic Review* 82 (September): 901–21.

Bernanke, Ben S., and Cara Lown. 1991. The credit crunch. *Brookings Papers on Economic Activity* (2), 205–39.

Friedman, Benjamin M., and Kenneth N. Kuttner. 1990. Money, income, prices and interest rates after the 1980s. Working Paper no. 90-11. Federal Reserve Bank of Chicago.

Kashyap, Anil K., Jeremy C. Stein, and David W. Wilcox. 1993. Monetary policy and credit conditions: Evidence from the composition of external finance. *American Economic Review* 83:79–98.

Stock, James, and Mark W. Watson. 1989. New indexes of coincident and leading economic indicators. *NBER Macroeconomics Annual,* 351–94.

6　Further Evidence on Business-Cycle Duration Dependence

Francis X. Diebold, Glenn D. Rudebusch, and
Daniel E. Sichel

Do business cycles exhibit duration dependence? That is, are expansions, contractions, or whole cycles more likely or less likely to end as they grow older? In recent work (Diebold and Rudebusch 1990; Sichel 1991), we argued that understanding business-cycle duration dependence is important for understanding macroeconomic fluctuations, we provided a framework for answering the questions posed above, and we provided some preliminary answers. More generally, we argued that the duration perspective may furnish fresh insight on important and long-standing questions in macroeconomics, such as the existence and the extent of a postwar stabilization of business cycles (Diebold and Rudebusch 1992).

Our earlier findings on the attributes of U.S. business cycles from a duration perspective can be compactly summarized:

1a. Prewar expansions exhibit positive duration dependence.
1b. Postwar expansions exhibit no duration dependence.
2a. Prewar contractions exhibit no duration dependence.

Francis X. Diebold is associate professor of economics at the University of Pennsylvania. Glenn D. Rudebusch and Daniel E. Sichel are economists at the Board of Governors of the Federal Reserve System.

Discussions with Christian Gourieroux, Jim Hamilton, Bo Honore, Nick Kiefer, Peter Schotman, and James Stock were extremely valuable. Participants at the World Congress of the Econometric Society, the 1990 NBER Summer Institute, the 1991 NBER Conference on Common Elements of Growth and Fluctuations, and the 1991 NBER Conference on New Research on Business Cycles, Indicators, and Forecasting provided useful input, as did seminar participants at Yale, Columbia, Stockholm, Georgetown, Washington, Santa Barbara, Maryland, Virginia, Pittsburgh, Johns Hopkins, and Michigan State. Diebold thanks the National Science Foundation (grant SES 89-2715), the University of Pennsylvania Research Foundation (grant 3-71441), the Institute for Empirical Macroeconomics, and the Federal Reserve Bank of Philadelphia for financial support. Hisashi Tanizaki provided superlative research assistance. The views expressed here are those of the authors and are not necessarily shared by the Board of Governors of the Federal Reserve System or its staff.

2b. Postwar contractions exhibit positive duration dependence.
3a. Postwar expansions are longer than prewar expansions, regardless of any shift in duration dependence pattern.
3b. Postwar contractions are shorter than prewar contractions, regardless of any shift in duration dependence pattern.

In this paper, we extend our earlier work in two ways. First, we reassess and elaborate on our earlier findings for U.S. data. We use a parsimonious yet flexible exponential-quadratic hazard model, developed for this paper and potentially applicable in other contexts. This model provides a good compromise between nonparametric hazard estimation procedures, for which the available samples are too small, and commonly used parametric hazard estimation procedures, which may impose undesirable restrictions on admissible hazard shapes.

Second, we confront our earlier findings for prewar U.S. business-cycle duration dependence (points 1a and 2a) with prewar data for three additional countries. This is desirable because there have been only about thirty U.S. business cycles since 1854; therefore, only a limited number of duration observations are available. An obvious strategy for obtaining more information about business-cycle duration dependence is to expand the information set by using the NBER chronologies of business cycles in other countries.[1] Such chronologies are available for France, Germany, and Great Britain during the prewar period.

6.1 Methodology

The distribution function of a duration random variable, $F(\tau)$, gives the probability of failure at or before time τ. The survivor function, defined as

$$S(\tau) = 1 - F(\tau),$$

gives the probability of failure at or after time τ. The hazard function is then defined as

$$\lambda(\tau) = f(\tau)/S(\tau),$$

so that an integral of the hazard over a small interval Δ gives the probability of failure in Δ, conditional on failure not having occurred earlier. If the hazard function is increasing (decreasing) in an interval, then it is said to exhibit positive (negative) duration dependence in that interval.

The obvious reference hazard, to which we shall compare our estimated hazards, is flat. That is,

$$\lambda(\tau) = \lambda, \quad \text{if } \tau > 0,$$

1. Similarly, international data have been used in attempts to refine estimates of macroeconomic persistence (see, e.g., Campbell and Mankiw 1989; and Kormendi and Meguire 1990).

where λ is an unknown constant that will of course be different for expansions, contractions, and whole cycles. The associated duration density, $f(\tau)$, for the constant hazard is exponential.

Various hazard models that nest the constant hazard are in common use and could be used to study business-cycle dynamics. Consider, for example, the hazard[2]

$$\lambda(\tau) = \lambda\alpha\tau^{\alpha-1}, \quad \text{if } \tau > 0.$$

This hazard function nests the constant hazard (when $\alpha = 1$, $\lambda(\tau) = \lambda$). The associated duration density is Weibull; thus, the log likelihood (without censoring) is

$$\ln L(\alpha, \lambda; \tau_1, \ldots, \tau_T) = T\ln(\alpha\lambda) + (\alpha-1)\sum_{t=1}^{T}\ln(\tau_t) - \lambda\sum_{t=1}^{T}(\tau_t)^{\alpha},$$

on which estimation and inference may be based for a given sample of observed durations, $\tau_1, \tau_2, \tau_3, \ldots, \tau_T$.

However, this hazard model, like other commonly used parameterizations, imposes strong restrictions on admissible hazard shapes. In particular, if $\alpha > 1$, the hazard is monotone increasing, and conversely for $\alpha < 1$. Nonmonotone hazard shapes (e.g., U or inverted U) are excluded. Although such restrictions may be natural in certain contexts, they appear unjustified in the business-cycle context.

Here we discuss a class of hazard models, developed for this paper but potentially more widely applicable, that we feel strikes a good balance between parsimony and flexibility of approximation, and on which we rely heavily in our subsequent empirical work. Consider the hazard

$$\lambda(\tau) = \exp(\beta_0 + \beta_1\tau + \beta_2\tau^2), \quad \text{if } \tau > 0.$$

This parsimonious hazard, which we call the exponential-quadratic hazard, is not necessarily monotone and is best viewed as a low-ordered series approximation to an arbitrary hazard.[3] In particular, the constant-hazard case of no duration dependence occurs for $\beta_1 = \beta_2 = 0$. Nonmonotone hazards occur when $\beta_1 \neq 0$, $\beta_2 \neq 0$, and sign $(\beta_1) \neq$ sign (β_2). The hazard is U shaped, for example, when $\beta_2 > 0$ and $\beta_1 < 0$ and inverted U shaped when $\beta_2 < 0$ and $\beta_1 > 0$.

The precise shape of the hazard is easily deduced. Immediately, $\lambda(0) = \exp(\beta_0)$, and rewriting the hazard as

---

2. For further details, see Sichel (1991).
3. Kiefer (1988) suggests that future research on hazard models of the form $\exp(\beta_0 + \beta_1\tau + \ldots + \beta_p\tau^p)$ would be useful. The exponential-quadratic hazard is, of course, a leading case of interest ($p = 2$). This hazard is also a special case of the Heckman-Walker (1990) hazard and is similar to the logistic-quadratic hazard of Nickell (1979).

$$\lambda(\tau) = \exp\left[\beta_2\left(\tau + \frac{\beta_1}{2\beta_2}\right)^2 - \frac{(\beta_1^2 - 4\beta_0\beta_2)}{4\beta_2}\right], \quad \beta_2 \neq 0,$$

makes obvious the fact that, when an interior maximum or minimum is achieved (i.e., when $\beta_1 \neq 0$, $\beta_2 \neq 0$, and sign $[\beta_1] \neq$ sign $[\beta_2]$), its location is at

$$\tau^* = -(\beta_1/2\beta_2),$$

with associated hazard value

$$\lambda(\tau^*) = \exp\left[-\frac{(\beta_1^2 - 4\beta_0\beta_2)}{4\beta_2}\right].$$

Before constructing the likelihood, we record a few familiar definitions that will be used repeatedly. First, by definition of the survivor function, we have

$$d \ln S(\tau)/d\tau = -f(\tau)/[1 - F(\tau)],$$

so that

$$\lambda(\tau) = -d \ln S(\tau)/d\tau.$$

We also define the integrated hazard as

$$\Lambda(\tau) = \int_0^\tau \lambda(x)dx,$$

which is related to the survivor function by

$$S(\tau) = \exp[-\Lambda(\tau)].$$

It is interesting to note that, for a hazard $\lambda(\tau)$ to be proper, it cannot be negative on a set of positive measure (otherwise, the positivity of probabilities would be violated) and it must satisfy $\lim_{\tau \to \infty} \Lambda(\tau) = \infty$ (otherwise, the distribution function would not approach unity). Thus, certain parameterizations of the exponential-quadratic hazard do not, strictly speaking, qualify as proper hazard functions. This is of little consequence for the results presented below, however, in which the exponential-quadratic hazard is used only as a *local* approximation.[4]

Construction of the log likelihood allowing for right censoring (as, e.g., with the last postwar trough-to-trough duration) is straightforward. Let $\beta = (\beta_0, \beta_1, \beta_2)'$. Then

$$\ln L(\beta; \tau_1, \ldots, \tau_T) = \sum_{t=1}^{T} \{d_t \ln[f(\tau_t; \beta)] + (1 - d_t)\ln[1 - F(\tau_t; \beta)]\},$$

where d_t equals one if the tth duration is uncensored, and zero otherwise. The form of the log likelihood is a manifestation of the simple fact that the contri-

---

4. Moreover, Heckman and Walker (1990) argue that, in certain contexts, it may be economically reasonable to place positive probability mass on durations of ∞.

bution of a noncensored observation to the log likelihood is the log density while the contribution of a censored observation to the log likelihood is the log survivor. But

$$f(\tau_i; \beta) = \lambda(\tau_i; \beta)[1 - F(\tau_i; \beta)],$$

so

$$\ln L(\beta, \tau_1, \ldots, \tau_T) = \sum_{t=1}^{T} \{d_t \ln[\lambda(\tau_i; \beta)] + \ln[1 - F(\tau_i; \beta)]\}.$$

Moreover,

$$[1 - F(\tau_i; \beta)] = \exp\left[-\int_0^{\tau_t} \lambda(x; \beta)dx\right],$$

insertion of which in the log likelihood yields

$$\ln L(\beta; \tau_1, \ldots, \tau_T) = \sum_{t=1}^{T} \left\{d_t \ln[\lambda(\tau_i; \beta)] - \int_0^{\tau_t} \lambda(x; \beta)dx\right\}.$$

Differentiating, we obtain the score

$$\partial \ln L/\partial\beta = \sum_{t=1}^{T} \left\{[d_t/\lambda(\tau_i; \beta)][\partial\lambda(\tau_i; \beta)/\partial\beta] - \int_0^{\tau_t} \partial\lambda(x; \beta)/\partial\beta dx\right\}$$

and the Hessian

$$\partial^2 \ln L/\partial\beta\partial\beta' = \sum_{t=1}^{T} \left\{[d_t/\lambda(\tau_i; \beta)][\partial^2\lambda(\tau_i; \beta)/\partial\beta\partial\beta']\right.$$
$$- [d_t/\lambda^2(\tau_i; \beta)][\partial\lambda(\tau_i; \beta)/\partial\beta][\partial\lambda(\tau_i; \beta)/\partial\beta']$$
$$\left. - \int_0^{\tau_t} \partial^2\lambda(x; \beta)/\partial\beta\partial\beta' dx\right\}.$$

Thus, specialization to the exponential-quadratic case yields the log likelihood

$$\ln L(\beta; \tau_1, \ldots, \tau_T) = \sum_{t=1}^{T} [d_t(\beta_0 + \beta_1\tau_t + \beta_2\tau_t^2) - \int_0^{\tau_t} \exp(\beta_0 + \beta_1 x + \beta_2 x^2)dx].$$

The derivatives of the exponential-quadratic hazard are

$$\partial\lambda(\tau_i; \beta)/\partial\beta = \begin{bmatrix} 1 \\ \tau_t \\ \tau_t^2 \end{bmatrix} \exp(\beta_0 + \beta_1\tau_t + \beta_2\tau_t^2)$$

and

$$\partial^2\lambda(\tau_i; \beta)/\partial\beta\partial\beta' = \begin{bmatrix} 1 & \tau_t & \tau_t^2 \\ \tau_t & \tau_t^2 & \tau_t^3 \\ \tau_t^2 & \tau_t^3 & \tau_t^4 \end{bmatrix} \exp(\beta_0 + \beta_1\tau_t + \beta_2\tau_t^2).$$

Insertion of the exponential-quadratic hazard derivatives into the general score and Hessian expressions yields the exponential-quadratic score and hazard

$$\partial \ln L / \partial \beta = \sum_{t=1}^{T} \left\{ (d_t \begin{bmatrix} 1 \\ \tau_t \\ \tau_t^2 \end{bmatrix}) - \int_0^{\tau_t} \begin{bmatrix} 1 \\ x \\ x^2 \end{bmatrix} \exp(\beta_0 + \beta_1 x + \beta_2 x^2) dx \right\}$$

and

$$\partial^2 \ln L / \partial \beta \partial \beta' = - \sum_{t=1}^{T} \int_0^{\tau_t} \begin{bmatrix} 1 & x & x^2 \\ x & x^2 & x^3 \\ x^2 & x^3 & x^4 \end{bmatrix} \exp(\beta_0 + \beta_1 x + \beta_2 x^2) dx.$$

Although construction of the likelihood, score, and Hessian is straight-forward, it is not clear that *maximization* of the likelihood will be numerically tractable, owing to the lack of a closed-form likelihood expression and the resulting necessity of numerically evaluating thousands of integrals en route to finding a likelihood maximum. It happens, however, that (1) the evaluation of the required integrals presents only a very modest computational burden, (2) the expressions derived earlier for the score and Hessian facilitate like-lihood maximization, and (3) the likelihood is globally concave, which pro-motes speed and stability of numerical likelihood maximization and guaran-tees that any local maximum achieved is global.

First, consider the requisite integral evaluation. This is done in standard fashion by approximating the integrand by a step function with steps at each integer duration value and adding the areas in the resulting rectangles. Thus, for example, the integral

$$\int_0^{\tau_t} x \exp(\beta_0 + \beta_1 x + \beta_2 x^2) dx$$

is evaluated as

$$\sum_{j=1}^{\tau_t} [x_j \exp(\beta_0 + \beta_1 x_j + \beta_2 x_j^2) + x_{j-1} \exp(\beta_0 + \beta_1 x_{j-1} + \beta_2 x_{j-1}^2)](x_j - x_{j-1})/2,$$

where $x_j = j$.

Second, consider numerical likelihood maximization. Given our ability to compute the likelihood value for any parameter configuration β, we climb the likelihood via the Newton-Raphson algorithm,

$$\beta^{(i+1)} = \beta^{(i)} - [\partial^2 \ln L^{(i)} / \partial \beta \partial \beta']^{-1} \partial \ln L^{(i)} / \partial \beta.$$

Convergence is deemed to have occurred if the change in the log likelihood from one iteration to the next is less than 0.01 percent.

Finally, global concavity of the likelihood (i.e., $\partial^2 \lambda(\tau; \beta) / \partial \beta \partial \beta' < 0$, for all β in R^3) is easily established. To prove global concavity, let H denote the Hessian of the exponential-quadratic model. We must show that $y'Hy \leq 0$, with equality, if and only if $y = 0$. Now,

$$y'Hy = -\sum_{t=1}^{T} \int_0^{\tau_t} y' \begin{bmatrix} 1 & x & x^2 \\ x & x^2 x^3 \\ x^2 x^3 x^4 \end{bmatrix} y \, \exp(\beta_0 + \beta_1 x + \beta_2 x^2) dx$$

$$= -\sum_{t=1}^{T} \int_0^{\tau_t} [(a'y)^2 \exp(\beta_0 + \beta_1 x + \beta_2 x^2)] dx,$$

where $a = (1, x, x^2)' >> 0$, and $y = (y_1, y_2, y_3)'$. Note that the integrand is nonnegative and zero if and only if $y = 0$. But the integral of a nonnegative function is nonnegative, as is the sum of such integrals. Thus, the entire expression is nonpositive and zero if and only if $y = 0$.

Finally, we note that we have obtained various generalizations and specializations of our results, which are not of particular interest in the present application but may be of interest in others. All are treated in the appendix. First, confidence intervals for the true but unknown hazard function may be computed. Second, models with covariates, Z, may be entertained, such as

$$\lambda(\tau, Z; \beta, \gamma) = \exp(\beta_0 + \beta_1 \tau + \beta_2 \tau^2 + Z\gamma).$$

Third, if it can be maintained that (locally) $\beta_2 < 0$, then the log likelihood can be written as a function of integrals of standard normal random variables, and numerical integration is not required.

6.2 Empirical Results

We take as given the NBER chronologies of business-cycle peaks and troughs for the prewar and postwar United States as well as for prewar France, Germany, and Great Britain, which are shown in tables 6.1 and 6.2.[5] The tables show durations of expansions, contractions, and whole cycles measured both peak to peak and trough to trough. The U.S. chronology in table 6.1 includes a ninety-month duration for the last expansion, a 106-month duration for the last peak-to-peak cycle, and a ninety-eight-month duration for the last trough-to-trough cycle. In the empirical work that follows, we treat them as right censored; that is, they are taken as lower bounds for the true durations, the values of which are as yet unknown.[6]

We are limited to prewar samples with the French, German, and British data because of the scarcity of true recessions, involving actual declines in output, in Europe during the 1950s and 1960s. After the devastation of Europe during World War II, there was a reconstruction of extraordinary pace; thus, it is often impossible to identify the classic business cycle in the early postwar period in the European countries. In the postwar period, growth cycles, which refer to periods of rising and falling activity relative to trend growth, have

---

5. These dates are taken from Moore and Zarnowitz (1986), which are the same as those in Burns and Mitchell (1946, 78–79), with minor revisions for some of the U.S. dates.

6. Thus, we assume that the great expansion of the 1980s ended no sooner than May 1990 and that the subsequent contraction ended no earlier than January 1991.

Table 6.1   Business-Cycle Chronology and Durations: United States

Trough	Peak	Contractions	Expansions	Trough to Trough	Peak to Peak
		Prewar			
December 1854	June 1857	. . .	30	. . .	. . .
December 1858	October 1860	18	22	48	40
June 1861	April 1865	8	46	30	54
December 1867	June 1869	32	18	78	50
December 1870	October 1873	18	34	36	52
March 1879	March 1882	65	36	99	101
May 1885	March 1887	38	22	74	60
April 1888	July 1890	13	27	35	40
May 1891	January 1893	10	20	37	30
June 1894	December 1895	17	18	37	35
June 1897	June 1899	18	24	36	42
December 1900	September 1902	18	21	42	39
August 1904	May 1907	23	33	44	56
June 1908	January 1910	13	19	46	32
January 1912	January 1913	24	12	43	36
December 1914	August 1918	23	44	35	67
March 1919	January 1920	7	10	51	17
July 1921	May 1923	18	22	28	40
July 1924	October 1926	14	27	36	41
November 1927	August 1929	13	21	40	34
March 1933	May 1937	43	50	64	93
June 1938	. . .	13	. . .	63	. . .
		Postwar			
	February 1945	. . .	. . .	. . .	. . .
October 1945	November 1948	8	37	. . .	45
October 1949	July 1953	11	45	48	56
May 1954	August 1957	10	39	55	49
April 1958	April 1960	8	24	47	32
February 1961	December 1969	10	106	34	116
November 1970	November 1973	11	36	117	47
March 1975	January 1980	16	58	52	74
July 1980	July 1981	6	12	64	18
November 1982	?	16	90	28	106
?		. . .	. . .	98	. . .

been identified for the European countries (see Moore and Zarnowitz 1986). However, the timing, and hence duration dependence, of these cycles is not comparable with the prewar business cycles.

Summary statistics, including the sample size, minimum observed duration, mean duration, and standard error, for each of the four samples from each country, are displayed in table 6.3. Also included in table 6.3 are summary statistics from pooled samples of all expansions, contractions, and

Table 6.2   **Prewar Business-Cycle Chronologies and Durations: Germany, France, and Great Britain**

Trough	Peak	Contractions	Expansions	Trough to Trough	Peak to Peak
		France, 1865–1938			
December 1865	November 1867	. . .	23	. . .	. . .
October 1868	August 1870	11	22	34	33
February 1872	September 1873	18	19	40	37
August 1876	April 1878	35	20	54	55
September 1879	December 1881	17	27	37	44
August 1887	January 1891	68	41	95	109
January 1895	March 1900	48	62	89	110
September 1902	May 1903	30	8	92	38
October 1904	July 1907	17	33	25	50
February 1909	June 1913	19	52	52	71
August 1914	June 1918	14	46	66	60
April 1919	September 1920	10	17	56	27
July 1921	October 1924	10	39	27	49
June 1925	October 1926	8	16	47	24
June 1927	March 1930	8	33	24	41
July 1932	July 1933	28	12	61	40
April 1935	June 1937	21	26	33	47
August 1938	. . .	14	. . .	40	. . .
		Germany, 1879–1932			
February 1879	January 1882	. . .	35	. . .	. . .
August 1886	January 1890	55	41	90	96
February 1895	March 1900	61	61	102	122
March 1902	August 1903	24	17	85	41
February 1905	July 1907	18	29	35	47
December 1908	April 1913	17	52	46	69
August 1914	June 1918	16	46	68	62
June 1919	May 1922	12	35	58	47
November 1923	March 1925	18	16	53	34
March 1926	April 1929	12	37	28	49
August 1932	. . .	40	. . .	. . .	77
		Great Britain, 1854–1938			
December 1854	September 1857	. . .	33	. . .	. . .
March 1858	September 1860	6	30	39	36
December 1862	March 1866	27	39	57	66
March 1868	September 1872	24	54	63	78
June 1879	December 1882	81	42	135	123
June 1886	September 1890	42	51	84	93
February 1895	June 1900	53	64	104	117
September 1901	June 1903	15	21	79	36
November 1904	June 1907	17	31	38	48
November 1908	December 1912	17	49	48	66

(*continued*)

Table 6.2   (continued)

Trough	Peak	Contractions	Expansions	Trough to Trough	Peak to Peak
September 1914	October 1918	21	49	70	70
April 1919	March 1920	6	11	55	17
June 1921	November 1924	15	41	26	56
July 1926	March 1927	20	8	61	28
September 1928	July 1929	18	10	26	28
August 1932	September 1937	37	61	47	98
September 1938	. . .	12	. . .	73	. . .

whole cycles. We shall not conduct our empirical investigation, however, on pooled samples. Although it might be appealing to pool durations across countries to expand the sample, the conformity of business-cycle timing across countries suggests that the observations across countries are not independent.[7] Hence, simple pooling would be inappropriate. Estimation and testing procedures that control for the degree of interdependence are likely to be very complicated, particularly because so little is known about the transmission of business cycles from one country to another.

There is one area, however, in which we *do* pool information from the four countries, namely, in the specification of a lower bound on admissible durations. This lower-bound criterion, which is denoted t_0, is necessary because, *by definition,* the NBER does not recognize an expansion or a contraction unless it has achieved a certain maturity. The exact required maturity is not spelled out by the NBER, but, in describing the guidelines enforced since Burns and Mitchell (1946), Moore and Zarnowitz (1986) indicate that full cycles of less than one year in duration and contractions of less than six months in duration would be very unlikely to qualify for selection.[8] Because this is a criterion of the NBER definition of business cycles, the choice of t_0 should be, not country specific, but uniform across countries. In particular, we set t_0 for expansions, contractions, or whole cycles equal to one less than the minimum duration actually observed in any of the four countries. We also require t_0 to be identical for peak-to-peak and trough-to-trough cycles, given evidence that the NBER makes no distinction between these two types of whole cycles (see Diebold and Rudebusch 1990). Operationally, the minimum duration criterion is incorporated into estimation of the hazard functions by subtracting t_0 from each of the observed durations before implementing the methodology described in section 6.1.

Let us first consider the United States, for which we can contrast the prewar

---

7. For qualitative descriptions of the conformity of international business cycles, see Moore and Zarnowitz (1986) and Morgenstern (1959).

8. Note that Geoffrey Moore and Victor Zarnowitz are two of the eight members of the NBER Business Cycle Dating Committee.

Table 6.3   **Business-Cycle Summary Statistics**

Sample	Sample Size (N)	Minimum Duration	Mean Duration	Standard Error
		Prewar		
France, 1865–1938:				
F1: Expansions	17	8	29.2	14.8
F2: Contractions	17	8	22.1	15.9
F3: Peak to peak	16	24	52.2	25.3
F4: Trough to trough	17	24	51.3	23.0
Germany, 1879–1932:				
G1: Expansions	10	16	36.9	14.2
G2: Contractions	10	12	27.3	18.1
G3: Peak to peak	10	34	64.4	27.5
G4: Trough to trough	9	28	62.8	25.5
Great Britain, 1854–1938:				
GB1: Expansions	16	8	37.1	17.8
GB2: Contractions	16	6	25.7	19.4
GB3: Peak to peak	15	17	64.0	32.9
GB4: Trough to trough	16	26	62.8	28.6
United States, 1854–1938:				
US1:Expansions	21	10	26.5	10.7
US2: Contractions	21	7	21.2	13.6
US3: Peak to peak	20	17	47.9	20.3
US4: Trough to trough	21	28	47.7	18.1
All countries:				
Expansions	64	8	31.5	14.8
Contractions	64	6	23.5	16.3
Peak to peak	61	17	55.7	26.7
Trough to trough	63	24	54.7	23.9
		Postwar		
United States, 1945–present:				
US1': Expansions	9	12	49.9	29.0
US2': Contractions	9	6	10.7	3.2
US3': Peak to peak	9	18	60.6	28.2
US4': Trough to trough	9	28	60.7	30.9

and postwar experiences. We start with prewar half-cycle hazards, estimates of which are graphed in figure 6.1. Each graph in this figure—and those in all subsequent figures—consists of three superimposed estimated hazards: the exponential constant ($\exp[\beta_0]$), exponential linear ($\exp[\beta_0 + \beta_1\tau]$), and exponential quadratic ($\exp[\beta_0 + \beta_1\tau + \beta_2\tau^2]$). These may be viewed as progressively more flexible approximations to the true hazard and are useful, in particular, for visually gauging the conformity of business-cycle durations to the constant-hazard model. The numerical values underlying the figures are given in tables 6.4–6.6, along with maximum-likelihood estimates of the underly-

(*a*) **Prewar expansions**

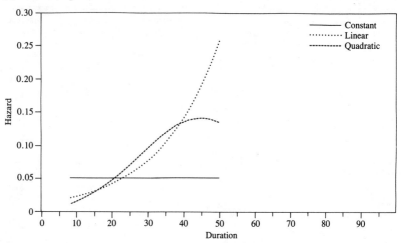

(*b*) **Prewar contractions**

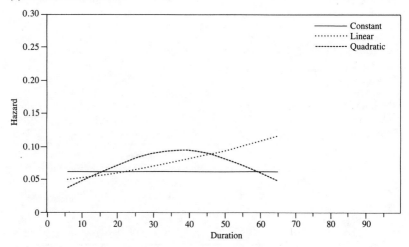

Fig. 6.1   Estimated hazard functions, United States

ing hazard function parameters. In keeping with our interpretation of the exponential hazard as a local approximation, the ranges of the tabled and
graphed hazard functions have been chosen to reflect observed historical maximum durations.

Prewar U.S. expansions display strong evidence of duration dependence.
The estimated exponential-linear expansion hazard rises sharply, from .03 to
.25 after fifty months. The estimated exponential-quadratic expansion hazard
rises more sharply at first, but subsequently less sharply, reaching .15 after

Table 6.4   **Estimated Exponential-Constant Hazard Functions**

Sample	β_0	$\exp(\beta_0)$	Sample	β_0	$\exp(\beta_0)$
	Prewar Expansions			Prewar trough to trough	
F1	−3.099	.045	F4	−3.564	.028
G1	−3.398	.033	G4	−3.875	.021
GB1	−3.405	.033	GB4	−3.846	.021
US1	−2.969	.051	US4	−3.457	.032
	Prewar Contractions			Postwar	
F2	−2.840	.058	US1′	−3.871	.021
G2	−3.105	.045	US2′	−1.735	.177
GB2	−3.030	.048	US3′	−3.910	.020
US2	−2.787	.062	US4′	−3.904	.020
	Prewar Peak to Peak				
F3	−3.589	.028			
G3	−3.850	.021			
GB3	−3.871	.021			
US3	−3.464	.031			

Note: For sample descriptions, see table 6.3.

fifty months. The p-values in table 6.7 indicate that we can soundly reject the constant-hazard null; the p-value for the null that $\beta_1 = 0$ in the exponential-linear model (p_1), for example, is .001.[9] The evidence against the linear-quadratic model, however, is less strong; the p-value for the null hypothesis that $\beta_2 = 0$ in the exponential-quadratic model (p_2) is .18.

Conversely, prewar U.S. contractions do not show strong evidence of duration dependence. The estimated exponential-linear expansion hazard rises only slowly, from .06 to .12 after seventy months. The estimated exponential-quadratic contraction hazard is inverted-U shaped, achieving a maximum of .09 after thirty-six months, but dropping back to .03 after seventy-two months. The p-values indicate that the constant-hazard null is hard to reject; p_1 is .17, and p_2 is .20.

The postwar U.S. results provide striking contrast. Postwar U.S. expansions display no duration dependence, while postwar U.S. contractions display strong positive duration dependence. In short, postwar duration dependence patterns, cataloged in figure 6.2 and tables 6.4–6.6, are precisely *opposite* those of the prewar period!

9. We report asymptotic p-values associated with the Wald statistics in the exponential-linear and exponential-quadratic models. The p-values give the probability of obtaining a sample test statistic at least as large in absolute value as the one actually obtained, under the null of no duration dependence. Small p-values therefore indicate significant departures from the null. p_1 is the p-value for the null hypothesis that $\beta_1 = 0$ in the exponential-linear model. p_2 is the p-value for the null hypothesis that $\beta_2 = 0$ in the exponential-quadratic model.

Table 6.5   **Estimated Exponential-Linear Hazard Functions**

Sample	β_0	β_1	12	18	24	36	48	72	96
					Duration in Months				
					Prewar Expansions				
F1	−3.76	.035	.028	.034	.042	.065	.099	.231	...
G1	−4.93	.065	.010	.015	.022	.047	.102	.481	...
GB1	−4.66	.050	.012	.016	.022	.041	.074	...	...
US1	−3.91	.060	.027	.039	.055	.113	.231	...	...
					Prewar Contractions				
F2	−2.95	.007	.055	.057	.060	.065	.070	.083	...
G2	−3.48	.019	.035	.039	.044	.055	.069	.108	...
GB2	−3.14	.005	.045	.047	.048	.051	.055	.062	.071
US2	−2.99	.014	.055	.060	.065	.077	.091	.127	...
					Prewar Peak to Peak				
F3	−4.06	.015	...	.018	.019	.023	.028	.040	.058
G3	−4.61	.020	...	.010	.012	.015	.019	.030	.048
GB3	−4.59	.018	...	.011	.012	.014	.018	.027	.041
US3	−4.05	.022	...	.018	.021	.027	.035	.060	.101
					Prewar Trough to Trough				
F4	−4.27	.024	...	.015	.017	.023	.030	.053	.093
G4	−5.35	.038	...	.005	.006	.010	.016	.040	.100
GB4	−4.55	.018	...	.011	.012	.015	.019	.029	.046
US4	−4.17	.028	...	.016	.019	.027	.037	.073	.142
					Postwar				
US1'	−4.20	.010	.016	.017	.018	.020	.022	.028	.035
US2'	−2.65	.195	.278	.897	...	...	...	...	...
US3'	−4.20	.008	...	.015	.016	.018	.019	.024	.029
US4'	−4.36	.013	...	.013	.014	.017	.019	.027	.036

Note: For sample descriptions, see table 6.3

The estimated exponential-linear and exponential-quadratic hazard functions for postwar U.S. expansions are hardly distinguishable from each other or from the estimated exponential-constant hazard, rising from .02 to only .03 after ninety-six months. Moreover, the p-values indicate that the data conform closely to the exponential-constant model ($p_1 = .23$, $p_2 = .43$). Conversely, the estimated hazards for postwar U.S. contractions rise extremely sharply. The estimated exponential-linear and exponential-quadratic hazards cannot be distinguished from each other but are readily distinguished from the constant hazard, rising from .07 to .29 in just twelve months. The deviation from constant-hazard behavior is highly statistically significant, with $p_1 = .03$.

It is important to note that the differences between prewar and postwar ex-

Table 6.6   **Estimated Exponential-Quadratic Hazard Functions**

Sample	β_0	β_1	β_2	12	18	24	36	48	72	96
						Duration in Months				
						Prewar Expansions				
F1	−3.80	.039	−.0001	.027	.034	.043	.066	.099	.207	...
G1	−5.13	.083	−.0003	.009	.014	.022	.050	.103	.340	...
GB1	−3.74	−.041	.0016	.020	.018	.019	.027	.063	...	...
US1	−4.44	.132	−.0017	.022	.041	.067	.124	.139	...	...
						Prewar Contractions				
F2	−2.98	.011	−.0001	.055	.058	.061	.066	.070	.074	...
G2	−3.24	−.014	.0006	.037	.036	.038	.047	.070	.270	...
GB2	−3.14	.006	−.0001	.045	.047	.048	.051	.055	.062	.070
US2	−3.28	.056	−.0009	.053	.067	.080	.093	.085	.033	...
						Prewar Peak to Peak				
F3	−4.54	.050	−.0004	...	.012	.016	.025	.035	.051	.047
G3	−5.16	.052	−.0003	...	.006	.008	.014	.022	.039	.048
GB3	−4.17	−.008	.0002	...	.015	.015	.015	.016	.022	.040
US3	−4.73	.075	−.0007	...	.010	.015	.030	.049	.069	.045
						Prewar Trough to Trough				
F4	−4.29	.026	.0000	...	.014	.017	.023	.030	.053	.089
G4	−5.06	.021	.0002	...	.007	.008	.010	.015	.037	.114
GB4	−5.14	.049	−.0003	...	.006	.009	.014	.021	.038	.050
US4	−5.10	.101	−.0010	...	.007	.013	.031	.055	.077	.034
						Postwar				
US1'	−4.32	.018	−.0001	.015	.016	.018	.021	.024	.029	.032
US2'	−2.72	.235	−.0034	.287	...	...	...	...	...	...
US3'	−4.17	.006	.0000	...	.016	.016	.018	.019	.023	.029
US4'	−4.76	.040	−.0003	...	.009	.012	.017	.023	.032	.033

Note: For sample descriptions, see table 6.3

pansion and contraction hazards are not limited to average *slopes*, although, as we have stressed, the slope changes are large and important. In particular, differences between the overall level of prewar and postwar expansion and contraction hazards exist—expansion hazards are higher in the prewar period, whereas contraction hazards are higher in the postwar period. These insights from the conditional perspective of hazard analysis—also noted in Sichel (1991)—lead to a deeper understanding of the unconditional distributional shifts documented in Diebold and Rudebusch (1992).[10]

10. Using exact finite-sample procedures, Diebold and Rudebusch (1992) also document the high statistical significance of the prewar-postwar change in business-cycle dynamics and estab-

Table 6.7   *p*-Values for Null Hypotheses That Hazard Parameters Equal Zero

Sample	p_1	p_2	Sample	p_1	p_2
	Prewar Expansions			Prewar trough to trough	
F1	.017	.472	F4	.015	.480
G1	.002	.425	G4	.004	.375
GB1	.002	.055	GB4	.010	.161
US1	.001	.181	US4	.002	.049
	Prewar Contractions			Postwar	
F2	.330	.468	US1'	.223	.433
G2	.169	.319	US2'	.027	.460
GB2	.328	.496	US3'	.264	.484
US2	.172	.201	US4'	.149	.295
	Prewar Peak to peak				
F3	.048	.176			
G3	.037	.245			
GB3	.024	.203			
US3	.011	.090			

Note: We report asymptotic *p*-values associated with the Wald statistics in the exponential-linear and exponential-quadratic models. p_1 is the *p*-value for the null hypothesis that $\beta_1 = 0$ in the exponential-linear model. p_2 is the *p*-value for the null hypothesis that $\beta_2 = 0$ in the exponential-quadratic model. For sample descriptions, see table 6.3.

Evidence of duration dependence in U.S. whole cycles, whether measured peak to peak or trough to trough, is also present in the prewar data. Moreover, the *p*-values indicate significance of the quadratic hazard term in the U.S. case. Finding duration dependence in prewar whole cycles is not surprising, in light of our finding of duration dependence in prewar expansions.[11] It is rather surprising, however, not to find significant duration dependence in postwar whole cycles, in light of our finding of significant duration dependence in postwar contractions. This may be due to low power, related to the fact that postwar whole-cycle behavior is dominated by expansion behavior (more than 80 percent of the postwar period was spent in the expansion state, as opposed to approximately 50 percent of the prewar period).

Now let us consider the evidence for France, Germany, and Great Britain. The estimated international exponential-constant, exponential-linear, and ex-

---

lish the robustness of that conclusion to issues of prewar data quality, the definition of *prewar*, and allowance for heterogeneity.

11. In fact, as pointed out by Mudambi and Taylor (1991), whole cycles may be expected to show duration dependence even in the absence of half-cycle duration dependence because the distribution of the time to *second* failure is not exponential when the distribution of the time to first failure is. (Moreover, the failure probabilities are of course different in expansions and contractions.)

(*a*) **Postwar expansions**

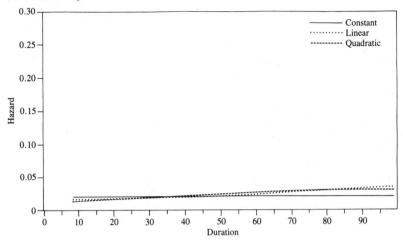

(*b*) **Postwar contractions**

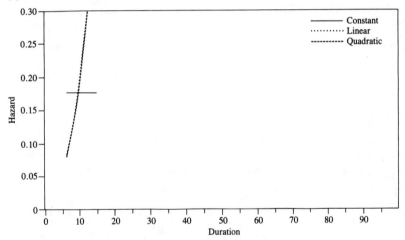

Fig. 6.2   **Estimated hazard functions, United States**

ponential-quadratic prewar hazard functions, shown in figures 6.3–6.5 and
tables 6.4–6.6, indicate striking cross-country conformity in prewar
business-cycle duration dependence patterns. All expansion hazards show
strong positive duration dependence. The estimated hazard for German expansions, for example, rises from near zero after twelve months to .34 after
seventy-two months. France and Great Britain also show substantial slope in
their expansion hazard functions. Like that of the U.S. hazard, the departures
of the French, German, and British hazards from constancy are highly signif-

(*a*) Prewar expansions

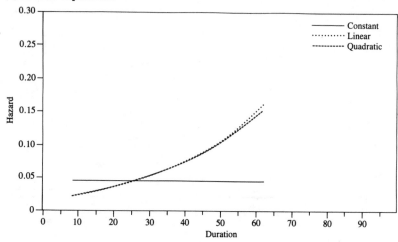

(*b*) Prewar contractions

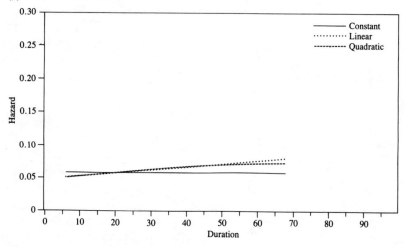

Fig. 6.3   Estimated hazard functions, France

icant, the respective values of p_1 being .02, .00, and .00. Also like the U.S. hazard, the quadratic term does not play a very important role, the respective values of p_2 being .47, .43, and .06.

For contractions, the U.S. prewar findings are again mimicked in France, Germany, and Britain: no evidence of duration dependence is found. All estimated contraction hazards are nearly constant, and the deviations from constancy are never significant. In contrast to the estimated expansion hazards, which start near zero and grow relatively quickly (and at increasing rates), the

(*a*) **Prewar expansions**

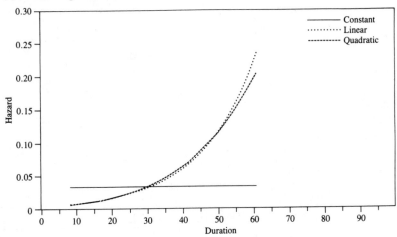

(*b*) **Prewar contractions**

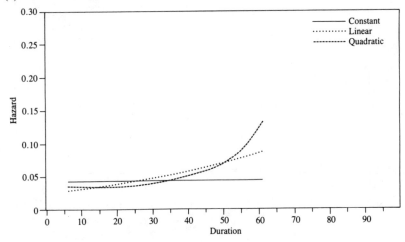

Fig. 6.4   Estimated hazard functions, Germany

estimated contraction hazards start near .05 and grow less quickly (and at decreasing rates).

Evidence for duration dependence in prewar whole cycles, which is strong in the U.S. samples, is also strong in the French, German, and British samples. For both peak-to-peak and trough-to-trough samples, all values of p_1 are less than .05. As in the United States, it would appear that the significant international prewar whole-cycle duration dependence is a manifestation of the significant half-cycle (expansion) duration dependence.

(*a*) Prewar expansions

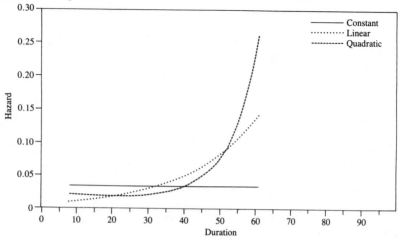

(*b*) Prewar contractions

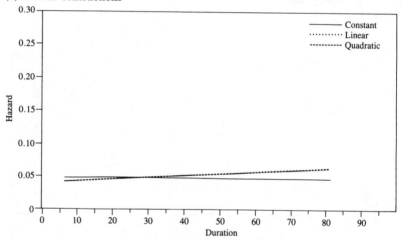

Fig. 6.5   Estimated hazard functions, Great Britain

6.3   Concluding Remarks

We began this paper by asking whether expansions, contractions, or whole cycles are more likely or less likely to end as they grow older, a question whose answer is of importance both methodologically and substantively. Methodologically, for example, the answer has implications for the proper specification of empirical macroeconomic models, such as the Markov-switching models proposed recently by Hamilton (1989). Substantively, for example, the answer has implications for turning-point prediction and business-cycle dating, as pointed out by Diebold and Rudebusch (1989, 1991).

Here we have investigated the patterns of duration dependence in U.S. pre-war and postwar business cycles using a parsimonious yet flexible hazard model, deepening our understanding of the nature of postwar stabilization documented in Diebold and Rudebusch (1992). We presented evidence of a postwar shift in U.S. business-cycle duration dependence patterns: postwar expansion hazards display less duration dependence and are lower on average, while postwar contraction hazards display more duration dependence and are higher on average.

Moreover, we compared our prewar U.S. results with those obtained using prewar data from France, Germany, and Great Britain. We found that, for prewar expansions, all four countries exhibit evidence of positive duration dependence. For prewar contractions, none of the countries do. The results paint a similar prewar picture for each country; statistically significant and economically important positive duration dependence is consistently associated with expansions and never associated with contractions. The similarities in the prewar pattern of duration dependence across countries suggest conformity across countries in the characteristics of business cycles.

The empirical results in this paper and in our earlier papers pose substantial challenges for the construction of macroeconomic models; we hope that our measurement stimulates fresh theory. Obvious questions abound: What types of economic propagation mechanisms induce duration dependence in aggregate output, and what types do not? What are the theoretical hazard functions associated with the equilibria of various business-cycle models, and how do they compare with those estimated from real data? What types of models are capable of generating equilibria with differing expansion and contraction hazard functions, and how do they relate to existing linear and nonlinear models? How can we explain and model secular variation in the degree of duration dependence in expansions and contractions? Some recent work has begun to address various of these questions (e.g., Murphy, Shleifer, and Vishny 1989 develop a model in which cyclical duration is influenced by the stock of durables), but much remains to be done.

Appendix
Specialization and Generalization of the Exponential-Quadratic Hazard Model

Confidence Intervals

Confidence intervals for the true but unknown hazard may be obtained in straightforward fashion. Taylor series expansion of $\lambda(\tau_i, \hat{\beta})$ around $\lambda(\tau_i, \beta)$ yields

$$\lambda(\tau_t; \hat{\beta}) \approx \lambda(\tau_t; \beta) + \partial\lambda(\tau_t; \beta)/\partial\beta'(\hat{\beta} - \beta),$$

where $\hat{\beta}$ denotes the maximum likelihood estimate of β. Mean squared error is therefore approximated by

$$E[\lambda(\tau_t; \hat{\beta}) - \lambda(\tau_t; \beta)]^2 \approx \partial\lambda(\tau_t; \beta)/\partial\beta'E[(\hat{\beta} - \beta)(\hat{\beta} - \beta)']\partial\lambda(\tau_t; \beta)/\partial\beta.$$

By asymptotic unbiasedness of the maximum likelihood estimate, $E[(\hat{\beta} - \beta)(\hat{\beta} - \beta)']$ is asymptotically just $\text{cov}(\hat{\beta})$, which we estimate in standard fashion as $-(\partial^2 \ln L/\partial\beta\partial\beta')^{-1}$ evaluated at $\beta = \hat{\beta}$. Thus, as $T \to \infty$,

$$E[\lambda(\tau_t; \hat{\beta}) - \lambda(\tau_t; \beta)]^2 \to \text{var}[\lambda(\tau_t; \hat{\beta})].$$

For the exponential-quadratic hazard, recall that the first derivate of the hazard is

$$\partial\lambda(\tau_t; \beta)/\partial\beta = \begin{bmatrix} 1 \\ \tau_t \\ \tau_t^2 \end{bmatrix} \exp(\beta_0 + \beta_1\tau_t + \beta_2\tau_t^2)$$

and that the Hessian is

$$\partial^2 \ln L/\partial\beta\partial\beta' = -\sum_{t=1}^{T} \int_0^{\tau_t} \begin{bmatrix} 1 & x & x^2 \\ x & x^2 & x^3 \\ x^2 & x^3 & x^4 \end{bmatrix} \exp(\beta_0 + \beta_1 x + \beta_2 x^2)dx,$$

thus producing the asymptotic variance of the estimated hazard

$$\text{var}[\lambda(\tau_t; \hat{\beta})] \approx \exp[2(\beta_0 + \beta_1\tau_t + \beta_2\tau_t^2)][1, \tau_t, \tau_t^2]$$
$$\left\{ \sum_{t=1}^{T} \int_0^{\tau_t} \begin{bmatrix} 1 & x & x^2 \\ x & x^2 & x^3 \\ x^2 & x^3 & x^4 \end{bmatrix} \exp(\beta_0 + \beta_1 x + \beta_2 x^2)dx \right\}^{-1} \begin{bmatrix} 1 \\ \tau_t \\ \tau_t^2 \end{bmatrix}.$$

The Likelihood Function for the Model with Negative Quadratic Coefficient

The log likelihood in hazard form is

$$\ln L(\beta; \tau_1, \ldots, \tau_T) = \sum_{t=1}^{T} [d_t \ln \lambda(\tau_t) - \Lambda(\tau_t)],$$

which in the exponential-quadratic hazard case is

$$(A1) \qquad \ln L(\beta; \tau_1, \ldots, \tau_T) = \sum_{t=1}^{T} [d_t(\beta_0 + \beta_1\tau_t + \beta_2\tau_t^2)$$
$$- \int_0^{\tau_t} \exp(\beta_0 + \beta_1 x + \beta_2 x^2)dx],$$

evaluation of which requires evaluation of the integrated hazard. The integration must be done numerically. Under the assumption that $\beta_2 < 0$, however, the integration may be greatly simplified because, as we shall show, the likelihood may be rewritten in terms of the standard normal cumulative density function (c.d.f.). The standard normal c.d.f. has been extensively tabulated and is available, for example, as a primitive function in many FORTRANs. We proceed by noting that

$$(A2) \quad \Lambda(\tau_t) = \int_0^{\tau_t} \exp(\beta_0 + \beta_1 x + \beta_2 x^2)dx$$

$$= \int_0^{\tau_t} \exp\left\{\beta_2[x + \beta_1/(2\beta_2)]^2 - \beta_1^2/(4\beta_2) + \beta_0\right\}dx$$

$$= \exp[\beta_0 - \beta_1^2/(4\beta_2)] \int_0^{\tau_t} \exp\left[\left(-1/\{2[-1/(2\beta_2)]\}\right)[x + \beta_1/(2\beta_2)]^2\right]dx$$

$$= \exp[\beta_0 - \beta_1^2/(4\beta_2)](2\pi)^{1/2}[-1/(2\beta_2)]^{1/2}$$

$$\int_0^{\tau_t} (2\pi)^{-1/2}[-1/(2\beta_2)]^{-1/2} \exp\left[\left(-1/\{2[-1/(2\beta_2)]\}\right)[x + \beta_1/(2\beta_2)]^2\right]dx,$$

which contains an integral of a normal density function with mean $-\beta_1/(2\beta_2)$ and variance $-1/(2\beta_2)$. (Recall our assumption that $\beta_2 < 0$, which is needed to ensure positivity of the variance.)

The integral may be rewritten as the difference of two integrals with left integration limit $-\infty$; that is,

$$\int_0^{\tau_t} (2\pi)^{-1/2}[-1/(2\beta_2)]^{-1/2} \exp\left[\left(-1/\{2[-1/(2\beta_2)]\}\right)[x + \beta_1/(2\beta_2)]^2\right]dx$$

$$= \int_{-\infty}^{\tau_t} (2\pi)^{-1/2}[-1/(2\beta_2)]^{-1/2} \exp\left[\left(-1/\{2[-1/(2\beta_2)]\}\right)[x + \beta_1/(2\beta_2)]^2\right]dx$$

$$- \int_{-\infty}^{0} (2\pi)^{-1/2}[-1/(2\beta_2)]^{-1/2} \exp\left[\left(-1/\{2[-1/(2\beta_2)]\}\right)[x + \beta_1/(2\beta_2)]^2\right]dx.$$

By standardizing appropriately, we can rewrite the difference of integrals as

$$(A3) \quad [-1/(2\beta_2)]^{-1/2}\Phi\left\{[x + \beta_1/(2\beta_2)]/[-1/(2\beta_2)]^{1/2}\right\}$$

$$- [-1/(2\beta_2)]^{-1/2} \Phi\left\{[\beta_1/(2\beta_2)]/[-1/(2\beta_2)]^{-1/2}\right\}$$

$$= [-1/(2\beta_2)]^{-1/2}\Phi\left\{[x + \beta_1/(2\beta_2)]/[-1/(2\beta_2)]^{1/2}\right\}$$

$$- [-1/(2\beta_2)]^{-1/2}\Phi\left\{[-\beta_1/(-2\beta_2)]^{-1/2}\right\},$$

where

$$\Phi(x) = \int_{-\infty}^{x} (2\pi)^{-1/2} \exp(-y^2/2)dx$$

denotes the standard normal c.d.f. Insertion of (A3) into (A2) yields

$$\Lambda(\tau_t) = \exp[\beta_0 - \beta_1^2/(4\beta_2)](2\pi)^{1/2}$$
$$\left(\Phi\left\{[x + \beta_1/(2\beta_2)]/[-1/(2\beta_2)]^{1/2}\right\} - \Phi\left\{[-\beta_1/(-2\beta_2)]^{1/2}\right\}\right),$$

which, when evaluated for $t = 1, 2, \ldots, T$ and inserted into (A1), yields the log likelihood function.

The Likelihood Function for the Model with Covariates

Consider the introduction of a vector of covariates into the hazard function; that is, consider

$$\lambda(Z_{\tau_t + s_t}, \tau_t; \beta),$$

where $s_t = \sum_{j=1}^{t-1} \tau_j$. Note that the total period used for estimation is $\sum_{t=1}^{T} \tau_t$. The log likelihood is

$$\ln L(\beta; \tau_1, \ldots, \tau_T) = \sum_{t=1}^{T} \left\{ d_t \ln[\lambda(Z_{\tau_t + s_t}, \tau_t; \beta)] - \int_0^{\tau_t} \lambda(Z_{x + s_t}, x; \beta)dx \right\}.$$

The score is

$$\partial \ln L/\partial \beta = \sum_{t=1}^{T} \left\{ [d_t/\lambda(Z_{\tau_t + s_t}, \tau_t; \beta)][\partial \lambda(Z_{\tau_t + s_t}, \tau_t; \beta)/\partial \beta] \right.$$
$$\left. - \int_0^{\tau_t} \partial \lambda(Z_{x + s_t}, x; \beta)/\partial \beta dx \right\},$$

and the Hessian is

$$\partial^2 \ln L/\partial \beta \partial \beta' = \sum_{t=1}^{T} \left\{ [d_t/\lambda(Z_{\tau_t + s_t}, \tau_t; \beta)][\partial^2 \lambda(Z_{\tau_t + s_t}, \tau_t; \beta)/\partial \beta \partial \beta'] - \right.$$
$$[d_t/\lambda^2(Z_{\tau_t + s_{tt}}, \tau_t; \beta)][\partial \lambda(Z_{\tau_t + s_t}, \tau_t; \beta)/\partial \beta']$$
$$\left. - \int_0^{\tau_t} \partial^2 \lambda(Z_{x + s_t}, x; \beta)/\partial \beta \partial \beta' dx \right\}.$$

In the exponential-quadratic case, we have

$$\lambda(Z_{\tau_t + s_t}, \tau_t; \beta) = \exp(\beta_0 + \beta_1 \tau_t + \beta_2 \tau_t^2 + Z_{\tau_t + s_t} \gamma),$$

where both $Z_{\tau_t + s_t}$ and γ are vectors, so that the score and Hessian are

$$\partial \ln L / \partial \beta = \sum_{t=1}^{T} \left\{ \left(d_t \begin{bmatrix} 1 \\ \tau_t \\ \tau_t^2 \\ Z_{\tau_t + s_t} \end{bmatrix} \right) - \int_0^{\tau_t} \begin{bmatrix} 1 \\ x \\ x^2 \\ Z_{x + s_t} \end{bmatrix} \exp(\beta_0 + \beta_1 x + \beta_2 x^2 + Z_{x + s_t} \gamma) dx \right\}$$

and

$$\partial^2 \ln L / \partial \beta \partial \beta' = -\sum_{t=1}^{T} \int_0^{\tau_t} \begin{bmatrix} 1 \\ x \\ x^2 \\ Z_{x + s_t} \end{bmatrix} (1, x, x^2, Z_{x + s_t}) \exp(\beta_0 + \beta_1 x$$

$$+ \beta_2 x^2 + Z_{x + s_t} \gamma) dx.$$

Each integration may be evaluated numerically as discussed in the text. Thus, for example,

$$\int_0^{\tau_t} Z_{x + s_t} \exp(\beta_0 + \beta_1 x + \beta_2 x^2 + Z_{x + s_t} \gamma) dx$$

is evaluated as

$$\sum_{j=1}^{\tau_t} [Z_{x_j + s_t} \exp(\beta_0 + \beta_1 x + \beta_2 x_j^2 + Z_{x_j + s_t} \gamma) + Z_{x_{j-1} + s_t} \exp(\beta_0 + \beta_1 x_{j-1}$$

$$+ \beta_2 x_{j-1}^2 + Z_{x_{j-1} + s_t} \gamma)](x_j + x_{j-1})/2,$$

where $x_j = j$.

References

Burns, A. F., and W. C. Mitchell. 1946. *Measuring business cycles.* New York: NBER.

Campbell, J. Y., and N. G. Mankiw. 1989. International evidence on the persistence of macroeconomic fluctuations. *Journal of Monetary Economics* 23:319–33.

Diebold, F. X., and G. D. Rudebusch. 1989. Scoring the leading indicators. *Journal of Business* 62:369–92.

———. 1990. A nonparametric investigation of duration dependence in the American business cycle. *Journal of Political Economy* 98:596–616.

———. 1991. Ex ante forecasting with the leading indicators. In *Leading economic indicators: New approaches and forecasting records,* ed. K. Lahiri and G. H. Moore. Cambridge: Cambridge University Press.

———. 1992. Have postwar economic fluctuations been stabilized? *American Economic Review* 82:993–1005.

Hamilton, J. H. 1989. A new approach to the analysis of nonstationary time series and the business cycle. *Econometrica* 57:357–84.

Heckman, J. J., and J. R. Walker. 1990. The relationship between wages and income and the timing and spacing of births: Evidence from swedish longitudinal data. *Econometrica* 58:1411–42.

Kiefer, N. M. 1988. Economic duration data and hazard functions. *Journal of Economic Literature* 26:646–79.

Kormendi, R. C., and P. G. Meguire. 1990. A multicountry characterization of the nonstationarity of aggregate output. *Journal of Money, Credit and Banking* 22:77–93.

Moore, G. H., and V. Zarnowitz. 1986. The development and role of the National Bureau of Economic Research's business cycle chronologies. In *The American business cycle,* ed. R. J. Gordon. Chicago: University of Chicago Press.

Morgenstern, O. 1959. *International financial transactions and business cycles.* New York: NBER.

Mudambi, R., and L. W. Taylor. 1991. A nonparametric investigation of duration dependence in the American business cycle: A note. *Journal of Political Economy* 99:654–56.

Murphy, K. M., A. Shleifer, and R. W. Vishny. 1989. Building blocks of market-clearing business cycle models [with discussion]. *NBER Macroeconomics Annual,* 247–86.

Nickell, S. 1979. Estimating the probability of leaving unemployment, *Econometrica* 47:1249–66.

Sichel, D. E. 1991. Business cycle duration dependence: A parametric approach. *Review of Economics and Statistics* 71:254–60.

Comment   Bruce E. Hansen

Let me pose the following question. Suppose that the economy is in an expansionary phase. What would be a reasonable estimate of the probability of entering a contractionary phase in the near future? What factors would your answer depend on? Is one factor the length (duration) of the current expansion? Similarly, if the economy is in a contractionary phase, does it seem reasonable that the probability of the contraction ending may depend on its past duration?

Quite frankly, I do not find it easy to come up with an intelligent answer to these questions. This is largely because the statistical models that are typically used to study aggregate output do not lend themselves easily to their analysis. A new approach has been proposed by Diebold, Rudebusch, and Sichel. In a series of papers, these authors have argued for the direct analysis of business-cycle duration data. This provides a statistical framework in which questions such as those listed above can be answered in a straightforward and easily interpretable manner.

Measuring the Business Cycle

The starting point for Diebold et al.'s analysis is dating the business cycle. The authors follow the NBER Business Cycle Dating Committee in assigning

Bruce E. Hansen is associate professor of economics at the University of Rochester.

the label *expansion* or *contraction* to each quarter. It is understood that the committee observes a large set of variables. Let us denote the vector of observables by Y_t and its history by $\{Y_t\}$. On the basis of a set of informal rules and internal discussion, the committee determines the appropriate label for each quarter, which we can denote by S_t, for *state of the economy*. The Business Cycle Dating Committee is in effect inducing a mapping from the observed series $\{Y_t\}$ to the reported labels $\{S_t\}$. If the committee's methods are stable over time, we can write this mapping as

$$S_t = \text{NBER} (\{Y_t\}).$$

I call this the NBER business-cycle filter.

Since the authors base their study on the series $\{S_t\}$, one has to think about the nature of the NBER filter that generated it. Does the Business Cycle Dating Committee impose some sort of prior reasoning on how it assigns the label *contraction* or *expansion* to a particular economic quarter? If so, then the dependence in the series $\{S_t\}$ may be a mixture of the committee's prior and the "true" dependence in the underlying economy. In order to justify working with $\{S_t\}$, we must be able to argue that the data are sufficiently informative to outweigh the prior beliefs of the committee members. Could small biases in the committee's dating conventions induce significant changes in the inferences made by the authors in their work? This is a difficult question, but it suggests that, if the questions raised in these papers are indeed important, then more in-depth empirical research needs to be done.

Are Business Cycles Duration Dependent?

The current paper reinforces the authors' past findings of duration dependence in business-cycle data. The general finding is that, regardless of country, time period, or measure of the business cycle (contractions, expansions, or full cycle), durations display *constant* or *increasing hazard*. The data suggest no significant evidence of decreasing hazard. So, the longer the economy has been in a state, the more likely a transition will occur. This suggests that some simple models of the business cycle are misspecified. For example, the Markov-switching model of Hamilton (1989) assumes a constant hazard. The finding by Diebold et al. of positive duration dependence suggests that it may be a useful avenue of research to generalize the Markov-switching model to allow for an increasing hazard. This poses some tricky econometric problems. Identification of the Markov-switching probabilities is known to be problematic in Hamilton's specification. A more complicated specification may suffer even deeper identification problems. Researchers who attempt to generalize Hamilton's approach in this direction should be aware of this problem before they begin and take it seriously when making inferences.

Has the Nature of the Business Cycle Changed?

Diebold et al. use their estimated duration model to argue that the stochastic nature of the business cycle changed after the Second World War. This claim is important for several reasons. If the distribution of business-cycle durations is the same in the prewar and postwar periods, then we can use the combined sample for learning about the nature of the business cycle. Since there are about twice as many cycles before the war as after, this may make a dramatic difference in the precision of estimation.

The authors make the claim that the business-cycle process changed during the war years by performing an informal sample split test. The model is separately estimated over the prewar and postwar periods and the parameter estimates informally compared. This approach, while suggestive, may lead to incorrect inferences. The problem is with the selection of the sample split point. The choice of the war period as the point at which to split the sample is not exogenous to the data. Since the choice has been made after (informally) examining the data, the tendency is to select a sample split point that is particularly tough on the null hypothesis. The critical values used implicitly by the authors to justify rejecting a constant model are too low, and a spurious rejection may have occurred.

The way to think about this is as follows. We want the correct distribution of the test statistic, under the null hypothesis of a constant model. Data generated from a constant-parameter model have a tendency to produce periods in which it appears as if the model is not constant over that period. An applied researcher who examines the data and then "tests" for model stability, conditioning on a sample split point at which the model looks particularly bad, will tend to overreject the hypothesis of constancy.

Recent developments in econometric methods allow us to circumvent this problem. Andrews (1990) and Hansen (1990) develop a unified theory of testing parameter constancy in parametric models. These tests are quite simple to apply, especially in maximum likelihood estimation (the framework used by the authors). In general, suppose that the log likelihood can be written as

$$L_n(\theta) = \sum_{i=1}^{n} l_i(\theta).$$

First, estimate the model over the full sample (prewar and postwar combined), yielding the parameter estimates $\hat{\theta}$. Then form a partial sum process in the estimated scores,

$$S_t = \sum_{i=1}^{t} \frac{\partial}{\partial \theta} l_i(\hat{\theta}),$$

and sequential estimates of the second derivative,

$$V_t = \sum_{i=1}^{t} \frac{\partial^2}{\partial \theta \partial \theta'} l_i(\hat{\theta}).$$

Then the statistic

$$L_C = \frac{1}{n} \sum_{t=1}^{n} S_t' V_n^{-1} S_t$$

is the Lagrange multiplier statistic for the test of the null of parameter stability against the alternative that the parameters follow a random walk. Asymptotic critical values are given in Nyblom (1989) and Hansen (1990, table 1). The statistic

$$\text{SupLM} = \max_{(t/n)\in\Pi} S_t' \left[V_t - V_t V_n^{-1} V_t \right]^{-1} S_t$$

is the Lagrange multiplier statistic for the test of the null of parameter stability against the alternative of a single structural break of unknown timing. Asymptotic critical values are given in Andrews (1990, table 1) for $\Pi = [.15, .85]$.

Both statistics are easy to calculate, and both have power against a much wider range of alternatives than that for which they were designed.

Table 6C.1 reports parameter estimates and asymptotic standard errors for the United States over the joint prewar and postwar periods. The model is the exponential-quadratic model advocated by Diebold et al. The likelihood was programmed in GAUSS386, and the calculations were performed on a 486/33 computer. Using numerical first and second derivatives, the model converged in only a few seconds, so I did not program the analytic derivatives, as recommended by the authors. The test statistics were also calculated using numerical derivatives.

These formal tests confirm the informal finding of Diebold et al. that the models for contractions and expansions are not stable over the joint sample. The SupLM statistic rejects parameter constancy for both contractions and expansions. The L_C statistic rejects parameter constancy for expansions. There are several possible interpretations of these findings. One, advocated by the authors, is that a regime change took place, possibly induced by changes in government macroeconomic policy. If this were indeed the case, we would expect that the SupLM statistic would be maximized for a break point during the war years. Unfortunately for this thesis, the statistic for expansions found the "break point" to be in 1969. We do not have standard

Table 6C.1	Estimated Quadratic Hazard Functions, United States, 1854–1990				
	β_0	β_1	β_2	L_C	SupLM
Expansions	−3.92	.046	−.0004	1.62**	16.0*
	(.44)	(.031)	(.0004)		
Contractions	−2.79	.032	−.0006	.72	24.8**
	(.36)	(.045)	(.0010)		
Peak to peak	−4.51	.051	−.0004	.68	6.8
	(.55)	(.034)	(.0005)		
Trough to trough	−4.94	.078	−.0007	.51	5.6
	(.60)	(.037)	(.0005)		

Note: Asymptotic standard errors are given in parentheses.
* Significant at the asymptotic 5% level.
* Significant at the asymptotic 1% level.

errors for this estimate of the break point, but it is not encouraging for the authors' thesis.

An alternative interpretation is that there is nothing particularly special about splitting the sample at the war years: instead, the finding of parameter instability is simply evidence against the hypothesis that the duration data come from a stationary distribution. The "parameter change" need not take the form of a simple regime shift. Instead, the distribution may be slowly shifting over time as the economy (or the "NBER filter") changes. We know that the underlying GNP process is nonstationary. Is it obvious that the NBER filter applied to this nonstationary process will process a stationary output? The finding of parameter instability is evidence against this hypothesis and is a reasonable interpretation of the evidence.

The formal tests also confirm the finding of Diebold et al. that full-cycle durations can be described well by a stable process over the entire sample. Neither the L_C nor the SupLM statistic is large for the peak-to-peak or trough-to-trough durations. This is indeed an interesting finding, when placed in contrast to the strong rejection of constancy by the contraction and expansion durations.

Questions for Future Research

The analysis contained in the paper by Diebold, Rudebusch, and Sichel implicitly assumes that the business cycle is well described by a two-state system. This assumption is also made by Hamilton (1989). It is not immediately apparent that this assumption is valid. Are the probabilities of leaving expansions and/or contractions dependent only on duration, or are they also dependent on amplitudes? That is, do these probabilities depend on the strength of an expansion or the severity of a contraction? I would expect so. If so, then the authors are inefficiently ignoring available information and, more important, are possibly distorting correct inferences. It is quite possible that, once amplitude is conditioned on, then the finding of positive duration dependence could disappear. A fruitful avenue for future research may be to explore how business-cycle durations depend as well on other variables.

References

Andrews, D. W. K. 1990. Tests for parameter instability and structural change with unknown break point. Discussion Paper no. 943. New Haven, Conn.: Cowles Foundation.

Hamilton, J. H. 1989. A new approach to the analysis of nonstationary time series and the business cycle. *Econometrica* 57:357–84.

Hansen, B. E. 1990. Lagrange multiplier tests for parameter, instability in non-linear models. University of Rochester. Typescript.

Nyblom, J. 1989. Testing for the constancy of parameters over time. *Journal of the American Statistical Association* 84:223–30.

7 A Dynamic Index Model for Large Cross Sections

Danny Quah and Thomas J. Sargent

In studying macroeconomic business cycles, it is convenient to have some low-dimensional characterization of economy-wide fluctuations. If an aggregate measure of economic activity—such as GNP or total industrial production—could be widely agreed on as accurately assessing the state of the economy, then all attention could focus on that measure alone. Econometric analysis and forecasting would then be, in principle, straightforward.

But any one given aggregate measure is likely affected by many different disturbances: understanding economic fluctuations then involves disentangling the dynamic effects of those different disturbances. For instance, much has been written on decomposing aggregate measures of output into different interpretable components. Some of this work uses multivariate time-series methods to analyze such decompositions. Little empirical work has been done, however, proceeding in the opposite direction, that is, using information from a wide range of cross-sectional data to shed light on aggregate fluctuations. In other words, in the business-cycle analysis triad of *depth, duration,* and *dispersion,* the third has typically been ignored.

We know that professional forecasters look at a variety of different indicators to predict aggregate activity. Interest rates, measures of consumer sentiment, the money supply, and the spectrum of asset prices are all candidates for helping predict economy-wide movements. There again, to understand

Danny Quah is reader in economics at the London School of Economics. Thomas J. Sargent is a senior fellow at the Hoover Institution, Stanford University, and professor of economics at the University of Chicago.

Conversations with Gary Chamberlain and Paul Ruud have clarified the authors' thinking on some of the issues here. John Geweke, Bruce Hansen, Mark Watson, James Stock, Jeff Wooldridge, and an anonymous referee have also provided helpful comments, not all of which the authors have been able to incorporate. Finally, the authors gratefully acknowledge the hospitality of the Institute of Empirical Macroeconomics, where portions of this paper were written.

aggregate fluctuations, one needs to go beyond examining a single time series in isolation.

This paper takes the natural next step in these observations: it provides a framework for analyzing commonalities—aggregate comovements—in dynamic models and data structures where the cross-sectional dimension is potentially as large, and thus potentially as informative, as the time-series dimension. Why might this be useful for analyzing macroeconomic business cycles?

When the aggregate state of the economy affects and is in turn affected by many different sectors, then it stands to reason that *all* those sectors should contain useful information for estimating and forecasting that aggregate state. It should then simply be good econometric practice to exploit such cross-sectional information jointly with the dynamic behavior to uncover the aggregate state of the economy.

Standard time-series analysis, however, is not well suited to analyzing large-scale cross sections; rather, it is geared toward the study of fixed-dimensional vectors evolving over time. Cross-sectional and panel data analysis, on the other hand, are typically not concerned with the dynamic forecasting exercises that are of interest in macroeconomics. It is this gap in macroeconometric practice between cross-sectional and time-series analyses that this paper addresses. While there are many interesting issues to be investigated for such data structures, we focus here on formulating and estimating dynamic index models for them.

The plan for the remainder of this paper is as follows. Section 7.1 relates our analysis to previous work on index structures in time series. Section 7.2 shows how (slight extensions of) standard econometric techniques for index models can be adapted to handle random fields. Section 7.3 then applies these ideas to study sectoral employment fluctuations in the U.S. economy. Appendices contain more careful data description as well as certain technical information on our application of the dynamic index model to random fields.

7.1   Dynamic Index Models for Time Series

This paper has technical antecedents in two distinct literatures. The first includes the dynamic index models of Geweke (1977), Sargent and Sims (1977), Geweke and Singleton (1981), and Watson and Kraft (1984). The second literature concerns primarily the analysis of common trends in cointegrated models, as in, for example, Engle and Granger (1987), King et al. (1991), and Stock and Watson (1988, 1990). Because of the formal similarity of these two models—the dynamic index model and the common trends model—it is sometimes thought that one model contains the other. This turns out to be false in significant ways, and it is important to emphasize that these models represent different views on disturbances to the economy. We clarify this in the current section in order to motivate the index structure that we will end up using in our own study.

Notice first that neither of these standard models is well suited to analyzing structures having a large number of individual time series. When the number of individual series is large relative to the number of time-series observations, the matrix covariogram cannot be precisely estimated, much less reliably factored—as would be required for standard dynamic index analysis.

Such a situation calls for a different kind of probability structure from that used in standard time-series analysis. In particular, the natural probability model is no longer that of vector-valued singly indexed time series but instead that of multiply indexed stochastic processes, that is, *random fields*. In developing an index model for such processes, this paper provides an explicit parameterization of dynamic and cross-sectional dependence in random fields. The analysis here thus gives an alternative to that research that attempts robust econometric analysis without such explicit modeling.

Begin by recalling the dynamic index model of Geweke (1977) and Sargent and Sims (1977). An $N \times 1$ vector time series X is said to be generated by a K-index model ($K < N$) if there exists a triple (U, Y, a) with U $K \times 1$ and Y $N \times 1$ vectors of stochastic processes having all entries pairwise uncorrelated and with a an $N \times K$ matrix of lag distributions, such that

(1) $$X(t) = a * U(t) + Y(t),$$

with $*$ denoting convolution. Although jointly orthogonal, U and Y are allowed to be serially correlated; thus (1) restricts X only to the extent that K is (much) smaller than N. Such a model captures the notion that individual elements of X correlate with each other only through the K-vector U. In fact, this pattern of low-dimensional cross-sectional dependence *is* the defining feature of the dynamic index model.

Such a pattern of dependence is conspicuously absent from the common trends model for cointegrated time series. To see this, notice that, when X is individually integrated but jointly cointegrated with cointegrating rank $N - K$, then its common trends representation is

(2) $$X(t) = aU(t) + Y(t),$$

where U is a $K \times 1$ vector of pairwise orthogonal random walks, Y is covariance stationary, and a is a matrix of numbers (Engle and Granger 1987; or Stock and Watson 1988, 1990). As calculated in the proof of the existence of such a representation, U has increments that are perfectly correlated with (some linear combination of) Y. It is not hard to see that there need to be no transformation of (2) that leaves the stationary residuals Y pairwise uncorrelated and uncorrelated with the increments in U. Thus, unlike the original index model, representation (2) is ill suited for analyzing cross-sectional dependence in general. In our view, it is not useful to call Y idiosyncratic or sector specific when Y turns out to be perfectly correlated with the common components U.

7.2 Dynamic Index Structures for Random Fields

While model (1) as described above makes no assumptions about the stationarity of X, its implementation in, for example, Sargent and Sims (1977) relied on being able to estimate a spectral density matrix for X. In trending data, with permanent components that are potentially stochastic and with different elements that are potentially cointegrated, such an estimation procedure is unavailable.

Alternatively, Stock and Watson (1990) have used first-differenced data in applying the index model to their study of business-cycle coincident indicators—but, in doing so, they restrict the levels of their series to be eventually arbitrarily far from each series's respective index component. Stock and Watson chose such a model after pretesting the data for cointegration and rejecting that characterization. Thus, their non-cointegration restriction might well be right to impose, but, again, the entire analysis is thereafter conditioned on the variables of interest having a particular cointegration structure.

When the cross-sectional dimension is potentially large, standard cointegration tests cannot be used, and thus the researcher cannot condition on a particular assumed pattern of stochastic trends to analyze dynamic index structure. (For instance, if N exceeds T, the number of time-series observations, no [sample] cointegrating regression can be computed.) Our approach explicitly refrains from specifying in advance any particular pattern of permanent and common components: instead, we use only the orthogonality properties of the different components to characterize and estimate an index model for the data. It turns out that, by combining ingredients of (1) and (2), one obtains a tractable model having three desirable features: (1) the cross-sectional dependence is described by some (fixed) low-dimensional parameterization; (2) the data can have differing, unknown orders of integration and cointegration; the model structure should not depend on knowing those patterns; and (3), finally, the key parameters of the model are consistently estimable even when N and T have comparable magnitudes.

Let $\{X_j(t), j = 1, 2, \ldots, N, t = 1, 2, \ldots, T\}$ be an observed segment of a random field. We are concerned with data samples where the cross-sectional dimension N and the time-series dimension T take on the same order of magnitude. We hypothesize that the dependence in X across j and t can be represented as

(3) $$X_j(t) = a_j * U(t) + Y_j(t),$$

where U is a $K \times 1$ vector of orthogonal random walks; Y_j is zero mean, stationary, and has its entries uncorrelated across all j as well as with the increments in U at all leads and lags; and, finally, a_j is a $1 \times K$ vector of lag distributions. Model (3) is identical to (1) except that (3) specifies U to be orthogonal random walks. A moment's thought, however, shows that the random walk restriction is without loss of generality: an entry in a_j can certainly sum to zero and thereby allow the corresponding element in U to have only transitory effects on X_j.

As is well known, model (3) restricts the correlation properties of the data: in particular, the number of parameters in X's second moments grows only linearly with N, rather than quadratically, as would be usual.[1] Further, it is useful to repeat that (3) differs from the common trends representation (2) in having the j-specific disturbances uncorrelated both with each other and with U; neither of these orthogonality properties holds for (2). Thus, (3) shares with the original index model (1) the property that all cross-correlation is mediated only through the lower-dimensional U—independent of N and T. Such a property fails for the common trends representation.

Since Y_j is orthogonal to U, (3) is a projection representation, and thus (relevant linear combinations of) the coefficients a_j can be consistently estimated by a least squares calculation: this holds regardless of whether X_j is stationary, regardless of the serial correlation properties of Y_j, and regardless of the distributions of the different variables. Notice further that, for this estimation, one does not require observations on U, but only consistent estimates of the conditional expectations of certain cross-products of U and X_j. Finally, since Y_j is uncorrelated across j's and the regressors U are common, equation-by-equation estimation is equivalent to joint estimation of the entire system. Many of these properties were already pointed out by Watson and Engle (1983); here we add that, if the parameters of (3) are consistently estimated as $T \to \infty$ independent of the value of N, then they remain consistently estimated even when N has the same order of magnitude as T.

The estimation problem is made subtle, however, by the U's not being observable. Nevertheless, using the ideas underlying the EM algorithm (see, e.g., Watson and Engle 1983; Wu 1983; or Ruud 1991), model (3) can easily be estimated. The key insight has already been mentioned above, and that is that, to calculate the least squares projection, one needs to have available only sample moments, not the actual values of U. When, in turn, these sample moments cannot be directly calculated, one is sometimes justified in substituting in their place the conditional expectation of these sample moments, conditional on the observed data X. Note, however, that these conditional expectations necessarily depend on all the unknown parameters. Thus, using them in place of the true sample moments, and then attempting to solve the first-order conditions characterizing the projection—even equation by equation— could again be intractable, for large N.

Instead, treat the projections in (3) as solving a quasi-maximum likelihood

---

1. If necessary, such statements concerning moments can be read as *conditional on initial values*. For brevity, however, such qualification is understood and omitted in the text.

problem, where we use the normal distribution as the quasi likelihood. Then the reasoning underlying the EM algorithm implies that, under regularity conditions, the algorithm correctly calculates the projection in (3).

This procedure has two features worthy of note: first, estimation immediately involves only least squares calculations, equation by equation, and thus can certainly be performed with no increased complexity for large N. To appreciate the other characteristic, one should next ask, Given this first property, how has the cross-sectional information been useful? The answer lies of course in the second feature of this procedure—the cross-sectional information is used in calculating the conditional expectation of the relevant sample moments.

To make this discussion concrete, we now briefly sketch the steps in the estimation. These calculations are already available in the literature; our contribution here has been just to provide a projection interpretation for the EM algorithm for estimating models with unobservables—thus, to distance the EM algorithm from any tightly specified distributional framework—and to note its applicability to the case when N is large.

Write out (3) explicitly as

$$(4) \qquad X_j(t) = \sum_{k=1}^{K} \alpha_{jk}(L)U_k(t) + Y_j(t);$$

in words, each X_j is affected by K common factors $U = (U_1, U_2, \ldots, U_K)'$ and an idiosyncratic disturbance Y_j. This gives a strong-form decomposition for each observed X_j into unobserved components: the first, in U, common across all j and the second Y_j specific to each j and orthogonal to all other X's. It will be convenient sometimes to add a term $d_jW(t)$ to (4), where W comprises purely exogenous factors, such as a constant or time trend.

The common factors in (4) have dynamic effects on X_j given by

$$\alpha_{jk}(L) = \sum_{m=0}^{M_a} a_{jk}(m)L^m, \quad M_a \text{ finite.}$$

Take U_k's to be integrated processes, with their first-differences pairwise orthogonal and having finite autoregressive representation

$$(5) \qquad \Gamma(L)\Delta U(t) = \eta_U(t),$$

where $\Gamma(L)$ is diagonal, with the kth entry given by

$$1 - g_k(1)L - g_k(2)L^2 - \ldots - g_k(M_g)L^{M_g} \quad M_g \text{ finite,}$$

and η_U is K-dimensional white noise having mean zero and the identity covariance matrix. As suggested above, the normalizations following (5) are without loss of generality because U affects observed data only after convolution with a. If X_j were stationary, the sequences a_j—provided that $M_a \geq 1$—

can contain a first-differencing operation to remove the integration built into (5).

Recall that the idiosyncratic or sector-specific disturbances Y_j are taken to be pairwise orthogonal as well as orthogonal to all ΔU. We now assume further that each Y_j has the finite autoregressive representation

(6) $$\beta_j(L)Y_j(t) = \varepsilon_j(t), \quad \text{for all } j,$$

with

$$\beta_j(L) = 1 - b_j(1)L - b_j(2)L^2 - \ldots - b_j(M_b)L^{M_b}, \quad M_b \text{ finite.}$$

Combining (4) and (5), and defining $\phi_{jk}(L) = \beta_j(L)\alpha_{jk}(L)$, we get

$$\beta_j(L)X_j(t) = \sum_{k=1}^{K} \phi_{jk}(L)U_k(t) + \varepsilon_j(t).$$

Notice that, because α and β are individually unrestricted, we can consider the model to be parameterized in β and ϕ, being careful to take the ratio ϕ/β whenever we seek the dynamic effects of U on X. When W—the set of exogenous variables—is lag invariant, as would be true for a time trend and constant, then $\beta_j(L)[d_j W(t)]$ spans the same space as just $W(t)$. Thus, without loss of generality, we can write the model as simply

(7) $$\beta_j(L)X_j(t) = \sum_{k=1}^{K} \phi_{jk}(L)U_k(t) + \varepsilon_j(t) + d_j W(t)$$

(possibly redefining d_j). Subsequent manipulations will exploit this representation (7) of the original strong-form decomposition of X given in (4).

Directly translating the model above into state space form—we do this in Appendix A below—gives

(8) $$X(t) = AZ(t) + dW(t) + Y(t),$$
$$Z(t+1) = cZ(t) + \eta(t+1).$$

The state vector Z, unfortunately, has dimension $O(N)$: this is computationally intractable for data structures with large N and T. Conceptually more important, however, such a state space representation (8) simply describes N time series in terms of an $O(N)$-dimensional vector process—certainly neither useful nor insightful. The reason for this is clear: from (7), lagged X_j's are part of the state description for each X_j owing to the β_j's being nontrivial, that is, owing to the serial correlation in each idiosyncratic disturbance.[2]

The solution to this is to notice that a large part of the state vector happens

---

2. This serial correlation pervades our model in particular and business-cycle data in general. It is this feature that distinguishes our work from many EM algorithm/unobservable common factor applications in finance, e.g., Lehmann and Modest (1988), where the data are either only a large cross section or, alternatively, taken to be serially independent.

to be directly observable; the unobservable part turns out to have dimension only $O(K)$, independent of N. Exploiting this structure gives Kalman smoother projections and moment matrix calculations that are, effectively, independent of N. (The assertions contained in this and the previous paragraph are detailed in Appendix A.)

The intuition then is that increasing the cross-sectional dimension N can only help estimate more precisely (the conditional expectations of) the (unobserved part of the) state and its cross-moments. This must imply the same property for estimates of the parameters of interest. Notice further that deleting entries of X leaves invariant the orthogonality properties on an appropriate reduced version of (8). Thus, if the model is correctly specified, estimators that exploit the orthogonality conditions in (8) remain consistent independent of N; at the same time, smaller N-systems must imply less efficient estimators. This observation is useful for building up estimates for a large N-system from (easier to estimate) smaller systems; additionally, it suggests a Wu-Hausman-type specification test for these index structures.[3]

Next, when the unknown distribution of (X, U, Y, W) generates a conditional expectation $E(U|X, W)$ that equals the linear projection of U on X and W, then standard Kalman smoother calculations yield the conditional expectations $E[Z(t)Z(t)'|X, W]$ and $E[Z(t)|X, W]$, taking as given a particular setting for the unknown parameters. We will assume that the underlying unknown distribution does in fact fall within such a class.[4]

Iteration on this scheme is of course simply the EM algorithm and, under weak regularity conditions, is guaranteed to converge to a point that solves the first-order (projection) conditions. Estimation of the dynamic index model for random fields with large N and T is thus seen to be feasible.

7.3   An Application: Sectoral Employment

This section gives a sectoral, employment-disaggregated description of U.S. economic fluctuations as interpreted by our index-model structure. We consider the behavior of annual full-time equivalent (FTE) employment across sixty industries.

The national income and product accounts (NIPA) report the number of full-time equivalent workers in different industries on an annual basis (NIPA, table 6.7b). Excluding the government sector and U.S. workers employed outside this country, there are sixty industrial sectors for which these data are

---

3. We do not follow up this testing suggestion below, leaving it instead for future work.

4. Elliptically symmetrical distributions would be one such class. Some researchers, such as Hamilton (1989), prefer to work with state vectors that have a discrete distribution—this of course need not invalidate the hypothesized equality of conditional expectations and linear projections, although it does make that coincidence less likely. In principle, one can directly calculate those conditional expectations using only laws of conditional probability. Thus, any simplification—whether by using linear projections or by discrete distributions—is not conceptual but only computational.

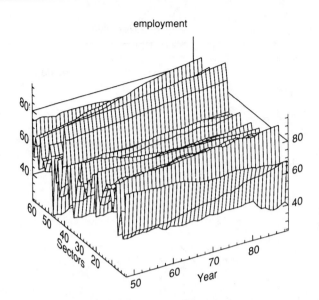

Fig. 7.1   Log (times ten) of employment, across sector and time

available from 1948 through 1989. The industries range from farming, metal mining, and coal mining through motion pictures, legal services, and private household services. (The entire set of sixty industries—complete with Citibase codes—is reported in Appendix B.) Figure 7.1 gives a three-dimensional depiction of these FTE employment data; the "sectors" axis in this graph arrays the different industries in the order given in NIPA table 6.7b and Appendix B. The vertical axis is the log (times ten) of employment in each sector. It is possible to give a more traditional time-series plot of these sixty series. Doing so, however, reveals very little information: the different time-series lines quickly merge, and the page is simply awash in black.

Since these employment figures are available only annually from 1948 through 1989, our data are larger in the cross-sectional than in the time-series dimension ($60 = N > T = 42$). No full rank (60×60) covariance matrix estimator is available; consequently, no full-rank spectral density estimator can be formed. From figure 7.1, it is also clear that the data are trending, with potentially differing orders of stochastic and deterministic permanent components. Again by $N > T$, no cointegrating regression could be calculated; no cointegration tests could be performed.

Figures 7.2–7.4 explore the extent to which the cross-correlation across sectors can be captured by two observable measures typically used by empirical researchers: first, (the log of annual) real GNP and, second, (the log times ten of) total—equivalently, average—employment across the sixty sectors. When we refer to total employment subsequently, we mean this second series, not total U.S. employment. These figures plot residual sample standard devia-

Standard·Deviation

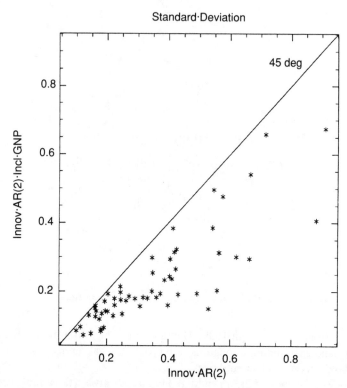

Fig. 7.2   **Residual standard deviations projecting on own two lags plus GNP, against those projecting on just own two lags**

tions from second-order autoregressions, fitted independently across individual sectors, over 1951–87, and always including a constant and time trend. (In a study with as high dimensionality as this one, presenting alternative specifications—varying lag lengths, e.g.—quickly becomes awkward; the signal-noise ratio in presentation falls rapidly and dramatically. Unless stated otherwise, the main conclusions hereafter should be taken as robust across small lag length increases.)

Figure 7.2 graphs the residual sample standard deviation when values for GNP at lag -2 through lag 2 are included as additional regressors (on its vertical axis) and when they are not (on the horizontal axis).[5] By least squares algebra, no point in figure 7.2 can lie above the forty-five-degree line. The further, however, that points fall *below* the forty-five-degree line, the more successfully does GNP—common to all sectors—explain employment in

5. Notice that these regressions include past, present, and future values of GNP. Below, we shall compare the residual variances from these regressions with residual variances from regressions on estimates of our indexes. Those estimates are projections of our indexes on past, present, and future values of all the employment series.

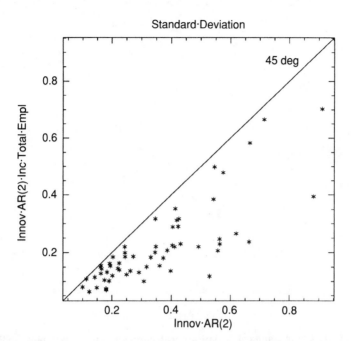

Fig. 7.3   Residual standard deviations projecting on own two lags plus total employment, against those projecting on just own two lags

each sector. From this graph, we conclude that aggregate GNP does appear to be an important common component in sectoral employment fluctuations.

Figure 7.3 is the same as 7.2, except GNP is replaced by total employment across the sixty sectors. The message remains much the same. There appear to be common comovements in sectoral employment, and those comovements are related to aggregate GNP and total employment movements. We emphasize that, in the regressions above, both lagged and lead aggregate measures enter as right-hand-side variables. The sample standard deviations increase significantly when lead measures are excluded.

Figure 7.4 compares these two measures of common comovements by plotting against each other the sample standard deviations from the vertical axes of figures 7.2 and 7.3. We conclude from the graph here that both GNP and total employment give similar descriptions of the underlying comovements in sectoral employment.

For the period 1948–89, we have estimated one- and two-index representations for sectoral employment.[6] (In the notation of the previous section, we take $M_a = 1$, $M_g = 1$, and $M_b = 2$; again, small increases in lag lengths do

---

6. All index-model and regression calculations and all graphs in this paper were executed using the authors' time-series, random-fields econometrics shell tsrf.

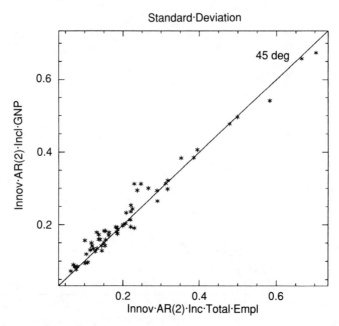

Fig. 7.4   Residual standard deviations projecting on own two lags plus GNP, against those projecting on own two lags plus total employment

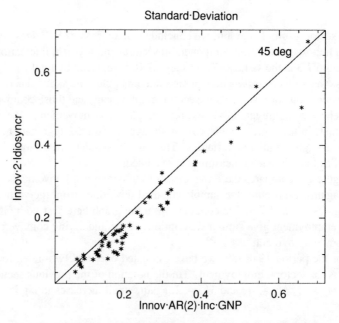

Fig. 7.5   Standard deviations of idiosyncratic disturbances in two-index model, against those of the residuals in the projection on own two lags plus GNP

not affect our conclusions materially.) Figure 7.5 plots standard deviations of the innovations in the idiosyncratic disturbances $\varepsilon_j(t)$, under the two-index representation, against the residuals in sector-by-sector projections including GNP (i.e., the vertical axis of fig. 7.2). In other words, the vertical axis describes the innovations on removing two common unobservable indexes and imposing extensive orthogonality conditions; the horizontal axis describes the innovations on removing the single index that is GNP and without requiring the resulting innovations to be orthogonal across sectors.[7] Since the models are not nested, there is no necessity for the points to lie in any particular region relative to the forty-five-degree line. Again, however, to the extent that these points fall below that line, we can conclude that the comovements are better described by the model represented on the vertical axis than that on the horizontal.

In this figure, twelve sectors lie marginally above the forty-five-degree line, six marginally below, and the remainder quite a bit below. Overall, we conclude that the two unobservable indexes provide a better description of underlying commonalities in sectoral employment than does aggregate GNP.

Figure 7.6 is the same as figure 7.5 except that GNP is replaced by total employment. We draw much the same conclusions from this as the previous graph.

Figure 7.7 replaces the horizontal axes of figures 7.5 and 7.6 with the standard deviation of idiosyncratic innovations from a single-index representation. Notice that the improvement in fit of the additional index is about the same order of magnitude as that of the two-index representation over either of the single observable aggregates.

We do not present here the calculations that we have performed comparing the single unobservable index with the two observable aggregates. The calculations show much what one would expect from the analysis thus far. Aggregate GNP and average employment are about as good descriptions of sectoral comovements as is the single unobservable index model.[8]

So what have we learned up until now? If one were concerned only about goodness of fit in describing the commonalities in sectoral employment fluctuations, then one might well simply use just total GNP or average employment.[9] In our view, index models should be motivated by a Burns-Mitchell kind of "pre-GNP accounting," dimensionality-restricted modeling. The idea

7. Thus, the vertical dimension of fig. 7.5 contains enough information to compute a normal quasi-likelihood value for the unobservable index model; for the horizontal dimension, however, the cross-correlations are nonzero and cannot, as a whole, be consistently estimated.

8. This finding is related to patterns detected in previous applications of unobservable index models to aggregate U.S. time series. For example, Sargent and Sims (1977) encountered so-called Heywood solutions at low frequencies: in those solutions, the coherence of GNP with one of the indexes is unity.

9. We should emphasize again that this is true only when one proxies for those common comovements using both leads and lags of these indicators. As already stated above, the projection residuals get considerably larger when future aggregates are excluded.

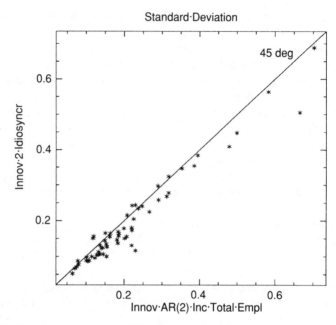

Fig. 7.6 **Standard deviations of idiosyncratic disturbances in two-index model, against those of the residuals in the projection on own two lags plus total employment**

is to allow a one-dimensional measure of "business activity" to emerge from analyzing long lists of different price and quantity time series. We have implemented one version of this vision and arrived at projection estimators of one- and two-index models. In computing these estimated indexes, we have used only employment series. Now we wish to see how, in particular dimensions, our estimated indexes compare with GNP, the most popular single "index" of real macroeconomic activity. GNP is, of course, constructed using an accounting method very different in spirit from that used by us and other workers in the Burns-Mitchell tradition.

Thus, we turn to some projections designed to explore this difference. A regression (over 1952–89) of GNP *growth rates* on a constant and first-differences of our fitted two indexes, lags 0–3, gives an R^2 of 83 percent. A similar regression using just the single index (estimated from the one-index model), again lags 0–3, gives an R^2 of 72 percent. GNP growth rates are thus highly correlated with the estimated index process. This correlation captures the sense in which a purely mechanical low-dimensional index construction yields an aggregate that closely tracks GNP growth.[10]

---

10. Note that sample versions of these indexes are estimated by a Kalman smoothing procedure and therefore use observations on sectoral employment over the entire sample, past and future. This is also why, in figs. 7.2 on, we always used future and past observable aggregates to make the comparison fairer.

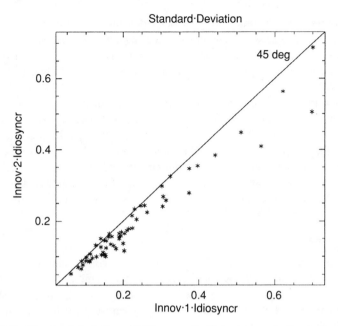

Fig. 7.7   Standard deviations of idiosyncratic disturbances in two-index model, against those in one-index model

We have also experimented with vector autoregressions in GNP growth, average employment growth, and first-differences of the indexes. Exclusion tests of lag blocks of the indexes here, however, *cannot* be viewed as Granger-causality tests because the estimated indexes are themselves two-sided distributed lags of employment. It would be possible to use the estimated parameters of our index representations to construct one-sided-on-the-past index projections. These one-sided projections could then be used to conduct Granger-causality tests. We have not done this here, but we think that it would be a useful exercise.

In concluding this empirical section, we judge that the unobservable index application to the large cross section here has been, in the main, successful. The empirical results here encourage us to be optimistic about continued use of large cross sections for dynamic analysis. There are, however, dimensions along which relative failure might be argued. Most notably, the refinement in the description of commonalities given by the unobservable index model was not spectacular relative to that given by observable measures, such as aggregate GNP or total employment. While the two-index representation is a better description of sectoral employment fluctuations, relative to a single-index representation, not both indexes turn out to be equally important for predicting GNP. For this exercise, the tighter parameterization implicit in a single index appears to dominate the marginal increase in information from a two-index representation. These failures should be contrasted with our two principal successes: (i) the tractability of our extension of standard index model analysis (simultaneously to encompass differing nonstationarities, large cross-sectional dimensions, and extensive orthogonality restrictions) and (ii) the strong informational, predictive content for GNP of our estimated common indexes.

Unlike in research on interpreting unobservable disturbances—such as in VAR (vector autoregressive) studies—we do not attempt here to name the two unobservable factors. Rather, the goal of the present paper has been to carry out the methodological extensions in point i above and to examine the forecasting properties of the resulting common factors in point ii. Future work could, in principle, attempt the same exercise for the unobservable index models here as has been performed for VAR representations elsewhere.

7.4 Conclusion

We have provided a framework for analyzing comovements—aggregate dynamics—in random fields, that is, data where the number of cross-sectional time series is comparable in magnitude to the time length. We have shown how, on reinterpretation, standard techniques can be used to estimate such index models.

In applying the model to estimate aggregate dynamics in employment across different sectors, we discovered that a model with two common factors turns out to fit those data surprisingly well. Put differently, much of the observed fluctuation in employment in those many diverse industries is well explained by disturbances that are perfectly correlated across all the sectors.

The econometric structure that we have used here seems to us quite rich and potentially capable of dealing with many different interesting questions. Among others, this includes issues of the relative importance of different kinds of disturbances (e.g., Long and Plosser 1983; and Prescott 1986), convergence across economic regions (e.g., Barro and Sala-i-Martin 1992; and Blanchard and Katz 1992), aggregate and sectoral comovements (e.g., Abraham and Katz 1986; Lilien 1982; and Rogerson 1987), and location dynamics, conditioning on exogenous policy variables (e.g., Papke 1989). Previous work, however, has used measurement and econometric techniques that differ substantially from that which we propose here; clearly, we think our procedure is closer in spirit to the relevant economic ideas. Questions about the appropriate definition and measurement of inflation, comovement in consumption across economic regions, and the joint behavior of asset prices observed for many assets and over long periods of time all can be coherently dealt with in our framework. In future research, we intend to apply our techniques to these and similar, related issues.

Appendix A
Technical Appendix

This appendix constructs a state space representation for the model of section 7.2; this is needed to compute the Kalman-smoothed projections that are in turn used in applying the EM algorithm to our estimation problem.

Recall that $\phi_{jk} = \beta_j \alpha_{jk}$ and that the maximum lags on β_j and α_{jk} are M_b and M_a, respectively. Define $M_f = M_b + M_a$; this is the maximum lag on ϕ_{jk}. From M_g, the maximum lag on Γ in (5), define $M_h = \max(M_f, M_g)$, and let

$$\tilde{U}(t) = [U(t)', U(t-1)', \ldots , U(t - M_h)']'$$

and conformably

$$\tilde{\eta}_U(t) = [\eta_U(t)', 0', \ldots , 0']'.$$

Then write (5) in first-order form as

(A1)
$$\tilde{U}(t) = C\, \tilde{U}(t-1) + \tilde{\eta}_U(t),$$

where C is $(1 + M_h) \times K$ square, with the following structure: Call a collection of K successive rows (or columns) a K-row (or -column) block. The last M_h K-row blocks comprise simply zeroes and ones, in the usual way, forming identities. Consider then the kth row ($k = 1, 2, \ldots , K$) in the first K-row block. The first K-column block of this row vanishes everywhere except in the kth position, where it contains $g_k(1) + 1$; the $(1 + M_g)$-th K-column block of this row vanishes everywhere except in the kth position, where it contains $-g_k(M_g)$. For K-column block m ($m = 2, 3, \ldots , M_g$), the entries again vanish everywhere except in the kth position, where they equal $g_k(m) - g_k(m - 1)$. This pattern of coefficients comes from (5) being in first-differences whereas (A1) is in levels.

Turning to the observables, write

$$X(t) = [X_1(t), X_2(t), \ldots , X_N(t)]';$$

since this is observed at time t, we denote

$$\text{info}(t) = \{X(t), X(t-1), X(t-2), \ldots \}.$$

Let

$$\tilde{X}(t) = [X(t)', X(t-1)', \ldots , X(t - M_b + 1)']'.$$

Also, write out $\phi_{jk}(L)$ explicitly as

$$\phi_{jk}(L) = \sum_{m=0}^{M_f} f_{jk}(m) L^m.$$

We can then rewrite equation (7) as

(A2) $X(t) = A \begin{bmatrix} \tilde{U}(t) \\ \tilde{X}(t - 1) \end{bmatrix} + dW(t) + \varepsilon(t) = aZ(t) + dW(t) + \varepsilon(t),$

where d has rows formed from d_j, and A has the following structure. Its jth row has the first $(1 + M_f)K$ entries given by

$$[f_{j1}(0), \ldots, f_{jK}(0), f_{j1}(1), \ldots, f_{jK}(M_f)];$$

the remaining entries in this row differ from zero only in M_b places. After the first $(1 + M_h)K$ entries (not the first $[1 + M_f]K$), there are M_b N-row blocks. Each such block vanishes except in the jth entry, which equals $b_j(m)$, for $m = 1, 2, \ldots, M_b$.

Now augment the transition equation (A1) with $\tilde{X}$ and W; that is, write

(A3) $Z(t + 1) = cZ(t) + \delta W(t) + \eta(t + 1),$

with

$$c = \begin{pmatrix} C & 0 \\ c_{21} & c_{22} \end{pmatrix},$$

where the first N rows of $(c_{21}\ c_{22})$ contain a, and the remaining rows comprise just zeros and ones; the matrix δ vanishes everywhere except in the N rows after the first $(1 + M_h)K$ (in those N rows it is composed of d); and, finally,

$$\eta(t + 1) = \begin{bmatrix} \tilde{\eta}_U(t + 1) \\ \varepsilon(t) \\ 0 \end{bmatrix}.$$

Notice that (A3) contains within it (A2).

Since all but the first $(1 + M_h)K$ entries of $Z(t + 1)$ are observed at time t, it will be natural to let $P[Z(t + 1) \mid \text{info}(t)]$ equal $\tilde{X}(t)$ except in its first $(1 + M_h)K$ entries. Similarly, we will choose the conditional mean square $\text{Var}[Z(t + 1) \mid \text{info}(t)]$ to be zero everywhere except in the leading $(1 + M_h)K$ square diagonal block.

In summary, our state space representation is

$$Z(t + 1) = cZ(t) + \delta W(t) + \eta(t + 1),$$
$$X(t) = AZ(t) + dW(t) + \varepsilon(t),$$

with $\text{Var}[Z(1) | \text{info}(0)]$ initialized to vanish everywhere except in the leading $(1 + M_h)K$ diagonal block. The disturbance vector $[\eta(t + 1)', \varepsilon(t)']'$ is serially uncorrelated and has covariance matrix

$$\Omega = \begin{pmatrix} \Omega_\eta & \Omega_{\eta\varepsilon} \\ \cdot & \Omega_\varepsilon \end{pmatrix},$$

where Ω_η is singular, $\Omega_{\eta\varepsilon}$ contains Ω_ε, and Ω_ε is $N \times N$ diagonal. We write $(\Omega_{\eta\varepsilon})_1$ to denote the first $(1 + M_h)K$ rows of $\Omega_{\eta\varepsilon}$ and Ω_{η_1} to denote the leading $(1 + M_h)K$ diagonal block of Ω_η.

Partition $Z(t)$ as $[Z_1(t)', Z_2(t)']'$, where

$$Z_1(t) = \bar{U}(t), \quad (1 + M_h)K \times 1,$$

and

$$c = \begin{pmatrix} c_{11} & c_{12} \\ c_{21} & c_{22} \end{pmatrix}, \quad \text{with } c_{11} = C(1 + M_h)K \text{ square, } c_{12} = 0.$$

Thus, $\eta(t)$ is also partitioned into $[\eta_1(t)', \eta_2(t)']'$, with $\eta_1 = \bar{\eta}_U[(1 + M_h)K \times 1]$. We can now write the measurement equation

$$X(t) = (a_1\ a_2) \begin{bmatrix} Z_1(t) \\ Z_2(t) \end{bmatrix} + \varepsilon(t),$$

where a_1 comprises the first $(1 + M_h)\ K$ columns of a. Note that $\text{Var}[Z_1(t)|\text{info}(s)]$ is thus only $(1 + M_h)K$ square and has dimensions that are invariant to N.

Appendix B
Data Appendix

Real GNP in the text refers to the annual version of GNP82 obtained from Citibase July 1991. This series is normalized to constant 1982 dollars and is no longer available—the new constant-dollar GNP series in Citibase is normalized to constant 1987 dollars and is available only from 1959. Since the employment data that we use go back through 1948, we decided to use the older GNP82.

Next, the sectoral description we study is from the national income and product accounts: employment (as listed below).

FTE Employees by Industry (annual)

Private Industries

1. Farms (GAFAF1)
2. Agriculture, forestry, and fisheries (GAFAF7)
3. Metal mining (GAFM10)
4. Coal mining (GAFM12)
5. Oil and gas extraction (GAFM13)
6. Nonmetallic minerals, except fuels (GAFM14)
7. Construction (GAFCC)

Manufacturing: Durable Goods

8. Lumber and wood products (GAFD24)
9. Furniture and fixtures (GAFD25)

10. Stone, clay, and glass products (GAFD32)
11. Primary metal industries (GAFD33)
12. Fabricated metal products (GAFD34)
13. Machinery, excluding electric (GAFD35)
14. Electric and electronic equipment (GAFD36)
15. Motor vehicles and equipment (GAF371)
16. Other transportation (GAFD37)
17. Instruments and related products (GAFD38)
18. Miscellaneous manufacturing industries (GAFM39)

Manufacturing: Nondurable Goods

19. Food and kindred products (GAFN20)
20. Tobacco manufacturing (GAFN21)
21. Textile mill products (GAFN22)
22. Apparel and other textile products (GAFN23)
23. Paper and allied products (GAFN26)
24. Printing and publishing (GAFN27)
25. Chemicals and allied products (GAFN28)
26. Petroleum and coal products (GAFN29)
27. Rubber and miscellaneous plastic products (GAFN30)
28. Leather and leather products (GAFN31)

Transportation and Public Utilities

29. Railroad transportation (GAFT40)
30. Local and interurban passenger transit (GAFT41)
31. Trucking and warehousing (GAFT42)
32. Water transportation (GAFT44)
33. Transportation by air (GAFT45)
34. Pipelines, except gas (GAFT46)
35. Transportation services (GAFT47)

Communication

36. Telephone and telegraph (GAF481)
37. Radio and television broadcastings (GAF483)
38. Electric, gas, and sanitary services (GAFUT)

39. Wholesale trade (GAFW)
40. Retail trade (GAFR)

Finance, Insurance, and Real Estate

41. Banking (GAFF60)
42. Credit agencies other than banks (GAFF61)
43. Security and commodity brokers (GAFF62)
44. Insurance carriers (GAFF63)
45. Insurance agents and brokers (GAFF64)

46. Real estate (GAFF65)
47. Holding and other investment companies (GAF67F)

Services

48. Hotels and other lodging places (GAFS70)
49. Personal services (GAFS72)
50. Business services (GAFS73)
51. Auto repair services and garages (GAFS75)
52. Miscellaneous repair services (GAFS76)
53. Motion pictures (GAFS78)
54. Amusement and recreational services (GAFS79)
55. Health services (GAFS80)
56. Legal services (GAFS81)
57. Educational services (GAFS82)
58. Social services and membership organizations (GAFS86)
59. Miscellaneous professional services (GAFS89)
60. Private households (GAFS88)

References

Abraham, Katherine G., and Lawrence F. Katz. 1986. Cyclical unemployment: Sectoral shifts or aggregate disturbances. *Journal of Political Economy* 94 (3): 507–22.

Barro, Robert J., and Xavier Sala-i-Martin. 1992. Convergence. *Journal of Political Economy* 100 (2): 223–51.

Blanchard, Olivier Jean, and Lawrence F. Katz. 1992. Regional evolutions. *Brookings Papers on Economic Activity* (1), 1–75.

Engle, Robert F., and Clive W. J. Granger. 1987. Cointegration and error correction: Representation, estimation, and testing. *Econometrica* 55 (2): 251–76.

Geweke, John. 1977. Labor turnover and employment dynamics in US manufacturing industry. In *New methods in business cycle research,* ed. Christopher A. Sims. Minneapolis: Federal Reserve Bank of Minneapolis.

Geweke, John, and Kenneth J. Singleton. 1981. Maximum likelihood "confirmatory" factor analysis of economic time series. *International Economic Review* 22 (1): 37–54.

Hamilton, James D. 1989. A new approach to the economic analysis of nonstationary time series and the business cycle. *Econometrica* 57 (2): 357–84.

King, Robert G., Charles I. Plosser, James H. Stock, and Mark W. Watson. 1991. Stochastic trends and economic fluctuations. *American Economic Review* 81 (4): 819–40.

Lehmann, Bruce N., and David M. Modest. 1988. The empirical foundations of the arbitrage asset pricing theory. *Journal of Financial Economics* 21 (2): 213–54.

Lilien, David M. 1982. Sectoral shifts and cyclical unemployment. *Journal of Political Economy* 90 (4): 777–93.

Long, John B., and Charles I. Plosser. 1983. Real business cycles. *Journal of Political Economy* 91 (1): 39–69.

Papke, Leslie E. 1989. Interstate business tax differentials and new firm location: Evidence from panel data. Working Paper no. 3184. Cambridge, Mass.: NBER, November.

Prescott, Edward C. 1986. Theory ahead of business cycle measurement. *Federal Reserve Bank of Minneapolis Quarterly Review* 10 (4): 9–22.

Rogerson, Richard. 1987. An equilibrium model of sectoral reallocation. *Journal of Political Economy* 95 (4): 824–34.

Ruud, Paul A. 1991. Extensions of estimation methods using the EM algorithm. *Journal of Econometrics* 49:305–41.

Sargent, Thomas J., and Christopher A. Sims. 1977. Business cycle modelling without pretending to have too much *a priori* economic theory. In *New methods in business cycle research,* ed. Christopher A. Sims. Minneapolis: Federal Reserve Bank of Minneapolis.

Stock, James H., and Mark W. Watson. 1988. Testing for common trends. *Journal of the American Statistical Association* 83 (404): 1097–1107.

———. 1990. Business cycle properties of selected U.S. economic time series. Working Paper no. 3376. Cambridge, Mass.: NBER, June.

Watson, Mark W., and Robert F. Engle. 1983. Alternative algorithms for the estimation of dynamic factor, MIMIC, and varying coefficient regression models. *Journal of Econometrics* 23:385–400.

Watson, Mark W., and Dennis F. Kraft. 1984. Testing the interpretation of indices in a macroeconomic index model. *Journal of Monetary Economics* 13 (2): 165–81.

Wu, C. F. Jeff. 1983. On the convergence of properties of the EM algorithm. *Annals of Statistics* 11 (1): 95–103.

Comment   John Geweke

The paper by Danny Quah and Thomas J. Sargent examines some possibilities for the application of index models of multiple time series in situations in which the number of cross sections (N) is large relative to the number of time periods (T). Since there are, in fact, many more of the former than there are of the latter, this is an interesting and worthwhile project. The paper argues that, when $N >> T$, one cannot estimate covariograms or autoregressions because the number of parameters grows quadratically with the number of observations but that one can estimate index models because the number of parameters grows linearly. In fact, stronger cases can be made for both approaches. In autoregressions, it is natural to regard sectors of the economy as exchangeable in a prior distribution, and either the Minnesota prior (Litterman 1986) or a hierarchical prior could be employed to yield a manageable inference problem. Bayesian inference for covariograms and spectra would follow at once. With regard to index models, it is clear that, given conventional normalizations and identifying restrictions, one can consistently extract the unob-

John Geweke is professor of economics at the University of Minnesota and adviser at the Federal Reserve Bank of Minneapolis. The views expressed here are the author's and not necessarily those of the Federal Reserve Bank of Minneapolis or the Federal Reserve System.

served indexes, as $N \to \infty$ with fixed T. Just how N must be related to T to do so as $(N, T) \to \infty$ would be a significant research question.

It would be useful to know how the authors resolved important identification questions. A necessary step in identifying the time series $U(t)$ is removal of the possibilities for rotating these latent factors through premultiplication by an orthonormal matrix. This problem arises in traditional factor analysis (Lawley and Maxwell 1971) and can be resolved in a variety of ways. If left unresolved, it must arise as a mechanical problem in application of the EM algorithm, but the technical appendix does not indicate what normalizations were used. Additional identification problems are introduced by the fact that $\Delta U(t)$ is a stationary time series. In particular, even after removal of conventional rotation possibilities, there are several ways to represent $\Delta U(t)$ as a linear combination of serially uncorrelated processes (Whittle 1983, chap. 2). Finally, dynamic-factor models that are "overfit" in the number of factors become underidentified in fundamental ways since a sector-specific disturbance can masquerade as a commonality. This has subtle but damaging effects on test statistics in the factor-analysis model (Geweke and Singleton 1980), and it is unlikely that these effects would be mitigated in a dynamic-factor model. It is difficult to see how a careful demonstration of the convergence of the EM algorithm to maximum likelihood estimates could proceed, without first dealing with these identification issues.

The development of an asymptotic distribution theory also depends on resolving identification questions: hence (presumably) the absence of standard errors, test statistics, or any other sort of formal statistical analysis in the paper. The development of an appropriate asymptotic foundation for inference is likely to be more difficult than resolution of identification questions. Asymptotics in T would require managing the unconventional unit root theory in the context of a nontrivial latent-variable model. Given the authors' motivation for examining these models, asymptotics in N is presumably of more compelling interest. Here the ratio of parameters to observations converges to a positive value, but the ratio of the number of latent variables to observations drops to zero: hence the opportunity to extract signals without error asymptotically. But, if T is fixed, and perhaps even if only $N/T \to \infty$, it may be sensible to abandon most of the time-series structure on the commonalities altogether, in the same way that it is not necessary to assume a time-series structure for disturbances in panel data when N is very large relative to T. There is a rich supply of nontrivial problems for the frequentist econometrician here.

For the authors' application, with $N = 60$ and $T = 37$, the presence or absence of such theory could turn out to be moot since no asymptotic theory might be applicable. It appears that the EM algorithm is used to estimate 540 parameters (nine for each of sixty sectors in the dynamic-factor model) and to extract forty latent variables, based on 2,400 initial degrees of freedom. For the two-factor model, the numbers rise to 780 parameters and eighty latent variables. Without any distribution theory, it would be difficult to evaluate the claim in the concluding section that "much of the observed fluctuation in employment in those many diverse industries is well explained by disturbances that are perfectly correlated across all the sectors." Summary statistics on proportion of variance accounted for by commonalities would help, but there would still be no basis for discriminating between statistical artifact and properties of the population. Nevertheless, two aspects of the reported empirical results cast doubt on this claim.

First, from the information given in section 7.3, a conventional test of the hypothesis that real GNP does not affect sectoral employment may be applied using an $F(5, 28)$ distribution. The hypothesis fails to be rejected at the 5 percent level for all those industries that lie above a ray from the origin with a slope of .828 and at the 1 percent level with a slope of .684. The hypothesis is not rejected for about one-quarter of the industries at the 5 percent level and for about half the industries at the 1 percent level. More informative would be confidence intervals for the fraction of variation accounted for by real GNP, but this cannot be reconstructed on the basis of the information provided. The outcome is similar when real GNP is replaced by the multisector employment measure (fig. 7.3).

Second, the presentation in figures 7.5 and 7.6 does little to support the case for the dynamic-index model. As the authors point out, neither of the models compared is nested in the other. However, the time-series structure of the commonality in the index model (i.e., the autocorrelation function of $\phi_{jk}[L]U[t]$) is very close to that of real GNP given that annual log real GNP is a random walk to a rough order of approximation and that coefficients can unwind modest departures from a random walk. Beyond this, in the index model, one is free to choose the time-series realizations of the commonality. From a strictly heuristic point of view—all one has here, given that no theory has been worked out—this appears to give an edge to the index model that goes beyond the usual counting rules of thumb for parameters. Further, notice that figures 7.5 and 7.6 report results for two-index models, which have, by my count, thirteen parameters per sector, whereas the real GNP regressions have only ten. (At this point, the two-index model still gets an additional eighty realizations of the commonality unavailable to the regressions!) The issue is somewhat clouded by the fact that sectoral employment in the regressions apparently extended from 1951 through 1987, whereas in the index models it ranged from 1948 through 1989. In this situation, figures 7.5 and 7.6 do nothing to dislodge the null hypothesis that the estimated index models reflect nothing beyond the regressions on real GNP.

Index models for large numbers of cross sections may well become an important tool in the decomposition of aggregate output. If they are to become a reliable and discriminating tool, however, substantial further development of the theory of inference for such models is needed.

References

Geweke, J. F., and K. J. Singleton. 1980. Interpreting the likelihood ratio statistic in factor models when sample size is small. *Journal of the American Statistical Association* 75:133–37.

Lawley, D. N., and A. E. Maxwell. 1971. *Factor analysis as a statistical method.* New York: American Elsevier.

Litterman, R. B. 1986. Forecasting with Bayesian vector autoregressions—five years of experience. *Journal of Business and Economic Statistics* 4:25–38.

Whittle, P. 1983. *Prediction and regulation by linear least-square methods.* Minneapolis: University of Minnesota Press.

8 Modeling Nonlinearity over the Business Cycle

Clive W. J. Granger, Timo Teräsvirta, and
Heather M. Anderson

There seems to be wide acceptance that the relations between economic time series are often nonlinear. This is certainly true for relations suggested by economic theory, and econometricians can propose estimates of the parameters of any explicitly nonlinear model. However, exploratory or specification search forms of modeling are used when a theory is not specific about the dynamics of a relation apply to linear (or log-linear) models, such as the Box-Jenkins transfer functions and vector autoregressive models. There is no generally accepted class of nonlinear models that can be applied to explore relations. One difficulty is that the number of alternative nonlinear models is enormous and that there has not been sufficient experience accumulated to decide which of these models are most appropriate in economics. In the past decade or so, there has been a greater deal of activity among statisticians, time-series analysts, and econometricians suggesting possible nonlinear models and techniques for their analysis. Tong (1990) surveys many of the univariate models, and Granger and Teräsvirta (in press) consider multivariate models but concentrate on single-equation nonlinear relations. The possible models include parametric forms (such as nonlinear autoregressive, bilinear, and doubly stochastic models), state space and flexible Fourier forms, many types of nonparametric models (including projection pursuit), and mixtures of these called semiparametric. These models are designed to be fairly general and to be flexible so that they can approximate a wide variety of actual nonlinearities. A problem that arises from this flexibility is that the models are in-

Clive W. J. Granger is professor of economics at the University of California, San Diego. Timo Teräsvirta is a research fellow at the Bank of Norway and visiting professor of economics at the University of California, San Diego. Heather M. Anderson is assistant professor of economics at the University of Texas at Austin.

This research has been funded by National Science Foundation grant SES-89-02950 and by the Yrjö Jahnsson Foundation.

clined to overfit in sample. We thus believe that it is important first to test linearity against the nonlinearity in which we are interested and then only if linearity is rejected to build a nonlinear model. Further, one way of judging the quality of this model should be its out-of-sample performance compared to other models, although there can be difficulties with this strategy, as will be seen later.

There exist many tests of linearity, and many of these are discussed in Lee, White, and Granger (1993), where a variety of simulations are presented, and in Teräsvirta (1990a), where theoretical power properties are discussed. A few tests are found to have good power under a variety of situations, including a new test based on neural network models. Let $\phi(X)$ be a so-called squashing function, being smooth, bounded, and monotonic nondecreasing, such as a probability density function or a logistic function, so that in this last case

$$(1) \qquad Y_t = c + \beta' \underline{X}_t + \sum_{j=1}^{p} \alpha_j \phi(\gamma_j' \underline{X}_t) + \text{white noise},$$

where $\underline{X}_t$ is the vector of explanatory variables including lagged Y's and present and lagged values of other variables. It is, of course, rather complicated to estimate the γ parameters, so a simple procedure has been suggested by White (1989) in which values of γ are chosen at random from some appropriate region and a rather large value of p is used, say 10 or 20. As the ϕ terms are now directly observable, $\underline{\beta}$ and the α's can be estimated by a standard regression procedure and the significance of the α's tested directly. If any are found to be significant, linearity can be rejected. In Lee, White, and Granger (1993), this test was found to have good power in most cases, but not for data generated by a bilinear model.

In Teräsvirta, Lin, and Granger (1993), it is proposed that a Lagrange multiplier (LM)–type test be used. As expected, simulations showed that it has comparable power to the neural network test and often better power. The test, here called the polynomial test, involves just adding squares and cross-products of the components of $\underline{\ddot{X}}_t$ (quadratic terms) and possibly also cubic terms (such as X_i^3, $X_i^2 X_j$, and $X_i X_j X_k$). These are added to a linear model, with constant, to form an artificial regression and an F-test used.

If such a test suggests that linearity can be rejected, the question naturally arises of what model to fit to the data. The polynomial test immediately suggests a model, involving the quadratic and cubic terms, but this form is not easily interpreted and may be explosive. It also suggests (1) because the test is an LM-type test against this alternative. However, difficulties in estimating (1) discourage use of that model.

The class of models that we propose is known as smooth transition regressions (STRs), which take the form

$$(2) \qquad Y_t = c_1 + \underline{\beta}_1 \underline{X}_t + \phi(Z_t)(c_2 + \underline{\beta}_2' \underline{X}_t) + e_t,$$

where $0 \leq \phi(Z) \leq 1$, and $\phi(Z)$ is zero, or small, for some values of Z and is near to one for other Z values. In (2), Z_t is the "indicator variable" and may be a linear combination of the components of $\underline{X}_t$ or just a single lagged component of $\underline{X}_t$, plus a constant, for example, $Z_t = m + \gamma Y_{t-d}$. The model is seen to be a smooth transition between the linear model

$$Y_t = c_1 + \underline{\beta}_1' \underline{X}_t + e_t$$

and the alternative linear model

$$Y_t = (c_1 + c_2) + (\underline{\beta}_1 + \underline{\beta}_2)' \underline{X}_t + e_t.$$

These two linear models can have quite different properties—one could be I(1) and the other I(0), for example—and can perhaps be interpreted as two regimes. The models thus represent a smooth regime-switching situation. There are plenty of examples in economic theory of regime switching, such as full-employment or full-capacity models being different from the nonfull cases. Similarly, there is evidence of stock market price changes being forecastable for certain indicator variable values, such as low volatility, but not otherwise. The following section considers the specification and testing of these models.

8.1   Specification of Smooth Transition Regression Models

Consider the following smooth transition regression (STR) model:

$$(3) \qquad y_t = \beta' x_t + (\theta' x_t) F(\alpha' z_t) + u_t,$$

where $u_t \sim$ i.i.d$(0, \sigma^2)$, $E(z_t u_t) = 0$, $\beta = (\beta_0, \beta_1, \ldots, \beta_m)'$, $\theta = (\theta_0, \theta_1, \ldots, \theta_m)'$, $\alpha = (\alpha_0, \alpha_1, \ldots, \alpha_{m+h})'$, $\sum_{j=10}^{m+h} \alpha_j = 1$, say, $x_t = (1, y_{t-1}, \ldots, y_{t-p}, x_{1t}, \ldots, x_{kt})'$, and $z_t = (x_t', v_t')'$ with $v_t = (v_{t1}, \ldots, v_{th})'$. Two different types of F will be considered. First,

$$(4) \qquad F(\alpha' z_t) = \{1 + \exp[-\gamma(\alpha' z_t)]\}^{-1}, \quad \gamma > 0,$$

which makes (3) a logistic STR (LSTR) model. Maddala (1977, 396) suggested this formulation. If $\gamma = 0$, (3) is a linear model. Second, if

$$(5) \qquad F(\alpha' z_t) = 1 - \exp[-\gamma(\alpha' z_t)^2], \quad \gamma > 0,$$

we have an exponential STR (ESTR) model. If $\gamma \to \infty$ in (4), (3) becomes a switching regression model with $\alpha' z_t$ as the linear combination of transition variables. If $\gamma \to \infty$ in (5), (3) becomes a linear model; its parameters switch if $\alpha' z_t = 0$, but that is an event with zero probability. Functions (4) and (5) describe two fundamentally different forms of parameter behavior. If (4) holds, the "stochastic parameter vector" $\beta + \theta F$ in (3) changes monotonically from β to $\beta + \theta$ with $\alpha' z_t$. If (5) is valid, this change is symmetrical about zero: the parameters change from $\beta + \theta$ to β and back again with increasing $\alpha' z_t$. Usually, (4) and (5) are still too general, in particular if the time series available for modeling are relatively short. A way of restricting them is to let $\alpha = (-c, 0, \ldots, 0, 1, 0, \ldots, 0)'$ so that $\alpha' z_t = z_{tj} - c$. Instead of a linear combination of variables determining the transition, a single variable is doing it. In practice, this variable may often be unknown; that is, it is not known to the investigator which $\alpha_j = 1$, and that has to be determined from the data. Furthermore, it is assumed here that, if the model is nonlinear, it is not known if the transition function is (4) or (5).

A successful application of (3) to data requires the following three steps: (i) Specify a linear model to form a basis for further analysis. (ii) Test linearity of (3) ($\gamma = 0$) against nonlinearity ($\gamma > 0$). If linearity is rejected, determine the transition variable from the data. Once this has been done, (iii) the transition function has to be selected, the choice being between (4) and (5). These steps may be carried out as follows:

i. Carry out the complete specification of a linear model. The maximum lag length p for lagged y_t has to be determined from the data as well as regressors $x_{t1}, \ldots, x_{tk}$ if economic theory is not fully explicit about them.

ii. Test linearity of (3) against STR using each element of z_t in turn as the transition variable. If linearity is rejected for more than one transition variable, choose the one for which the p-value of the test is the lowest. The rationale behind this procedure is that the linearity test has the highest power against the correctly specified alternative. If a wrong transition variable is selected, the power of the test suffers from the erroneous choice.

iii. Treat the selected transition variable as given, and choose between (4) and (5) using an auxiliary regression already needed in testing linearity.

It is seen that linearity testing plays a central role in this specification strategy. In this case, not the only, but the most convenient, way of expressing the null hypothesis of linearity is

$$(6) \qquad H_0^*: \gamma = 0 \quad \text{against} \quad H_1^*: \gamma > 0.$$

It is clear from (3) that the model is not identified under this null hypothesis. A Lagrange multiplier–type test may be derived for testing (6) using the suggestions in Davies (1977). The test is described in detail in Granger and Teräsvirta (in press, chaps. 6 and 7). It is based on the following artificial regression:

$$(7) \qquad y_t = \delta_0 + \delta_1' \tilde{x}_t + \delta_2'(\tilde{x}_t z_{td}) + \delta_3'(\tilde{x}_t z_{td}^2) + \delta_4'(\tilde{x}_t z_{td}^3) + \tilde{u}_t,$$

where $\tilde{u}_t \sim \text{i.i.d.}(0, \sigma^2)$, $\tilde{x}_t = (y_{t-1}, \ldots, y_{t-p}, x_{1t} \ldots, x_{kt})'$ and z_{td} is the transition variable, which is an element of $\tilde{x}_t$. The null hypothesis (6) translates into

$$(8) \qquad H_0: \delta_2 = \delta_3 = \delta_4 = 0.$$

Table 8.1   **Alternative Choices of STR Model Type Based on Outcomes of a Sequence of F-Tests within the Artificial Model (7)**

	Hypothesis		
$\delta_4 = 0$	$\delta_3 = 0 \mid \delta_4 = 0$	$\delta_2 = 0 \mid \delta_3 = \delta_4 = 0$	Choice
Reject	. . .	. . .	LSTR
Accept	Reject	Accept	ESTR
Accept	Accept	Reject	LSTR
Accept	Reject	Reject	No decision

The alternative is that at least one element in either δ_2, δ_3, or δ_4 is not equal to zero. The fourth-order terms are needed in the case that the true model is an LSTR model in which the most important nonlinearity parameters is the intercept in the nonlinear part, θ_0.

If the true model is an ESTR model, then $\delta_4 = 0$ (see Granger and Teräsvirta, in press, chap. 7). Also, if $\delta_3 = 0$, the model can be only an LSTR model. This suggests the following testing sequence. First, test H_0 in (7), and continue as follows:

i. If (8) is rejected, test H_{04}: $\delta_4 = 0$ against H_{14}: $\delta_4 \neq 0$ in (7).
ii. If H_{04} is accepted, test H_{03}: $\delta_3 = 0 \mid \delta_4 = 0$ against H_{13}: $\delta_3 \neq 0 \mid \delta_4 = 0$.
iii. If H_{03} is accepted, test H_{02}: $\delta_2 = 0 \mid \delta_3 = \delta_4 = 0$ against H_{12}: $\delta_2 \neq 0 \mid \delta_3 = \delta_4 = 0$.

In practice, it is advisable to carry out these three tests automatically independent of the outcome of the previous test. The outcomes help us decide between LSTR and ESTR models (see table 8.1).

The only problem is the case where both H_{03} and H_{02} are rejected after H_{04} is accepted. Then this scheme does not provide a clear-cut answer to the problem of choosing between the two models (see Granger and Teräsvirta, in press chap. 7). Recomputing the test statistic after shifting z_{td} may provide some guidance, as in the univariate case that Teräsvirta (1990b) discussed.

The situation is less complicated if the transition variable is not an element of $\tilde{x}_t$ but one of $v_t = (v_{t1}, \ldots, v_{th})'$, say, v_{td}. Then an artificial regression corresponding to (7) is

$$y_t = \delta_0 + \delta_1' \tilde{x}_t + \delta_2 v_{td} + \delta_3 v_{td}^2 + \delta_4' \tilde{x}_t v_{td} + \delta_5' \tilde{x}_t v_{td}^2 + \tilde{u}_t.$$

The null hypothesis of linearity is

$$(9) \qquad H_0: \delta_2 = \delta_3 = 0; \delta_4 = \delta_5 = 0,$$

the alternative being that (9) is not valid. The test has power against both LSTR and ESTR alternatives. If, after rejecting (9), we test H_{05}: $\delta_5 = 0$ and reject it, the conclusion is that (3) is an ESTR model.

The steps of the specification strategy outlined above leave open the question of the dynamic structure of (3). Specifying that may be best carried out by estimating different specifications and learning from them. This has turned out to be a successful way in univariate STAR (smooth transition autoregression) modeling (for examples, see Teräsvirta 1990b; and Teräsvirta and Anderson 1992). The specification of STAR models follows the same principles as those presented above. The main difference is that $x_t = (1, y_{t-1}, \ldots, y_{t-p})'$ and the transition variable is $z_{td} = y_{t-d}$ where d is not known a priori (for discussion, see Teräsvirta 1990b).

8.2 Modeling the Relations between GNP and the Index of Leading Indicators

This section describes an exploratory modeling exercise between y_t = real GNP and x_t = the Department of Commerce quarterly index of leading indicators. The objective of the exercise is to consider if a nonlinear model provides better forecasts of GNP. The results are indecisive, with some evidence of nonlinearity being found but no clear-cut improvement in forecastability. The series used are those designated GNP82 and DLEAD in the Citibase data bank. The series are quarterly, real, and seasonally adjusted, with 166 observations from the period 1948: I–1989: II. Models were constructed using the full sample, and then twenty terms were held back for use in a forecast comparison, so that the models were reestimated using just the first 146 observations. The leading indicator series was originally recorded monthly but was summed over the adjacent values to obtain a quarterly series. It was decided to use GNP as the variable of interest as it is probably the best available approximation to the variable that the leading indicators were designed to lead. The problem is that this variable is available only quarterly. The alternative would be to use the index of industrial production, which is available monthly, but, with the growth in the importance of the service industries, the industrial sector now provides a poor approximation of GNP.

To help decide what models to fit, the two series, y_t and x_t, and their logs, Ly_t and Lx_t, were tested for unit roots and then for cointegration.

Augmented Dickey-Fuller τ-tests (see Dickey and Fuller 1979) suggest that both y and x are I(1), that Lx is also I(1), but that Ly is less clearly so. (Details are shown in appendix 8A.1.) The first-differences of all these series are all clearly I(0). The fitted univariate linear model for y_t is

(10) $y_t = 1.28y_{t-1} - 0.14y_{t-2} - 0.14y_{t-3} + 3.64 + e_t,$
              $(.08)$ $(.13)$ $(.08)$ (5.67)

     $R^2 = .9992,\ \text{D-W} = 1.97,\ \tau_0 = -12.22$

where standard errors are shown in brackets, and τ_k is the augmented Dickey-Fuller τ-statistic applied to the residuals using k lags of the differenced variable. It is seen that the coefficients add to one, and the errors e_t seem to be I(0) (or stationary), suggesting that y_t is I(1), possibly with drift.

To investigate possible cointegration, it will be assumed that all the series are I(1). The Engle-Granger (1987) two-step tests found no evidence of cointegration in levels and weak evidence of cointegration for logs, as the following regressions show:

(11) $y_t = 520.3 + 9.10t + 4.57x_t$, D-W $= .133, \tau_1 = -2.82$;
       $\quad\;\;\;(25.6)\quad (.52)\quad\;\; (.27)$

(12) $\quad\; y_t = 155.5 + 9.27x_t$, D-W$= .15, \tau_4 = -3.35$;
       $\quad\quad\quad\;(25.3)\quad (.10)$

(13) $Ly_t = 5.07 + .004t + .421Lx_t$, D-W $= .11, \tau_1 = -4.02$;
       $\quad\;\;\;\,(.19)\quad (.0003)\quad (.04)$

(14) $\quad\; Ly_t = 2.59 + .85Lx_t$, D-W $= .18, \tau_4 = -3.61$.
       $\quad\quad\quad\;(.05)\quad\;\; (.009)$

The critical value for the τ-statistics is -3.44, so the null hypothesis that the residuals are I(1) is rejected only in (13) and (14). It should be noted that the standard errors given here cannot be used to evaluate the significance of parameters in the model because of the very low Durbin-Watson statistics. However, these results are confused by different results obtained by using the Johansen (1988) maximum likelihood procedure, which find cointegration for both levels and logarithms of the series. (Again, details are shown in appendix table 8A.2.) The Johansen procedure is known to be more powerful than the two-step procedure (as shown by Gonzalo [1991]), but the results do not suggest that it is necessarily a good modeling strategy to impose cointegration on further models, so a flexible specification was adopted.

For later purposes, it is relevant to ask if various nonlinear transforms of our series seem to be I(1) or not. Using both simulations and simple theory, Granger and Hallman (1988) show that polynomials in I(1) variables also contain linear roots if a linear model is constructed. Table 8.2 shows Dickey-Fuller τ-test statistics for several of these polynomials. A critical value of -3.44 or less allows one to reject the null hypothesis of a unit root with 95 percent confidence. It is seen that, using x, y, in no case is the null rejected, but it is rejected twice using Lx, Ly.

The modeling experiment used the following steps:

i. Construct a few alternative models for y, with and without the constraints suggested by possible cointegration, using the full sample.

ii. Use Lagrange multiplier tests to test for missing variables that are second- and third-order polynomials of lagged dependent (GNP) and explanatory (leading index) variables.

iii. Reestimate the model using the shorter sample, and compare the one-step forecasting ability of the alternative models over the final twenty terms of the sample.

Table 8.2   Augmented Dickey-Fuller (D-F) Tests for Quadratic and Cubic Functions o
x and y

Variable	y^2	xy	x^2	y^3	y^2x	yx^2	x^3
D-F stat.	.59	$-.17$	$-.77$	1.93	.79	.64	.10
Variable	$(Ly)^2$	Lx,Ly	$(Lx)^2$	$(Ly)^3$	$(Ly)^2Lx$	$Ly(Lx)^2$	$(Lx)^3$
D-F stat.	-3.01	-3.17	-3.26	-3.71	-4.33	-3.19	-3.19

These steps were repeated for the logarithms of the variables, Ly_t and Lx_t. Once evidence for nonlinearity has been found, the best procedure is to try to build specific models, such as nonlinear autoregressive or neural network models, but this has been attempted just with an STR model, as reported in the next section.

Two of the preliminary models considered for y_t are reported (together with specifications tests and the Lagrange multiplier test results, for possible augmenting nonlinear variables). Denoting these models as M1 and M2, M1 is given by,

$$\Delta y_t = .06\Delta y_{t-1} + 12.55 + 2.45\Delta x_{t-1},$$
(15)   (.08)   (2.04)*   (.35)*

$$N = 164 \ (1948:\text{III}-1989:\text{II}),$$

$$R^2 = .33, \text{D-W} = 2.14, \tau_1 = -7.78^*, \text{SE} = 21.17,$$

Serial Correlation: $F(6,155) = 1.26$, ARCH: $F(6, 149) = .52$,
    Normality: $\chi^2 = 24.51^*$,

$$\text{LM}(\Delta y)_{-1}^2 (\Delta x)_{-1}: F(1, 160) = 5.17^*,$$

and M2 is given by

(16) $\Delta y_t = 14.90 - .06(\text{ECT})_{-1} + (2.05)\Delta x_{t-1},$
            (1.75)*   (.02)*   (.31)*

$$N = 159 \ (1949:\text{IV}-1989:\text{II}),$$

$$R^2 = .38, \text{D-W} = 2.08, \tau_0 = -13.41^*, \text{SE} = 20.38,$$

Serial Correlation: $F(6, 150) = .72$, ARCH: $F(6, 144) = .67$,
    Normality: $\chi^2 = 18.76^*$,

$$\text{LM}(\Delta y_{-1}^2 \ \Delta x_{-1}) = F(1, 155) = 5.31^*.$$

Here ECT is the error-correction term from (12), ECT $= y_t - 155.5 - 9.27x_t$.

We provide a variety of statistics to help evaluate the models, and these include R^2, Durbin-Watson (D-W), the standard error (standard deviation of

Table 8.3   **In Sample and Postsample Standard Errors for Models M1 and M2 and Their Nonlinear Extension**

	Standard Error		
Model	Long Sample	Short Sample	Postsample
M1	21.17	20.83	24.47
M1 augmented		20.75	23.11
M2	20.38	20.33	21.13
M2 augmented		20.10	20.50

residuals), and τ_k, the augmented Dickey-Fuller test statistic based on the residuals using k lags. Standard specification test statistics for serial correlation, ARCH, and normality are also given. The Lagrange multiplier test results, with the apparently successful augmenting nonlinear variables, are shown after the specification statistics.

A linear trend was added to M1 but was not found to be significant. In both models, the LM tests suggested that some nonlinearity in mean may be present. These models were augmented by adding a term $(\Delta y_{t-1})^2(\Delta x_{t-1})$. Table 8.3 shows the standard errors in sample for both the long and the shortened sample plus the postsample forecast standard errors.

Using the test outlined in Granger and Newbold (1986, 278–79) to compare the sum of squared forecast errors, the M1 augmented model is significantly better than M1. However, the error correction model M2, which is superior both in and out of sample, does not produce a clearly superior forecast when augmented by a nonlinear term.

A more extensive experiment was conducted using the log series and three models, denoted L1, L2 and L3, are reported here. L1 is given by

(17)
$$Ly_t = .85Ly_{t-1} + .56 + .0003t + .11Lx_{t-1},$$
$$\quad\quad\;\;(.02)^* \quad\; (.13)^* \;\; (.0001)^* \quad (.01)$$

$N = 165$ (1948:II–1989:II),

$R^2 = .9994$, D-W $= 1.519$, $\tau_2 = -7.94^*$, SE $= .0093$,

Serial Correlation: $F(6, 155) = 2.78^*$, ARCH: $F(6, 149) = 2.69^*$, Normality: $\chi^2 = 1.17$,

LM$(LxLy)_{-1}$: $F(1, 160) = 4.55^*$, LM $(Ly)^3_{-1}$: $F(1, 160) = 3.91^*$,

LM $(Ly)^2_{-1}(Lx)_{-1}$: $F(1, 160) = 4.42^*$, LM $(Ly)_{-1}(Lx)^2_{-1}$:

$F(1, 160) = 4.68^*$, LM$(Lx)^3_{-1}$: $F(1, 160) = 4.77^*$.

L2 is given by

(18) $\Delta L y_t = .11 \Delta L y_{t-1} + .005 + .23 \Delta L x_{t-1},$
           (.07)   (.0009)* (.03)*

$N = 164 \ (1948:\text{III}-1989:\text{II}),$

$R^2 = .34$, D-W $= 2.19$, $\tau_0 = -13.24*$, SE $= .0090,$

   Serial Correlation: $F(6, 155) = 1.40$, ARCH: $F(6, 149) = 1.69,$
   Normality: $\chi^2 = 4.58*,$

   $\text{LM}[(\Delta L y)^2_{-1}, (\Delta L y \Delta L x)_{-1}, (\Delta L x)^2_{-1}]: F(3, 158) = 4.30*,$

   $\text{LM}[(\Delta L y)^3_{-1}, (\Delta L y)^2_{-1}(\Delta L x)_{-1}, (\Delta L y)_{-1}(\Delta L x)^2_{-1}, (\Delta L x)^3_{-1}:$
   $F(4, 157) = 3.08*,$

and, finally, L3,

(19) $\Delta L y_t = .007 - .08(\text{ECT})_{-1} + .18 \Delta L x_{t-1},$
           (.0007)* (.016)*   (.03)*

$N = 159 \ (1949:\text{IV}-1989:\text{II}),$

$R^2 = .42$, D-W $= 1.99$, $\tau_6 = -4.22*$, SE $= .0084,$

   Serial Correlation: $F(6, 150) = .73$, ARCH: $F(6, 144) = .24,$
   Normality: $\chi^2 = 2.49*,$

   $\text{LM}\left[(\Delta L y)^2_{-1}, (\Delta L y_{-1})(\Delta L x)_{-1}, (\Delta L x)^2_{-1}\right]: F(3, 153) = 3.79*.$

In each of the models, the LM tests found evidence of nonlinearity. Table 8.4 shows the in-sample and postsample values of the standard errors of the various models.

It is seen that the augmentations of L1 all involve particular single quadratic and cubic terms and that all the augmented models forecast better than the original linear models, and the improvement in forecasting ability is found to be significant. The best linear model, both in and out of sample, is L3, which is an error-correction form, and the augmentation with quadratic lagged terms gives a slight improvement. Thus, the initial conclusion is that there does appear to be some evidence of nonlinearity in mean and that the nonlinear models can lead to an improvement in forecasts.

The augmented models are considered just for the purpose of testing for nonlinearity and are not proposed as serious, interpretable, nonlinear models. Their postsample performance is presented just for general interest.

One final experiment included the current value of the index of leading indicators in the model for GNP, in which case the LM tests found no evidence of missing nonlinearity in mean using lagged quadratic or cubic terms. Although this result has no direct forecasting implications for GNP, it suggests that a nonlinear model for the leading index is worth exploring. A modeling

Table 8.4   **In-Sample and Postsample Standard Errors for Models L1, L2, and L3**

Model	Additional Nonlinear Terms	In Sample	Postsample
L1		.0096	.0076
L1A$_1$	$(Lx_{-1} Ly_{-1})$	.0096	.0057
L1A$_2$	$(Ly_{-1})^3$	.0096	.0061
L1A$_3$	$(Ly_{-1})^2(Lx_{-1})$	.0096	.0058
L1A$_4$	$(Ly_{-1})(Lx_{-1})^2$	.0096	.0056
L1A$_5$	$(Lx_{-1})^3$	.0096	.0055
L2		.0094	.0054
L2A$_1$	$(\Delta Ly_{-1})^2, (\Delta Ly_{-1})(\Delta Lx_{-1}),$ $(\Delta Lx_{-1})^2$	.0091	.0059
L2A$_2$	$(\Delta Ly_{-1})^3, (\Delta Ly_{-1})^2(\Delta x_{-1}),$ $(\Delta Ly_{-1})(\Delta Lx_{-1})^2, (\Delta Lx_{-1})^3$	.0091	.0061
L3		.0087	.0055
L3A	$(\Delta Ly_{-1})^2, (\Delta Ly_{-1})(\Delta Lx_{-1}), (\Delta Lx_{-1})^2$	.0085	.0054

exercise, not reported here in detail, did find that a univariate LSTAR model of the index fitted better in sample than a linear model but did not forecast better. It should be noted that we could not find a suitable univariate STAR model for GNP.

8.3 Application of STR Models

The tests of linearity suggest that nonlinear models are appropriate, and this section presents and evaluates a pair of models for the changes in log GNP. A critical decision in the specification of these models is the choice of the switching variable. From the justification of these models presented earlier, this variable should itself be slowly changing, and it should not contain a dominant deterministic trend as the variable is inserted into a bounded function. The variable selected was the linear detrended log of the index of leading indicators, denoted by

$$LI_t = \log(\text{index leading indicator}) - 4.73 - .008t.$$

A linear error-correction model which relaxes Ly_t and Lx_t was estimated to be

$$(20) \quad \Delta Ly_t = \underset{(.002)}{.006} - \underset{(.02)}{.09\text{ECT}_{-1}} - \underset{(.08)}{.08\,\Delta\,Ly_{t-1}}$$

$$+ \underset{(.08)}{.10\Delta Ly_{t-2}} - \underset{(.08)}{.11\Delta Ly_{t-3}} - \underset{(.08)}{.03\Delta Ly_{t-4}}$$

$$+ \underset{(.07)}{.02\Delta Ly_{t-5}} + \underset{(.07)}{.11\Delta Ly_{t-6}} + \underset{(.07)}{.06\Delta Ly_{t-7}}$$

$$+ \ 0.22\Delta Lx_{t-1},$$
$$(.04)$$
$$SE \ = \ 0.0085,$$

where $ECT_t = Ly_t - 2.50 - .96 \, Lx_t$. The model is clearly overparameterized, but the standard reduction procedure has not been used.

Testing this error correction model against STR alternatives that use lags of the log of the leading indicator index as indicator variables found strong evidence of nonlinearity when $z_t = LI_{t-2}$. (The p value of this test was $p = .001$.) The corresponding STR model was estimated to be
.001.) The corresponding STR model was estimated to be

$$(21) \qquad \Delta Ly_t = .011 - .16ECT_{-1} - .27\Delta Ly_{t-1}$$
$$(.002) \quad (.02) \qquad (.09)$$
$$- \ .17\Delta Ly_{t-3} - .13\Delta Ly_{t-4} + .13\Delta Ly_{t-6} + .010\Delta Ly_{t-7} + .19\Delta Lx_{t-1}$$
$$(.08) \qquad\qquad (.08) \qquad\qquad (.07) \qquad\qquad (.06) \qquad\qquad (.04)$$
$$+ \left[-\ .015 + .14ECT_{-1} + .54\Delta Ly_{t-1} + .44\Delta Ly_{t-3} + .32\Delta Ly_{t-4} \right]$$
$$(.003) \quad (.06) \qquad\quad (.19) \qquad\qquad (.20) \qquad\qquad (.17)$$
$$\left\{ 1 + \exp[-221(LI_{-2} - .036)] \right\}^{-1},$$
$$(.005)$$

$$SE \ = \ 0.007,$$

There are seen to be quite substantial differences in the two regimes, which approximately correspond to the troughs and peaks of the business cycle. The models were constructed using just the in-sample data. The forecasting performance of the two models (20) and (21) over the following twenty-six quarters (i.e., 1984:III–1990:IV) is presented in table 8.5.

It is noteworthy that both these models produce forecasts that are too high, giving negative forecast errors on every occasion except for three. Neither model performed satisfactorily in forecasting the most recent downturn, as shown in figure 8.1. Figure 8.2 shows the movement of the detrended leading indicator LI over time, which is the switching variable used in the model. Using a lag of two, it is seen that the switching variable has changed little

Table 8.5   **In-Sample and Postsample Standard Errors for Models (20) and (21)**

	Root Mean Squared Errors	
	In Sample	Postsample
Linear (20)	.0085	.0072
STR (21)	.0077	.0109

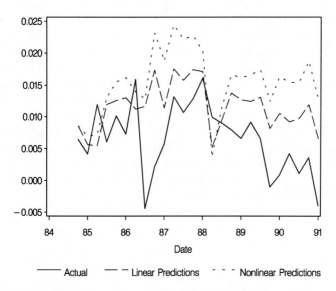

Fig. 8.1   Postsample forecasting performance of the model

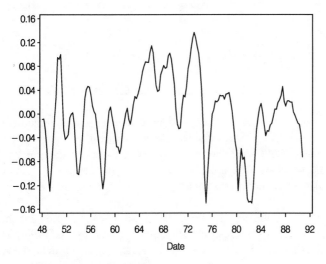

Fig. 8.2   Detrended leading indicator

from its recent high at the end of the postsample period and so was not helpful in forecasting the downturn.

8.4   Conclusions

A number of linear models have been compared to nonlinear ones. It has often been found that the nonlinear models appear to be superior in sample but not out of sample. When using nonlinear models, there is always the possibility of overfitting due to data mining, although this is less likely to occur when tests for linearity have first found evidence against it before model estimation. The postsample evaluation of models is thus particularly important for distinguishing real versus spurious nonlinearity. However, a practical question arises that the postsample period will be limited in extent, and, in this period, both regimes in an STR model may not occur sufficiently often for the inherent advantage of a true nonlinear model to become apparent. For example, if one of the regimes occurs when z_t takes a large value, as in the STR example given above, but this large value occurs less often in the postsample evaluation period, again as in the example, the advantage of the nonlinearity will not be apparent.

Appendix

Table 8A.1 shows the augmented Dickey-Fuller τ_t-test statistics, together with the number of lags used. The 5 percent critical value is -3.44.

The lag k was chosen in each case so that the residual in the Dickey-Fuller equation

$$\Delta y_t = a + by_{t-1} + \gamma t + \sum_{j=1}^{k} \beta_j \Delta y_{t-j} + \text{residual}$$

appears to be white noise. The Dickey-Fuller test statistic is the t-value for the estimate of b.

The Johansen maximum likelihood procedure uses as an alternative test statistic the maximum eigenvalue (λ) and the value of the trace (τ) of an estimated matrix. Table 8A.2 shows the values of these statistics for levels and logs of the variables. The notation r represents the number of cointegrating vectors, and, with only two variables (x and y), r can take only the values zero or one.

The 5 percent critical values for λ_1 and λ_0 are 4.08 and 14.60 and those for τ_1 and τ_0 8.08 and 17.84, respectively (Johansen and Juselius 1990). The evidence suggests that there exists a single cointegrating vector in both levels and logs.

Table 8A.1   Augmented Dickey-Fuller Test Statistics

Variable	No. of Lags Used	D-F Test Statistic	Variable	No. of Lags Used	D-F Test Statistic
y	2	-1.69	Δy	0	-8.98
x	4	-2.13	Δx	3	-7.56
Ly	2	-3.71	ΔLy	2	-6.67
Lx	4	-3.16	ΔLx	3	-8.14

Table 8A.2   **Maximum Eigenvalue and Trace Statistics**

	Series in Levels			Series in Logs	
Null	λ	τ	Null	λ	τ
$r \leq 1$	2.03	2.03	$r \leq 1$	1.37	1.37
$r = 0$	35.70	37.73	$r = 0$	40.09	41.46

References

Davies, R. B. 1977. Hypothesis testing when a nuisance parameter is present only under the alternative. *Biometrika* 64:247–54.

Dickey, D., and F. W. Fuller. 1979. Distribution of the estimators for autoregressive time-series with a unit root. *Journal of the American Statistic Association* 74:427–31.

Engle, R. F., and C. W. J. Granger. 1987. Cointegration and error-correction representation, estimation and testing. *Econometrica* 55:251–76.

Gonzalo, J. 1991. Estimation of long-run equilibrium relationships and common long memory components in cointegrated systems. Ph.D. diss., University of California, San Diego, Economics Department.

Granger, C. W. J., and J. Hallman. 1988. The algebra of I(1). Finance and Economics Discussion Series. Washington, D.C.: Federal Reserve Board.

Granger, C. W. J., and P. Newbold. 1986. *Forecasting economic time series*. New York: Academic.

Granger, C. W. J., and T. Teräsvirta. In press. *Modelling dynamic nonlinear economic relationships*. Oxford: Oxford University Press.

Johansen, S. 1988. Statistical analysis of cointegration vectors. *Journal of Economic Dynamics and Control* 12:231–54.

Johansen, S., and K. Juselius. 1990. Maximum likelihood estimation and inference on cointegration with applications to the demand for money. *Oxford Bulletin of Economics and Statistics* 52:169–210.

Lee, T.-H., H. White, and C. W. J. Granger. 1993. Testing for neglected nonlinearity in time series models: A comparison of neural network methods and alternative tests. *Journal of Econometrics* 56:269–90.

Maddala, G. S. 1977. *Econometrics*. New York: McGraw-Hill.

Teräsvirta, T. 1990a. Power properties of linearity tests for time series. Economics Discussion Paper no. 90–15. University of California, San Diego.

Teräsvirta, T. 1990b. Specification, estimation and evaluation of smooth transition autoregressive models. Economics Discussion Paper no. 90–39. University of California, San Diego.

Teräsvirta, T., and H. M. Anderson. 1992. Characterizing nonlinearities in business cycles using smooth transition autoregressive models. *Journal of Applied Econometrics* 7:S119–S136.

Teräsvirta, T., C.-F. Lin, and C. W. J. Granger. 1993. Power of the neural network linearity test, *Journal of Time Series Analysis* 14:205–20.

Tong, H. 1990. *Non-linear time series analysis: A dynamic system approach*. Oxford: Oxford University Press.

White, H. 1989. An additional hidden unit test for neglected nonlinearity in multilayer feedforward networks. In *Proceedings of the International Joint Conference on Neural Networks,* vol. 2. San Diego, Calif: SOS Printing.

Comment   Andrew Harvey

Data mining is always a problem in time-series modelling. As Granger, Teräsvirta, and Anderson point out, this problem is particularly acute with nonlinear models, and it is certainly very important to assess the performance of models out of sample as well as in sample. The range of nonlinear models is very wide, and it seems virtually impossible to work within a particular class. Indeed, I have not been very convinced by attempts to work within classes of models such as bilinear or state dependent. In order to be useful, nonlinear models should have some economic meaning and a reasonably straightforward interpretation. As a simple example, we might consider an unobserved components model, consisting of a stochastic trend and a stochastic cycle of the kind considered in Harvey (1985) but with the period changing according to whether the change in observations in the previous period, Δy_{t-1}, is negative or positive.

The model described at the end of the previous paragraph is a nonlinear univariate model. The paper considers models with explanatory variables, and an additional source of nonlinearity here comes from nonlinearity in the functional form. This then raises the question of what kind of nonlinearity it is that the tests are picking up. Another issue surrounding the tests is that, if several are applied, it becomes difficult to say much about the Type I error. If enough powers of lagged variables are put into the test statistics, one is probably bound to reject at some stage. This being the case, the comment in the conclusion that overfitting due to data mining "is less likely to occur when tests for linearity have first found evidence against it before model estimation" becomes less convincing.

I feel that the tests for cointegration are a bit tangential since there is no strong economic reason for GNP and the index of leading indicators to be cointegrated and the tests are not being used to find other variables that might go in a set of cointegrated variables. More generally, the whole autoregressive distributed lag framework is not ideal for the kind of exercise being carried out here. Equation (21), with its large number of parameters and arbitrary lag structure, is not particularly appealing. Coupled with the difficulty of specifying the switching mechanism, and the associated lag, I suspect that the equation may not be very robust.

Reference

Harvey, A. C. 1985. Trends and cycles in macroeconomic time series. *Journal of Business and Economic Statistics* 3:216–27.

Andrew Harvey is professor of econometrics at the London School of Economics.

Contributors

Heather M. Anderson
Department of Economics
University of Texas at Austin
Austin, TX 78712

Ben S. Bernanke
Woodrow Wilson School
Princeton University
Princeton, NJ 08544

Phillip Braun
Northwestern University
Kellogg School of Management,
    Finance Dept.
2001 Sheridan Road
Evanston, IL 60208

Francis X. Diebold
Department of Economics
University of Pennsylvania
3718 Locust Walk
Philadelphia, PA 19104

Ray C. Fair
Cowles Foundation for
    Research in Economics
Yale University
Box 2125 Yale Station
New Haven, CT 06520

Benjamin M. Friedman
Department of Economics
Littauer 127
Harvard University
Cambridge, MA 02138

John Geweke
Room 1035
Management and Economics
University of Minnesota
Minneapolis, MN 55455

Clive W. J. Granger
Department of Economics, 0508
9500 Gilman Drive
University of California, San Diego
La Jolla, CA 92093

James D. Hamilton
Department of Economics, 0508
9500 Gilman Drive
University of California, San Diego
La Jolla, CA 92093

Bruce E. Hansen
Department of Economics
Harkness Hall
University of Rochester
Rochester, NY 14627

Andrew Harvey
Statistics Faculty
London School of Economics
Houghton Street
London WC2A 2AE
ENGLAND

Kenneth N. Kuttner
Research Department
Federal Reserve Bank of Chicago
230 South LaSalle Street
Chicago, IL 60604

Pierre Perron
Department of Economics
University of Montreal
P.O. Box 6128 Station A
Montreal, Quebec HC3 3J7
CANADA

Danny Quah
London School of Economics
Houghton Street
London WC2A 2AE
UK

Glenn D. Rudebusch
Mail Stop #71
Federal Reserve Board
20th and Constitution Avenue, NW
Washington, DC 20551

Thomas J. Sargent
Hoover Institution
HHMB Room 243
Stanford University
Stanford, CA 94305

Daniel E. Sichel
Mail Stop #80
Federal Reserve Board
20th and Constitution, NW
Washington, DC 20551

Christopher A. Sims
Department of Economics
Yale University
37 Hillhouse
New Haven, CT 06520

Allen Sinai
Chief Economist
Lehman Brothers Economic Advisors
200 Vesey, 12th Floor
New York, NY 10285
also:
Visiting Professor
Lemberg Program for International
    Economics
Brandeis University
Waltham, MA 02254

James H. Stock
Kennedy School of Government
Harvard University
Cambridge, MA 02138

Timo Teräsvirta
Bank of Norway
Research Department, C-51
PB 1179 Sentrum
N-0107 Oslo
NORWAY

Kenneth F. Wallis
Department of Economics
University of Warwick
Coventry CV4 7AL
ENGLAND

Mark W. Watson
Department of Economics
Northwestern University
2003 Sheridan Road
Evanston, IL 60208

Victor Zarnowitz
Graduate School of Business
University of Chicago
1101 East 58th Street
Chicago, IL 60637

Author Index

Subject Index